PROMISES AND PERILS IN HOSPITALITY AND TOURISM MANAGEMENT

PROMISES AND PERILS IN HOSPITALITY AND TOURISM MANAGEMENT

SAURABH KUMAR DIXIT

AMAN PUBLICATIONS

NEW DELHI

Published by
Rajiv Jain for Aman Publications
LG-4A, Ganpati Bhawan,
4675-B/21, Ansari Road,
Darya Ganj, Delhi - 110002
PH: 23255012, 23282127
E-mail: sshjbs@yahoo.com

First Published – 2006

ISBN–81-8204-010-8

SOLE DISTRIBUTOR
JINDAL BOOK SERVICES
LG-4A, Ganpati Bhawan,
4675-B/21, Ansari Road,
Darya Ganj, Delhi - 110002

Jacket Designed by :
S.M. Graphics

Printed by:
NCT Printers & Publishers, Delhi, India

Dedicated
To
My Loving Parents,
DR. RAJESH DIXIT
and
MRS. SUNITA DIXIT

PREFACE

The second half of the last century has witnessed tremendous developments in the tourism and hospitality sectors. The international tourist arrivals increased from 25 million in the year 1950 to 67 million in 2000 registering an annual growth rate of 7 per cent. Now tourism industry is enjoying one of the top most positions in the overall business scenario worldwide. It is accepted world over that tourism is a major force in the economy of the world, an activity of global importance and significance. This most rapidly expanding industry is contributing over ten per cent to global GDP and generating employment for 200 million people. The WTO's Tourism Vision 2020 forecasts the international arrivals are expected to cross 1.56 billion by the year 2020. Among that, 1.18 billion will be intra regional and .371 billion will be long haul travelers.

The first decade of the millennium has brought with it no shortage of significant events - each creating new challenges for the hospitality and tourism industries. Some of them worked as the catalyst for the growth of hospitality and tourism industries, while other acted in reversible manner. September 11, 2001, was the most significant event and the one most still in worlds' collective minds. While September 11th has come and gone, concerns about safety and security remain. Further compounding effects of the lingering recession are all to a very slow recovery. Tensions in the Middle East, war in Iraq, December 2004, Tsunami and new and mis-understood diseases are all being used as excuses not to travel. SARS (Severe Acute Respiratory Syndrome) is perhaps the most recent and best example of how an illness can create widespread concern.

Like any other business, tourism and hospitality operators too witness some promises and perils in its regular operation. The key of success of any enterprise lies on the endeavor it used while unfavorable stage and maximum exploitation its resources during happy days. The work atmosphere and employees are made ready to handle any such situation. Therefore, in the present edited book an effort has been put in to give a clear picture of the pros and cons concerning to the global hospitality and tourism industries. The book will serve and reflect the tremendous growth in tourism and hospitality which has come about as a result of the growing appreciation of the economic and social importance of the these fields and their rapid expansion. It is probably time to reinforce the importance, the challenge and the excitement of working in our industries and try to change the negative image and create a more positive future.

With the clear thinking and intellectual caliber the contributors of the book have brought to bear on a selection of important themes of tourism and hospitality industries. It has compiled together the twenty contributions of the renowned subject experts on vivid areas. The collection embraces the original rigorously conducted research, opinion pieces, applied practice and conceptual contributions of hospitality/ tourism and other related fields. On the basis of the specialized nature of their themes, all papers have rationally been classified into five sections - **(A)** Contemporary Issues of Hospitality and Tourism Management **(B)** Ecological Perspectives **(C)** Economic Implications of Hospitality and Tourism Development **(D)** Destination Management **(E)** Human Resource Management in Hospitality and Tourism Operations. The papers have been selected to publish after proper editing and review.

Section A of the book has incorporated five research papers covering vivid *Contemporary Issues Concerning to the Industry* ranging from Cruise competition and Quantitative analysis of passenger trends; Application of Marketing strategy in tourism and hospitality industries; Semantic Web Technologies in tourism Information Systems; Demographic and Economic Patterns In Italian Tourism In The Last Century and Crisis Management in Tourism industry.

Section B comprises the articles dealing with the *Ecological Perspectives to the Industries*. The section starts with the research paper titled Environmental Impacts of nature based tourism in

South Africa followed by The Opportunities and Pitfalls in Ecotourism Development; The Impact of Ecotourism Development in Kenya: Environmental Issues of Planning and Management and Tourism Development as an Alternative for Agricultural Production – The Case of E. Slovakian Wine Tourism.

Section C dealing with *Economic Implications of Hospitality and Tourism Development* starts with the research paper Implications Of The Development Of Hospitality And Tourism In The Economy and followed by The Decision About The Increase Of Income And The Reduction Of Costs In Hospitality Corporations; The Impact Of Management Accounting Systems On Performance: An Exploratory Study Of Hotels In Slovenia and The Cretan Resort Cycle From Wealthy Explorers And Cruisers To Mass Tourism.

Section D of the book possesses the contributions on *Destination Management.* The areas covered in this section include Politics Of Place And The Role Of Policy Makers In The Creation Of Opportunities For Community Orientated Events And Festivals; The Cluster Effect Of The Tourism Industry In Pearl River Delta and An Analysis of tourism infrastructure in Madhya Pradesh, India.

Section E is themed on *Human Resource Management in Hospitality and Tourism Operations* has four research papers. The first paper is on Pay Satisfaction in the Hospitality and Tourism Industry: Theories, Realities and the Possibilities; Second paper is on Customers' Emotional and Behavioral Responses to Complaint Handling; Third paper is on Changing Scenario Of Human Capital Development In Indian Hospitality Operations and the fourth one is Empowerment levels and complaining behaviors: A case of hotel customers' behavioral intentions.

I have received cooperation and help from a number of dignitaries at various stages of the venture. Prof. R.P. Agrawal, Hon. Vice Chancellor, Bundelkhand University, Jhansi; Prof. O.P. Kandari, Pro V.C. and HOD, Institute of Tourism and Hotel Management; Prof. S. C. Bagri, Dean and HOD, Centre for Mountain Tourism and Hospitality Management, H.N.B. Garhwal University, Srinagar Garhwal, Uttaranchal; Dr. Aparna Raj, Coordinator, Institute of Tourism and Hotel Management have been quite liberal in extending their help and cooperation at various stages of the publication. I extend my heartfelt thanks to the entire staff of Institute of Tourism and Hotel Management, Bundelkhand University, Jhansi for making this book to see light of the day. I acknowledge my immense gratitude to the publisher M/s Aman Publications, New Delhi for accepting the manuscript for the publication.

Saurabh Kumar Dixit

Jhansi (M.P), India

CONTENTS

Section C

ECONOMIC IMPLICATIONS OF HOSPITALITY AND TOURISM DEVELOPMENT

Section D

DESTINATION MANAGEMENT

Section E

HUMAN RESOURCE MANAGEMENT IN HOSPITALITY AND TOURISM OPERATIONS

ABOUT THE ...

John Moustakas ...

from Dal...

MSc in ...

Safety ...

Newcastle ...

respectively ...

and offshore ...

with support ...

He has ...

publications ...

papers and ...

interests ...

design and ...

E-Mail: ...

Petros ...

He obtained ...

Accountancy ...

in 1991 ...

professional course leading to the qualification of the Association of Accounting Technicians (AAT). He obtained the Accountancy Foundation Degree from Southbank University (UK) in 1993 and also completed the ... Level of the Association of Chartered Certified Accountants (ACCA) in 1994. He ... Accounting and Finance from De Montfort University (UK) ... He received his PhD (Marine Technology) from Liverpool John Moores University, UK ... He has been ...

ABOUT THE CONTRIBUTORS

Jin Wang is Professor of Marine Technology at Liverpool John Moores University. He received his BSc in Marine Automation from Dalian Maritime University, P. R. China, MSc in Marine Engineering and PhD in Maritime Safety Engineering from the University of Newcastle upon Tyne, UK in 1989 and 1994, respectively. He has been involved in marine and offshore research for the past 15 years with support from the EPSRC, EU, HSE, etc. He has written more than 200 technical publications including over 60 refereed journal papers and 2 research books. Professor Wang's major research interests include marine leisure studies, safety and reliability based design and operations of large marine and offshore systems.

E-Mail: j.wang@livjm.ac.uk

Petros Lois is an Assistant Professor at Intercollege, Cyprus. He obtained a Diploma in Accounting from BPP College of Accountancy and Business Studies (Cyprus) in 1991 and following that, attended the professional course leading to the qualification of the Association of Accounting Technicians (AAT). He obtained the Accountancy Foundation Degree from Southbank University (UK) in 1993 and also completed the Certificate Level of the Association of Chartered Certified Accountants (ACCA) in 1994. He also obtained an MSc in Accounting and Finance from De Montfort University (UK) in 1995. He received his PhD (Marine Technology) from Liverpool John Moores University, UK in 2004. He has been involved in marine

tourism research for the past 6 years. He has written technical publications including refereed journal papers and research book chapters. He has presented research work in several conferences and been involved in the Socrates programme of the E.U. (Faculty exchange). Dr. Lois' major research interests include safety, and financial and economic issues of passenger cruise ships.

E-Mail: plois@cytanet.com.cy

Marios D. Soteriades is Associate Professor and Head of the Department of Tourism Industry, Technological Educational Institute of Crete, Greece. He received his MSc in Hospitality Management and his PhD in Tourism Management from the Université de Nice – Sophia Antipolis, Nice, France. He has undertaken a variety of research and consultancy projects for both the public and private sectors of industry. He is the author of three books and three distance learning manuals on aspects of hospitality management and marketing. His research and writing interests include hospitality and tourism management and marketing. He has published journal articles and conference papers in these fields.

E- Mail: marsot@sdo.teicrete.gr

Dimitris Kanellopoulos is a Lecturer in the Department of Tourism Management at the Highest Technological Education Institute of Patras, Greece. He received a diploma in electrical engineering and a Ph.D. degree in electrical and computer engineering from the University of Patras, Greece. Since 1990, he was a research assistant in the Department of Electrical and Computer Engineering at the University of Patras and involved in several EU R&D projects. His research interests include: multimedia communications, the Semantic Web, knowledge representation, web-based education and intelligent tourism information systems. He has more than 30 publications to his credit in *International Journals* and *Conferences* in these areas.

E-Mail: dkanellop@teipat.gr

Adriana Galvani is a Lecturer in the Department of Economics and teacher of Sociology of Tourism at the University of Bologna (Italy). She obtained a specialization diploma in Geography and attended several post-doc schools. She is corresponding member of IGU, member of Italian Geographical Associations, referee for two Spanish and one Italian reviews. She is expert evaluator in environment and agriculture for European Commission and for INTAS (Cooperation network among EU and East European Countries) and responsible on Sustainable Tourism Sector in the European Regional Network on Sustainable Development, based on EU-DG Regio. She also regularly collaborates with the EU Group on Life Sciences, working on the EU project Life in Extreme Environments. She is foreign responsible for a national project at the University of Oujda (Morocco) on desertification. She participated at the AAG Center for Global Geography Education project supported by the USA National Science Foundation. She has 170 publications in Italian, French and English published in international reviews.

E-Mail: galvani@spbo.unibo.it

Senol Cavus is an Assistant Professor in the School of Tourism & Hotel Management at the Adnan Menderes Univer-sity, Turkey. He is interested in the research within the fields of destination management, tourism planning and policy, hotel management and organization, sustainable tourism, and special interest tourism.

E-Mail: scavus@adu.edu.tr

Abdullah Tanrisevdi is an Assistant Professor in the School of Tourism & Hotel Management at the Adnan Menderes University, Turkey. He is engaged in the research within the fields of crisis management, travel agency operations, and special interest tourism.

E-Mail: atanrisevdi@adu.edu.tr

Anna Spenceley works across Africa on the design and implementation of environmentally, socially and economically

sustainable nature-based tourism operations within protected areas; socio-economic development emanat-ing from responsible tourism in rural areas; sustainable livelihoods; commu-nity based tourism; the promotion of conservation of biodiversity in and around protected areas; and catalysing financial and educational benefits. Her PhD through the International Centre for Responsible Tourism at the University of Greenwich led to the development of a Sustainable Nature-Based Tourism Assessment Toolkit (SUNTAT). Her post-doctoral research at the Transboundary Protected Areas Research Initiative based at the University of the Witwatersrand evaluated responsible tourism investment in the Great LImpopo Transfrontier Conservation Area. Ms. Spenceley is a member of the IUCN WCPA (World Commission on Protected Areas) Tourism Taskforce and the IUCN Southern Africa Sustainable Use Specialist Group. More information can be found at www.anna.spenceley.co.uk

E-Mail: annaspenceley@hotmail.com

Ian Rotherham is Reader in Tourism Leisure and Environmental Change at Sheffield Hallam University' Centre for

Tourism and Cultural Change. His background is in ecology and landscape history and currently researches into the economics of sustainable rural development linked to leisure and tourism. His studies have included major projects on nature reserves and tourism for the Wildlife Trusts, the Heritage Lottery Fund, the Countryside Agency, and the RSPB. He chairs the International Working Group on Socio-economic Aspects of Forestry and Forest History, for IUFRO.

E-Mail: i.d.rotherham@shu.ac.uk

Roselyne Nyawiri Okech is a Lecturer at the Department of Ecotourism, Hotel and Institution Management, Maseno University, Kenya. She obtained Masters in Tourism Administration degree from Institute for Social Sciences and Research Vellore, Tamil Nadu, India in 1997. She received her PhD (Tourism) from the University of KwaZulu-Natal (Westville Campus), South Africa in 2004. She has been involved in tourism and hospitality research for the past 6 years. She has written a couple of technical publications including refereed journal papers, newsletters, conference reviews and research book chapters. She has presented papers in a dozen of National and International conferences.

E-Mail: rnokech@yahoo.com

Gejza M. Timcak is a professor at the Dept. of Geotourism of the BERG Faculty, Technical University, Kosice, Slovakia. He was awarded an MSc Diploma at the same university in 1964 and a PhD in applied mineralogy at Imperial College, London in 1975. He was a visiting scientist at Indian School of Mines in Dhanbad, at the National Technical University Athens, Nottingham Trent University and a number of other Universities. At present he is teaching applied informatics and human potential development related subjects. His research is presently oriented towards tourism development strategies, human resource development and tourism related information systems. Since 1967 he manages national and international (mainly EU) research projects and offers consultancy to companies like MicroCAD systems Kosice and Brainy Zilina. He is the manager of the MSc study at his Dept. He authored and co-authored more than 200 publications in the mentioned areas published as monographs, textbooks and papers.

E-Mail: gmtkg@tuke.sk

Waclaw Kotlinski is presently working as a Lecturer at the Faculty of Economics, Department of Marketing and Management, University of Technology, Rzeszow, Poland. He has contributed around 60 research papers and popular articles on Tourism in various national as well as international conferences. He is also author and co-author of five books titled "Social and economic factors of tourism development in Podkarpackie region", "Marketing tourism services", "Strategy of tourism development in the Podkarpackie region". His didactical and scientical activities focus on the tourism issue in the aspect of socio-economic development of the region and an analysis of the size, structure and dynamics of touristic movement.

E-Mail: wackot@prz.rzeszow.pl

Dragan Nikolic was born in 1955 in Valjevo, Serbia, SCG. He is working at The College of Hotel Management in Belgrade as a professor of Economics in Hotel Industry and Business Finances in Hotel Industry as well as at the Faculty for Tourist and Hotel Management in Belgrade as an Assistant Professor for a narrower scientific field of Economics and Management in Hotel Industry and Tourism. He graduated at the Faculty of Tourism and Foreign Trade in Dubrovnik, Croatia. He has completed Master of Science as well as Doctor of Science Degree at the Faculty of Economics of Belgrade University, SCG. He has authored a few dozens of specialized and scientific works, of one monograph and two textbooks in the field of hotel management and tourism.

E-Mail: jov99@ptt.yu

Slavka Kavcic is a Full Professor of Management Accounting and Financial Accounting at the Faculty of Economics of the University of Ljubljana. She is a Verified Accountant, a Certified Auditor, an Expert of Court of Audit and also a Member of the Professional Council of Slovenian Institute of Auditors, a Chairman of the Board of Accounting Section at the Slovenian Institute of Auditors and a Member of the Commission for Changes of Slovenian Accounting Standards. Before joining the Faculty of Economics, she was a Head Accountant at big Slovenian company. Her areas of research interest include accounting in public sector, hospitality management accounting, environmental management accounting, cost management in insurance companies and ethics. She has published over 200 scientific papers and professional articles in variety of journals and many books.

E-Mail: slavka.kavcic@ef.uni-lj.si

Gordana Ivankovic is an Assistant Professor in Accounting and Finance at TURISTICA, College of tourism, University of Primorska, Slovenia. Her main research interests are in accounting and finance in hospitality management accounting as well as in management of tourism companies. She is very active in presenting conference papers, both nationally and internationally, and in publishing scientific papers and professional articles in variety of journals.

E-Mail: gordana.ivankovic@k2.net

Konstantinos Andriotis holds a first degree in Tourism Management and Administration (TEI of Crete, 1993), an MSc in International Hospitality Management (University of Strathclyde, 1995) and a PhD in Tourism Development and Planning (Bournemouth University, 2000). He is currently working at the Greek Open University and the Technological Educational Institute of Crete. His principal research interests are concerned with tourism development and planning, community perceptions and island tourism. His work has appeared in various journals including: Journal of Travel Research, Tourism Management and Journal of Sustainable Tourism. He has also acted as referee in various tourism journals including Tourism Management and Journal of Sustainable Tourism.

E-Mail: andriotis@eap.gr

Razaq Raj is Senior Lecturer in Events Financial and Strategic Management and Course Leader of MSc Events Management for Leeds Metropolitan University. His research interests include community events, outdoor events, economic impacts, religious tourism, cultural festivals and sustainable tourism, cultural diversity in events management and financial management for events. He has published work on special events, financial management in events, information technology, events sponsorship, cultural festivals and events sustainable tourism and religious tourism. He regularly attends and presents papers at national and international conferences and recently edited a special edition of the International Journal of Management Cases. He also sits on a number of voluntary sector management boards.

E-Mail: r.raj@leedsmet.ac.uk

Zhang mu is a professor in the Department of Tourism Management at the Shenzhen Tourism College of Jinan University, P.R.China. He received a diploma in Geography and a Ph. D degree in Geography from Fujian Normal University, China. Since 1985, he was a teacher in the Department of Tourism & Environment at the Guangxi Institute of education and involved in several national and local government R&D projects. His research interests include: geography, land use & planning, tourist resources development & planning and the GIS application. He has more than 60 publications to his credit in Chinese and international journals or conferences in these areas.

E-Mail: zhangmu@ 163.com

Amitabh Mishra is currently working as Asst. Professor of Tourism Management at Gondar University, Federal Democratic Republic of Ethiopia. He is a M.T.A. from A.P.S.University Rewa, India and D.H.M. from Devi Ahilya University, Indore, India. He holds Ph.D. degree in tourism management under the supervision of Prof. S.C.Bagri, Center for Mountain Tourism and Hospitality Studies, H.N.B.Garhwal University Srinagar, Garhwal, India. His areas of interest are Tourism Marketing, Travel and Tour Operation, Tourism Transportation and Computer Application. He has been associated with institutes of repute viz, Garhwal University - Srinagar, Kumaon University – Nainital and S.M.J.N. (P.G.) College, Haridwar, etc. He has participated and presented the research paper in two international and about a dozen national conference and workshops on tourism.

E-Mail: amitabh_mishra@rediffmail.com

Sumeetra M Thozhur is a Lecturer in Hospitality Management at the School of Management, University of Surrey, UK. She received her Masters in International Hospitality Management in 1999, with a distinction, at the University of Surrey, following which she gained a PhD at Surrey, in 2005. Her area of interest and specialization is pay and low pay in the service industries. She has explored methods of applying theories of Organizational Behaviour to explain why people stay in low paid jobs. In doing so, she goes beyond traditional economic explanations of job worth and low accumulation of human capital as well psychological explanations of satisfaction with pay. She has presented her research work in several conferences and has been involved in looking at Student Employability Skills Project funded by the Higher Education Academy.

E-Mail: s.thozhur@surrey.ac.uk

Atila Yuksel (BA in Tourism and Hotel Management, Dokuz Eylul University; MSc in Tourism Management, the University of Wales; Ph. D. at Sheffield Hallam University) is a faculty of School of Tourism and Hospitality Management, Adnan Menderes University, Turkey. He has published articles on tourist satisfaction and complaint management, destination planning and marketing, and tourism research in prestigious scientific journals, including Annals of Tourism Research, Tourism Management, Journal of Hospitality and Tourism Research, Journal of Travel and Tourism Marketing, Journal of Vacation Marketing, the Cornell Hotel and Restaurant Administration Quarterly, and the Journal of Travel and Tourism Research.

E-Mail: ayuksel@adu.edu.tr

Saurabh K. Dixit has done his four years Bachelors Degree in Hotel Management and Catering Technology (2000) from Rohilkhand University, Bareilly. After his graduation in Hotel Management, he pursued Masters Degree in Tourism Management (2003) from I.G.N.O.U., New Delhi. He has qualified J.R.F.-N.E.T. (Tourism Management) exam being conducted by University Grants Commission, New Delhi and received Junior Research Fellowship for doing D.Phil. (Tourism). He has work experience from CMTHS, H.N.B.Garhwal University, Srinagar Garhwal and C.Z.Patel College of Business and Management, Anand, Gujarat as Lecturer (Hotel Management). Presently, he is working as Assistant Professor in Institute of Tourism and Hotel Management, Bundelkhand University, Jhansi, India. He has six books to his credit. So far his eight research papers have been published in national / international refereed journals and edited books, besides he has participated in a number of national and international seminars.

E-Mail: saurabh5sk@yahoo.com

Murat Hancer (B.A. in Tourism and Hotel Management, Dokuz Eylul University; M.Sc. in Hospitality and Tourism, University of New Haven; Ph.D. in Hospitality and Foodservice Management, The Ohio State University) is a faculty of School of Tourism and Hospitality Management, Adnan Menderes University. He has published articles in Journal of Hospitality and Tourism Research, International Journal of Hospitality Management, and Psychological Reports on the topics of psychological empowerment, job satisfaction, leader-member exchange theory about hospitality and foodservice employees.

E-Mail: mhancer@adu.edu.tr

Ugur K. Kilinc (BA in Tourism and Hotel Management, Adnan Menderes University; MSc in Hotel Management, Adnan Menderes University) is a research assistant and PhD candidate at the Graduate School of Adnan Menderes University. She has published scientific papers in national and international journals.

E-Mail: ukkilinc@adu.edu.tr

SECTION A

CONTEMPORARY ISSUES OF HOSPITALITY AND TOURISM MANAGEMENT

1

CRUISE COMPETITION AND QUALITATIVE ANALYSIS OF PASSENGER TRENDS

JIN WANG and PETROS LOIS

ABSTRACT

This contribution investigates an approach to cruising, including an explanation of the different segments of the cruise market and the typology (i.e. characteristics) of cruisers. It also examines how the participants within the cruise market try to find which type of cruise is more advantageous and beneficial with respect to the several different types of cruise defined. Consumer attitudes to cruise tourism and fundamental considerations of competition at sea, and the factors considered for choosing a destination in the Cyprus and Mediterranean regions are extensively examined by analysing the results of cruise passenger surveys carried out in the examined cruise regions. A generic qualitative assessment methodology is proposed in order to synthesize the competition factors for decision-making purposes.

Kaywords: ***Cruise, cruise market, marine tourism, passenger attitude, qualitative analysis.***

INTRODUCTION

Cruise lines that wish to succeed in the future will pay very close attention to the needs and desires of this generation. As the conspicuous consumption mentality of the 1980s gives way to the value conscious consumer of the 1990s, the cruise industry will do well to heed this trend. Not only are today's consumers more value conscious, but also their levels of expectations are higher and their desires for something different are all-important factors in the purchasing decision.

Due to the expansion of the cruise market and the development opportunities for new destinations, competition becomes very strong. The fundamental considerations of competition are of paramount importance and, therefore, the cruise lines will have to pay significant attention to these factors. This will enable them to overcome the problems of intensive competition.

The demand and supply issues are essential as the phenomenal growth of the industry over the last decade has fuelled many discussions and much hand-wringing over whether or not the continuous increase in berths can be absorbed. The question arises as to whether the industry will be required to absorb a large number of new buildings, over the next few years.

RECENT APPROACH TO CRUISING

Cruises

The word "cruise" is difficult to define. This is because cruise lines use different routes and destinations with different types of passengers. The cruise market can be divided into the following segments [Cruise Industry News, 2000]:

1. **Contemporary market:** it includes cruises offered on older ships with an average length of seven days or shorter and is value-priced.
2. **Premium market:** it includes cruises with a broader range of amenities and services, which often sail worldwide, and which appeal to more affluent passengers.
3. **Budget market:** it includes inexpensively priced cruises with fewer amenities.
4. **Luxury market:** it includes cruises with an average of 14 days or longer on medium- sized or smaller ships, which offer a full range of upscale services and amenities.

5. **Niche market:** it includes explorations, sail or other specialty ships.

Cruises can also be defined as travel accommodation on board ship between two or more destinations with the objective of leisure, where no passenger can embark or disembark before their final destination. These cruises can be classified into:

1. **Mini cruises:** cruises with the objective of leisure taken on an irregular basis all year round between two cities.
2. **Overnight cruises:** cruises with the objective of leisure sometimes combined with transportation, on a regular basis all year round between two cities.
3. **Short cruises:** cruises with the objective of leisure on an irregular basis from one city to a destination or to nowhere.
4. **Long cruises:** cruises of more than seven days with the objective of leisure and sightseeing.

The participants within the cruise industry need to find out what type of cruise is the most advantageous and beneficial. This depends on various factors, including the market within which the cruise lines operate. For example, if a particular liner operates within the mass market (i.e. budget market), it would be suggested that such a liner offers short cruises. This is because the majority of people who love to go on a cruise are reasonably price conscious [Lois P., Wang J., Wall A. D., Ruxton T., 2000, 2001]. They also prefer to stay on board the ship no longer than three days in order not to spend too much money aboard. The operators take into account the type of cruise, consumer attitudes and the market they choose. They may then decide what type of vessel will be introduced for the particular cruise.

TYPOLOGY OF CRUISERS

The requirements of cruisers are derived from those generic to holidaymakers. Various authorities have considered models for describing tourists. Cohen (1972) provided four categories for describing tourists (Cohen E., 1972):

1. **The organised mass tourist:** tourists like to travel in a fairly large group of similarly minded companions and are happy to trade off individuality for safety.

2. **The individual mass tourist:** tourists go to the same places as the organised mass tourists but gain some personal satisfaction in making some of their own arrangements.
3. **The explorer:** explorers arrange their own travel. They want to visit less developed destinations but still wish to retain a level of comfort.
4. **The drifter:** drifters do not see themselves as tourists and wish to get to know the host community.

Other researchers have looked at the importance of the psychological determinants in the tourist industry, such as escape, relaxation, play, education, social interaction, shopping and others [Crompton J., 1979; Mathieson A., Wall G., 1982; Ryan C., 1991].

Based on the above ideas, it is essential to describe the cruiser profile, that is, the tendency of any one person on a cruise to require certain ingredients to make that cruise a success. Two researchers, Cartwright and Baird [Cartwright R., Baird C., 1999], in developing the cruisers' profile, have used the development concepts of Belbin [Belbin M., 1981] and Honey and Mumford [Honey P., Mumford J., 1986]. The characteristics of the cruisers can be described as follows:

1. The partygoer:

The partygoer is on a cruise for the activities and nightlife. They are likely to be the happiest on a ship that has the latest in entertainment features, a lively casino and plenty of organised activities.

2. The relaxer:

The relaxer will not object to days spent at sea and may well only venture ashore briefly on port days. The relaxer is on the cruise to unwind and whilst he or she may well take in a degree of the action at night, the daytime is likely to find them lying on deck chair and devouring the ship's library.

3. The enthusiast:

The enthusiast is addicted to cruising. The itinerary is not important, the ship may not be a major priority but the cruise is.

4. The stroller:

Strollers take the opportunity to escape from normality and to experience a perception of a glamorous yesteryear.

5. The seeker:

The seeker is concerned with finding out a great deal about the area he visits and will wish to try to become a part of the culture.

6. The explorer:

The explorer wishes to see those places few have seen before. Explorers do not need shopping malls but they seek different lifestyles.

7. The dipper:

The dipper is truly the 'been there, seen that, experienced this and bought a T shirt' person. He is satisfied with an explanatory leaflet, a briefing from the port official and a tour of the highlights.

NEW TIMES, NEW CRUISE SHIPS

The ship of tomorrow seems to be a very hot topic today. Everyone wants to know what the cruise ship is going to look like. Added to the increasing number of new buildings, there has also been an increase in the size of cruise passenger vessels being built in recent years [Cruise Industry News, 1999; Shipping World and Shipbuilder, 1996]. Table 1 shows the number and capacity of vessels added to the fleet since 1995. In 2000, 13 new ships were introduced [Cruise Industry News, 2000] and another 15 new ships in 2001 [Cruise Industry News, 2000]. It is estimated that by the year 2006, 29 new ships will have been introduced into the cruise market [Cruise Industry News, 2000].

The differentiation in geographical destination and product expectation may greatly influence the type of ship that is introduced not only now, but also in the coming decade. To satisfy a continuing strong demand in the established cruising areas, large mass-market ships may continue to come in line [Paige M. M., 1994]. This results from the fact that demand grows through more first-time cruisers becoming aware of the many benefits of cruising, as the vacation alternative of choice. Through stricter safety rules and increased passenger expectations, many older ships may

Table 1: Analysis Of Oceanic Fleet Additions From 1985 By Size

	Pax												
	Up to 500		500-999		1,000-1,499		1,500-1,999		2,000+		Total		Average
Year	No	Pax	No	Pax	No	Pax	No	Pax	No	Pax	No	Pax	Size
1985-9	19	3,358	2	1,330	8	10,510	1	1,526	1	2,282	31	19,006	613
1990-4	24	4,794	5	3,662	12	14,938	3	4,790	6	12,872	50	41,056	821
1995-9	6	1,684	6	4,236	6	7,962	13	24,008	13	28,419	44	66,309	1,507
Total	49	9,836	13	9,228	26	33,410	17	30,324	20	43,573	125	126,371	1,011

Source:* *Cruise Industry News (1999), Shipping World and Shipbuilder (1996)

become obsolete, necessitating investment in new ships. However, not all the new ships will be mass-market ships catering to the established cruise areas. Other types of ships may be introduced.

Many of the world's most attractive and interesting ports and waterways are accessible only to ships of a smaller size. For example, the ships that dock in Limassol are small in both size and capacity. Limassol is an attractive port because tourist attractions and interesting places are located within a short distance from the port, but it is a small harbour that does not allow big ships to dock. Even if large ships could dock, it may simply not be appropriate to disembark thousands of passengers in many of these destinations. Certainly, judging from the rising popularity of small ship cruising and the generally very high passenger satisfaction being registered from cruise passengers on smaller ships, the trend towards more cruise passengers seeking upscale and adventure-oriented cruises offering fascinating and unusual destinations is more likely to continue. This is evidenced by the survey carried out in the Cyprus cruise region and the results are shown in section "survey results". This high degree of satisfaction may result in a very high level of repeat business, and as a result the small ship cruise market may continue to expand.

In addition, the ships may be expected to feature on-board amenities. This may ensure a level of comfort that encourages passengers to return frequently, rather than viewing a voyage as a one-time hardship for the sake of adventure. Comfortable cruising might become the means of choice for visiting many of the world's most remote destinations.

The cruisers with the means to travel to these remote destinations will demand a high quality of service. Fine cuisine and wine, swimming pools, spacious staterooms, saunas and a well-trained staff will be the order of the day. In short, by combining a small hull size and luxurious features, a cruise line may be able to cater to the emerging class of adventurous "empty nest baby boomers".

SUPPLY AND DEMAND BALANCE

Passenger growth was continuous from 1995 to 2002. Demand-side growth for 1995, 1996 and 1997 was put at 6.0%,

6.5% and 8.0%, respectively [Wild G. P., 1995]. This took account of the continuing higher annual growth rates in Europe and USA combined with a boom in the Asia market. The figures have never failed to increase year after year. For the years 1998 to 2000 it was assumed that whilst most countries had moved out of recession, the economic climate within the USA and Europe continued to the end of the century and that passenger growth remained below the historic average of 9%.

Table 2: Supply and Demand Scenario

	1999	2000	2001	2002	2005
Ships	**228**	**240**	**255**	**268**	**292**
Berths	199,116	219,337	245,213	269,353	319,843
Market capacity	10,279,639	11,465,135	12,801,391	14,134,311	16,715,011
Passengers (million)	8.7	9	9.8	10	11.9
Utilisation (%)	84.6%	78.4%	76.5%	70.7%	71.1%

Source: Cruise Industry News (2000)

Table 2 shows that utilisation levels remain below 90% and decrease from year to year. The utilization level is measured by dividing the number of passengers by the market capacity in berths. The decrease in utilization level may be a result of the increase in new tonnage and of the fact that older tonnage discarded by the major operators is utilised by smaller ones. The industry's reaction to a surplus of supply over demand is to squeeze prices, together with yields, as discounting is employed to ensure that ships sail as close to full capacity as possible [Lloyd's Shipping, 2001]. The cruise industry does not appear to generally follow economic indicators and is normally regarded as supply-driven, with demand stimulated by effective marketing. However, when the market becomes saturated, it is likely to change, although there is no evidence that the market is currently saturated [Lloyd's Shipping, 2002].

The cruise market has been buoyed by unbroken expansion since 1990. The industry's total revenue increased from $5.1 billion in 1990 to $15 billion in 2000 [Lloyd's Shipping, 2002], carrying an increased total of 9 million passengers. In 2001, there were 255 ships offering a total capacity of 245,213 berths and in 2002, 268 ships offered 269,353 berths. It is estimated that in 2003, 271 ships will offer 297,169 berths and by the year 2005 the number of berths will increase to 319,843 [Cruise Industry News, 2000]. Europe's capacity is set to receive an unprecedented supply boost due to the new ships already contracted and targeted at the European market. The European capacity was estimated to pick up with 5-10% annual growth between 2001 and 2004 [Cruise Industry News, 2000].

Figure 1 shows the market share of the world four big cruise companies in capacity terms. The capacity includes the fleet of the companies in service and their newbuildings. The big four cruise operating groups that make up 82% of projected world capacity [Lloyd's Shipping, 2001], are set to take over the next five years, as their new buildings come into service. Figure 2 shows an indication of the capacity share in the Mediterranean region, including Cyprus. Worldwide Carnival Corporation remains first in terms of capacity and the Cyprus-based Louis Cruise Lines holds the highest capacity share in the whole Mediterranean region.

COMPETITION AT SEA: FUNDAMENTAL CONSIDERATIONS

With the rapid increase in the world's cruise fleet, cruising has become a realistic vocational option for the travelling public. The high density of cruise ships sailing certain popular regions of the world presents the potential cruiser with a dilemma resolved by more than the itinerary alone. Fundamental considerations such as service, food and entertainment are of paramount importance and the lines paying significant attention to these factors are amongst those likely to overcome the problems of intensive competition [Lois P., Wang J., Wall A. D., Ruxton T., 2000, 2001; Paige M. M., 1994].

In other words, in today's political, economic and social climate, tourism providers and destinations are faced with a growing concern for maintaining and developing their infrastructure to

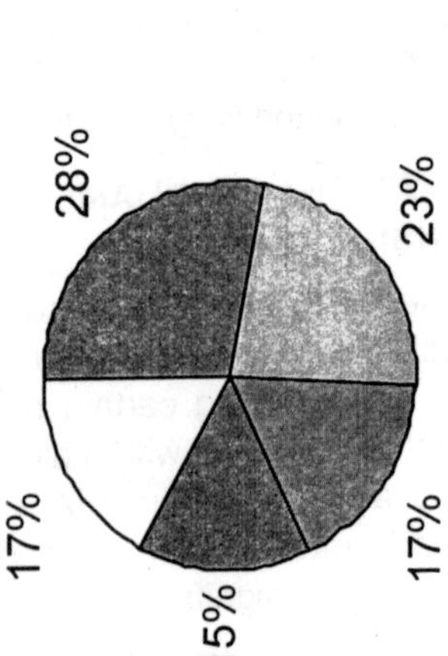

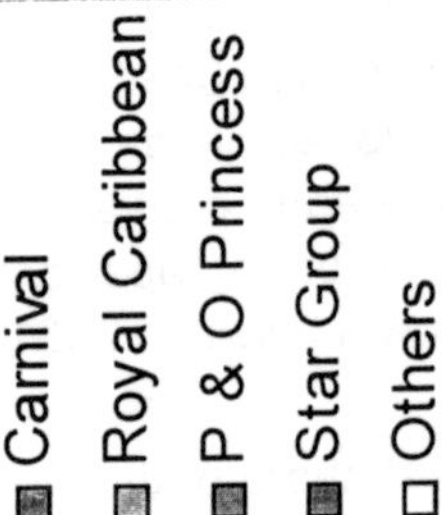

Figure 1: World Projected Berths Capacity Share (Fleet In Service And Newbuildings)
Source: Lloyd's Shipping (2001)

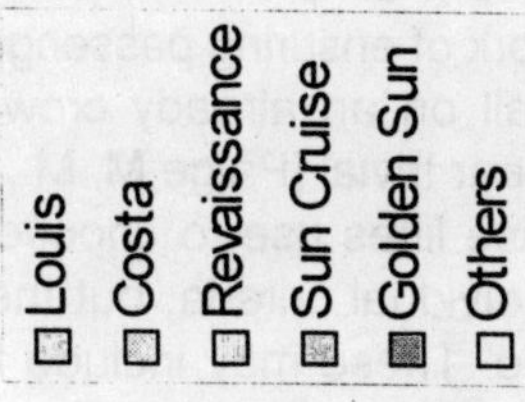

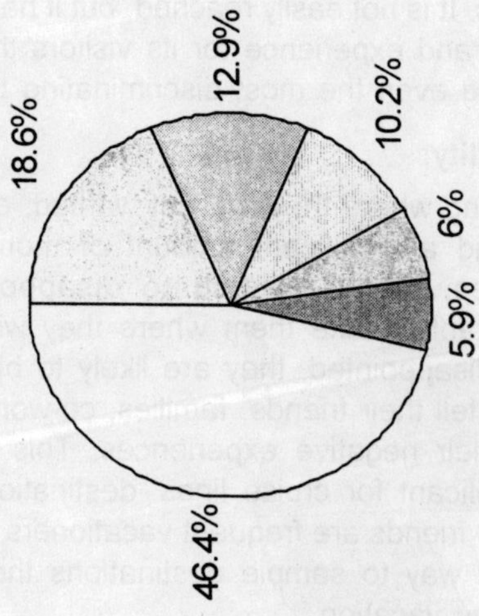

Figure 2: Mediterranean Berths Capacity Share
Source: Cruise Industry News (2001)

remain competitive. The cruise industry is faced with the same challenges. They must develop their onboard products including food, entertainment and sale destinations. Marketing a cruise package, particularly one that has already made its established mark in the industry, may seem simple. To those not involved with the behind-the-scenes work of ensuring passenger satisfaction through the right ports of call on an already crowded itinerary, such a task will probably appear trivial [Paige M. M., 1994]. There are no set formulas that cruise lines use to choose destinations and each line has its own individual criteria, but there are some basic principles that hold true. These may include the following:

Location:

Location is the hardest selling point for a destination to overcome. Therefore the cruise lines must work harder to create a demand from passengers wanting to travel there. Bermuda is a prime example of this. It is not easily reached, but it has created such a terrific product and experience for its visitors that it has a loyal following among even the most discriminating travellers.

Attitude and Hospitality:

No one enjcys going where they are not wanted, especially tourists who have paid a significant amount of money for a vacation. Cruise lines, never wanting to disappoint their passengers, are reluctant to take them where they will not be welcome. If they are disappointed, they are likely to blame this on the cruise line and tell their friends, families, co-workers and travel agents about their negative experiences. This negative response can be significant for cruise lines' destinations alike, since cruisers and their friends are frequent vacationers and look at a cruise as a good way to sample destinations they would consider for a long-stay vacation.

Political Stability:

Cruise lines must be responsible for their passengers' safety. Therefore it is not surprising that they look for destinations with a stable political environment. Political stability also allows for a continuity of good relations between the cruise line and destination tourism partners. Since both have a lot to gain by maintaining a positive experience for visitors, cruise lines look for destinations where there is mutual respect and cooperation to develop long-term relationships.

Ship Support Facilities:

This category is the one that most impacts upon the operations of a cruise ship and its abi1ity to call at a given port. Before any other consideration can be made, cruise lines require decent and safe docking facilities and/or launch or tender services, water, food, suppliers and possible waste handling facilities, repair services and re-fuelling capacity.

Catering and entertainment are of great importance and the cruise lines must be ready to meet and satisfy the needs of their passengers.

Value and Cost:

Overall cruise lines must determine the value of a destination related to the costs associated with calling there. The most visible of these costs is the passenger head tax, but other costs might include those relating to pilots, tenders and longshoremen. These costs are weighed in with the operational costs of cruising and provisioning a ship properly (e.g. with fuel) for that stop in the full itinerary. This cost is then evaluated with the overall passenger satisfaction with the destinations. Not all destinations are equivalent in what they offer, therefore not all carry the same value to passengers. The value to customers can be measured in quantitative terms by taking into the account the related costs associated with a particular voyage. It can also be measured in qualitative terms by evaluating the passengers' satisfaction of their expectations.

Shopping:

One important aspect of tourism is that destinations enjoy the economic benefits that visitors bring. One of the largest benefits stems from tourist shopping. Cruise passengers like to be able to buy either a known product at a bargain price, or something unique to the destination visited.

Other Factors:

The travel agency community is an important factor in recommending new destinations to cruise lines and in assessing existing destinations. Since the majority of cruises are sold through travel agents, as stated in the analysis of survey's results, their attitudes and comments are respected. Marketing and research techniques are used to measure the advantages and disadvantages of different itineraries. The marketing and research department of cruise lines uses this information in order to improve the existing destinations or to recommend new attractive itineraries and destinations. Sometimes, selections are based upon reaction to competition, either to match what they are doing or to provide exclusivity in an itinerary. Destination marketing and advertisement can greatly enhance a destination's image in the minds of both decision-makers and prospective passengers.

Apart from the major factors mentioned above, there are several other principles that the cruise companies must take into account. Such principles may include sightseeing, infrastructure, attractions and historical interest, and cultural individuality. Since competition within the cruise market has grown dramatically, the cruise companies need to be genuinely aware of the importance of the above factors.

SURVEY RESULTS

In order to consider the primary factors of competition at sea, to investigate the consumer attitudes to cruise tourism in the Cyprus and Mediterranean regions, and then to apply cost-benefit analysis to these findings, two surveys were conducted during April 2000. The first survey was carried out on board the cruise ship *Atalante* and outside the Limassol port terminal in Cyprus. Three hundred respondents were asked to rate certain factors as being the most important in making a cruise holiday enjoyable. The respondents were also asked to consider the major factors in their choice of voyage, their impression of the ship, its activities and the shore excursions. Then, they were requested to provide information as to how they had booked their cruise and whether they would like to take another cruise within the next three years.

In carrying out the first survey, a "quota sampling technique" was used. The sample selected was 300 passengers. 186 were foreigners since 62% of cruisers are overseas. 100 passengers selected were British because 53.7% of tourists visiting Cyprus come from Great Britain.

The second survey was conducted with tourists who visited Cyprus during April 2000 and covered all the tourist areas in Cyprus. This was carried out by the method of personal interview and 300 respondents were asked to rate certain factors that make the cruise enjoyable, their expectation and satisfaction levels after having taken a cruise. Those who had never taken a cruise were requested to state whether they would plan to take a cruise within the next three years.

The method of "quota sampling" was also used for the second survey. The survey covered the four major tourist areas in Cyprus. 53.7% were British and 46.3% came from other countries. The percentages used to divide the sample size were collected from the Department of Statistics and Research of the Cyprus government [Republic of Cyprus, 2000].

Analysis of Consumer Attitudes to Cruise Tourism - Survey 1

Attitudes to cruising differ in many countries. For example, in the US and Canada cruising was not a traditional vacation option in the 19th century and many North Americans in the past were more interested in building infrastructure for internal tourism and vacationing at home than in looking outwards to the sea. To many in Europe, there has been a feeling that cruising was for the old and wealthy and the industry will have to continue to work hard for some years in order to ensure that these traditional attitudes are dropped [Wild G. P., 1995]. Table 3 sets out the attitudes of consumers in the Cyprus and Mediterranean regions to cruising, following the survey.

Consumers who have already taken a cruise were most likely to be over 45 years of age, and particularly over 65 years. A large proportion of people of the latter age would not consider taking a cruise. A much larger proportion of younger people appear to be receptive to the idea of taking a cruise with around 58% to 62% of those interviewed between 15 and 34 years of age expressing interest in taking a cruise. This is a very encouraging result for cruise tourism. A large proportion of interviewees come from the UK, as most of the tourists who visit the Cyprus and Mediterranean regions are British citizens [Republic of Cyprus, 2000].

Table 3: Consumer Attitudes Towards Cruising By Demographics

Category	Have been on a cruise (%)	Would consider taking a cruise (%)	Wouldnever take a cruise (%)
All	40	35	25
Men	36	38	26
Women	44	40	16
15-19	6	60	34
20-24	7	62	31
25-34	9	58	33
35-44	11	55	34
45-54	14	38	48
55-64	12	27	61
65+	16	20	64
Cyprus	5	70	25
Greece	6	65	29
England	55	38	7
Others	29	47	24
Working	10	50	40
Retired	10	42	48
Married	15	47	38
Single	8	45	47
Divorced	4	55	41
Children	3	52	45
No children	10	45	45

Source: Survey 1 - (2000).

Despite the competition, the future outlook for the cruise industry is promising. More than 7.66 million North Americans are estimated to have cruised in 2002. Despite the challenges faced in 2002, the industry not only met but exceeded its projections and easily bettered the record number of 7.49 million passengers who had cruised in 2001 [Cruise Lines International Association, 2003]. The industry had the opportunity to welcome 1 million more guests in 2003 compared to 2002 – a potential of 8.66

million passengers from North America and 9.66 million worldwide [Cruise Lines International Association, 2003]. It is obvious that, since Europe is now the fastest growing source market for cruise passengers, the Mediterranean region tends to increase its market share and further tonnage will be deployed in the region. According to CLIA's survey [Cruise Lines International Association, 2003], a large proportion of around 75% of the respondents said that they would consider taking a cruise and 56% of these people said that they are planning to go on a cruise within three years.

Table 4: Cruiser Demographics

Category	First time cruisers (%)	Frequent cruisers (%)
Married	78	72
Single (including divorced)	22	28
Do vacation with children	20	17
Do not vacation with children	80	83
Males	52	49
Females	48	51
Age 25-40	29	24
Age 41-59	40	36
Age 60 or older	25	24

Source: Survey 1 - (2000).

It is clear from Table 4 that most of the cruisers are married, and they do not prefer taking a cruise with children. In addition, the results of the authors' first survey are analyzed as follows:

1. Of those polled (300 passengers), 60% were first-time cruisers and 40% were frequent cruisers.
2. The passengers considered destination as the major factor in their choice of voyage. The destination rate came to 61%, followed by convenient dates and safety factors with 45% and 27%, respectively.
3. The overall impression of the ships was excellent. The passengers were happy about cleanliness of cabins and

public areas, quality and quantity of food, service in the dining rooms, hospitality of staff and social programmes. On the other hand, adverse comments were expressed regarding the limitations in duty free shops and casino entertainment. As mentioned by the passengers, they wanted to buy things that they could not get at home at reasonable prices. The passengers also suggested that the cruise line companies must extend the casino area of the ships, as it does not accommodate those who like to make use of it.

4. The passengers considered the options “Go sightseeing” and “Visit tourist attractions” as the most important factors in their decision to go on a cruise in specific regions. In particular, the rate of these options came to 65%, followed by the options “Visit museums etc.”(55%) and “Go shopping”(25%). This means that the cruise operators, in choosing cruise destinations, will need to ensure that they find places where passengers can go sightseeing and buy things they cannot get at home.

5. The overall impression of the land tours was very good, but the main problem was the amount of time spent at each destination. Although passengers were happy about the tour service and sightseeing attractions, the limited time did not allow them to do their shopping and have lunch at a local restaurant.

6. The passengers also expressed their opinion on the abolition of duty free shops in ports by the European Union. 68% of those polled said that the abolition would have an adverse effect on the profits of the companies and not on the passengers' spending. With the increase in prices, the passengers would save some money as they can get everything at home at the same or similar price. Due to the fact that the profit of the companies will decrease, some of the “duty free shop” staff will become redundant. 32% of the passengers said that there would be little or no effect on their decision because duty free shopping is not an important factor in choosing a cruise destination.

7. Another point that is considered important for the passengers was the size of the ship. The majority of the passengers indicated that they prefer to go on a cruise on bigger cruise ships. For example, 28% of the passengers would prefer a 600 to 799-foot long cruise ship and 19% would prefer an even bigger cruise ship (i.e. more than 800 feet long).
8. 49% of the passengers booked their cruise through Tour Operators and 44% through Travel Agents.
9. Finally, 84% of the passengers said that they would like to take another cruise within three years. They said that the main reason luring them into taking another cruise is that a cruise vacation is an excellent combination between a land-based holiday and sea travel, where they can enjoy certain things like entertainment, quality service and hotel comfort.

CONCLUDING REMARKS – SURVEY 1

It was concluded that destination is the major factor in the passengers' choice of cruise. The cleanliness of cabins and public areas, the quality of food and service, the staff hospitality, and social and entertainment programmes are considered important.

The distribution system of the Tour Operators and Travel Agents plays a major role within the cruise industry as both liners and agents become close partners.

A cruise vacation is an excellent combination between a land-based holiday and sea travel, where they can enjoy certain things like entertainment, quality service and hotel comfort. This shows that the Cyprus and Mediterranean cruise market will see continued growth, and the future of the international industry looks bright. This is indicated by the fact that most passengers expressed the desire to take a cruise in the international seas, such as Western Mediterranean and the Caribbean. It was also indicated that the future prospects of the companies offering cruises in the Cyprus and Mediterranean regions is good. This is because 88% of the passengers would like to take a cruise on the same ship, sailing in the Eastern Mediterranean.

ANALYSIS OF CONSUMER ATTITUDES TO CRUISE TOURISM – SURVEY 2

Expectations regarding the cruise experience are high, and focus particularly on the freedom of cruisers to do as much or as little as they want, on getting good value for money, on having fun and relaxing. Table 5 sets out the importance of various aspects of cruising to first time cruisers and their satisfaction levels after having taken the cruise.

According to people who have taken both cruise and land-based vacations, cruise holidays seem to have certain significant differences. The people were asked to rate their satisfaction on some important items during their cruise and land-based vacations. In the Cyprus and Mediterranean cruise regions, when compared to land-based vacations by people who have taken both, cruise vacations rate exceptionally well over all key descriptive characteristics. Table 6 details all these items.

Table 5: Cruising Attributes According To First-Time Cruisers

Item	Importance (%)	Satisfaction (%)	Gap (%)
Offers a variety of activities	70	80	+10
Allows you to relax	82	85	+3
Is a learning experience	48	76	+28
Is a way to meet interesting people	38	50	+12
Allows you to do as much or as little as you want	86	87	+1
Is a fun vacation	83	84	+1
Is a good value for money	84	82	-2
Gives you the chance to visit different places	74	80	+6
Offers comfortable accommodation	71	78	+7
Allows you to be pampered	49	69	+20

Source: ***Survey 2 - (2000).***

Table 6: Cruising Versus Resort Vacations

Item	Cruises %	Resorts %
Well organised	88	83
Relaxing	92	90
Good value for money	89	77
Pampered by staff	69	61
Active	58	51
Safe	78	75
Romantic	79	60
Good way to try out a vacation	80	56
Able to meet interesting people	58	55
Hassle-free	75	67

Source: Survey 2 – (2000).

The fact that people consider that a cruise vacation is a good "value for money" as opposed to a land-based vacation rates high among cruisers. The characteristic with the highest difference between cruise and land-based vacations is that of a "good way to try out a vacation".

Other remarkable features were identified by the survey. Table 7 sets out the number of days that people prefer to spend on a cruise holiday. Clearly, most of the people (40%) prefer to spend 8-15 days on a cruise holiday. A large proportion of 38% indicated that they prefer the option of 4-7 days and 12% prefer taking a mini cruise (i.e. less than 3 days).

Table 7: Number of Days Preferred for a Cruise Holiday

Item (No of Days)	Cruise %
Less than 3 days	12
4-7 days	38
8-15 days	40
16-30 days	4
Others	6
Total	**100**

Source: Survey 2 – (2000).

Table 8 shows the places that people have been to, on a cruise. 33% said that they had visited other places not mentioned above, and in particular, 27% had been on a cruise in the Western Mediterranean and 6% in the Caribbean region. With respect to UK cruisers, Egypt was their first option, but Cypriots, Greeks, Russians, and Germans preferred Israel and the Greek islands, especially for historical and religious reasons.

Table 8: Visiting Places

Places	Cruisers%
Egypt	24
Israel	19
Greek islands	24
Others	33
Total	**100**

Source: Survey 2 – (2000).

CONCLUDING REMARKS – SURVEY 2

Clearly, in most areas satisfaction levels were in excess of expectations, particularly in the areas of learning experience, pampering, activities and meeting interesting people. Most also thought that cruising offered comfortable accommodation and was a good way to visit different places.

The fact that tourists consider that they are more attentively looked after on a cruise as opposed to a land-based holiday rates high among cruisers. This is a key aspect of ship life with staff to guest ratios being higher aboard ship than in a resort.

According to the survey, mini cruises are not preferable by the tourists. It was investigated that tourist attractions and sightseeing are the most important factors in their decision to go on a cruise. With the mini cruises they do not have enough time to go sightseeing and visit tourist attractions.

QUALITATIVE ASSESSMENT OF PASSENGERS' ATTITUDES

It would be important to propose an approach in order to synthesise the above factors for making decisions qualitatively.

With the continuous development of the social sciences, and especially through the introduction of new statistical and quantitative techniques which can be used in commerce and industry, an attempt needs to be made to 'measure the immeasurable' [Harvey M., 1982] before making decisions.

The development of a generic qualitative assessment model is proposed as an attempt to measure the cruise passengers' attitudes to cruise tourism. This model is used in order to help cruise companies, particularly in the Cyprus and Mediterranean cruise regions, to determine the factors in choosing a destination, analyse those factors in qualitative terms, and then make the most appropriate decisions that may be beneficial for them. A simple way to do this is to incorporate the factors and alternatives on a matrix. Then, a point measurement weighting system is used to assign relative values to the factors being considered. The matrix in Table 9 shows the factors that might affect the decision to choose a destination, to any of the possible options.

Table 9: A Measurement Matrix

FACTORS	**Destination Score**			**WEIGHTING**	**Weighted Destination Score**		
	A	**B**	**C**		**A**	**B**	**C**
Location							
Attitude & Hospitality							
Political Stability							
Ship Support Facilities							
Value and Cost							
Shopping							
Others							
TOTAL							

The two stages in the completion of the matrix are:

a. To use some point scale (1 to 10) to assign ratings to the various factors concerned.

b. To assign weightings to the factors being considered based upon their importance to the organisation.

After this has been done, it is clear that a simple totting up of these factors will not provide a deterministic solution, although it may appear to do so. However, even if the actual figures finally obtained are not conclusive, at least the analysis of the factors and discussion of them will make the participants become more aware and consider the influences of all factors on the decision more carefully.

The approach described above can be demonstrated by an example, where "XYZ Cruises" will have to take a decision as to where to operate its first ship acquired recently. In particular, "XYZ Cruises" has three alternative itineraries shown below:

Itinerary A: Cyprus-Israel-Egypt-Cyprus (4 -day cruise)

Itinerary B: Cyprus- Lebanon- Rhodes-Cyprus (4-day cruise)

Itinerary C: Piraeus-Mykonos-Patmos-Crete-Santorini-Piraeus (4-day cruise)

The ratings and the weightings of the factors concerned can be described as follows:

Ratings of the various factors concerned:

1 2 3 4 5 6 7 8 9 10

Least important Most important

Weightings of the factors being considered based upon their importance to the organization:

1 2 3 4 5 6

Least important Most important

The weights used to arrive at the final decision are based on the analysis of the survey's results carried out by the authors in the Cyprus and Mediterranean regions [Lois P., Wang J., Wall A. D., Ruxton T., 2000, 2001]. In particular, the passengers were asked to indicate the main factor(s) in choosing to travel on a cruise ship. The response to this question was as follows:

Factors	Location	Attitude & Hospitality	Political Stability	Ship Support Facilities	Value and Cost	Shopping	Others
%	65	50	60	58	27	25	62

The above results can then be used to find the weight of each factor. Using the weighting system, as shown in Table 10, each factor will correspond to a weight as presented in Table 11. Multiple expert judgments can also be incorporated into the above analysis.

Table 10: Weighting System

Class intervals (%)	Weighting system
0-20	1
21-35	2
36-50	3
51-65	4
66-80	5
81-100	6

Source: Survey 2 – (2000).

Table 11: Level Of Importance Of Travelling Factors By Cruise Ship

Factors	%	Weights
Location	65	5
Attitude & Hospitality	50	3
Political Stability	60	4
Ship Support Facilities	58	4
Value & Cost	27	2
Shopping	25	2
Others	62	4

Source: Survey 2 – (2000).

The results of the qualitative assessment matrix, as shown in Table 12, show that Itinerary C is the best solution for the company.

It is clear that "Location" is the major factor in the choice of itinerary. Therefore, the company must work hard in order to create a demand from passengers who want to travel there. The factor "Others" ranks second and includes the travel agency community, the marketing and advertising techniques, sightseeing, attractions and historical interest. The importance of the above factors is well indicated in the results of the survey where 65% of the total passengers expressed the opinion that "Go sightseeing" and "Visit tourist attractions" are considered as the most important affecting their cruise vacation. In addition, 44% and 49% of the passengers booked their cruise through a travel agency and a tour operator respectively. "Ship support facilities" is also an important factor because it impacts upon the operations of a cruise ship.

Table 12: Qualitative Assessment Matrix

FACTORS	Destination Score			WEIGHTING	Weighted Destination Score		
	A	B	C		A	B	C
Location	7	8	9	5	35	40	45
Attitude & Hospitality	6	6	8	3	18	18	24
Political Stability	9	7	4	4	36	28	16
Ship Support Facilities	8	8	8	4	32	32	32
Value & Cost	6	6	8	2	12	12	16
Shopping	4	5	7	2	8	10	14
Others	7	6	9	4	28	24	36
Total	**47**	**46**	**53**		**175**	**170**	**191**

Source: Survey 2 – (2000).

The cruise line must pay great attention to the passengers' wants because the 'word of mouth' technique is an excellent advertising element for the company. The company must ensure that all the support facilities of its cruise ship can satisfy the needs of the passengers. This factor is also important for both Itinerary A and Itinerary B. Then the factors "Attitude and hospitality" and "Value and cost" follow. The company must not ignore the importance of these factors. 50% of the passengers said that their impression of the staff hospitality was "Very Good" and 32% said that the impression was "Good". "Value and cost" is an important element for both the passengers and the cruise line. The cost can be evaluated by the overall satisfaction of passengers with the destinations. It is obvious that not all itineraries carry the same value to passengers because not all destinations are equivalent in what they offer. The next factor that needs to be addressed is "Political stability". This factor ranks first for Itinerary A. It is clear that passengers look for destinations with a safe political environment. The political environment in Israel is unstable compared to Egypt and Greece. Therefore, the company must be responsible for the passengers' safety. "Shopping" ranks last in all Itineraries. This means that it is not very important in their choice of destination. 25% only expressed the opinion that shopping is a factor but not a major one during their cruise vacation.

Although passengers would like to buy something unique, this does not affect their decision regarding the cruise destination. The results obtained are a good indication for the cruise company to understand that they need to have good communication with the passengers. This may enable the company to discuss and evaluate the passengers' expectations and wants, and also create a situation that will win back the repeating passengers.

CONCLUSION

According to various studies and surveys carried out throughout the decade [Loizou C., 1997; Peisley T., 2002; Wild P., Dearing J., 1999; Wild G. P., 1995], the cruise industry enjoyed growth despite continuing recession, and has been more successful than almost any other tourist industry. This is also proved by the authors' surveys [Lois P., Wang J., Wall A. D., Ruxton T., 2000, 2001]. The cruise industry has prospered in the current economic environment, and the major lines are increasing their market share, earning good profits, and signalling optimism for a bright future with orders for new ships. A key reason of this prosperity is that a cruise provides greater value to the consumer compared to resorts and other types of vacation.

The cruise product and new ships will play a key role in the future of the cruise market. The cruise ships are becoming more innovative and, in many cases, larger to meet the needs of the changing cruise passenger. Destination development is also important. Another reason for the industry's success is the support of the travel agency community. Because a cruise sale offers one of the highest commission opportunities available and also depends on the level of customer satisfaction [Lois P., Wang J., Wall A. D., Ruxton T., 2000], agents have aligned themselves with the cruise business to become close partners.

The continuing expansion of the cruise lines, the building of new ships and the new passengers' expectations may indicate that the competition will be strong. Therefore, the cruise lines need to take into account certain considerations. These may be beneficial for their customers, and only certain lines will be able to survive within the cruise market. The findings from the surveys [Lois P., Wang J., Wall A. D., Ruxton T., 2000, 2001] revealed that due to the expansion of the cruise market and the development opportunities for new destinations, the competition becomes increasingly strong. The fundamental competition considerations are of paramount importance and therefore, the cruise lines will have to pay great attention to these factors. This will enable them to overcome the problems of intensive competition. The factor found as the most important for passengers in choosing to travel on a cruise ship is Location with 65.3%. Other factors of paramount importance include "Attitude and hospitality" with 50%, "Political stability" with 60% and "Ship support facilities" with 58%.

The proposed methodology was developed in order to synthesise competition factors and carry out a qualitative analysis on the consumers' attitudes to cruise tourism. This will enable the cruise companies to make proper decisions, and it can also be used to carry out a quantitative analysis of those factors and further analyse each factor separately. For example, an analysis may be carried out to investigate the main areas and reasons why the passengers consider "Location" as the primary factor when choosing to travel on a cruise ship.

The factors that were examined in this contribution can be used by cruise companies, particularly in the Cyprus and Mediterranean regions, to build up their marketing and pricing strategies. The price of the cruise product, the impact of discounting and the manner of distribution and promotion of the product play a vital role in the successful operation of cruise companies. The main objectives of such companies are to divert revenue opportunities into profits and increase their market share. In order for the companies to achieve these objectives, they will have to construct an appropriate business strategy.

REFERENCES

Belbin, M. (1981) *Management Teams, Why They Succeed or Fail.* Oxford: Heinemann.

Cartwright, R. and Baird, C. (1999) *The Development and Growth of the Cruise Industry.* Oxford: Butterworth/Heinemann.

Cohen, E. (1972). Towards a sociology of international tourism. *Social Research* 39 (1), 164-182.

Crompton, J. (1979) Motivations for pleasure vacations. *Annals of Tourism Research* 6, 408-424.

Cruise Industry News (1999) *Annual Report.* International Guide to the Cruise Industry, 12th Edition, New York.

Cruise Industry News (2000) *Annual Report* International Guide to the Cruise Industry, 13th Edition, New York.

Cruise Industry News (2001) The Largest Cruise Companies Worldwide 2001 and 2006. International Guide to the Cruise Industry, 14th Edition, New York.

Cruise Lines International Association (CLIA) (2003) CLIA lines host 8.66 million cruise vacationers in 2002. Online documents at URL http://www.cruising.org/cruisenews [14 February 2003].

Harvey, M. (1992) *Management Accounting: Relevant Costs, Information for Decision-Making.* Revision Course Paper. UK: Chartered Institute of Management Accountants (CIMA).

Honey, P. and Mumford, J. (1986) *A Manual of Learning Styles.* Maidenhead: Peter Honey.

Lloyd's Shipping (2001) Is the Cruise Industry Oversupplied?. *Lloyd's Shipping Economist* 23 (3), 7-9.

Lloyd's Shipping (2002) Cruise Trade Picks up again. *Lloyd's Shipping Economist* 24 (3), 10-14.

Lois, P., Wang, J., Wall, A. D. and Ruxton, T. (2000) Consumer attitudes to cruise tourism and fundamental considerations of competition at sea in Cyprus and Mediterranean regions. *2nd International Congress on Maritime Technological Innovations and Research*, Cadiz (Spain), 8-11 November.

Lois, P., Wang, J., Wall, A. D. and Ruxton, T. (2001) Fundamental considerations of competition at sea and the application of cost-benefit analysis. *Tourism Today*, 1, 89-102.

Loizou, C. (1997) The outlook for the European cruise market. *Maritime*

Cyprus Conference: A New Era in Shipping, Cyprus, 7 October.

Mathieson, A. and Wall, G. (1982) *Tourism, Economic, Physical and Social Impacts.* Harlow: Longmans.

Paige, M. M. (1994) Factors involved in choosing a cruise destination, *International Cruise and Ferry Review*, London, Autumn/Winter, 195.

Peisley, T. (2003) *Global changes in the cruise industry 2003-2010* - a Seatrade research report. Online documents at URL http://www.seatrade-global.com/cruise_report/cruise_focus.htm [14 March 2003].

Republic of Cyprus (2000) *Tourism and Travel Statistics. Number* 158, Cyprus: Department of Statistics and Research.

Ryan, C. (1991) *Recreational Tourism.* London: International Thomson Business Press.

Shipping World and Shipbuilder (1996) In focus: cruise and ferry industry, p.8.

Wild, G. P. (1995) *Maritime Tourism to the Year 2000.* Sussex: G. P. Wild International Limited.

Wild, P. and Dearing, J. (1999) *Maritime Tourism to the Year 2004*. UK: G. P. Wild International Limited.

2

THE APPLICATION OF MARKETING STRATEGY IN THE TOURISM AND HOSPITALITY INDUSTRY

MARIOS D. SOTERIADES

ABSTRACT

The marketing planning process occurs on two levels. Strategic decisions should be taken prior to operational decisions. Essentially a marketing strategy contains a series of analyses. The results of these analyses should be documented in a marketing action plan (operational marketing). Therefore, strategy must be transformed into action by determining the various marketing components and the appropriate communications mix. This paper provides an outline of the principal marketing strategy issues and its application in the tourism and hospitality industry. In the first section, definitions for the main terms being discussed are provided. Attention will then be directed toward the main issues, which play a significant role in the marketing strategy. The industry faces new and increasing marketing challenges arising from changing tourist behaviour and environmental conditions. The imperative for a careful environment analysis and assessment is addressed in the second section. The main aspects related to the distinct nature of marketing tourism services are presented in the third section. In the tourism context, the product is an experience that is achieved through the combination of a diverse range of products and services. In addition, the marketing mix for tourism and hospitality services has changed; the traditional four Ps have been redefined and have become seven Cs in order to reflect consumer orientation. Strategies are needed to suit the changing and more demanding competitive environment. Moreover, the unique attributes of tourism and hospitality services provide challenges that must be addressed when developing strategies. This is the topic of the fourth section which highlights the aspects of strategy formulation and implementation. The next section provides a brief overview of some specific strategic issues, such as Destination marketing, Customer Relationship Marketing and E-marketing in the tourism and hospitality industry. Recommendations contributing to the effective implementation of marketing strategy are presented in the last section.

Keywords:* *marketing strategy, tourism and hospitality industry, strategic analysis and assessment, marketing mix, strategic issues.

INTRODUCTION

The tourism and hospitality industry today faces a set of new challenges arising from changing consumers and environment. It is estimated that only those operators who recognize the changes occurring in the marketplace and proactively respond to these challenges will continue to be successful in the future. Thus, strategies are necessary in order to address the more demanding competitive environment. The tourism and hospitality industry needs to be more forward thinking than ever before. It is suggested that strategic marketing decision-making is the management process responsible for coordinating an organisation's marketing activity. The purpose of this paper is to examine the application of strategic marketing in the tourism and hospitality industry and provide an outline of principal marketing strategy issues.

DEFINITIONS

A comprehensive definition of marketing is suggested by Kotler (2003): Marketing is the analysis, planning, implementation and control of carefully formulated programs designed to bring about voluntary exchanges of values with target markets for the purpose of achieving organizational objectives. Thus, marketing is a managerial process involving several activities (WTO, 1997): establishing marketing goals and objectives, formulating marketing strategy, preparing and implementing plans.

According to Mazanec (1994: 99-100), contemporary marketing theory and advanced marketing practice distinguish between strategic and operational marketing planning. Strategic decisions should be taken prior to operational decisions. The objective of operational planning is to design the appropriate marketing mix. Strategy must be transformed into action by determining the communications mix.

Marketing Strategy

Marketing strategy specifies the long-term goals and objectives of a business, identifying opportunities and the scope of activities needed to realize them. Strategies therefore show how to pinpoint objectives. Calver (1994: 285-286) pointed out that the use of the term 'strategy' as a description of longer-term planning is helpful, but unless it provides the right guideposts, it is equally ineffective. The strategic plan should provide a blueprint for action that can be interpreted at any organizational level. Marketing strategy must therefore provide clear indications of which markets are to be targeted and the means by which they will be targeted in the long term. The following description of what marketing strategy does emphasize the dynamic aspect of the process and the importance of strategy as an action-based discipline: 'Marketing strategy is the process by which the organization translates its business objectives and business strategy into market activity' (Filfield, 1992: 13). The two terms '**marketing planning**' and '**marketing strategy**' are often used interchangeably. Marketing plans should be prepared for the long term with clear guidelines for action. The marketing plan contains the tactical details for implementation, dealing with specific marketing activities. Marketing strategy provides the overall analysis of the organization and its environment with a means of achieving its overall objectives. The strategic plan may therefore be regarded as a substantial preface to the marketing plan.

From the above brief discussion, it might be pointed out that:

- Strategy shows how to pinpoint objectives.
- Strategic marketing entails a stream of decisions and

actions, which lead to the development and implementation of effective strategy (Crawford-Welch, 1996: 167-169).

- Strategy is not only about deciding on future direction but also the actual implementation at operational level. The crucial point is how to convert strategy into action.
- Strategic marketing is as much an art as a science and is not a panacea or a prescription for success.

Marketing strategy in the tourism and hospitality industry faces a particular challenge as it deals with a multifaceted, poorly standardized product, and a volatile, fastidious customer.

ENVIRONMENT ANALYSIS AND ASSESSMENT

To be successful in the hospitality and tourism markets, businesses must be able to interpret the needs of their customers, identify appropriate ways of segmenting the markets in which they compete, develop and launch the appropriate products and effectively communicate with potential consumers. These issues are closely interrelated as they form the basis of the marketing interface between the organization and its business and market environment. Tourism takes place in a complex, dynamic and constantly changing environment that must be monitored and adapted to by all tourism and hospitality enterprises. The industry today faces a set of new and increasing challenges arising from changing tourist behaviour and environment conditions (Calver, 1994; Crawford-Welch, 1996; Middleton, 2001). These challenges include:

- the reconciliation of the need to consolidate the industry's service offerings to the consumer and maintain a market position with the need to remain flexible enough to respond to changes in its operational environment.
- to design and properly deliver products and services corresponding to the needs of the various markets.

It is estimated that only those businesses that recognize the changes occurring in the marketplace and proactively respond to these challenges will continue to be successful in the future (Chon & Singh, 1995). These tasks require a strategic marketing approach, as well as more reliable information through proper long-term strategic planning and decision-making.

Both the general and market environments create opportunities and pose threats to the tourism and hospitality businesses. Within a perspective of strategic marketing planning formulation, the first major task is a situation analysis, which consists of two analyses: environmental and resources (Heath & Wall, 1994):

- In the environmental analysis, an assessment of the major environments - macroeconomic, competitive and market – is emphasized in order to identify opportunities and threats.
- The purpose of a resource analysis is to identify the strengths and the weaknesses in the tourism and hospitality industry.

These analyses should be followed by business's goal and strategy formulation. These steps form the foundation for the development of an enterprise's marketing strategy. It should be noted that information is the basis of planning and decision-making, and is needed in order to develop meaningful and effective strategies. Thus, a marketing information system becomes a valuable tool and an essential support for the decision-making process in tourism and hospitality organisations, complementing the intuition and entrepreurial ability that have been responsible for the success of the industry in the past few decades (Calver, 1994).

The importance of monitoring and analyzing the tourism and hospitality environment has been documented by several authors (among others Witt & Moutinho, 1995; Porter, 1995; Knowles, 1996; Middleton, 2001; Varvaressos & Soteriades, 2005). Scanning the environment for trends that dictate strategic postures is a necessary and vital part of strategic marketing. The one certainty of the future is that change will continue and those tourism businesses and destinations which are both aware of economic, social and technological changes, and develop effective responses to them, will achieve longer-term viability (Moscardo, *et al.*, 2000: xxxi). Predictions are that the industry will continue to be volatile, consolidation will continue, consumer satisfaction will become even more important and technology will play an increasingly more important role (Matovic & McCleary, 2003). Therefore, environment and resource analysis and assessment are essential to the organisations in order to identify and respond to changes incurring in any field and to undertake the appropriate marketing actions.

THE DISTINCT NATURE OF MARKETING TOURISM SERVICES

The nature and particularities of tourism have a number of important marketing implications. The tourism product is an experience that is achieved through the combination of a diverse array of products and services (Heath & Wall, 1994: 3-7). For the tourists, the product is the complete experience that covers the entire amalgam of all the components of the product, including their attitudes and expectations. According to Middleton (2001), the overall tourism product is a package and might be defined in terms of five main components, comprising destination attractions, destination facilities and services, accessibility of the destination (including transport), images, brands and perceptions, and price to the customer. Thus, it might be argued that the tourism and hospitality industry is a provider of experiences. The unique attributes of tourism services include (Crawford-Welch, 1996; Middleton, 2001):

- Intangible and variable nature
- Simultaneous nature of production and consumption
- The consumer's participation in the production process by making choices and interacting with service staff. The interaction dynamics are influenced by the specific needs and expectations of each customer (consumption experience).
- Difficulties in ensuring reliabilities and consistencies of service delivery.

Because of these characteristics, which are inherent in the tourism and hospitality product, their marketing is a special case of marketing at both a strategic and an operational level.

An organisation's marketing mix is traditionally defined as comprising the four P's - product, price, promotion and place - but this definition has been redefined to encompass the unique aspects of service. The original four core variables have been expanded to encompass People, Process and Physical Evidence or design. Kotler & Armstrong (1999: 111) later redefined the 'Ps' as 'Cs' to reflect the consumer orientation that is central to modern services marketing thinking:

- Product means Customer value (the perceived benefits provided to meet needs and wants, quality of service received and the value for money delivered).
- Price means Cost to the consumer (cost is the consumer-focused equivalent of price).
- Promotion means Communication (embracing all forms of producer / customer dialogue, not just sales promotion).
- Place, distribution, access means Convenience (in terms of consumer access to the products they buy).
- People mean Visitors; Employees; and Host community.
- Process (The service delivery process): the tourism and hospitality product experience consists of both process and outcome.
- Physical evidence and design: Style and ambience of the offer judged appropriate to the image and price of the product.

The unique attributes of tourism services provide challenges that must be addressed when developing marketing strategies and plans: identifying and determining target markets or segments of those markets will help an organisation to decide how it can best meet customer expectations, and so help to determine service styles and levels.

STRATEGY FORMULATION AND IMPLEMENTATION

The strategic marketing approach involves the appropriate choices in the following major fields:

- Setting marketing goals and objectives
- Selecting market targets, based on marketing objectives.
- Formulating the marketing strategy, including positioning and marketing mix strategies.
- Preparing the promotion /communication plan, the strategic choices take the form of a marketing action plan.

Hence, marketing strategy is based upon and reflects the environmental analysis, resource analysis, and goal formulation stages. Based on strategic marketing principles and approaches that have been suggested by several authors on the subject (Buckley & Papadopoulos, 1986; Calver, 1994; Heath & Wall, 1994; WTO, 1997), the following strategic marketing process is proposed (Table 1).

Table 1 The strategic planning process: the stages of developing a marketing strategy

Stages – Key elements	Content
Situation Analysis	Environmental Analysis Resource Analysis
Goal Formulation: Organisation's Mission, Goals and Objectives	- Determine: - Organisation's mission - Goals (qualitative variables to pursue) - Specific objectives (quantitative goals).
Strategy Formulation	Develop a broad strategy to achieve goals and objectives, taking into account all constraints (market, competition, resources, capabilities, etc.)
Marketing Objectives & Strategy - Target Strategy - Positioning Strategy- - Marketing Mix Strategy	The components of marketing strategy: Select the target market segment(s) - Chose a competitive position (select a desired position in the market and plan a strategy to achieve the desired position). - Develop an effective marketing mix strategy to reach and serve the selected market segments (including the strategies for Product, Price, Distribution and Promotion).

Stages – Key elements	**Content**
Marketing Supporting Systems	Develop marketing systems that are required for the successful implementation of strategic marketing: Information, Planning and Evaluation.
Communications / Promotional Mix	This mix is composed of every factor and variable that influences the marketing effort.
Operational Marketing / Action Plans	Implement the marketing strategy with the appropriate marketing plans.

From the above table, it can be seen that it is of paramount importance to have a strategic approach to all crucial areas of marketing function. Strategies allow the organisation to address the more demanding competitive environment. As for implementation, it is worth noting that (Witt & Moutinho, 1995):

- In order to implement a strategic marketing approach effectively, appropriate marketing systems - information, planning, and evaluation - are required.
- One aspect of strategy implementation is resource planning, at both the organisational and operational levels. The former refers to the allocation of resources within the various parts of the organisation to support the strategy. The later refers to the identification of critical success factors needed at the operational level.
- There is a need to develop and implement action plans in all related fields, such as human resources and quality (Varvaressos & Soteriades, 2005).

Recent studies have suggested innovative approaches; for example, Edgell *et al.* (1999) proposed a new approach to strategic marketing planning in the tourism industry, emphasizing quality, efficiency and effectiveness in the marketing process. The authors recommend a six-step approach to strategic marketing planning, including needs analysis, research and analysis, creative infusion, strategic positioning, marketing plan development, as well as training, implementation, evaluation and adjustment. The suggested framework is designed to provide a road map for almost any tourism organization or destination and to help improve their marketing efforts. It is a strategic marketing system, but it is also action-oriented to benchmark and counter competitors' strategies.

Calver (1994: 290-295) pointed out that discussions of marketing strategy development often ignore the significant impact of the context in which it takes place.

Tourism and hospitality enterprises, like any other, contain a large number of interest groups anxious to maintain their own status quo to the detriment of strategy implementation. It is therefore important that having assessed all environmental influences, both internal and external to the organization (Smith, 1998: 144-163), the market remains the primary focus for strategic action.

Completing this section it is worth noting the following issues:

- The organization must ensure that an efficient marketing information system informs the strategic planning process and that the organizational culture is able to respond to market trends and be proactive in the identification of new strategic directions.
- Segmentation is a valuable marketing strategy. It is simply a means of achieving efficient resource allocation in an increasingly competitive marketplace and environment (Crawford-Welch, 1996). In tourism and hospitality, the diversity of products and customers has justified the intensive use of segmentation methods as strategic tools. Among these techniques, benefit segmentation has extensive use in tourism research, and seems to receive wide approval by academics and practitioners alike (**Frochot & Morrison, 2000).**
- During the past two decades, hospitality operations have been implementing product differentiation and branding strategies in response to their own maturation. Often the key to successful differentiation lies not in modifying the hospitality product for different market segments, but in careful promotion in order to modify the perception of the

product by consumers and their experience of it (Teare & Calver, 1996).

SPECIFIC STRATEGIC ISSUES

This section provides a brief overview of some issues of special interest in strategic marketing, such as destination marketing, customer relationship marketing and information and communication technologies.

Destination Marketing:

Tourism destination marketing involves many stakeholders and a complex product offer (Goodall & Ashworth, 1997). The strategic marketing approach makes the coordinated marketing of all actors involved feasible. This includes inter-relating the tourist attractions, activities, facilities and services and the various and increasingly fragmented tourist markets.

Given the variety of businesses operating from a particular destination, and the geographic dispersion of source markets, cooperative marketing arrangements are quite common and offer clear advantages. Complexity and interdependency among stakeholders have resulted in the creation of many local tourism marketing alliances and partnerships between the private and public sectors (Jefferson, 1994; Palmer & Bejou, 1995; WTO, 1997). These forms of cooperative marketing are particularly efficient in destination marketing. A well-known example of destination marketing partnership is 'Maison de France'. This body has the responsibility of coordinating French tourism marketing and is generally recognized as a model of good practice.

There is an increased demand in destination marketing due to rising customer expectations and growing competition between destinations. The destination marketing partnerships are important because most destinations have to compete at a global level. The preponderance of small businesses in destinations and the diversity of objectives in larger organizations is an impediment to the implementation of strategic destination marketing (Scott *et al.*, 2000). Recent studies stress the crucial role that knowledge management and information and communication technology (ICT) could play for these partnerships and other joint schemes in the field of destination marketing (You *et al.* 2000; Scott *et al.*, 2000; Riege *et al.*, 2002; Mistilis & Daniele, 2005). The virtual marketplace is an ideal tool for all destination management organisations that can implement marketing facilitation strategies, by using Websites (B2B) simultaneously for information, promotion, distribution, relationship marketing and marketing research (WTO, 1999; Middleton, 2001). These strategies are particularly valuable for both smaller-sized and medium-sized companies that lack the resources to undertake marketing activities.

Customer Relationship Marketing:

Customer Relationship Marketing (CRM) is essentially about getting and keeping customers. (Christopher *et al.,*1991: 3-28). There are many reasons why a tourism and hospitality business wishes to identify, deal differently and generally form relationships with its loyal customers. The marketing of services anged orientation from a product management to a customer relationship management. has changed orientation from product management to customer relationship management. Once again relationships with customers are brought to the forefront of marketing activities (Gummesson, 2002). The concept is derived from the links between customer service, quality and marketing. The rising prominence of CRM, which seeks to offer a holistic rather than a discipline-bounded perspective, underpins the need to adopt a more rigorous approach to understanding and responding to the needs of customers. In essence, the nature of CRM is to achieve a form of integration between customer service, quality and marketing (Laws, 1991; Teare & Gummesson, 1996). CRM strives to create a competitive advantage for the organisation. This goal can be reached by implementing the appropriate strategies, such as loyalty, indirect competition, cooperation network and creation of value for the customer. A valuable tool is a CRM system, defined as the total of methodologies, tools and technology to implement the relationship marketing strategy (Gordon, 1998).

The network of relationships between customers and markets requires a strategic focus. One key issue in the concept of strategy is the delivery of value to the customer. CRM essentially offers a broader view of marketing and offers a framework that operates more openly and builds inter-functional customer and value chain-based links (Teare & Calver, 1996:33-36). Middleton (2001: 166-167) notes that the concept has been one of the buzzwords of the last decade and it is primarily driven by knowledge gained and communicated by connected customer databases, which have a powerful market research value in generating detailed knowledge of repeat customers and in reducing marketing expenditure.

Information and Communication Technology:

The rapid advancement of information technology (ICT), notably the Internet and the World Wide Web, has created challenges and opportunities for the tourism and hospitality industry. ICT developments permeate every aspect of tourism marketing. A rapidly changing business environment, largely brought about by the Internet, requires companies to quickly implement new business methods, develop new networks and alliances, and be creative in their marketing. In the late 1990s the Internet and e-commerce systems have come to dominate the strategic thinking of the entire industry (O'Connor, 1999). Evidence shows that ICT influences nearly every aspect of marketing and the main stages in the marketing mix. The Web gives rise to a new and very effective tool and changes the way marketers define marketing mix variables (Middleton, 2001; Kotler, 2003; Siegel, 2003). The main implications of ICT on the principal processes in marketing include:

- Market research and marketing information systems.
- Strategic Planning and Networking: Virtual marketing companies provide distribution and marketing services. The Internet also allows the creation of virtual enterprises in which ICT provides the linkages – especially networks for micro-businesses (Braun, 2002).
- Customer Relationship Marketing (CRM): The Internet has a catalyst role in CRM applications (Demetriades & Baltas, 2003).
- Advertising and Public Relations: The Internet provides a completely new medium to communicate to targeted customer groups.
- Sales Promotion and Pricing: The Internet is an ideal medium for communicating prices, special offers and late availability of a product.

- Distribution and Access: As a new channel for direct marketing communications, the Internet is also reinventing distribution. Distribution channels are the new forums for product innovation and development.

The digital marketplace not only brings rapid proliferation of new products and services, but also new ways of marketing. ICT slash marketing cost, remove intermediaries and redefine marketing relationships (Rayport & Jaworski, 2001). It is obvious that marketing in the digital age requires dynamic and innovative strategies. Therefore, there is an imperative need for tourism and hotel businesses to actively select between business models that can best support an effective online marketing strategy. It has been suggested (Porter, 2001; Christian, 2001) that it is necessary to have a strategic approach to e-commerce as a medium to accomplish business objectives. Such an approach allows businesses to overcome the challenges and exploit the opportunities presented by ICT. Soteriades *et al.* (2004) have proposed a methodological framework, which would enable tourism and hotel enterprises to develop and implement their electronic marketing and commerce activities. This framework reflects a strategic approach in order to integrate e-commerce initiative into business operations as a medium to serve the corporate strategy. Within this framework, the following issues should be noted (Soteriades *et al.* 2004):

· Apart from the formulation of a strategy and organizational planning, the development of a business presence on the Internet requires appropriate actions in order to ensure its quality, thereby, contributing to the general marketing strategy's effectiveness.

· Evidence indicates that failing to introduce innovations, such as ICT, is due either to the lack of strategic planning or to the non-acceptance and implementation of the strategy in-house (Porter, 2001). Therefore, the integration of e-commerce activities into business operations should be considered as a 'top-down process'.

· The e-commerce operation is not an aim *per se*, neither an activity that might be developed independently and implemented separately. It should be incorporated as a new media that serves current and future corporate general strategy and aims.

RECOMMENDATIONS

Tourism marketing represents the systematic, coherent and consistent effort of hospitality and tourism businesses to develop, formulate, and implement their strategies in order to achieve their main goal: making the tourism product a successful experience for their guests / visitors. In a strategic approach, tourism marketing has taken on new dimensions which increasingly reflect the perspective of tourists and those hosting them. In simple terms, a marketing strategy is an integrated plan for marketing orientation; encompassing definitions of mission and target markets; detailed specification of marketing objectives; and a commitment to implementation. This paper has outlined some of the main considerations in developing and implementing a marketing strategy within the tourism and hospitality industry.

There are several important benefits to undertaking a strategic approach to marketing. These advantages include: establishing the overall objectives and strategies, providing a rational basis for decision-making on marketing and laying the foundation for effective implementation of the marketing plan.

The strategic approach to marketing at the business and destinations levels is now widely adopted as a principle, although implementation of the action plans is still weak in some instances. Founded on accumulated experience, the approaches and techniques of strategic marketing tourism are now reasonably well understood.

The following recommendations could be put forward to hospitality and tourism operations in order to effectively formulate and implement strategic marketing:

- Marketing strategy is based on a careful analysis and assessment of the marketplace and depends on the use of appropriate marketing information. Relevant and accurate information is required in order to carry out effective strategic marketing plans.
- In order to implement a strategic marketing approach effectively, appropriate management support is required.
- In order to ensure that marketing objectives, strategies and tools are optimally adapted to the dynamic

environment, an evaluation system should be developed (Varvaressos & Soteriades, 2005).

This paper, by no means exhaustive, has attempted to cover several issues that should be considered by tourism and hospitality operations while they are formulating and implementing their marketing strategies.

REFERENCES

Braun, P. (2002) Networking Tourism SMEs: E-commerce and E-marketing Issues in Regional Australia. *Information Technology & Tourism* 5(1), 13-23.

Buckley, P. and Papadopoulos, S. (1986) Marketing Greek tourism – the Planning Process. *Tourism Management* 7(2), 86-100.

Calver, S. (1994), Strategic Marketing Communication. In R. Teare, J. Mazanec, S. Crawford-Welch and S. Calver (eds.) *Marketing in Hospitality and Tourism: A Consumer Focus*. London: Cassell, 213-311.

Chon, K-S. and Singh, A. (1995) Marketing Resorts to 2000: Review of Trends in the USA. *Tourism Management* 16(6), 463-469.

Crawford-Welch, S. (1996) International Marketing in the Hospitality Industry. In R. Teareiety industry" In Richard TEAREghtligthed ategic marketing and A. Boer (eds.) *Strategic Hospitality Management: Theory and Practice for the 1990s (*4th edn). London: Cassell, 166-193.

Christian, R. (2001) Developing an Online Access Strategy: Issues facing Small to Medium-sized Tourism and Hospitality Enterprises. *Journal of Vacation Marketing* 7(2), 170-178.

Christopher, M., Payne, A. and Ballantyne, D. (1991) *Relationship Marketing*. Oxford: Butterworth-Heinemann.

Demetriades, S. and Baltas, G. (2003) *Electronic Commerce and Marketing*. Athens: Rosili Publications.

Edgell, D.L., Ruf, K. and Agarwal, A. (1999) Strategic Marketing Planning for the Tourism Industry. *Journal of Travel & Tourism Marketing* 8(3), 111-120.

Fifield, P. (1992) *Marketing Strategy*. Oxford: Butterworth-Heinemann.

Frochot, I. and Morrison, A. (2000) Benefit Segmentation: A Review of its Applications to Travel and Tourism Research. *Journal of Travel & Tourism Marketing* 9(4), 21-45.

Goodall, B. and Ashworth, G. (eds.) (1997) *Marketing in the Tourism Industry: Promoting Tourist Destinations*. London: Routledge.

Gordon, H.I. (1998) *Relationship Marketing*. New York: J. Wiley & Sons.

Gummesson, E. (2002) *Total Relationship Marketing*. Oxford: Butterworth-Heinemann.

Heath, E. and Wall, G. (1994) *Marketing Tourism Destinations: A Strategic Planning Approach*. New York: J. Wiley & Sons.

Jefferson, A. (1994) Marketing in National Tourist Offices. In C. Cooper (ed.) *Progress in Tourism, Recreation and Hospitality Management*, Vol. 2, Chichester: J. Wiley & Sons, 82-95.

Knowles, T. (1996) *Corporate Strategy for Hospitality*. Essex: Longman.

Kotler, P. (2003) *Marketing Management* (11th edn). New York: Prentice-Hall.

Kotler, P. and Armstrong, G. (1999) *Principles of Marketing* (8th edn). New York: Prentice-Hall.

Laws, E. (1991) *Tourism Marketing, Service and Quality Management Perspectives*. Cheltenham: Stanley Thornes.

Matovic, D. and McCleary, K. (2003) Marketing in the Next Decade: A Qualitative Study of the U.S. Hotel Industry. *Journal of Travel & Tourism Marketing* 14(2), 47-65.

Mazanec, J. (1994) Segmenting Travel Markets. In R. Teare, J. Mazanec, S. Crawford-Welch and S. Calver (eds.) *Marketing in Hospitality and Tourism: A Consumer Focus*. London: Cassell, 99-164.

Middleton, V.T.C. (2001) *Marketing in Travel and Tourism* (3rd edn). Oxford: Butterworth-Heinemann.

Mistilis, N. and Daniele, R. (2005) Challenges for Competitive Strategy in Public and Private Sector Partnerships in Electronic National Tourist Destination Marketing Systems. *Journal of Travel & Tourism Marketing* 17(4), 63-73.

Moscardo, G., Faulkner, B. and Laws, E. (2000) Introduction: Moving Ahead and Looking Back. In B. Faulkner, G. Moscardo and E. Laws (eds.) *Tourism in the Twenty-first Century; Lessons from Experience*. London: Continuum, xviii – xxxii.

O'Connor, P. (1999) *Electronic Information Distribution in Tourism and Hospitality*. Oxford: CAB International.

Palmer, A. and Bejou, D. (1995) Tourism Destination Marketing Alliances. *Annals of Tourism Research* 22(3), 616-629.

Porter, M. (1995) *Competitive Advantage: Creating and Sustaining Superior Performance*. New York: Free Press.

Porter, M. (2001) Strategy and the Internet. *Harvard Business Review* 79(3), 63-78.

Rayport, J. F. and Jaworski, B. J. (2001) *E-Commerce*. Boston: McGraw-Hill.

Riege, A., Perry, C. and Go, F.M. (2002) Partnerships in International Travel and Tourism Marketing: A Systems-Oriented Approach between Australia, New Zealand, Germany and the United Kingdom. *Journal of Travel & Tourism Marketing* 11(1), 59-77.

Scott, N., Parfitt, N. and Laws, E. (2000) Destination Management: Co-operative Marketing, a Case Study of the Port Douglas Brand. In B. Faulkner, G. Moscardo and E. Laws (eds.) *Tourism in the Twenty-first Century; Lessons from Experience*. London: Continuum, 198-221.

Siegel, C. (2003) *Internet Marketing: Foundations and Applications*. Boston: Houghton Mifflin Company.

Smith, P. R. (1998) *Marketing Communications: An Integrated Approach* (2nd edn). London: Kogan Page.

Soteriades, M., Aivalis, C. and Varvaressos, S. (2004) E-Marketing and E-Commerce in the Tourism Industry: A Framework to Develop and Implement Business Initiatives. *Tourism Today* 4 (autumn), 157-169.

Teare, R. and Calver, S. (1996) *Consumer Marketing: A Resource-Based Approach for the Hospitality and Tourism Industries*. London: Cassell.

Teare, R. and Gummesson, E. (1996) Integrated Marketing Organization for Hospitality Firms. In R. Teare and A. Boer (eds.) *Strategic Hospitality Management: Theory and Practice for the 1990s* (4th edn). London: Cassell, 144-157.

Varvaressos, S. and Soteriades, M. (2005) Tourism Services Marketing: Evaluation Approaches to the Parameters Market, Quality and Price. *Review of Economic Sciences* 8 (forthcoming).

Witt, S. and Moutinho, L. (eds.) (1995) *Tourism Marketing and Management Handbook*. Hertfordshire: Prentice-Hall Europe.

World Tourism Organisation (1997) *National and Regional Tourism Planning; Methodologies and Case Studies* (3rd edn). London: International Thomson Business Press.

World Tourism Organisation, Business Council (1999) *Marketing Tourism Destinations Online: Strategies for the Information Age*. Madrid: WTO.

You, X., O'Leary, J. and Fesenmaier, D. (2000) Knowledge Management through the Web: A New Marketing Paradigm for Tourism Organizations. In B. Faulkner, G. Moscardo and E. Laws (eds.) *Tourism in the Twenty-first Century; Lessons from Experience*. London: Continuum, 181-197.

3

SEMANTIC WEB TECHNOLOGIES IN TOURISM INFORMATION SYSTEMS

DIMITRIS KANELLOPOULOS

ABSTRACT

The tourism industry depends on complex value creation chains involving a large number of participants (travel agencies, tour operators, hotels etc.) that change frequently and rapidly. In addition, the products of tourism industry are complex and they will perish if they are not sold in time. For these reasons, the ideal tourism information systems require a lot of flexibility of underlying systems. Moreover, they comprise accurate access to any tourism service that provide, and they are usable by corporate and private customers alike. The management and interoperation of semantically diverse tourism information systems are facilitated by Semantic Web technologies that provide methods and standards, which allow accurate access to information as well as flexibility to comply with needs of tourism information system users and administrators. This paper considers state-of-the art issues: *Ontologies, Semantic modelling and querying, Semantic portals and Semantic-based E-markets*, concerning the exploitation of the Semantic Web technologies and applications in tourism information systems.

***Keywords*: Tourism Information Systems; Semantic Web; Ontologies; Semantic Web**

INTRODUCTION

The travel industry was one of the earliest e-Commerce adopters (Werthner and Ricci, 2004) and one of the most important kinds of commerce through the Web, representing almost 40% of all global e-Commerce. The travel industry reflects the impact that web-based commerce can have in the business process itself (Carroll, 2002). Currently, the travel industry has developed open specifications messages, based on XML (eXtensible Markup Language), to ensure that messages can flow between industry segments as easily as within (Dell'Erba et al., 2002). For example, the OpenTravel Alliance (OTA, 2004) is an organization pioneering the development and use of specifications that support e-business among all segments of the travel industry. The cumulative effort of various teams, individuals, associations, companies, and international organizations, including air, car, cruise, rail, hotel, travel agencies, tour operators and technology providers, has produced a fairly complete set of XML-based specifications for the travel industry.

The OTA adopted the *Web Services model* that provides the travel industry with an ideal platform to confront the difficult problem of data heterogeneity. Web Services technology is a collection of standards that allows tourism web server applications to *talk* to each other over the Internet. In the context of Web Services, three main protocols are used:

1) UDDI (Universal Description, Discovery and Integration: http://www.uddi.org/), a registry system to find tourism resources and Web Services;
2) WSDL (Web Service Description Language: http://www.w3.org/TR/wsdl/), an interface description language; and
3) SOAP (Simple Object Access Protocol: http://www.w3.org/TR/soap), the communication protocol for tourism Web Services.

All three protocols are based on XML (http://www.w3.org/XML) for driving web application services, that is, XML schema is used in requests and replies.

On the other hand, the real benefits of the web-based information revolution will come from enabling the interoperability of content (Berners-Lee et al., 2001). The current generation of web delivery is designed for human users who struggle to make effective use of the billions of pages of information currently accessible. When we search for something at the moment, we sometimes discover suitable candidate information but more often than not this is far from being the case. More than this, the entire process of searching, discovery, and use is designed to be driven by humans. Certainly, the proliferation of web-based tourism resources makes finding what you are looking for increasingly difficult. The current ways tourism content is represented on the web makes it nearly impossible for machines to search the web meaningfully and effectively – even with the limitations of their skills and tools humans are better at searching the web than the most powerful of the current generation of software agents. The emergence of the *Semantic Web* would solve this problem. The tourism industry is a good candidate for taking up Semantic Web technologies, as information dissemination and exchanges are the key backbones of the tourism industry.

THE SEMANTIC WEB INITIATIVE

The Semantic Web enables better machine processing of tourism information on the Web, by structuring web documents in such a way that they become understandable by machines (Berners-Lee et al., 2001). The Semantic Web allows tourism content to become aware of it. This awareness allows users and software agents (viz. Internet-based programs that are created to act autonomously) to query and infer knowledge from tourism information quickly and automatically. The Semantic Web forms a platform for search engines, information brokers and ultimately the 'intelligent' software agents. It propagates interoperability, reusability and shareability, all grounded over an extensive expression of semantics with a standardized communication among intelligent tourism information systems (Maedche and Staab, 2002).

Furthermore, semantics can be used in the discovery, composition and monitoring of Web Services (Ouzzani and Bouguettaya, 2004). Definitely, semantically isolated pieces of tourism information can be connected, and the user can find the tourism information sources more easily, while individual tourism offers can be achieved. The development of the Semantic Web proceeds in steps, each step building a layer on top of another. The layered design is shown in Figure 1, which is outlined below.

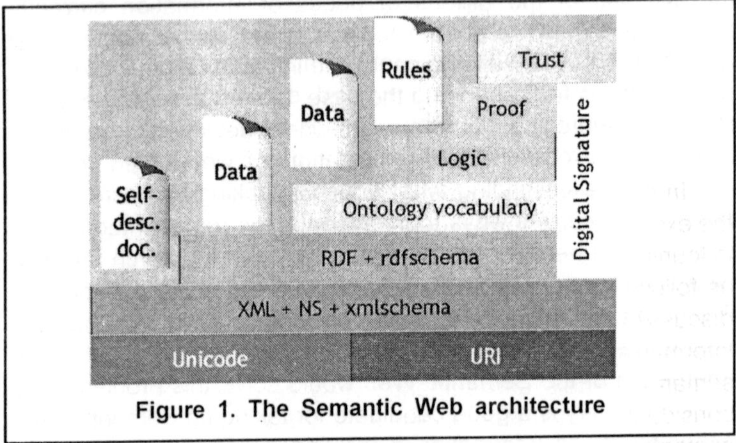

Figure 1. The Semantic Web architecture

- At the bottom layer we find XML, a language that lets one write structured Web documents with a user-defined vocabulary. XML is particularly suitable for sending documents across the Web, thus supporting syntactic interoperability.
- RDF is a basic data model for writing simple statements about Web objects (resources). The RDF data model does not rely on XML, but RDF has an XML-based syntax. Therefore, it is located on top of the XML layer.
- RDF Schema provides modeling primitives for organizing Web objects into hierarchies. RDF Schema is based on RDF. RDF Schema can be viewed as a primitive language for writing ontologies.
- But there is a need for more powerful ontology languages that expand RDF Schema and allow the representation of more complex relationships between Web objects. Ontology languages, such as OWL (Web Ontology Language), are built on the top of RDF and RDF Schema.
- The *logic layer* is used to enhance the ontology language further, and to allow writing application-specific declarative knowledge.

- The *proof layer* involves the actual deductive process, as well as the representation of proofs in Web languages and proof validation.
- Finally *trust* will emerge through the use of digital signatures, and other kind of knowledge, based on recommendations by software agents we trust, or rating and certification agencies and consumer bodies.

In this paper, we consider state-of-the-art issues concerning the exploitation of the Semantic Web technologies and applications in tourism information systems. The rest of this paper is organized as follows: Section 2 presents tourism ontologies and Section 3 discusses applications of them. Section 4 describes tourism information semantic modelling and querying. Section 5 presents semantic portals and semantic Web services, while Section 6 considers e-markets and intelligent software agents that exploit semantics. Lastly, Section 7 concludes the paper with some interesting remarks.

ONTOLOGIES AND INTEROPERABILITY

For the Semantic Web to succeed it will require not only modelling languages, such as XML, RDF and OWL (OWL, 2004), but it will also require methodologies for extracting and defining the knowledge that is to be represented. The success of the Semantic Web will depend heavily upon the creation of suitable ontologies. According to Hendler (2001: 30), an ontology is '*a set of knowledge terms, including the vocabulary, the semantic interconnections, and some simple rules of inference and logic for some particular topic.*' In particular, an ontology comprises the classes of entities, relations between entities and the axioms which apply to the entities of that domain (Mizoguchi, 2004).

For the tourism industry, the development of ontologies is fundamental to allow machine-supported travel-related data interpretation and integration. Furthermore, ontologies offer a promising infrastructure to cope with heterogeneous representations of tourism web resources. Data heterogeneity implies that various tourism information systems use different *meta-data* (viz. objective data about data) for representing tourism resources. Data heterogeneity is solved, if semantic reconciliation with respect to the domain ontology is provided between the different tourism information systems. By adding descriptive information to tourism content and resources, and representing both the descriptive information and the content in well defined, consistent, and structured ways, 'mechanised agents' could be enabled to use web information 'intelligently'.

The TOVE (http://wwweil.utoronto.ca/tove/toveont.html) project resulted in several e-business ontologies, which specify various aspects of a tourism enterprise. The modelling of a tourism enterprise was guided by different sets of constraints on the processes executed inside of it. Core tourism ontologies will contain knowledge about the domain of travel and tourism for developing intelligent tourism information systems. In the OnTour project, a working group at the Digital Enterprise Research Institute (DERI) deployed the *e-Tourism ontology* (Prantner, 2004) using OWL (Web Ontology Language). This ontology was based on an international standard: the *Thesaurus on Tourism & Leisure Activities* of the World Tourism Organization (WTO, 2002). This standard is a very extensive collection of terms related to the area of tourism. The *e-Tourism Ontology* describes the domain of tourism and it focuses on accommodation and activities (http://e-tourism.deri.at/ont/).

Mondeca's tourism ontology (http://www.mondeca.com) defines tourism concepts based on the WTO thesaurus (WTO, 2002). These concepts include terms for tourism object profiling, tourism and cultural objects, tourism packages and tourism multimedia content.

The development of another comprehensive and precise reference ontology named COTRIN (Comprehensive Ontology for the Travel Industry) is the major result of another research group (Cardoso, 2004). Major airlines, hoteliers, car rental companies, leisure suppliers, travel agencies and others will use COTRIN to bring together autonomous and heterogeneous tourism Web services, Web processes, applications, data, and components residing in distributed environments. The objective of COTRIN is the implementation of the semantic XML-based OTA specifications. In the LA_DMS project, an interesting ontology for tourism destinations was deployed in order Destination Management Systems (DMS) to become adaptive to user's requirements concerning information about tourism destinations (Kanellopoulos et al., 2005a).

An overview of development methodology and applications for tourism ontologies is given in (Jakkilinki et al., 2005). In particular, ontologies are created using ontology development tools, such as Protégé 2000 (Protégé, 2000). Protégé is a Java-based ontology editor with OWL Plugin: it allows ontology implementation as an *applet* on the Web. This permits multiple users to share the ontology.

The W3C (World Wide Web Consortium) has recently finalized the OWL as the standard format in which ontologies are represented online. OWL provides greater machine interpretability of web content than that supported by XML, RDF and RDF-Schema (McGuinness and Van Harmelen, 2003). With OWL it is possible to implement a semantic description of a tourism/travel domain by specifying its concepts and the relationships between the concepts.

In the near future, providers of travel-related services (e.g. accommodation and holiday activities) will advertise their services on the Semantic Web, so that intelligent software agents can find them dynamically. These intelligent agents could then make suggestions on vacation planning and make travel arrangements in consideration of user preferences. For these agents, the Semantic Web infrastructure would be based on core ontologies that would be published on fixed URI's (Universal Resource Indicators) as OWL files. Ontologies would allow these providers to publish metadata about their travel services and contact information.

SEMANTIC-BASED PROJECTS IN TOURISM

"Harmonise is an ontology-based mediation and harmonisation tool" (Dell'Erba, 2004), that, in conjunction with other initiatives (EnjoyEurope, Fetish: http://www.fetish.t-6.it/) and with the involvement of International Tourism Organizations (ETC, IFITT, NTOs, and so on), establishes the bridges between existing and emerging online marketplaces. The Harmonise project allows participating tourism organizations to keep their proprietary data format and use ontology mediation while exchanging information (Missikoff et al., 2003; Dell'Erba, 2004).

The Satine project developed a secure semantic-based interoperability framework for exploiting web service platforms in conjunction with Peer-to-Peer (P2P) networks in the tourist industry (Dogac et al., 2004). The essence of P2P computing is that nodes in the network directly exploit resources present at other nodes of the network without intervention of any central server. The advantages of web semantics and P2P computing for service interoperation and discovery in the travel domain have been analyzed in (Maedche and Staab, 2003). The EU-IST project SWAP (http://swap.semanticweb.org/) demonstrated that the power of P2P computing and the Semantic Web could actually be combined to share and find "knowledge" easily with low administration efforts. The LA_DMS project (Layered Adaptive semantic-based DMS) aims at providing semantics-based tourism destination information by combining the P2P paradigm with Semantic Web technologies (Kanellopoulos and Panagopoulos, 2005b). Semantic Web methodologies and tools for intra-European sustainable tourism were developed in the Hi-Touch project (Hi-Touch, 2003). These tools are used to store and structure knowledge on customers' expectations and tourism products. The top-level classes of the Hi-Touch ontology are *Documents*, *Objects* and *Publication*. *Documents* refer to any kind of documentation, advertisement, about a tourism product. *Objects* refer to tourism offers themselves, while a *Publication* is a document created from the results of a query. Machines, as well users, can process the knowledge on customers' expectations and tourism products in order to find the best matching between supply and demand. The Hi-Touch platform has already been adopted in several French regions.

TOURISM INFORMATION SEMANTIC MODELING AND QUERYING

Semantic annotation is the process of inserting tags in documents in order to assign semantics to the text. The success of the Semantic Web in tourism will depend on the availability of ontologies as well as the proliferation of web pages annotated with metadata conforming to these ontologies. Therefore, a crucial question is *where* and *how* to acquire these metadata. Kiryakov et al. (2005) proposed a promising approach. However, the presentation of their approach is beyond the scope of this paper.

The semantic modelling of tourism information enables intelligent tourism information systems to provide personalized services. An intelligent tourism information system includes ontology-driven subject domain and repository of tourism information. It is adaptive to consumers' needs (e.g. information for transportation, restaurants, accommodation, services, weather, events, itinerary tips, shopping, nightlife, daily excursion, car rental, sport activities...). In intelligent tourism systems information management tasks are incorporated and annotated in terms of subject domain concepts. System's adaptive behavior to consumers' requirements is obtained by attaching semantic metadata to its information modules. For achieving this, tourism concepts ontologies (being used) must be also aligned with the ontologies defining its context and the user's profile. System's adaptation requires the tourism information of the *knowledge base* to be modeled using multiple descriptions (viz. using various templates associated with the user's needs).

Kanellopoulos et al. (2005a) proposed a layered approach with appropriate semantic labeling for DMS. The layers of their approach reflect a higher level of semantics, such as domain model, user and machine characteristics. Furthermore, they introduced the Layered Adaptive DMS model (LA_DMS), which enables DMS to provide to consumers personalized information services for tourism destinations.

SEMANTIC QUERYING FOR TOURISM INFORMATION

The need for searching information is one of the fundamental needs of a prospective tourist. Maedche and Staab (2002) presented semantic search scenarios for tourism information. Semantic-based search enhances current search engines with semantics: It goes beyond superficial keyword matching by adding semantic information, thus allowing easy removal of non-relevant information from the result set. Semantic-based search can be provided by Semantic Web tools, such as the *Ontobroker* System that provides an ontology-based crawling and answering service (Fensel et al., 1999).

Semantic browsers, such as Magpie (Dzbor et al., 2003), use ontologies to identify important concepts in a document and provide access to relevant material. Semantic browsing locates metadata and assembles point-and-click interfaces from a combination of relevant information: It should be able to allow easy navigation through tourism resources, since users with any level of computing knowledge may use it.

SEMANTIC INTEROPERABILITY

The evolution towards semantic-based knowledge tourism systems must be supported by the complement of the technical interoperability with 'semantic interoperability'. This includes making available tourism information about the data elements and value spaces adopted by the components in the global infrastructure, in a way that can be processed by software agents and other Semantic Web-enabled applications. It also includes examining how to make the relations between different data elements and value spaces available to such applications, thereby enabling semantic extension and refinement of vocabularies.

SEMANTIC PORTALS AND SEMANTIC WEB SERVICES

Existing tourism portals on the Web have the limitation that they only present accommodations and tourism facilities that are in their databases. Furthermore, existing portals rely on existing Web technologies that are not able to perform efficient searches-really giving the users what they need. A tourism knowledge (semantic) portal can be seen as a web application providing access to tourism data in a semantically meaningful way, making available a variety of tourism resources for diverse target audiences. Differently from "dumb" web portals, semantic portals are "smarter" and carry out intelligent reasoning behind the scenes. They should offer semantic services including semantics-based browsing, semantic search and smart question answering. Knowledge portals provide views onto tourism information on the Web, thus facilitating their users to find relevant specific information.

The objective of the OnTour project (Prantner, 2004) was the building of a portal that searches semantically annotated websites and retrieves efficient and optimal results using Semantic Web technologies. The KAON portal is a simple tool for generating of ontology-based web portals. In order to create the portal, the user needs to create an ontology containing the information, which will be presented on the Web. Then, the KAON Portal may be used to provide default visualization and navigation through this ontology (http://km.aifb.uni-karlsruhe.de/kaon/Members/rvo/

kaon portal). There is also the SEAL portal (SEmantic portAL) that exploits semantics for providing and accessing information at a portal as well as constructing and maintaining the portal (Maedche et al. 2001).

The semantic web services purpose is to describe web services' capabilities and content in a computer-interpretable language and improve the quality of existing tasks, including web services discovery, invocation, composition, monitoring, and recovery. They have major impact on the tourism industry as they allow the automatic discovery, composition, integration, orchestration, and execution of inter-organization tourism business logic, making the Internet become a global common platform (McIlraith et al., 2001).

Tourism semantic web services can be: 1) the automated identification of tourism information, 2) personalized tourism services, 3) semantic discovery and interoperability of tourism web services, and 4) P2P-based semantic web services. Sakkopoulos et al. (2005) proposed techniques to facilitate semantic discovery and interoperability of web services that manage and deliver web media content. Besides, Kanellopoulos et al. (2004) proposed a novel management system of semantically enriched web travel plans, which evaluates how on-line travel plans are consumed and identifies the individual differences among the users in terms of travel plan content usage.

E-MARKETS AND INTELLIGENT SOFTWARE AGENTS EXPLOITING SEMANTICS

In the tourism domain, new offers and requests typically come in by the minute and late vacancies of rooms, flights or lodging easily can be lost. Therefore, there is a need for a fast match between providers and requestors. In electronic-markets that exploit semantic descriptions, semantics-based matching of products and requirements is made fast between tourism providers and requesters, while a large volume of transactions is executed. Antoniou et al. (2005) studied the brokering and matchmaking problem in the tourism domain, that is, how a requester's requirements and preferences can be matched against a set of offerings collected by a broker. Their proposed solution uses RDF to represent the offerings, and a deductive logical language for expressing the requirements and preferences.

Sycara et al. (1999) described a comprehensive software agent framework that allows the set up of semantic-based e-markets. In semantic-based e-markets, intelligent software agents can exploit semantics on the Web. The Semantic Web can utilize a variety of *traveler, hotel, museum* and other software agents to enhance the tourism marketing and management reservation processes (Hendler, 2001). For example, a *hotel* software agent operating on the Semantic Web might undertake many of the routine administrative tasks that currently consume large amounts of a hotel manager's time. On the other hand, *traveler* software agents can assist travelers in finding sources of tourism products and services and in documenting and archiving them. An additional capacity of the Semantic Web is realized, when software agents extract information from one application and subsequently utilize the data as input for further applications. In this way, software agents create greater capacity for large scale automated collection, processing and selective dissemination of tourism data.

DYNAMIC PACKAGING TOURISM SYSTEMS

The Web has permanently changed the manner vacation packages can be created. Consumers can now acquire packages from a diversity of websites including online agencies and airlines. In the travel industry, one of the fastest-growing categories is the creation of dynamic vacation travel packages. The objective of *dynamic packaging* is to pack all the components chosen by a traveller to create one reservation. Regardless of where the inventory originates, the package that is created is handled seamlessly as one transaction, and requires only one payment from the consumer. Dynamic packaging systems create customized tourism packages for the consumers. Cardoso (2005) proposed a platform to enable dynamic packaging using semantic web technologies. A dynamic packaging application allows consumers or travel agents to bundle trip components. The range of products and services to be bundled is too large: *Guider Tour, Entertainment, Event/Festival, Shopping, Activity, Accommodation, Transportation, Food and Beverage* etc. Dynamic packages can be created and booked effortlessly with private and published air, car hire, hotels, attractions and insurance rates.

SEMANTIC MINING

Semantic data mining allows precise targeting, personalization of tourism products, and measurability; viz. tools for effective tourism marketing strategies. For example, semantic mining can be very useful for the management of tourism destinations or the management of travel plans (Kanellopoulos et al., 2004). Semantic mining process can be applied to record and analyze users' preferences concerning in specific elements of a tourism information module. Intelligent tourism information systems can generate users' profiles by recording users' preferences. *User profile* is used for expressing the characteristics and features of a person. A user profile consists of a static part (e.g. demographic info such as name, sex, age, country of origin etc) and a dynamic part (interests, filters, traces). *Filters* describe the mechanism for expressing user's interests (e.g. museums), while *traces* describe the interactions of users with the tourism information system and the mechanism for recording these actions.

CONCLUSIONS AND OPPORTUNITIES FOR RESEARCH

Delivering the Semantic Web to the tourism sector depends upon: (a) the syntactical and semantic mark-up of content, (b) the development of better knowledge analysis and modelling tools, (c) widespread adoption of interoperable knowledge representation languages, and (d) the construction of suitable ontologies. A semantic web application allows consumers or travel agents to create, manage and update itineraries. Moreover, it permits the customer to specify a set of preferences for a vacation and query a set of information sources to find components such as air fares, car rental, and leisure activities in real-time. Intelligent tourism information systems offer full integration, flexibility, specialization and personalization.

- ***Full Integration***: Intelligent tourism information systems can integrate the management and marketing of the various local tourism products and services (Bussler, 2003). They can facilitate interconnectivity of Small and Medium Tourism Enterprises (SMTEs) via full integration in order to increase margins on the products sold. Tools for sales assistance, such as '*intelligent*' software agents, can provide various products and services into an integrated tourism package, which is personalized to tourist's requirements.

- ***Flexibility***: Intelligent tourism information systems can combine the individual tourism products and services. They are platform independent and can change their data without affecting the data representation.
- ***Specialization and personalization***: Precise targeting, personalization, privacy and measurability can be achieved through *web direct marketing* that is interactive, immediate, and accurately timed. Through web direct marketing, tourism products and services can be personalized to the user's requirements (Murphy, 2003).

The tourism industry is facing rapid changes with the advent of the Semantic Web technologies. There is now the need for developing an infrastructure to manage the online tourism information and deliver to consumers what they want. New superior consumer services can be deployed such as tourism *market overview* and *price comparison*. Ontologies will play an important role as they promise a shared and common understanding of tourism and travel concepts that reaches across people and application systems.

Despite, proof and trust is emerging as another central issue. How do we know that what our intelligent software agent has discovered through its trawl of the Semantic web can be trusted? Even in the case of ontologies how should we decide whose ontology to trust? This is especially important where the two ontologies may conflict with one another. Similarly we are faced with the difficulties of ensuring and maintaining semantic integrity and a lack of methods for testing its presence. The requirements of future systems raise several technical research issues, such as: (a) semantic interoperability and mediated architectures; (b) e-business frameworks supporting processes across organizations; (c) mobility and embedded intelligence; (d) personalization and context-based services; and (e) information-to-knowledge transformations – data mining and knowledge management.

REFERENCES

Antoniou, G., Skylogiannis, T., Bikakis, A., Bassiliades, N. (2005) A Semantic Brokering System for the Tourism Domain 2005,

Information Technology & Tourism, 7.

Berners-Lee, T., Hendler, J. and Lassila, O. (2001) The Semantic Web, *Scientific American*, 279(5), 34-43.

Bussler, C. (2003) The Role of Semantic Web Technology in Enterprise Application Integration, *IEEE Data Engineering Bulletin*, 26(4), 62-68.

Cardoso, J. (2004) Semantic Web Processes and Ontologies for the Travel Industry, *AIS SIGSEMIS Bulletin, The official Quarterly Newsletter of AIS Special Interest Group on Semantic Web and Information Systems*, 1(3), 25-28.

Cardoso, J. (2005) E-Tourism: Creating Dynamic Packages using Semantic Web Processes, *In W3C Workshop on Frameworks for Semantics in Web Services*, Innsbruck, Austria, June 9-10. Online, Available: http://www.w3.org/2005/04/FSWS/Submissions/16/paper.html

Carroll, W. J. (2002) *Hotel & Lodging Commerce 2002-2005: Distribution Strategies and Market Forecasts*, In L. Sileo (Ed.): PhoCusWright Inc.

Dell'Erba, M. (2004) Exploiting semantic web technologies for data interoperability, *AIS SIGSEMIS Bulletin*, *The official Quarterly Newsletter of AIS Special Interest Group on Semantic Web and Information Systems*, 1(3), 48-52.

Dell'Erba, M., Fodor, O., Ricci, F. and Werthner, H. (2002) Conceptual normalization of XML data for interoperability in Tourism, *In Proc. of the Workshop on Knowledge Transformation for the Semantic Web, KTSW*, 69-76, Lyon, France, July. Online, Available: http://xml.coverpages.org/KTSW2002.pdf

Dogac, A., Kabak, Y., Laleci, G., Sinir, S., Yildiz, A., Kirbas, S. and Gurcan, Y. (2004) Semantically Enriched Web Services for the Travel Industry, *ACM Sigmod Record* 33(3), 21-27, New York: ACM Press.

Dzbor, M. Domingue, J.B., and Motta, E. (2003) Magpie - Towards a Semantic Web Browser, *In Proc. of the 2nd International Conference (ISWC 2003)*, 690-705. Florida, USA, October. Online, Available: http://kmi.open.ac.uk/people/domingue/papers/magpie-iswc-03.pdf

Fensel, D., Angele, J. Erdmann, M., Schnurr, H., Staab, S. Studer, R. and Witt, A. (1999) On2broker: Semantic-based access to information sources at the WWW, *In Proc. of WebNet*, 366-371.Online, Available: http://www.aifb.unikarlsruhe.de/WBS/Publ/1999/webnet_dfeetal_1999.pdf

Hendler, J. (2001) Agents and the Semantic Web, *IEEE Intelligent Systems*, 16(2), 30-37.

Hi-Touch Working Group (2003). Semantic Web methodologies and tools for intra-European sustainable tourism. Online, Available: http://www.mondeca.com/articleJITT-hitouch-legrand.pdf

Jakkilinki, R., Sharda, N. and Ahmad I. (2005) Ontology-based Intelligent Tourism Information Systems: An overview of development methodology and applications, *In Proc. of TES2005: Tourism Enterprise Strategies: Thriving – and Surviving – in an Online Era,* Melbourne, Australia, 11-12 July, Centre for Hospitality and Tourism Research (CHTR), Victoria University.

Kanellopoulos, D., Panagopoulos, A. and Psillakis, Z. (2004) Multimedia applications in Tourism: The case of travel plans, *Tourism Today*, 4, 146-156.

Kanellopoulos, D., Panagopoulos, A. and Karahanidis J. (2005a) How the Semantic Web revolutionizes Destination Management Systems, *In Proc. of Int. Conference on Tourism Development and Planning 2005*, 11-12 June, Patras, Greece.

Kanellopoulos, D. and Panagopoulos, A. (2005b) Exploiting tourism destinations' knowledge in a RDF-based P2P network. *Hypertext 2005, 1st International Workshop WS4 – Peer to Peer and Service Oriented Hypermedia: Techniques and Systems*, ACM Press.

Kiryakov, A. Popov, B., Terziev, I., Manov, D. and Ognyanoff, D. (2004) Semantic Annotation, Indexing, and Retrieval, *Journal of Web Semantics,* 2(1), 49-79.

Maedche, A. and Staab, S. (2002) Applying Semantic Web technologies for tourism information systems, *In K. Woeber, A. Frew, and M. Hitz, (Eds), Proc. of the 8th International Conference for Information and Communication Technologies in Tourism 2002, ENTER 2002*, Innsbruck, Austria: Springer Verlag.

Maedche, A. and Staab, S. (2003) Services on the Move: Towards P2P-Enabled Semantic Web Services, *In Proc. of Information and Communication Technologies in Tourism 2003, ENTER 2003*, 124-133, Helsinki: Springer.

Maedche, A., Staab S., Stojanovic, N., Studer, R. and Sure, Y. (2001) SEmantic PortAL - The SEAL approach. In D. Fensel, J. Hendler, H. Lieberman, W. Wahlster (eds.) In *Creating the Semantic Web*. Boston: MIT Press, MA, Cambridge.

McGuinness, D. and Van Harmelen, F. (2003) *OWL Web Ontology Language Overview.*

Online, Available: http://www.w3.org/TR/owl-features/

McIlraith, S., Cao Son, T. and Zeng, H. (2001) Semantic Web Services, *IEEE Intelligent Systems*, 46-53, March/April 2001.

Missikoff, M., Werthner, H. Höpken, W., Dell'Ebra, M., Fodor, O. Formica, A. and Francesco, T. (2003) HARMONISE: Towards Interoperability in the Tourism Domain, *In Proc. of Information and Communication Technologies in Tourism 2003, ENTER 2003,* 58-66, Helsinki: Springer.

Mizoguchi, R. (2004) Ontology Engineering Environments. In S. Staab, R. Studer (Eds.) *Handbook on Ontologies*, Berlin: Springer, 275-298.

Murphy, H.C. (2003) An Investigation into how data collected by destination websites are utilised as a direct marketing tool, *In Proc. of Information and Communication Technologies in Tourism 2003, ENTER 2003,* 316-325, Helsinki: Springer.

OTA (2004) *OpenTravel Alliance.* Online http://www.opentravel.org.

Ouzzani M. and Bouguettaya, A. (2004) Efficient Access to Web Services, *IEEE Internet Computing*, March-April 2004, 8(2), 34-44.

OWL (2004) *Web Ontology Language*, World Wide Web Consortium (W3C).

Online, Available: http://www.w3.org/2004/OWL/

Prantner, K. (2004) OnTour: The Ontology, DERI Innsbruck, Austria. Online, Available:

http://e-tourism.deri.at/ont/docu2004/OnTour%20-%20The%20Ontology.pdf

Protégé-2000 tool (2000) *User's Guide.*

http://protege.stanford.edu/publications/UserGuide.pdf

Sakkopoulos, E., Kanellopoulos, D. and Tsakalidis, A. (2005) Semantic mining and web service discovery techniques for media resources management, *International Journal of Metadata, Semantics and Ontologies,* 1(1), 34-46.

Sycara, K., Klusch, M., Widoff, S. and Lu, J. (1999) Dynamic service matchmaking among agents in open information environments, *ACM SIGMOD Record,* 28(1), 47-53, ACM Press.

Werthner, H. and Ricci, F. (2004) E-commerce and Tourism, *Communications of the ACM,* 47(12), 101-105, New York: ACM Press.

World Tourism Organisation - WTO (2002). *Thesaurus on Tourism & Leisure Activities of the World Tourism Organization*. Online, Available: http://www.world-tourism.org

4

DEMOGRAPHIC AND ECONOMIC PATTERNS IN ITALIAN TOURISM IN THE LAST CENTURY

ADRIANA GALVANI

ABSTRACT

Public organizations are charged to provide public health, and when, at the end of the 19th century, doctors recognized that thalassic therapy for children could prevent adult diseases, local and national institutions created seaside resorts for children whose parents weren't able to afford a vacation. Today industrial evolution and social insurance allow people to work less and earn more, so almost all families have the means to take holidays all together. Most of the buildings, once able to recover hundreds of children, are now abandoned. The disappearance of the *summer colonies*, once seen throughout Western Europe, reflects these enormous changes and the passage from social to individual tourism. The earlier form of social tourism has been modified from a health service into leisure and recreation.

Keywords: colony, children, social tourism, health, public assistance

FOREWORD

In antiquity people used to move only for practical reasons: for religious, health, or family visits (Casson, 1974). The origins of tourism are also related to concrete motivations, mostly health related; on the other hand, tourism for amusement is only a very recent occurrence, deriving from mass tourism since the sixties. Health reasons include visits to sanctuaries in order to pray for miracles, or to mineral or hot water sources, both useful for physical rehabilitation. This gave origin to the fashion of the "baths" from which some resorts derived their names. The baths were an elite form of travel, used by the rich, for whom they also offered the opportunity of social meetings, balls, and receptions.

At the end of the 19th century it was discovered that sea environments were good treatments for some illnesses such as rheumatism, respiratory infections, and children's growth problems. Mountain climate is also good for children and the elder, but the seaside has, since then, attracted an increasing number of people around the world. The seaside was judged so effective that charities and governments started, at the beginning of the last century, to send poor children to sea resorts and to host them in public facilities created for this purpose. Marine climate was reputed the best solution for a widespread children's illness: the *scrophula*[1].

Scrophula wasn't dangerous in itself, but as it could evolve into tuberculosis for which no medicines existed until 1946[2].

---

1. Scrofula (Scrophula or Struma) refers to a variety of skin diseases; in particular, a form of tuberculosis, affecting the lymph nodes of the neck. In adults it is caused by *Mycobacterium tuberculosis* and in children by nontuberculous mycobacteria. The word comes from the Latin *scrofulae*, meaning *brood sow (Microsoft Wikipedia, 2005)*.
2. Tuberculosis caused the most widespread public concern in the 19th and early 20th centuries as the endemic disease of the urban poor. The bacillus-causing tuberculosis, *Mycobacterium tuberculosis*, was described on March 24, 1882 by Robert Koch. He received the Nobel Prize in physiology or medicine for this discovery in 1905. Koch announced a glycerine extract of the tubercle bacilli as a "remedy" for tuberculosis in 1890, calling it tuberculin, but it was not effective. It was not until 1946 with the development of the antibiotic *streptomycin* that treatment, rather than prevention, became a possibility (*Microsoft Wikipedia*).

INTRODUCTION

At the beginning of the 20th century, governments generally initiated policies concerning social issues, and frequently they associated social policies with health issues.

Public organizations were charged to provide public health, and when doctors recognized that thalassic therapy for children could prevent adult diseases and that this proactive sanitization would cost less than lasting infirmities and help assure a healthy work force, local and national institutions tried to create seaside resorts for children whose parents weren't able to sustain a long residential vacation.

The success of marine resorts also led to the construction of mountain resorts[3].

These organized vacations related to health issues were named in France "*colonies de vacances*"; in Italy "*colonie estive*" which we can translate as "*summer colonies*".

I will refer to these places and to these buildings as "colonies" throughout this paper, also utilizing this word for the system itself.

Now most of the buildings, once able to recover hundreds of children, are abandoned. As they fall apart, they have a strong physical impact on territory, involving planning managers in discussions about how to utilize them in new forms[4].

The end of this era permits a discussion about the pros and cons of these summer colonies, contextualized by the lived experiences of the author, both as an involved child, and later counselor, after having obtained the title of teacher.

FROM SOCIAL TO INDIVIDUAL TOURISM

The new millennium marked 100 years of elite tourism and 50 years of mass tourism history in most of the Western countries. During this century, leisure, more than other activities, has been

3. In effects in 1972 the school non profit agency of Ferrara Province declared that the mountain climate was better than the marine one, and teachers recommended that parents send their sons and daughters there.

4. After the Second World War the colonies were used by Allied Forces (Sanjust, 1951: 44).

conditioned by demographic changes such as declining birth rates. The lowest birth rate of the entire world is now found in Italy[5], and very low birth rates also characterize some other European countries such as Germany and Spain. This factor, combined with the decreasing of agricultural work force and high performances in industrial and technological production is also strongly influencing the time and the money people have for vacation.

In Italy the effort to build summer colonies reached its peak during the dictatorship of Mussolini (1922-1943) who wanted to assure a healthy population to a deprived nation. Today, on the other hand, the phenomenon of colonies, as collegial forms of holidays, is receding because children are not as subject to these illnesses due to chronic under-nutrition, and the improvements in living conditions can offer the entire range of vitamins and proteins they need. Industrial evolution allows people to work less and earn more, and permits a more balanced distribution of welfare; the social insurance provides employees with paid free time, so now almost all families have the means to take holidays all together: children and parents.

The disappearance of the colonies, once seen throughout Western Europe, reflects these enormous changes and the passage from social to individual tourism or from a holiday to restore health to one intended for primary amusement.

THE ORIGINS OF SOCIAL TOURISM

The creation of sea hospitals began in the UK in 1796, in France in 1861, and in the Netherlands and Belgium in 1888.The first forms of children's assistance in Italy dates from the second half of the 19th century. Milan was the first local government to organize colonies in 1881, and the second was Bologna in 1889, as two of the richest cities in Italy. In 1867 there were 21 health hospices for youth in Italy; in 1876 there were 70, then 100 in 1885, but a systematic network of organizations dates only from the first years of the 20th century.

For Italy these were the years of post unification, of the creation of a new unitarian state, and philanthropists desired to create a

---

5. The age for State colonies was generally between 6 and 12, the private ones accepted older children, but not younger.

strong nation based on health population (Fabbri and others, 2003: 19).The creation of colonies was first an idea of private charities; with the Royal Decree of 3.20.1910, the government created a moral corporation or "Institution of Public Assistance and Beneficence" (IPAB) to care for children. The colonies appeared at the same time the sanatoria were closing, as a passage towards a proactive health policy. Unfortunately, the benefits of summer treatments vanished during the winter, because of poor nourishment conditions and a lack of hygiene at home. One solution to these disappearing benefits was the creation of clinics in residential towns, which organized weekly controls for children. The best solution, however, has been procured by the general economic development and increases in workers salary that came decades later.

In Italy, hospitals were constructed along the two seasides of the peninsula, especially in northern and central Italy, sponsored by middle class charity groups and later by industrial or workers' associations. Statistics indicate that 2,500 assisted children in 1902 became 100,000 in the year 1922; 350,000 in 1932, 700,000 in 1936; 940,000 in 1942 (Sanjust, 1951, p.6); and, in a more recent work of 1969, Ferrua (p. 320) quotes 2 million assisted children in Italy[6]. Reggiani states that in the period 1868-1910, the religious institution of *Opera Pia* in Bologna hosted 8,121 children, out of which 1,460 were healed; 3,723 improved greatly, 2,270 were healed a little, and 13 died.

The national statistics generally estimated that 44% of scrophula children improved, but 100 per cent were healed in France because the children stayed for six months instead of one.

Along the 14 miles of coast by the Adriatic Sea in northern Italy, from Marina di Ravenna to Cattolica, it has been estimated that, until the seventies, 246 buildings with 2.5 millions cubic meters and 1.5 million quadratic meters existed (Tamini, 2003: 72). The constructions were open toward the sea, on a large surface, as counseled by the French doctor Meseurer (1908) to take advantage of the marine air. In these buildings boys and girls were hosted for one month, or, in some cases, 20 days.

6. Only 2% had a loss.

One might think that one month is a too short period for recovery: we have to remember that it was necessary in order to host the maximum number of fragile children through several rotations during the summer season. Some documents testify in favor of the 30 days period to ameliorate situations. Doctor Azzi, at the beginning of the last century in Rimini, claimed that even one month is sufficient to do well, and supported his statement with pictures of children before and after the sojourn. The collected statistics he published demonstrated that 3,500 children gained weight, on average 1.220 kg, which was 4.81% of their original body mass, much more than the usual, even considering that spring and summer are the months of major physical increase[7]. Doctor Azzi states that only 2.5% of children had a decrease (1934:14). Pictures too demonstrate the betterment of assisted infants (Dall'Olio, Manservisi, 1956). The Ministry of Education published a document in November 1946 declaring an average weight increase of 1.5-2.5 kilograms, more than the usual increase.

However, when shorter periods were organized, the Ferrara Prefecture pointed out that 15 days were not enough. The Prefecture was also in charge of controlling the hygienic conditions and in 1948 noticed some inadequacies in old buildings. The Prefecture confirmed the sanitary goal of colonies and requested that, at least, one doctor, nurses, and a first aid post would be provided. The Prefecture also decided the dimensions of the spaces, and the number of hygienic services.[8]

FASCIST PROPOSALS

Hospitality mansions were created for proactive reasons, due to the fact that in Italy, in the period 1921-25, child mortality was more than 30% for those aged 0-5 (Luminasi, 1932). It is important to evaluate the social and economic situation of the Italian families of this period: usually families were composed of a dozen members, less than 50% had water in the house, and in popular buildings, bath and shower were not existent; 1.9% didn't have a latrine, children didn't have their own beds. This health policy

8. The dormitory space were scientifically organised by Ministry of Education rules, so each bed had 6.55 square metres of space and 32.75 cubic metres.

aspect changed during the Mussolini dictatorship, in order to increase the number of inhabitants to make the nation stronger.

At the beginning of the last century, colonies were utilized to care and to teach children how to learn basic hygienic and nutritional habits not known at home, because of extreme poverty. Some educators remind us that poor children didn't enjoy varied and rich food, because their families couldn't share it with them. It was only during these summer months that these children first slept in a bed, especially a single bed. A large part of the population didn't know, a century ago, a mattress. Mattresses then were made from sacks of cornhusks. However, these conditions were drastically altered by the economic boom of the seventies (Manaresi, 2002: 44-45).

In the inter-world wars period, the colonies were proposed to the University students too. At the University of Bologna a document exists, published in 1934 (PUF), informing university students about the possibility of attending for 1 week, a marine colony in Venice in the framework of the program "Marine Weeks", organized by the GUF (Jung University Fascists Organization). For seven days, they had to pay 130 Liras (about ten cents in dollars), a big amount in those years, but we have to remember that the beach of Venice is one of the most elegant in Italy and that participants could enjoy all the elite sports, such as fencing, rowing, sail, tennis, golf, and riding, in addition to several excursions and celebrations in Venice. The students were furnished with a city guide, public transport schedules, and they were informed about the presence of a telephone booth on the main avenue.

University students had, also, in those times, the opportunity to enjoy cheaper camping in southern Italy, at the price of 15 Liras (one tenth of the Venice colony), but all the students were obliged to wear the fascist uniform: white trousers, white shoes, black shirt, blue neckerchief, and student's panama.

ENPAS, the State employee charity, required (4. 30. 1947) guests to arrive at the summer stay with underwear, a white cotton sun-hat, one swimming costume, sandals, two towels, one comb, and one toothbrush.

THE ECONOMIC COSTS

At the end of the nineteenth century, expenditure per child in the colonies was 93 Liras (one dime), but managers were able to reduce it to 80 Liras and to 62.7 Liras in 1912 by direct acquisition of food supplies[9]. In 1950 the prices for children in public-owned facilities were established at 10 dollars for one month, and a half dollar more for transport; the prices doubled in 1972. Obviously, the institutions were economically sustained by local Governmental bodies and banks as well as by the Ministry of Education (Dall'Olio, Manservisi, 1956: 36). Although sugar was one of the most expensive nourishments, some recoveries of health were noticed after the introduction of sweet afternoon snacks.

There were four types of accommodation: one sustained by charities, free of charge; the second was half paid by the hosts, and half by local, regional, or State governments; the third was offered by big enterprises to employees' sons and daughters, free of charge. This last arrangement has always been the most luxurious and has persisted until today.

Another form of hospitality was organized by the Ministry of Education in 1950, but it shouldn't be considered a colony, because it did not offer overnight stay: schools would stay open during the summer, to host the peasant-women's or rice-harvesters' kids during the day. Especially rice-harvesters women were migrant workers, because in the rice field localities, workers weren't numerically sufficient. Today this form of migration doesn't exist anymore, because of better economic conditions and decreasing rice production in Italy.

THE EVOLUTION OF TOURISM: FROM HEALTH TO LEISURE THROUGH EDUCATION

The earlier form of social tourism has been modified from a health service into leisure and recreation. Now, more game time is inserted in public hostels instead of the military discipline of a century ago or of the dictatorship years. Decades ago, children would attend flag-hoisting in the mornings and evenings; they had to march in order, to pray before eating, to go to bed and wake

---

9. The most expensive aliment was the sugar.

up at the same time, also to sleep in the afternoon, even if some of them weren't used doing so at home. Evening free time was used for watching films or documentaries. Even the excursions were organized in lines, two by two, and the little guests weren't allowed to enter the city. Effectively the residences were separated from the villages in which they were situated by gates and high walls[10]. As the buildings were located outside the urban profile, even the inmates' promenades were conducted in separate territories.

In 1950 the Ministry of Education declared that colonies should add an educational function to their sanitary function, in order to develop principles and rules of community life[11]. Living together can become a democratization process, and a good pedagogic experiment should favor a horizontal dynamic society, instead of one with vertical impositions. But these suggestions, deriving from the social change that invested Western society in the seventies, didn't find an opportunity to be realized in these situations, because the democratic process favored by economic and industrial evolution advanced the workers' economic conditions, and with compulsory legal paid holidays to the employees, children started to go on sea or mountain holidays with their parents. More than this, new forms of collectivism were offered by charities or by the evolving market, such as camping for teen-agers or hostels for youth. These opportunities aren't much offered in Italy, but may be more common in Anglo-Saxon countries. In effect, if this

10. A negative aspect, present in all the colonies, was a separate building-hosting children with a communicable disease. To assist to a segregation of a child in a specific separate house, without allowing visits, is the most sad scene for all the hosts, both the healthy ones and the ill ones. Nobody sustained the right choice: that means to send ill person to the hospital. No! Every day the phantom house stayed in front of children playing on the court. Some witnesses affirm that some ill children were restored after the visit of their mother, even if the poor women had to see her child only outside the window (Reggiani, 1911, p. 24).

11. A leaflet published by national school charity on 3.31.1969 and diffused in all the school, was reporting these words: "The holiday house is the fittest site to develop the gradual children inclusion into society".

holiday solution were more accepted, colony buildings would today be utilized for that, instead of being abandoned.

As tourist flows were increasing on the seaside, the hostels area progressively declined, and as more families could enjoy a summer holiday, the situation of the regimented children become more absurd. According to some psychologists, this experience displaces the family, the school, the friends, the neighborhood, the streets, and all other personal habits: because of this it can be disruptive; it would be preferable for hostel life to be as similar as possible to family life.

Some Criticism

During the summer of 1970 a group of representatives of 5 colony institutions denounced through a leaflet presented to tourists, children's parents, and the inhabitants too, the precarious situations in which operators and children were living, in particular:

The military discipline,

The adults' moral impositions,

The inadequacy of living conditions and spaces,

The lack of preparation of all degrees of workers,

The low salary of employees;

In conclusion, the supervisors expressed their hope that the colony institutions could change, offering children better conditions and opportunities to develop, rendering them able to enjoy a peaceful community and to receive the education to make them responsible citizens, not merely obedient puppets.

The leaflet cited also the unacceptable conditions of colonies managed by religious institutions, maybe worse than others. (Several depositions, on Italian television, confirmed this statement).

(Frabboni, 1971: 153-55).

THE PEDAGOGIC PERSPECTIVE

Professor Frabboni of the Education Department at Bologna University is very critical of the military aspect of scheduled days.

He suggests children should decide how to spend their free time. Frabboni thinks summer colleges should integrate the physical and psychological experiences of kids, instead of disrupting their lives. He suggests they derive experiences from the community, enlarging their mental perspective, instead of restricting it. For these reasons, in the seventies, professor Frabboni organized a cultural revolution in this rigid scheme: with Bologna University students he entered into a colony to do some experiments.

First of all, they requested guests to fill out some forms in order to know the children's preferences. In fact, the answers were not consistent with adults' decisions: they preferred to organize their games by themselves and, ideally, they preferred to choose eventually their counselors. If the first option is easy to accept, the second one involves a more psychological concern, justified by the fact that children and counselors would live together day and night, 24 hours a day. This habit can create a sort of psychological dependence once children have accepted the counselors assigned to them. Other mental unbalances occurred when counselors left the institute during their free day each week, substituted by another.

Frabboni drastically changed the organized life of the colony. The result was impressive, children were given a freedom never before experienced in a way that tutors, directors, health and service employees, and parents too, didn't accept, and that children weren't able to manage. The only positive aspect was the relief of the anxiety generated by the old system in itself; not only had children been oppressed by a rigid authority, but all people working in the organization had been distressed by the responsibility and moral load of hundreds of little guests.

Frabboni suggests interaction with the environment and social communities as a process of discovery for emotional growth. According to him, such a period can be utilized as a break between the disciplined time of institutional education and free time at home (1971: 84).

OTHER PERSPECTIVES

The author of these pages would propose a compromise between the old system of organization and the new one proposed by Frabboni. The author thinks the summer colony should become an educational event, not only to develop community life, as asked by the Italian Ministry of Education, but in a systematic sense, because it is no longer a health resort and new perspectives are seeing education as the most compelling exigency of modern life. Better nutrition and improved quality of life make climatic adjustments unnecessary, but the post industrial or consumerist society requires a more communitarian integration than that offered by mononuclear families.

The national birth rate in Italy is today 1.2 children per female; the one child family is the norm, so children aren't used to living with others, or sharing experiences and perspectives with mates, so individualism and ego-centrism are pervading everywhere. The solipsistic form of personality lets children grow feeble, collapsing in front of the difficulties of life. Lengthening the school days or extending the school calendar into the holidays is a good policy: study and homework shouldn't be judged a penalty, but a joy for children and adults, because education is one of the principal aspects of scientific progress.

The colony system is today very expensive; so all the structures should be utilized in a systematic way, to form a complete personality. The temporary sea colonies were in Italy a typical fascist institution, but, at the same time, they introduced a democratization process, sending poor children and ill children to the same beach where rich children were going with their families for leisure.

Certainly the locality of Rimini was the first site where doctors discovered the good effects of the seaside influence, but this was the area where the dictator of the interwar period was born, his preferred coast, where he usually took his sunbaths; during his government the colonies institution reached its peak. He strongly supported this idea as a way to have a numerous and healthy population. This organization was a logical extension of the demographic policy that promoted family planning, with prizes for big families with numerous children and penalties for single men. The hidden goal of this policy wasn't to have healthy people, but to have strong men able to fight in war, in what turned out to be the Second World War.

POST COLONIES ENVIRONMENT

The presence of huge abandoned old buildings on the most famous beaches is today very impressive. Some of them are semi-destroyed, some have lost windows and doors; grass is invading the gardens. It is important to note that they occupy the sea front, very near the shoreline, where new buildings are prohibited. For this reason they have become very attractive from a business point of view, especially for investors trying to modify the colonies into residences or hotels, but this operation isn't easy for public owned properties, for which all the administrative processes are slow. The function change is also very expensive, due to the large dimensions and to the transformation from communitarian use to a personal one. The easiest change has been the transformation into schools; one big colony is now a youth hostel, another Sea-World, another a fitness center; some are administered by religious groups hosting clients at an inexpensive cost, some are transformed into residences or luxury hotels, but architects are protesting about the demolition of a lot of them: "Erasing the witnesses of the past, that is characterizing the territories identity, tourist resorts would become homogeneous with urban degraded slums, reaching a progressive economic devaluation" (IBC, 1986, p. 13).

Very curious to note is that the colonies occupied the same beaches, which are today the most famous for leisure time and for VIP society. On 8. 6.1951 a Ministry of Education Decree prohibited the construction of new colonies in specialized tourist localities, especially in downtown, in order to avoid "detriments". The document doesn't specify what these detriments or damages were, but it states that some managers or administrators were complaining about the presence of buildings modeled like prisons, overshadowing the reputation of famous resorts. The aspect of captivity was underlined by the necessity of diphtheria, smallpox, and typhus fever vaccination.

According to the actual economic perspectives we suggest a perennial exploitation of buildings, instead of abandoning them. In my opinion, these great buildings can and should host children in a recreational way during the entire year. During the winter season, too, they can host school students with their teachers, engaging in schoolwork, sports and, surely, leisure, because, if the location is the means for health, it would have essentially the same effect during cold periods. The learning experience would be more inserted in the children's routine, the hostels would be more efficient with year-round guests, and education would be integrated with knowledge and leisure time, as in modern colleges around the world.

By utilizing the colonies on a year-round basis, charities could enable more children to gain the benefits of this environment, and the area would have a more lovely inhabited landscape

THE AUTHOR'S PERSONAL EXPERIENCE

I have the chance to say something about a phenomenon, which I experienced at different stages of my life, because of all the situations I have encountered. My father was a strong supporter of the colony idea, so enthusiastic that he sent me to this sort of college until the age of fifteen and before the legal age of six. He fought to obtain my inclusion and he succeeds as my sixth birthday was in November, few months after the summer period. More over, my parents didn't allow themselves a summer holiday, because they worked only during the summer, my mother as a peasant, my father a sugar industry employee; in the Italian north plains, sugar beets are harvested in August and soon transformed, as such this work only continues until October.

Summer holidays weren't possible for my family, nor were holidays in general, because with only 3 or 4 months of work, their earnings had to sustain the family all year round. In these conditions my first experience occurred in 1954, and it was disruptive. My family conditions were poor, but so were the Italian conditions in general. One aspect of the colonies system in particular was very expensive: the transport. A solution was to amass children on a truck like animals, and like animals we were herded up a ramp into the truck. Upon our arrival, the situation worsened. I remember a big, too big, sleeping room with dozens of unknown mates. I arrived at the hostel with new clothes, but after only a few days I was robbed of them, covering myself with the old clothes the thief left. I lost the first toothpaste and toothbrush I had in my life, robbed not for their value or attractiveness, but for the candies that accompanied the package as advertisement (stupidly joined to the toothpaste tube to attract children to use it). Unfortunately the thief didn't steal my sandals, which became my trial all through the month of my stay there: I wasn't able to tie them, and during the promenades I remained the last in the line, unsuccessfully tying them every moment.

Worse than that was the bath in the sea: 1,300 children[12], males and females separated by a few meters, were compelled to run into the sea at the whistle ring. The bath would only last a few allowed minutes; for this reason the first day I went on the front line, to profit more from these few minutes of amusement, but.... I was submersed by the mass behind me, and I fell face down in five centimeters of water. My love for the sea sustained me in fighting against difficulties, so, on the second day, I stayed at the back of the line, but this was not a good idea, because before I could touch the water, the exit whistle rang, so immediately hundreds of children, running out of the sea, submersed me. This time, I not fell on my face, but on my back in the sand.

Years and years passed before I could find the serenity to learn to swim. I went on colony until 15 years, a very late age, for which only a few possibilities were available, at high cost. Finally, I became adult, and with my title of schoolteacher I became a caretaker. I haven't remarkable remembrances of this experience because I only remained at this post for a year.

THE LAST COLONY

In order to bring myself up to date, last summer I visited the area where most of the colonies are located. I walked past one of the last existing colonies, owned by the national phone company. Without knowing who I was, one boy approached me behind the fences and asked me if I appreciated his hat. I answered affirmatively, but I didn't understand why he had to ask me that. He explained later that he colored his hat red because he didn't accept the rule that he had to dress the same way as his peers, all in white.

I discovered during the conversation, that he tried to distinguish himself from others because he was the oldest, aged thirteen, and he didn't accept the discipline, even if the hostel was elegant with a green garden and a nice swimming pool; he was rich, at home he had more than a boy could desire and he was missing his toys.

In few minutes our entertainment was interrupted by the children's supervisor asking the boy to come back to his mates.

CONCLUSIONS

We can state that the phenomenon of the colonies has persisted for a hundred years, very slow at its birth, very fast at its disappearance. We remember it as one bad thing, even with some sentimental remembrances, but the same could be said about colleges. Surely it has been an important way to enable holidays for all, and encourage mass tourism. The phenomenon lost its opportunity to become a source of educational knowledge and interplay with other people and with the environment.

Stereotypic judgments see the organization as a prison, and effectively, as in prisons, boarders become aggressive towards one other. Socially damaging for that time was a system in which a lot of money has been spent for vacation, at the same time during which not enough schools were offered to the population, and when poor children attended only two or three years of school. Certainly the system has been organized for poor infirm people, but the solution should have gone into the roots of the illnesses, or it would have been necessary to nurse a malnourished population with sound food. Certainly healthy climate is important, but in addition to a sound style of life. The Italian State wasn't able in the past to give the entire population what needed, but it tried to offer to the poor an aspect of what the elite class enjoys, and in this way it was forecasting the future development of Italian tourism.

REFERENCES

Azzi E., *Su l'incremento ponderale nei bambini dai sei ai dodici anni dopo un mese di soggiorno al mare*, Rimini, Tip. Grattoni, 1934.

Casson L., *Travel in the ancient world*, London, Allen & Unwin, 1974.

Cipolla C., *Oltre la delega*, Milano, F. Angeli, 2004.

Dall'olio A., Manservisi A., *Colonie scolastiche bolognesi*, Bologna, Comune di Bologna, 1956.

Fabbri E., *La riconversione urbana delle grandi aree dismesse: attori, strategie, pratiche di trasformazione urbana*, in NATALICCHIO S.

e TAMINI L., *Grandi aree e stazioni ferroviarie*, Milano, Egea, 2003: 52-72.

Ferrua A., *Anacarsi o delle colonie estive in* «Scuola e Città», n. 6, 1969: 71-77.

Frabboni F., *Tempo libero infantile e colonie di vacanza*, Firenze, La Nuova Italia, 1971.

IBC- Emilia Romagna, *Colonie a mare: il patrimonio delle colonie sulla costa romagnola quale risorsa urbana e ambientale*, Bologna, Grafis, 1986.

Innocenti P., *Geografia del turismo,* Roma, La Nuova Italia Scientifica, 1992.

Kertzer D.,White M., *Explaining Very Low Fertility in Italy,* Workshop at Brown University, December, 8, 2005.

Luminasi I., *Bonifica Umana: la colonia marina del fascio bolognese*, Bologna, SPR, 1932.

Manaresi F., *Date Pauperibus: storia ed indici de "La Strenna delle Colonie Scolastiche estive Bolognesi*" in «L'Archiginnasio», n. 97, Bologna, 2002: 362-434.

Marcovigi G., *L'Ospizio marino provinciale bolognese in Rimini*, Torino, UTET, 1915.

Maroni O., Piraccini O., *Un relitto moderno: la colonia novarese di Rimini*, Bologna, Tip. Moderna, 2002.

Mesureur A., *Les nouveaux pavillons de l'hôpital de l'assistance publique à Berk-sur-Mer*, Paris, Masson, 1908,

Montanari M., *Le città del sole: le colonie marine sulla costa romagnola tra politica e salute dal primo novecento ad oggi*, Tesi di laurea, Università di Bologna, relatore prof. Dogliani P., 1995.

PNF, *Settimane Marinare dell'Anno XII, Seconda Colonia Marina dei GUF*, 16 luglio-16 settembre 1934-XII, Zanetti, Venezia, 1934.

Reggiani A., *L'Opera Pia degli ospizi marini di Bologna, 1888-1910*, Bologna, Stabilimento Poligrafico Emiliano, 1911.

Ruffino A., *Servizi estivi di vacanza*, in «Assistenza d'oggi», n. 3, 1967: 53-59.

Sanjust F., *Un problema ricorrente: le colonie estive*, in "Assistenza d'oggi", n. 8, 1951: 32-45.

5

CRISIS MANAGEMENT IN TOURISM INDUSTRY

SENOL CAVUS and ABDULLAH TANRISEVDI

ABSTRACT

Crises have become everyday phenomena in all industries affecting a number of people and subjects. Simply put "Any action or failure to act that interferes with an (organization's) ongoing functions, the acceptable attainment if its objectives, its viability and survival, or that has a detrimental personal effect as perceived by majority of its employees, clients or constituents" (Selbst, 1978). In spite of the fact that crises are considered as usual in all categories of both daily routines and business environment are most affected due to their complex and harmful nature. Like many other types of business, tourism industry can find itself in a downward of events that are difficult to overturn. In other words most business is at risk extremely to a wide range of unexpected events that could cause vast damage, occasionally very quickly and tourism is one of the most vulnerable industries (Richter, 1999). In relation to a widespread ignorance of their size and complexity, the tourism has frequently exposed into the crises.

Crises related to tourism industry can be defined as any occurrence which can threaten the normal operation and conduct of tourism related businesses; damage a tourist destination's overall reputation for safety, attractiveness, and comfort by negatively affecting visitor's perceptions of that destination; and, in turn, cause a downturn in the local travel and tourism economy, and interrupt the continuity of business operations for the local travel and tourism industry, by reduction in tourist arrivals and expenditures (Sonmez, et al., 1994 : 22). Basic classification of the crises in relation to tourism industry is to appear as: Security related crises such as war, terrorist attacks against tourists and/or tourism establishments, natural disasters (earthquake, flood, and volcano), criminal incidents, economic or financial crises, political instabilities, and technology related crises and so on.

The development of the industry is negatively affected by those types of crises: external and internal factors that both have potential to affect industry as a whole. External factors can be explained such as natural disasters or other events over which those involved have little or no control. In contrast to those, internal factors include some control mechanisms inside; additionally anticipating signals in terms of internal crises may be easier and more effectively. Organizational based crises such as stuff illness, accidents, robberies, product tampering and stuff challenges/breakdowns can be given as examples.

Crises are becoming increasingly more complex, more difficult to anticipate and to manage effectively. As nearly whole business operating under the tourism industry umbrella are susceptible and vulnerable to crises, management of crises should be taken into account by both single operators and destination managers.

In this framework, the purpose of this study is to discuss concept of crisis and crisis management by giving examples for about tourism field. The expected outcome of this study is to contribute to the limited research in this area and to provide managers with better strategies in crisis management.

Keywords: Crisis, disaster, crisis management, types of crisis, tourism industry.

THE CONCEPT OF CRISIS AND ITS DEFINITION

The concept of 'crisis' has got several definitions in different literatures. However; in whatever literature or terminology it's defined, some common points which the word meaning of the concept 'crisis' never changes. Almost all the definitions of crisis defines a time at which a big problem occurs. Nevertheless, this problematic time is at the same time a turning point and it results the situation at present (Brown, 2003 : 194). Besides, crises are not only problem creating events. They have both positive and negative sides (Faulkner, 2002 : 279). At that point, it is possible to relate crisis with the concept 'opportunity'. Because crisis not only means failure but also includes the seeds of success, creates opportunities and transforms it into a turning point (Fink, 1986; Haþit, 2000; Augustine, 2000; Faulkner and Vikolov, 2001; Çiçek and Kýlýç, 2001). In many of the studies in literature; crises are dealt with their both negative and danger creating (upsetting, complicated and indefinite environment creating, distressing) and positive and opportunity creating (mobilizing, creating solidarity environment, increasing the power of getting along with the environment, creating a learning from the experiences) features. The symbol which best expresses the two dimensions that include danger and opportunity of crisis is the word *wei-ji* which is created by the combination of two words in Chinese and which means 'crisis'. These two words mean the concepts 'danger' and 'opportunity' (Keown and McMullan, 1997: 4). Fink (1986), defines the concept of 'crisis', by attributing it's meaning in Chinese, as 'turning point towards better or worse' (Wrigley et al., 2003, in Fink, 1986; 282).

Faulkner (2002) indicates an important point, which separates the concept 'crisis' from the concept 'disaster'. According to the writer, crisis is human-resourced events and has both positive and negative sides. At that point, to be able to investigate crisis management in tourism industry accurately, externalizing the areas in which human factor has little or no activity like nature based disasters can be a precise approach. Because, administering such disasters in their occurrence period or turning their negative conducts to positive is very difficult and even impossible.

When dealt on the point of tourism industry, it can be noticed that industries are vulnerable to crises and disasters. On account of this, the possibility that tourism destinations may face with crisis is not low (Faulkner, 2002: 279). Factors such as local or national problems about security, economical depressions, political instabilities, environmental and technological problems are noticed as important titles among basic factors, which can alert crisis events in touristic destinations (Tanrýsevdi, 2002). Security is one of the basic needs of individuals and is a basic condition, which plays a role in the development of attraction places (Cavlek, 1997; Mikacic et al, 1999). Although tourism industry has become one of the most important industries in the world in spite of the several risks it carries, taking their individual securities under protection has the first importance on point of guests. It is very hard for the attraction places to prevent the problem creating events. These events may occur in different types such as terror, war, crimes, and natural disasters (Mansfeld, 1999). For instance, although the year 1985 was a year in which important steps for international tourism activities were made, the same year was also a year in which terror, civil revolts, aircraft crashes and natural disasters were also mostly experienced (Lerhman, 1986).

Crisis originating from political factors indicates the results of the decisions that the decision makers make and the negative reflections of these decisions on society. These reflections, especially which political quarrels and ideological polarizations create, provides a base for military strikes. To provide the political stabilization is an important component for the development of tourism industry. Because, the lack of political stabilization or the frequent changes of the regime or the politic decisions prevents the foreign investors and managers from investing on developing countries (Yarcan, 1998), effects the entrance of foreign capital towards the attraction places negatively, and causes a decrease in the number of guests. Moreover, government changes which occurs in a short time also causes political inconsistencies, and this situation makes it hard to take important decisions in the issue of tourism industry and applying them (Akova et al, 2000).

Environmental and technological factors also cause crisis in tourism industry. For instance, between the years 1900 and 1987, 29 important industry accidents occurred. Especially the 80's are noticed as the years in which crisis originating from commercial and industrial factors were dense (Mitroff and Pearson, 1993; Santana, 1995).

The most important ones among these events are; Bhopol accident, Chernobil Nuclear Disaster, the crisis of syanur mixing in Tylenol capsules which Johnson & Johnson firm produced, Piper Alpha petrol platform explosion, Challenger space craft explosion, King Cross subway station fire, Exxon Valdez petrol fire and the petrol leak it caused, Lockerbie/Pan Am and Kegworth/

M1 plane crashes, Bradford subway, Heisel and Hillsbourg stadium disasters.

None of the Tourism destinations have protections for the negative effects of crisis. For example such crisis instances as terror, political violence, diseases, crime waves, wars affect all tourism industries. Global tourism industries need crisis management strategies which will determine the negative effects of crisis at the very beginning, or which will turn it reverse if there is any defect (Beirman, 2003).

CRISIS MANAGEMENT

Crisis management, when taken into account as an institution, expresses the groups the people responsible for administrating crises and the responsibilities they have. These groups consist of people who have the most important responsibilities in functional crisis management. When crisis management is dealt as a function, it explains the process starting from the time the crisis occurs, the duties to be done within this process and the changes in these duties (Glaesser, 2003). When dealt generally, crisis management is the general planning to be able to answer emergencies and disaster affairs (Young, 1996). The aim here is to decrease the threats the crisis creates on security, to decrease the wealth loss of public or firms, and to provide the continuity of the normal functions of the institutions in the destination. Crisis management, first of all, makes it necessary to be ready for crisis. The realization of the crisis in the very beginning, the definition of the situation and the destruction at present, the determination of choices for the solution, the selection of the most suitable choice and moving very fast during these actions creates the base of an effective crisis management (Arslan, 2001).

The basic duty of a crisis manager is to prevent a control loss that is possible to occur in the future before the crisis occurs. If the crisis has occurred and a control loss is faced, the manager should try to reacquire the control lost. The effort to reacquire the control lost has been the base principle of crisis management (Heath, 1998: 140).

Fink (1986) is one of the most attribution-taking scholars of the literature about crisis management. Fink dealt with the crisis management processes as *prodramatic process* (pre-crisis), *akut process* (sudden and severe crisis process), *chronic process* (continuous crisis process) and *crisis analysis process.*

Mitroff and Pearson (1993), just like Fink (1986) is one of the mostly accepted scientists of the science community for his studies on crisis. Mitroff evaluated the crisis management processes as taking crisis signals, preparation/protection, taking crisis under control, recovery, and learning a lesson processes. These processes are shown on Figure 1.

Figure 1. The Processes of Crisis

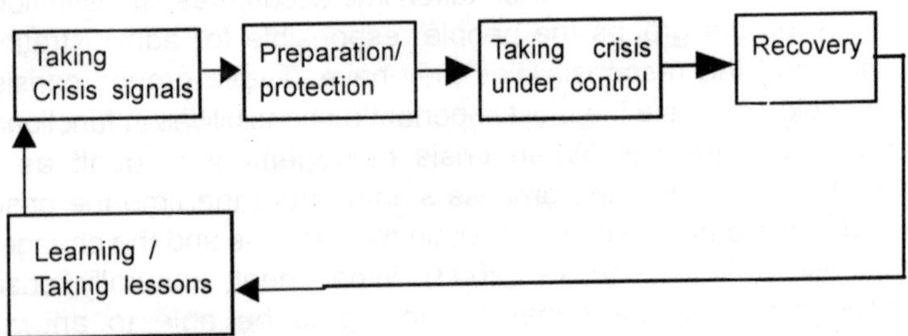

Source: Mitroff, I. and Pearson, C. (1993) From Crisis Prone to Crisis Prepared: A Framework for Crisis Management, Academy of Management Executive 7(1), 48-59 In Santana, G. (1999) Tourism: Toward A Model for Crisis Management. *Turizam* 47(1), 4-12.

In 1998 Chong (1998) developed a crisis management plan, which consists of six processes by summarizing the literature dealing with the crisis management. The steps of the six process model which Chong (1998) developed is, in sequence as; *'approach, reconsider, start, sensation, interference, and taking precautions'* processes. The steps of the six process model which Augustine (1995) developed is, in sequence, as; *'staying away from crisis, getting prepared for crisis management, crisis detection, stopping crisis, solving crisis, and benefiting from it'* processes. Glasser (2003) has shown the crisis management processes on an easier and more different diagram.

Figure 2. Crisis Management Processes

<table>
<tr><th colspan="4">Crisis Preview</th><th>Coping with Crisis</th></tr>
<tr><td colspan="2">Crisis Precautions</td><td colspan="2">Staying Away From Crisis</td><td rowspan="2">The Usage of the Resources Available</td></tr>
<tr><td>Planning</td><td>Applying the Plan</td><td>Warning at the Very Beginning</td><td>Adaptation</td></tr>
</table>

Source:* *Glaesser, D. (2003) Crisis Management In The Tourism Industry. Great Britain: Butterworth-Heinemann.

CRISIS MANAGEMENT IN TOURISM INDUSTRY

In every industry in which competition advantage can be attacked or harmed by means of negative affairs, crisis management plays a very important role to prevent from such negative events. For the industries like tourism industry, which do not look like the other industries, which work with mental and imaginary values, and which makes the dreams come true, the crisis management efforts have more importance. Especially if it is dealt from the point of view of tourism sector, it can be noticed that fore-definition of the negative affairs which can affect the sector is one of the chief duties of crisis management. The important thing here is not the observation of how the already known events occur, but the analysis of the dangers and the determination of their possible results (Glasser, 2003).

Tourism demand especially shows sensitivity to negative conditions related with security and health (Blake and Sinclair, 2003). Besides, the point of view of a tourist to crisis or the degree of his or her being affected from crisis will be different from an ordinary individual. Cassedy (1991) developed a crisis action strategy for tourism destinations, which is composed of five steps. In the first step, the issue is the selection of a team leader. This leader should be authoritarian and his or her orders should be respected. In the second step, a team should be developed. This team should define crisis and analyze it. At the same time, it should create conspiracy theories related with the destination. In the third step, probable crisis and disaster scenarios about the destination should be guessed. Solution plans for these bad scenarios should be formed. In the fourth step, action plans about how crisis will be interfered should be developed. It should be determined how the duties will be distributed, how the information will be collected, and how the relationships with the other groups, public, media etc. will be created. Finally, a crisis management center should be set up. It should be taken into account that this center has a strategic position considering the communication (Faulkner, 2000).

In the recent years, global tourism industry has subjected to several disasters including terrorist attacks, political ignorances, economical stagnitions and natural disasters. Natural disasters may cause the best prepared managements to such disasters be unsuccessful by defecting especially service managements' electric, communication, and other critic background compounds. The lack of defense of service managements to such crisis have been noticed in human-resourced events like The Corruption of Twin Towers and The Bomb Attack in Bali. These attack shave affected tourism and travel industries negatively. Tourism industry has a deficiency in investigating disaster and crisis cases (Ritchie, 2004).

THE IMPORTANCE OF CRISIS/DISASTER MANAGEMENT FROM TOURISM INDUSTRY POINT OF VIEW

Globalization tendencies in tourism industry have progressed the market shares and profits of tourism managements to international scales. However, this globalization has also progressed the risks that tourism industries take and the problems they can face to international scales, and made it more complicated. Globalization and the world getting smaller and smaller have caused that everything depends on and is related with each other. That is, a small crisis occurring in one part of the world have become to affect the other parts of the world extremely.

As can be easily noticed in the Gulf War in 1991, and the Iraq War, the wars and the political indecisiveness in one part of the world unfortunately affects the tourists' travel and participation desires negatively. Such instances indicate that tourism industry has a strong sensitivity to external factors and constraints (Ritchie, 2004). When the managers working for tourism industry face with such crises, they have to decide too fast with too little information in the situation of uncertainty. This situation creates a big pressure on them. For example, the corruption of Twin Towers on the 11 of September drove the hotels in Washington into a difficult situation. The terrorist attacks in this event include the kidnapping of commercial planes and cruiser ships, and the tourists being killed. When the hotel managers faced this situation, first they wanted to acquire the truths and the true information about terrorist attacks. Then, they assigned some of the employees in order that they make the public and the tourists stay calm and inform them by sending the employees to public places. And then, they started their emergent operation plans and crisis plans. From the external point of view, by communicating with the travel agencies, the hotels provided a permanent communication web with their external connections (Stafford et al., 2002).

Apart from this, the student protests and the political in decisiveness, which occurred on the fourth of June 1989, affected the international image of tourism industry negatively. Consequently, the hotel prices decreased 30%, 300 tourist groups (nearly 11.500 people) delayed their travel plans and these affairs gave the country economical harm which is an income of 430 million dollars.

The Islamic terror organization Al-Gama'at al Islamiyya in Egypt systematically attacked Egypt's tourism industry in order to end the government of President Hüsnü Mübarek and govern the country with religious laws. During these attacks between 1992 and 1995, 13 tourists died. Thus, Egypt lost 22% of its foreign newcomers and 43% of its tourism income. International tour operators cancelled their tour programs to Egypt. Finally, during the attacks in April 1996, 18 Greek tourists killed in Cairo.

In Turkey the attacks of PKK since 1991, which also aims tourism, have affected tourism industry negatively. The bombing of hotels and some tourism sites decreased the number of foreign newcomers 8% between the years 1992 and 1993. After the truce in 1996, Turkey was able to have a record as 9.5 million guests (Sönmez, 1998).

According to Sausmarez (2004), tourism destinations should apply proactive crisis management model before the crisis, and reactive crisis management model if the crisis weren't prevented.

The basic aim of the proactive crisis management is to detect early warning signals and to prevent the crisis before it occurs. If proactive crisis management process is achieved, there will be no need for reactive crisis management. If it is not enough and the crisis isn't prevented, reactive crisis management can be applied. The aim in this process is to decrease the defect insofar as it is possible and to cure it as long as possible.

SOME CRISIS TYPES THAT TOURISM DESTINATIONS MAY COME ACROSS

Among the crisis types, which can affect tourism destinations, terror and political violence, natural disasters, diseases, crime and war are the initials. Tourism demand for a specific country is very sensitive to economical crises which decrease the income of travel investments, to political affairs that can give harm to touristic country's or region's image, and to immediate crises such as diseases, natural disasters, wars or terrorist attacks which threat the consumers' life and property security (Yýlmaz and Yýlmaz, 2005). The probability of such crises is a risk for tourists. This subject has a discussion base in literature with the concept *risk percepted*. Roehl and Fesenmaier (1992) divide the tourists into three groups on risk perceptions of destinations point of view. These are neutral, functional and regional risk groups. Among these risk groups, especially the tourists having regional risk perception mostly considers the attraction place risks. The risk perceptions of tourists aimed at destinations can prevent the tourists from realizing their plans for visiting a specific attraction place. For instance, the perception of terror as a risk can prevent the travel plans to Middle East regions (Lepp and Gibson, 2003).

At that point, the necessity that crisis management plans aimed at destinations should take the risk factor percepted into account arouses. In fact, the crisis management plans formed in literature up to now, are built on models generally starting from signal stabilization process, and including recovery and learning process after crisis. However, like in the Middle East example, possible risk factors that destinations may have as location or image and the control of them are out of these models. Nevertheless, it is under discussion that tourism industry from macro point of view; attraction places from micro point of view need continuous crisis management models that aim at minimizing

FIG. 3. THE COMPOUNDS OF CRISIS MANAGEMENT

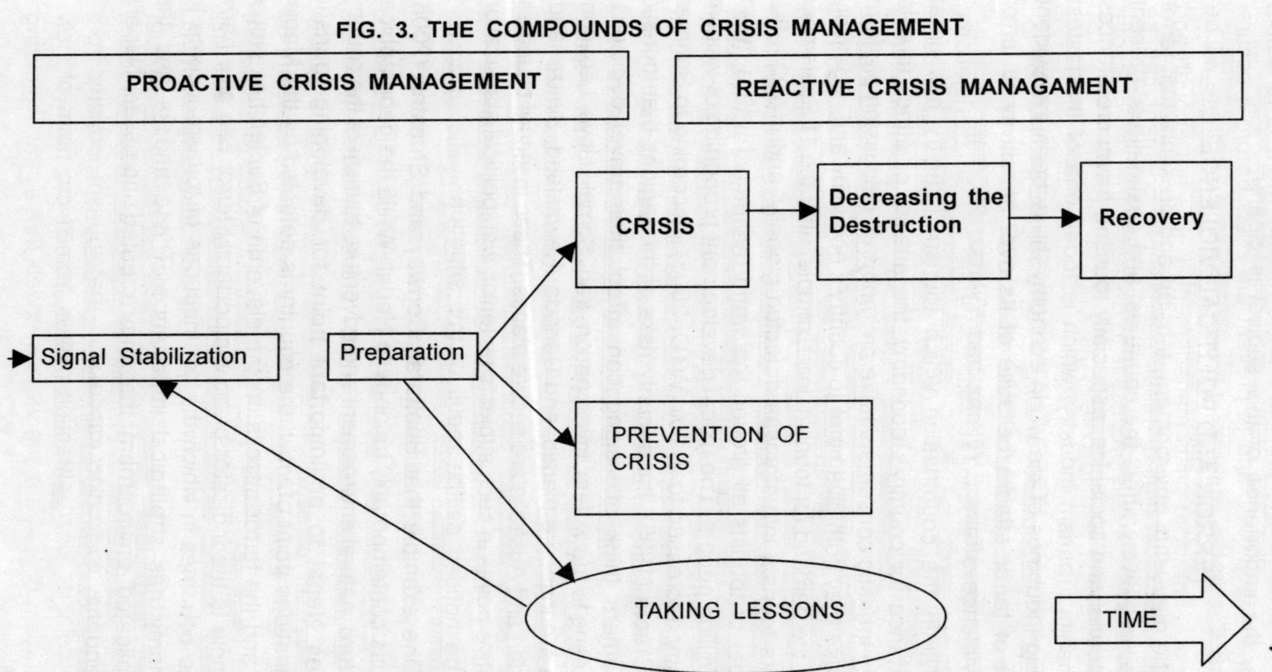

Resource: ***Sausmarez, N. D. (2004) Crisis Management for The Tourism Sector: Preliminary Cosiderations in Policy Development. Tourism and Hospitality Planning & Development 1(2).***

such risk perceptions. If we consider that risks are the seeds of crises, the importance of this subject is clearer.

TERROR AND POLITICAL VIOLENCE

The distrustful environment, tension and pressure that terror create, negatively affect the countries' and destinations' present commercial and social life; especially tourism, travel preferences and habits. Tourism industry, which is today one of the fastest growing industries of the world economy; have been the evident target of terror attacks because of its over sensitivity to terror and violence affairs (Yýlmaz and Yýlmaz, 2005).

Within the countries in which tourism industry has great importance for country's economy, the attacks or attack threats aiming touristic consumers have an important discussion platform because they both give harm to country's economy and negatively affect the demand for tourism. For example, after the 11 September attacks tourism industry was defected globally, and in 2001, the number of tourists all around the world decreased with a mean of 2 million people. The global development proportion of tourism industry decreased to -0,3% (WTO, 2005). According to Sönmez and Graefe (1995), the security risks of the regions that touristic consumers think of visiting can affect their travel decisions. According to the writers' investigation, Iraq, Somali, Libya, Lebanon, Syria are insecure places, and Canada, Newzeland, Switzerland, Sweden and Australia are secure places. These insecure countries' negative points in such subjects as terror, war, political stabilization can be noticed as the result of this situation.

One example that Bhattarai, Conway and Shrestha (2005) discuss contemporarily belongs to Nepal. While the geographical structure, natural environment and adventure tourism of the country carries Nepal to an important point for developing touristic destinations point of view; the country is defected by the Maoist War and the terror attacks on the eleventh of September. Nepal example is the indicator of how importantly terror can give harm in the countries in which the contributions of tourism income to economy has strategical importance. These attacks and the complicated environment that they created increased Nepal's dependency to foreign capital.

NATURAL DISASTERS

Such natural disasters as fire, flood, and earthquake are the basic reasons for tourism related crises. The possibility of managing and controlling such crisis affairs is very low (Atay, 2005). Such crisis events can hinder the normal flow of the events and activities, and cause tragedies on the lives of people (Spillan and Hough, 2003). Such wide-scaled natural disasters can give harm to tourism industry not only regionally but also nationally. For instance, Ýzmit Earthquake that Turkey experienced in 1999 caused the cancellation of the reservations to the country. After it, Turkey has performed many recovery activities. Among these, the followings can be listed; Ministry of Tourism's financial and morale support to tourism market by the support of the government; Ministry of Tourism's developing a crisis management plan without wasting time and by means of this having control on media, relationships with public, and travel industry; and restoration of market image as a whole (Beirman, 2003).

Another instance to natural disasters is the earthquake, which Assisi destination at the center of Italy faced on the 26th of September 1997. In the earthquake, it was reported that 11 people passed away and nearly 100 people were wounded. Furthermore, this earthquake gave harm to historical remains and monumental heritage in the region. After the earthquake, a decrease in tourist flow to the region was observed (Mazzocchi and Montini, 2001).

DISEASES

Diseases can be dealt as another crisis category that has the possibility of affecting the country's economy and destinations. It is a discussion worthy subject that fatal bird influenza was encountered in Manyas borough of Balýkesir in Turkey in October 2005, and a person died because of bird influenza in England, and that may negatively affect the risk perceptions of the potential consumers.

It is possible to observe SARS disease occurred in 2003 as an example which best shows the concrete effects of diseases on tourism. This disease especially affected Malezia very negatively. According to World Tourism Organization statistics, Malezia, which had been the 15th with 13.2 million tourists among the most tourist attracting countries in 2002, had great decreases in visitor numbers because of the SARS disease and that number decreased to 10.5 million tourists. After the SARS disease, Malezi decreased to the 17th among the most tourist attracting countries standings (www.tursab.org.tr).

Another example is the foot and mouth disease (FMD), which spread from the farm animals in England in 2001. In England, this disease gave more harm to the markets, which have especially more potential to be affected from media. The effect of the disease to England was not very huge, but many park and rural tourism areas were closed down. Because of this, after the disease, there was a decrease in the visits to farms, van parks and camp sites (Beirman, 2003).

CRIME

When compared with terrorist activities, the possibility of tourists being crime victims is higher. As tourist demand to a specific destination increases, and the proportion of tourism investment increases, the crime proportion (especially crimes directed to properties) of that destination also increases. Another of the most important reasons is that tourism resources are the chief targets of crime activities. The case of crime affects especially tourists more than ordinary people, and makes them have a stronger sense of being a victim that is created by being exposed to crime. The last thing the tourist hopes is to be the victim of a theft or robbery. Because tourists travel to relax and enjoy, personal security is a subject having secondary importance for them (Albuquerque and McElroy, 1999).

According to Pizam (1995), in every moment of a day, in any destination of any part of the world, a crime or violence affair occurs. However, comfort, safety and security are the basic conditions necessary for countries, regions and tourism destinations' normal development continuity (Pizam, 1995; in Cavlek, 2002). The case of crime, which such negatively affects tourists and destinations, is so accepted that of course it is a critical approach on touristic attraction places point of view. Consequently, tourism destinations are more sensitive and indefensible than the other destinations. Their approach to the case of crime and violence should be more sensitive than the other normal destinations or regions.

WAR

War is a very important security subject that is discussed in a more different position than crimes and terror because of those wars extensive social effects and long-term results are caused. In literature, the effects of wars on tourism industry are discussed as being negative (Smith, 1998). The chief two years in which decreases were experienced in tourism incomes of Turkey were 1991 and 1999. The most important factor in 1991 was the Gulf War. And in 1999, the Gulf Earthquake. If 'tourist flow is bound to the trust environment' is taken into account, the frame in which earthquake and war atmosphere exists and the rumors accordingly are effective, affects tourism negatively (Emsen and Deðer, 2004).

As an example to the negative effects of wars, we can show the Croatia-Yugoslavia War occurred between the years 1991 and 1995. After this war, the seashore regions of Croatia and the city Dubrovnik had a dramatic decrease was experienced in tourist flows to Croatia. This war sabotaged and paralyzed especially Croatia's tourism industry.

CONCLUSION

This paper has investigated the importance of understanding crises related to tourism field. As previously indicated, crises are becoming increasingly more complex, more difficult to anticipate and to manage effectively. Full recovery for visitor arrivals may take longer period for the destinations (Huang and Min, 2002) exposed specifically security related crises, developing a management plan for the tourism and hospitality organizations are crucial to deal with negative effects of crises. Despite the fact that every crisis is unique, this nature leads taking into account studying within the context of tourism industry specifically (Henderson, 2003). Hence, a number of measures taken by the administrators should be recognized, both single operators and destination managers. Size and location are inconsequential to crisis.

The basic objective of the crisis plan is to minimize the negative impacts on the destination or tourism and hospitality organizations. Preparing for the worst is a good approach aiming at minimizing the risks in advance. Besides this approach some opportunities are also merit to detecting during actual problems and after the crisis. Because it should be known that crises could occasionally contain some positive impacts. From this point of view, while developing a more efficient crisis plan, decision-makers should take into account this basic nature of crisis. Surviving and prospering in highly competitive and unpredictable business environment force operators to pay attention this characteristic.

Being pro-active in management process will help administrators to deal with the existing problems in advance by collecting related data in outside or inside due to crises may have unique nature. That's why measures should be taken before crises. The types of measures can be differentiated up to company scale, crisis characteristic, period, market segments, limited resources, geographical penetration, and your own special products. Planners must audit every signal that has a potential to damage. A crisis management team formation may be helpful to overcome these types of difficulties as suggested in literature.

Personal experiences and knowledge are both crucial components to manage crisis properly (Okumus et al., 2005). Administrators who had experienced many different crises seem take reliable precautions in comparison with others. However it is not important having enough experiences to deal with, more importantly those should show capability to take precautions to prevent any further crises. In other words, not only with words but also with actions (Okumus et al., 2005), hence overall experiences should put into practice in terms of lessons learned.

Just have previous studies have found that crisis management becomes more popular research field nowadays. However more research is needed because of nature of crises. Additionally it is essential to provide further insights to this complex area; scholars rather concentrate on different characteristics of crises. As previously indicated they have unique nature and becoming more complex day by day. Overcoming strategies should be determined in this regard. Because in order to deal with crises one must analysis in detail the situation and find out reliable solutions according to findings that hidden inside. That is having an anatomy of problem easily take one to the correct path. In this term future studies might find the effects of each crisis regarding tourism industry, and then contribute new findings to existing literature. In this way information and knowledge about crises will increase and direct researchers to find out new strategies to overcome them.

REFERENCES

Akova, O., Çetinkaya, A., Saritas, E. and Aksu, A. (2000) 1999 Yilinda Seyahat Acentalarinin Karþilaþtiklari Sorunlar Üzerine Bir Araþtirma. *Turizmde Seçme Makaleler* (34). Istanbul : Turizm Geliþtirme ve Eðitim Vakfi Yayini (51).

Albuquerque, K. and McElroy, J. (1999) Tourism and Crime In The Caribbean. *Annals of Tourism Research*, 26(4), 968-984.

Arslan, M. (2001) Yönetim ve Organizasyonun Bazi Temel Kavramlari. *Yönetim ve Organizasyon*. Ankara : Nobel Yayin Daðitim, Yayin No: 265.

Atay, H. (2005) Seyahat Acentalarinda Içsel Kaynakli Krizler: Kuþadasi'nda Faaliyet Gösteren A Grubu Seyahat Acentalari Üzerinde Bir Araþtirma. *Basilmamiþ Yüksek Lisans Tezi*. Aydin : Adnan Menderes Üniversitesi Sosyal Bilimler Enstitüs.

Augustine, N. R. (2000) Önlemeye Çaliþtiðimiz Krizi Yönetmek. In Crisis Management, Harvard Business Press. (Çev. Atay, S.) *Kriz Yöneti*. Istanbul : Mess Yayinlari (328).

Beirman, D. (2003) *Restoring Tourism Destinations In Crisis A Strategic Marketing Approach*. USA : CABI Publishing.

Bhattarai, K., Conway, D. and Shrestha D. (2005) Tourism, Terrorism and Turmoil In Nepal. *Annals of Tourism Research* 32(3), 669-688.

Blake, E. and Sinclair, M. T. (2003) Tourism Crisis Management US Response To September 11. *Annals of Tourism Research* 30(4).

Brown, S. (2003) Crisis, What Crisis? Marketing, Midas, and the Croesus of Representation. *Qualitative Market Research: An International Journal*. 6(3).

Cavlek, N. (1997) *Tour Operators – Gages of Destination Safety. In War Terrorism Tourism Times of Crisis and Recovery*. International Conference Absracts. Dubrovnik: Organized by The Institute for Tourism, Zagreb and The Faculty of Economics, University of Zagreb.

Cavlek, N. (2002) Tour Operators and Destination Safety. *Annals of Tourism Research* 29(2), 478-496.

Chong John, K. S. and Donald R., E. (1998) Anticipating and Dealing with Financial Crisis. *Management Decision* 36(9).

Çiçek, O. and Kiliç, H. (2001) Konaklama Endüstrisinde Kriz Yönetim Planlari ve Uygulama Aþamalari. *II. Ulusal Türkiye Turizmi Sempozyumu Tebliðler Kitabi.* Izmir : Türkiye Turizmi Araþtirma Enstitüsü.

Emsen, Ö. S. and Deðer, M. K. (2004) Turizm Üzerine Terörizmin Etkileri: 1984-2001 Türkiye Deneyimi. *Akdeniz I.I.B.F. Dergisi* (7), 67-83.

Faulkner, B. (2001) Towards A Framework For Tourism Disaster Management. *Tourism Management* (22).

Faulkner, B. and Vikolov, S. K. (2001) Washed Out One Day, Back On Track The Next: A Post Mortem of A Turism Disaster. *Tourism Management* (22).

Fink, S. (1986) *Crisis Management: Planning for the Inevitable.* New York: American Management Association.

Glaesser, D. (2003) *Crisis Management In The Tourism Industry.* Great Britain: Butterworth-Heinemann.

Haþit, G. (2000) *Iþletmelerde Kriz Yönetimi ve Tükiye'nin Büyük Sanayi Iþletmeleri Üzerinde Yapilan Araþtirma Çaliþmasi.* Eskiþehir : Anadolu Üniversitesi Yayinlari (616).

Heath, R. (1998) Dealing with the Complete Crisis – the Crisis Management Shell Structure. *Safety Science* (30).

Henderson, J.C. (2003) Communicating in a crisis: Flight SQ 006. *Tourism Management* (24), 279-287.

http://www.tursab.org.tr/content/turkish/istatistikler/akrobat/ULKE/05myMlzC.pdf. 01.11.2005.

Huang, J. H. and Min, J.C.H. (2002) Earthquake devastation and recovery in tourism: the Taiwan case. *Tourism Management* (23), 145-154.

Keown-McMullan, C. (1997) Crisis: When Does A Molehill Become A Mountain. *Disaster Prevention and Management* 6(1).

Lee, Y.J. and Harrald, J.R. (1999) Critical Issue for Business Area Impact Analysis in Business Crisis Management: Analytical Capability. *Disaster Prevention and Management* 8(3).

Lepp, A. and Gibson, H. (2003) Tourist Roles, Perceived Risk and International Tourism. *Annals of Tourism Research* 30(3), 606-624.

Lerhman, K. (1986) When Fact and Fantasy Collide: Crisis Management in the Travel Industry. *Public Relations Journal* (42).

Mansfeld, Y. (1994) The Middle East Conflict and Tourism To Israel. *Middle East Studies* 30(3).

Mazzocchi, M. and Montini, A. (2001) Earthquake Effects On Tourism In Central Italy. *Annals of Tourism Research* 28(4), 1031-1046.

Mitroff, I. and Pearson, C. (1993) From Crisis Prone To Crisis Prepared: A Framework for Crisis Management. *Academy of Management Executive* 7(1), 48-59:53. In Santana, G. (1999) Tourism: Toward A Model for Crisis Management. *Turizam* 47(1), 4-12.

Okumus, F., Altinay, M. and Arasli, H. (2005) The Impact of Turkey's Economic Crisis of February 2001 on the Tourism Industry in Northern Cyprus. *Tourism Management* (26), 95-104.

Richter, L. K. (1999) After Political Turmoil: The Lessons of Rebuilding Tourism in three Asian Countries. *Journal of Travel Research* (38), 41-45.

Ritchie, B.W. (2004) Chaos, Crises and Disasters: A Strategic Approach To Crisis Management In The Tourism Industry. *Tourism Management* (25).

Roehl, W. and Fesenmaier, D. (1992) Risk Perceptions and Pleasure Travel: An Exploratory Analysis. *Journal of Travel Research* 2(4), 17-26.

Sausmarez, N.D. (2004) Crisis Management For The Tourism Sector: Preliminary Considerations In Policy Development. *Tourism and Hospilality Planning & Development* 1(2).

Selbst, P. (1978) Crisis Management Strategy: Competition and Change in Modern Enterprises. In Booth. S. (1993). New York: Routhledge.

Smith, V. L. (1998) War and Tourism An American Etnography. *Annals of Tourism Research* 25(1), 1031-1046.

Sonmez, S., Backman, K. and Lawrence, A. (1994) *Managing Tourism Crisis: A Guidebook*. Clemson, SC: Clemson University.

Sönmez, S.F. and Graefe, A.R. (1998) Influence of Terrorism Risk On Foreign Tourism Decisions. *Annals of Tourism Research* 25(1), 112-144.

Sönmez, S.F. (1998) Tourism, Terrorism, and Political Instability. *Annals of Tourism Research* 25(2).

Spillan, J. and Hough, M. (2003) Crisis Planning In Small Businesses: Importance, Impetus and Indifference. *European Management Journal* 21(3).

Stafford, G., Yu, L. and Armoo, A.K. (2002) Crisis Management and Recovery How Washington, D.C., Hotels Responded To Tourism. *Cornell Hotel and Restaurant Administration Quarterly*-October.

Tanrisevdi, A. (2002) Krizlerin Seyahat Acentalari Üzerindeki Etkileri ve Bu Etkilerin Çözümüne Yönelik Stratejiler. *Basilmamiþ Doktora Tezi.* Aydin: Adnan Menderes Üniversitesi Sosyal Bilimler Enstitüsü.

WTO (2005). World Tourism Barometer 3(1), http://www.world-tourism.org/facts/barometer/WTOBarom05_1_en_expc.pdf, 30.10.2005.

Yarcan, Þ. (1998) *Seyahat Ýþletmeleri.* Ýstanbul : Boðaziçi Üniversitesi Yayinevi 2(549).

Yýmaz, Ö. Yýlmaz, D. (2005) Terörizm ve Terörizmin Hedefi Olarak Turizm Endüstrisi. *Elektronik Sosyal Bilimler Dergisi* 4(13), 39-58.

SECTION B

ECOLOGICAL PERSPECTIVES

6

ENVIRONMENTAL IMPACTS OF NATURE-BASED TOURISM IN SOUTH AFRICA

ANNA SPENCELEY

ABSTRACT

Assessments of environmental factors contributing to sustainable tourism are described in relation to four photographic wildlife tourism enterprises in South Africa. A series of qualitative and quantitative results are presented to demonstrate how nature-based tourism enterprises in protected areas address their environmental impacts. Field based evaluations and interviews with local community members show how a new Sustainable Nature-based Tourism Assessment Toolkit (SUNTAT) was used to evaluate enterprise performance. Motivations underlying environmentally responsible activities undertaken by private and public sector enterprises are described, in addition to their limitations and constraints. Conclusions are made regarding the need for environmentally responsible activities to utilise commercially appropriate best practice, and to consider both the local level and neighbouring livelihood strategies.

Key words: sustainable development; environmental impacts; nature-based tourism; protected areas, South Africa

INTRODUCTION

The purpose of this paper is to describe the environmental sustainability of four tourism enterprises in South Africa. Data is provided to illustrate how environmental information was obtained through the application of a holistic Sustainable Nature-based Tourism Assessment Toolkit (SUNTAT). Qualitative and quantitative results from the field studies have been evaluated and presented. Examples of environmentally responsible processes and performance are used to demonstrate how the toolkit may be applied to collect reliable and comparable data. Complementary to the empirical data, this paper also discusses motivations underlying environmentally responsible activities by private and public sector enterprises. Limitations and constraints to environmental sustainability that relate to commercial and political forces are also reviewed. The article highlights the importance of applying commercially and locally appropriate environmental best practice.

The importance of this work rests in four main areas. Firstly, it presents data from the evaluation of sustainable tourism development in developing countries, which tends to be underrepresented in the literature (Tosun, 2001). Secondly, the paper illustrates how progress has been made to move past the debate surrounding what sustainable tourism is or is not, and towards tangibly assessing the constituent factors of sustainability, as defined by regional experts. Thirdly, instead of focusing narrowly on one level of environmental impacts (e.g. wildlife behavioural change), the research demonstrates the importance of evaluating both micro- and macro-level issues to strategically address sustainability. Fourthly, the article provides examples of benchmarks that may be used to demonstrate how environmentally responsible interventions at the local-level have cumulative implications for a sustainable nature-based tourism industry at a strategic-level.

BACKGROUND

Research and discussion regarding sustainable tourism development has grown in volume since the Brundtland Report proposed that intergenerational equity could not be achieved unless the environmental impacts of economic activities were considered (WCED, 1987: 43). Concern for sustainable tourism arose from the increasing realisation that mass tourism could have significant detrimental environmental impacts in destinations if it was not controlled. Nature-based tourism, which incorporates the enjoyment of wildlife or undeveloped natural areas (WTTERC, 1993), was of special concern. This was in part because degradation of the environment fundamentally undermines the potential for nature-based tourism to be attractive to visitors (Roe *et al.* 1997). Researchers have produced comprehensive reviews of sustainable tourism issues that consider the 'triple bottom line' of sustainability (Elkington, 1997): economic, social and environmental factors (for example, Archer & Cooper, 1994; Bramwell & Lane, 1993; Harris & Leiper, 1995; Mowforth & Munt, 1998).

Although the field studies undertaken addressed the triple bottom line, only the environmental aspects of sustainable tourism are reviewed within this paper. Environmental impact studies attempt to generalise relationships between tourism activities and impacts with respect to specific ecosystems and disturbance characteristics (Knight & Cole, 1995). Evaluation techniques used to predict and avoid development impacts that are detrimental to the environment include the Limits of Acceptable Change (Stankey *et al.* 1984), Environmental Impact Assessment (Bagri *et al.* 1998), Strategic Environmental Assessment (Therivel *et al.* 1992), Ecological Impact Assessment (Beanlands & Duinker, 1983) and Cumulative Effects Assessment (Peterson *et al.* 1987). Aspects of these and other tools were incorporated within the research where appropriate to the SUNTAT.

There have been a number of reviews of environmental impacts research (e.g. Knight & Gutzwiller, 1995; Mathieson & Wall, 1982; Speight, 1973). A summary of environmental impact research in Table 1 highlights the dominance of interest in tourism assessments linked to habitats and wildlife rather than issues regarding air, water, geology and landscape. Given the diversity of environmental issues that may be evaluated, this research focused on environmental factors that were prioritised by regional stakeholders.

TABLE 1: OVERVIEW OF ENVIRONMENTAL IMPACTS OF TOURISM (SPENCELEY, 2003A)

AIR:	Impacts of transport activity and facility power include: • air and noise pollution from vehicles (Mathieson & Wall, 1982); and • increased carbon dioxide ($C0_2$) emissions from fossil fuel combustion which contributes to global climate change (Adams, 1990).
WATER:	Impacts of the disposal of waste into water bodies include the: • introduction of minerals, nutrients, sewage, petrol and toxins to the environment (FAO, 1972; Mathieson & Wall, 1982); and • contamination reduces water quality and may lead to potential health hazards to animals (Mathieson & Wall, 1982; Wang & Miko, 1997).
GEOLOGY & SOIL:	Impacts of collection, vandalism, erosion include:· removal of minerals, rocks, fossils and items of archaeological interest, and graffiti (Mathieson & Wall, 1982); • physical and chemical changes in soil (Mathieson & Wall, 1982); and • erosion (Sun & Walsh, 1998) and soil compaction, which affects invertebrate fauna (Duffey, 1975).
LANDSCAPE:	Impacts of Formal and informal development include: • visual impact of settlements on the landscape (Sindiyo & Pertet, 1984); and • potential improvement in the landscape's appearance (Perdue *et al.* 1990) through preservation of heritage structures (Lui *et al.* 1987).
HABITATS:	Impacts of clearing for construction and tourism facility include: • decrease in natural habitat (e.g. wetlands) due to resource use and/or tourism construction (Burton, 1998);

- competition between native and invasive plant species from resort gardens; and
- increased fire frequency (Buckley, 1991) leading to habitat change (Mathieson & Wall, 1982).Impacts of pedestrian and vehicular traffic include: changes germination, establishment, growth and reproduction (Cole & Landres, 1995), species diversity, composition, and plant morphology (Sun & Liddle, 1993); and
- disappearance of fragile species (Sun & Liddle, 1993) and replacement by more resilient species (Mathieson & Wall, 1982).Impacts of plants and fungi collection include: changes in species composition and disappearance of rare species (Rogers, 1981).

WILDLIFE: Impacts of hunting and fishing include:

- changes in species composition and social behaviour (e.g. elephants, lions); disappearance of rare species; and
- reduction of habituated animals (Sindiyo & Pertet, 1984).Impacts of pollution include:
- effects on health including; psychological stress, behavioural changes, reductions in productivity due to noise pollution (Bowles, 1995); and
- use of waste disposal areas as sources of food (Speight, 1973; Spenceley, 1997). Impacts of wildlife harassment resulting from viewing and photography include:
- *behavioural changes:* Avoidance, habituation or attraction to humans resulting from interactions (Knight & Cole, 1995);
- *physiological changes*: Change in heart rate (Gabrielsen & Smith, 1995), affects on growth rates and abundance (Anderson, 1995);
- *species composition and distribution*: Changes in species composition, diversity and abundance and interspecific interactions (Gutzwiller, 1995; Knight & Cole, 1995).

Displacement due to recreational activity (Klein *et al.* 1995);

- *disruption of feeding:* Found in birds (Hulbert, 1990), rhinoceros (McCoy, 1995), hunting behaviour in lions (Ceballos-Lascuráin, 1996), wolves and bears (Knight and Cole, 1995); and
- *effects on breeding success:* Direct destruction (Burger, 1981) or abandonment, and increased predation on bird nests (Burger *et al.* 1995). Disruption of reproductive behaviour in antelope (Edington & Edington, 1986) and reptiles (Cott, 1969).Impacts of the development of highways and trails in natural areas include:
- species-specific disturbance caused by roads, buildings and plantations (van der Zande *et al.* 1980);
- barrier effects to carnivores, collisions, increased accessibility to wild areas by poachers (Noss *et al.* 1986); and
- vehicles kill and/or maim wildlife during collisions, from which scavengers profit (Mathieson & Wall, 1982).

Environmental impact research has a number of limitations, which include (Briassoulis, 1991; Mathieson & Wall, 1982; van der Duim & Caalders, 2002; Whittaker & Knight, 1998):

- tourism involves linked activities, making it difficult to distinguish between impacts arising from different activities (including other industries, and natural changes) and therefore to connect cause and effect;
- cumulative, synergistic, indirect and long-term impacts are difficult to identify and assess;
- changes in wildlife behaviour may be species-specific and not actually be detrimental to their survival; and
- the extent to which ecosystems can recuperate following impacts are poorly understood.

The development of the new assessment toolkit addressed these issues by incorporating a mixture of simple and practical techniques that addressed activities both inside and outside tourism enterprises. Appreciating that ecosystems are complex and poorly understood, tools from process- and performance-based environmental management systems were combined with expert stakeholder opinion and baseline ecological information to provide practical approaches to address aspects of environmental sustainability (Spenceley, 2003a).

Historically, the lack of responsibility shown by tour operators towards environmental and cultural resources in destinations has been attributed to the lack of ownership and control over ground operations (Ashworth & Goodall, 1990), coupled with intense competition between tour operators and low profit margins (Evans & Stabler, 1995). However, evidence suggests that tour operators are increasingly requiring that their ground handlers report on their environmental performance (e.g. the Association of Independent Tour Operators {AITO}). This is in part due to the growing market demand from consumers for environmentally sensitive holidays (see Table 2).

Although most tourists make purchasing decisions based on price, climate, facilities and quality, it is clear from the Tearfund and Mori surveys (see Table 2) that the sustainability of their travel experiences are becoming *increasingly* important. Therefore, it is the responsibility of the tourism industry to transparently demonstrate that they are operating responsibly and making progress towards environmental sustainability: an objective that the new SUNTAT may facilitate.

Research addressed within this paper concerned the environmental sustainability of nature-based tourism enterprises in South Africa. South Africa provided the ideal context for the work given the nation's rich biodiversity; its established nature-based tourism industry; and the strong national policy basis for responsible tourism development.

Biodiversity has been acknowledged by the South African government as one of the mainstays of economic sectors such as tourism, recreation, agriculture, forestry, horticulture and fisheries. In cognisance of this, South Africa ratified the Convention

TABLE 2: CONSUMER ATTITUDES TO THE ENVIRONMENT AND SUSTAINABLE TOURISM (SPENCELEY, 2003A)

Issue	Proportion of sample	Source
Importance of environmentally sensitive policies and practices		
More likely to book hotels with a good environmental attitude	87% British 60% Australians 54% Americans	IHEI study, cited in Anon, 2002(n = 300 travellers at airports in UK, Australia and US)
It was important that their holiday did not damage destination environments	71%	Stueve *et al.* 2002. (n=4300 adults in the USA)
Importance that the holiday should not damage the environment	2000 - 85% 2002 - 87%	MORI study for ABTA, cited by Goodwin and Francis, 2003 (n=963 British public in 2000; n=713 in 2002)
At least fairly important to deal with a company that took into account environmental issues when arranging holidays and business trips	1995 - 52% 1997 - 61%	MORI, 1995, 1997, cited in Martin & Stubbs, Undated(British Public)

Importance of socially responsible policies and practices

More likely to book a holiday with a company that had a written code guaranteeing good working conditions, protection of the environment and support of local charities in the tourist destination	1999 – 45% 2001 – 52%	Tearfund, 2001; 2002(1999: nationally and regionally representative sample of n = 2032 adults in the UK; 2001 n=927)
Knowing that they had booked with a company with good ethical practice made their holiday enjoyable	24%	Mintel, 2001(n =2028; UK holiday makers = 1636) July 2001
Importance of the holiday benefiting people in the destination (e.g. through jobs and business opportunities)	2000 - 71% 2002 – 76%	MORI study for ABTA, cited by Goodwin and Francis, 2003 (n=963 British public in 2000; n=713 in 2002)
Respect towards the ways of living and the traditions of the local host population was the most important criteria for them when booking a holiday	95%	Forschungsinstitut für Freizeit und ourismus (FIF), Müller & Landes, 2000 T(German tourists)

* The sample size is indicated, where known

on Biological Diversity in 1995 (DEAT, 2000) within the 1997 National Policy on the Conservation and Sustainable Use of South Africa's Biological Diversity (DEAT, 1997). South Africa has 422 formally protected areas and 160 privately owned reserves covering approximately 6% of the land surface area (DEAT, 1999). There is a major demand for nature-based tourism, and approximately 60% of all foreign visitors experience wildlife in a game or nature reserve during their visit (DEAT, 1996) (see Figure 1).

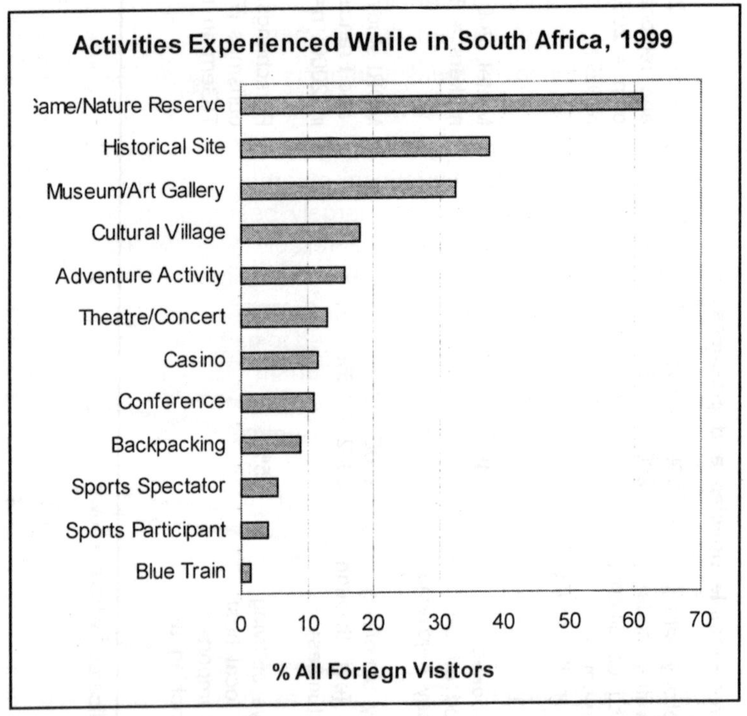

FIGURE 1: ACTIVITIES EXPERIENCED BY FOREIGN VISITORS IN SOUTH AFRICA (ADAPTED FROM DSI, 1999A, 1999B)

The South Africa government aims to manage the nation's tourism industry in the interests of sustainable development in such a way that it contributes to the improvement of the quality of life of all its citizens. The White Paper on the *Development and Promotion of Tourism in South Africa* (DEAT, 1996) proposed that tourism development should be underpinned by responsible environmental practices and should encourage the conservation and sustainable use of tourism resources. Specifically, the White Paper promoted the (ibid):

- maintenance and encouragement of natural, economic, social and cultural diversity;
- sustainable use of local resources;
- avoidance of waste and over-consumption;
- assessment of environmental, social and economic impacts of tourism developments; and
- monitoring of tourism impacts with open disclosure of information.

South Africa, similarly to other countries, has not reported on the progress made by tourism enterprises towards achieving responsible tourism. This has largely been due to the lack of availability of appropriate tools that reliably measure environmental performance. Therefore, this research aimed to address the shortfall by developing and testing a range of performance and process-based tools that could be used to gauge the environmental sustainability of nature-based tourism. Existing information regarding sustainable tourism development has predominately been produced within developed countries (Tosun, 2001), and therefore this research emphasised that stakeholders from developing countries should be active participants in the process. Consulting southern African experts and stakeholders regarding factors that they considered essential to sustainable nature-based tourism ensured the regional relevance of the new toolkit.

The four tourism enterprises located in and around Kruger National Park (KNP) were evaluated using the toolkit. Each operated photographic safari tourism as their core business, and did so within lowveld savannah habitats where charismatic fauna including elephant, rhino, buffalo, lion and leopard could be found. In all four cases, the enterprises were located within a protected area and had a rural community as an immediate neighbour on one border. Land on other borders of the enterprises was also protected, and either privately or publicly owned (see Table 3).

TABLE 3: VARIATION OF INDEPENDENT VARIABLES BETWEEN ENTERPRISES (SPENCELEY, 2003A)

Ngala	Pretoriuskop	Jackalberry	Sabi Sabi
Land context			
In the Timbavati Private Nature Reserve (PNR) Kruger National Park (KNP)	A camp in KNP	In the Thorny-bush Game Reserve close	In the Sabi Sands Wildtuin, unfenced from to KNP
Conservation status			
National Park	National Park	PNR	PNR
Area land ~ 147 km^2 within ~789 km^2 PNR	~620 km^2 for region within ~20 000 km^2 park	~ 43 km^2 within ~124 km^2 PNR	~ 32 km^2 within ~750 km^2 PNR
Land ownership			
Privately owned land	Government owned land	Privately owned land	Privately owned land
Land tenure			
Land leased from private owner by management company	Land owned by public management company	Land owned by private management company	Land owned by private management company
Infrastructure ownership			
Privately owned	Publicly owned	Privately owned	Privately owned
Number other operations managed by same organisation			
22 lodges in six African countries	18 national parks in South	None	None

Ngala	Pretoriuskop	Jackalberry	Sabi Sabi
	Africa. In KNP: 13 rest camps (plus 6 bushveld & 5 private camps		
Capacity			
1 camp with 21 rooms (42 beds)	1 camp with 136 units (352 beds) & 40 camp sites	1 camp with 5 rooms (10 beds)	3 camps with 46 rooms (92 beds)
Price range (approximate figures given where converted from Rands)			
US$340 to $475 p/p per night Price includes meals, game drives, game walks	~US$7 to ~$245 per site/room/guest house Accomm-odation only	~US$170 to ~$205 p/p sharingPrice includes meals, game drives, game walks	~US$410 to ~$1050 p/p sharingPrice includes meals, game drives, game walks
Closest rural community			
Welverdiend	Numbi	Timbavati	Huntingdon
Population			
7 000 (1996 census)	4 130 (1996 census)	11 240 (1999 census)	6 507 (1999 census)
No. interviewees (and proportion of the community surveyed)			
168 (2.4%)	226 (5.5%)	314 (2.8%)	350 (5.4%)

As Table 3 indicates, the enterprises varied with respect to their land context, ownership, traversing area, land tenure, traversing rights, capacity, price range and the type of interactions with local people. These variations allowed the reliability of the toolkit to be tested under different conditions.

The case studies took place between 23 July 2000 and 4 May 2001. On-site planning of the assessments took place with the enterprise managers; and included familiarisation with the enterprise structure, their staff and contractors, local stakeholders and documentation that was available for review.

The environmental issues identified are described here in relation to three levels:

- **the context,** regarding the wider environment; overarching policies and frameworks; management practices by neighbouring landowners; collaboration, and conflicts; and environmental costs and benefits to local communities;
- **the land,** in relation to the protected area that the enterprise operated within, and details from management plans; management of water, flora and fauna; infrastructure maintenance; and commercial activities; and
- **the enterprise,** with regard to operational resource use and waste disposal.

ENVIRONMENTAL CONTEXT

Factors considered in relation to the environmental context of the enterprises *within* their private nature reserves (PNRs) were:

- overarching policies and plans, including those relating to land management, development, and tourism; and
- cooperation, conflicts and control of activities within the protected area.

OVERARCHING POLICIES AND ENVIRONMENTAL MANAGE-MENT

Each of the enterprises based within PNRs were signatories to voluntary constitutions that promoted the conservation of flora and fauna. These agreements were needed because the majority of properties within the PNRs were unfenced from one another, and therefore wildlife could move freely between them. The parastatal South African National Parks (SANParks) managed the land that two of the enterprises were based on, while the others managed their land privately. The land around Ngala and Pretoriuskop was managed in line with detailed masterplan for

KNP, which specified fire, water, elephant, recreational zoning, and neighbouring community programmes. The location of Ngala meant that under the constitution of the Timbavati PNR consumptive wildlife management activities took place on neighbouring properties. The PNRs that Jackalberry and Sabi Sabi lay within had more fragmented environmental management plans. Both the Thornybush PNR and the Sabi Sands Wildtuin actively managed wildlife populations over the entire reserves, and set hunting quotas based on annual aerial surveys (although neither enterprise hunted itself). The habitat management planning in the Thornybush GR was divided into two sections in relation to the two land management companies contracted by different landowners. There was cooperation between the management parties and an increasing tendency to create consistency between management efforts. However, the Sabi Sands Wildtuin had no strategic environmental management plan and fragmented management practices took place across the PNR. Essentially, each landowner within the Sabi Sands Wildtuin independently employed their own land managers in order to prioritise the management of their land. The majority of landowners focussed on maximising the game viewing potential on their own property, rather than strategically to improve the conservation value of the whole reserve.

The constitutions of the PNRs provided different limits on density of commercial beds that could be operated by landowners in the PNRs, and in some cases the number of vehicles (see Table 4).

TABLE 4: ENTERPRISE LAND AND TOURISM CONTEXT (SPENCELEY, 2003A)

Ngala	Pretoriuskop	Jackalberry	Sabi Sabi
Tourism development limits			
Limits on bed density (15 beds per 856 ha) and vehicle density (2 per 856 ha)	Visitors limited by gate day-visitor limits and accommodation capacity at camps.	Limit on bed density (15 beds per 1000 ha)	Limit on commercial bed density (1 bed per 150 ha)

COOPERATION AND CONFLICTS

Cooperation between PNR members consistently took place through formal meetings and committees. Democratic processes, with different systems of determining majority votes, were used to govern PNR issues - such as selecting individual animals for off-take during hunting operations. The PNR constitutions contained provisions for dealing with members who infringed their obligations. Financial penalties could be imposed on members, in addition to the last resort of fencing landowners out of the PNR (e.g. for gross misconduct). Monitoring landowner activities within PNRs were undertaken by members policing one another and also by the PNR wardens.

Factors that were considered in relation to the case study enterprise's land and tourism management context *outside* the protected area with members of rural communities, were:

- natural resource use;
- human-wildlife conflict;
- environmental education; and
- perceptions of wildlife.

NATURAL RESOURCE USE

There were a number of reports from neighbouring community members interviewed that they had been able to access natural resources prior to the creation of the four protected areas. The vast majority of community members (between 61% and 97% of the samples) reported that they could currently access some natural resources within the four protected areas. To different extents the enterprises provided bush-cleared wood, thatch and grass to local community members. There were formal mechanisms that allowed people from the Numbi community to obtain a proportion of the natural resources and revenue generated from annual harvests of thatching material from their land within KNP. Although they also wished to access river water, SANParks was concerned about the potential for disease transmission between wildlife and domestic animals. SANParks therefore arranged pumping and piping systems to divert water from the river into the community (although this infrastructure was subsequently destroyed by vandals).

Subsistence poaching occurred within all four protected areas at low levels, and presumably this allowed some members of the communities to benefit by obtaining meat from wildlife. The poachers used snares and dogs to hunt wildlife, and in the case of Pretoriuskop the most common form of poaching encountered was actually fishing! Anti-poaching patrols were operated around all four enterprises - either organised by the PNR or the landowner concerned. Wildlife managers used informers within neighbouring communities, and informal communication forums with local tribal authorities, in attempts to control the problems. Poaching of trophy species (e.g. elephant for their tusks; rhinos for their horns) was rare in all four cases, although isolated incidences were reported. Pretoriuskop maintained the most detailed reports of poaching incursions, including the number of alleged poachers caught and their punishment if they were found guilty in a court of law. Only in the case of Jackalberry had antipoaching staff initiated active attempts to create a mutually beneficial relationship with neighbouring tribal groups, and to develop incentives for community policing.

HUMAN-WILDLIFE CONFLICT

Between 31% and 56% of neighbouring community members interviewed reported problems with wildlife from the protected areas. Problems included elephants and baboons raiding their crops; lion and hyena killing livestock; and disease transferred between wildlife and livestock (e.g. *Theileriosis*). There were also isolated incidents reported where lion and leopard had attacked and killed people. Interviewees indicated that the conflict did not appear to take place on a daily basis, but that there were more frequent incidents of crop-raiding around harvest times – obviously the most critical times for the poor people inhabiting these communities. There was overwhelming agreement that there was no compensation for damage to property or person inflicted by wildlife. Only a handful of people reported that they had obtained money or meat as compensation.

Incidents of human-wildlife conflict are rarely compensated in South Africa, because the law states that the *land that it is situated on* dictates the ownership of wildlife. Therefore wildlife *leaving* a park or reserve is no longer owned nor the responsibility of that park or reserve. This means that landowners who 'lose' dangerous game, which then damages property in neighbouring communities, are not legally obliged to compensate people for those damages. It should also be noted that wildlife not only emanated from the enterprise properties studied, but also from other nearby protected areas. This created some confusion over the source of wildlife causing damage to local property, and was particularly true in the case of Welverdiend (which bordered two other protected areas in addition to Ngala).

ENVIRONMENTAL EDUCATION

Both the private and public sector enterprises engaged with local community members to provide environmental education. Ngala channelled donations from tourists and philanthropic institutions to provide academic bursaries, conservation lessons, environmental debates, and educational weekend trips to the reserve. In collaboration with the other landowners in the Thornybush GR, Jackalberry funded conservation education for local children at a nearby environmental centre, while Sabi Sabi supported the rehabilitation of existing infrastructure to create a community environmental education centre and library - using both donations and its own funds. The extent of enterprise assistance depended upon the financial and human resource capacities of the enterprises, and their access to donations and support from other organisations and individuals. Through the extended human resources capacity of KNP, members of Numbi benefited from a variety of environmental education programmes. These provided woodcarvers with ecological information regarding the use of alien tree species for materials; assisted traditional healers with seedlings and the establishment of a cultural centre; and provided courses, workshops, projects and educational trips. Pretoriuskop itself has not promoted these activities, but instead the Social Ecology department within KNP has driven them independently.

PERCEPTIONS OF WILDLIFE

When asked about the net benefits and costs of living in proximity to wildlife, the majority of local community members interviewed stated that the benefits were not sufficient to offset their costs. Interviewees also made it clear that the benefits were not sufficient to encourage conservation of wildlife or the protected area in question. The majority of the benefits that were desired by the community members were socio-economic rather than environmental. They desired employment, money, compensation for damages, more tourists and improved communication with protected area stakeholders (see Table 5).

LAND MANAGEMENT

A series of factors were assessed in relation to the environmental management activities and impacts of the tourism enterprises on their properties. The factors considered were:

- habitat management;
- wildlife management;
- roads and access; and
- control of commercial activities.

HABITAT MANAGEMENT

There was a stark difference between the habitat management activities undertaken by the public and private sector. In the case of the public sector land around Pretoriuskop, a 'natural' regime was encouraged in relation to bush clearing and fire management - although in the past both of these tools had been used extensively throughout the park in an almost trial-and-error experimental approach. Experience, and also the geographical scale of KNP, meant that a low level of active management was perceived as viable for biodiversity conservation. In contrast, the three private sector enterprises undertook more intensive habitat management (although Ngala to a lesser extent). Aerial photographs from the 1940's and 1970's were used by the three private sector enterprises to indicate the extent of encroachment on grasslands by woody vegetation. Land managers believed that historically unsustainable livestock numbers, before the predominant land use had changed to wildlife, had caused the encroachment. In all cases, regimes of fire management and bush clearing took place, in addition to mowing of some areas around Sabi Sabi. In each case maps were maintained to indicate where and when activities had taken place. Fires caused naturally (e.g. by lighting strikes) were allowed to run their course on the land around Ngala and Pretoriuskop, while human-ignited fires were fought.

TABLE 5: BENEFITS AND COSTS OF WILDLIFE (SPENCELEY, 2003A)

Welverdiend	Numbai	Timbavati	Huntingdon
Are the benefits of tourism enough to make up for problems with wildlife?			
No – 63%	No – 74%	No – 49%	No - 80%
Are the benefits sufficient to encourage conservation of wildlife or the Protected Area?			
Not asked	No - 81%	No – 55%	No - 17.1%[1]
What would be required to encourage conservation of wildlife and the Protected Area?			
Benefits shared with communities (21%) Resources/money (13%) Development projects (11%) Employment (3%)	Employment (33%) Money (32%) More tourists in the area (4%)	Compensation (9%) Meetings and discussion (9%) More protection (7%) Better opportunities (6%) Environmental education (3%)	Compensation and money (62%) Employment (3%) A committee to deal with problems (3%)

***Footnote:** 1. 62% of this sample did not answer this question, but the 'No' response was the most frequent.*

All four of the protected areas provided artificial sources of water for wildlife, by artificially pumping groundwater into pans and by constructing dams. Although this practice was motivated to encourage increases in wildlife populations within a semi-arid region, research in KNP had revealed that this strategy had led to declines in sensitive species such as tsessebe, roan, sable and Lichenstein's hartebeest, with associated increases in wildebeest, zebra, elephant and buffalo populations. Therefore, the 1997 water management plan for the park recommended decommissioning some artificial water sites, while retaining others along tourist roads for game viewing purposes. Water management within the three private enterprises, however, continued to provide artificial water *despite* land manager's appreciation of the negative ecological implications this caused for species diversity. None of the enterprises had access to information regarding groundwater aquifers that they pumped from to their artificial pans, nor did they monitor volumes pumped. In addition, none employed strategies to rotate water resources in order to encourage the movement of game between different areas (and so reduce localised impacts). The financial pressure to create good game viewing opportunities for guests appeared to be greater within the private sector enterprises than the public sector.

WILDLIFE MANAGEMENT

All four enterprises actively promoted the conservation of wildlife on their land and chose not to stock their properties with domestic livestock. The Thornybush GR had translocated the majority of wildlife onto the reserve over the previous decade, at major financial cost. All three PNRs set hunting quotas annually for various species on the reserve, but Ngala and Sabi Sabi had chosen not to utilise their quotas. The hunting quotas were set in relation to annual aerial wildlife counts and revenues generated from hunting in the Timbavati PNR were used finance maintenance on the reserve. Culling of elephant had taken place historically in KNP, but local and international public pressure had stopped the activity. Instead, live translocations of species including elephant and rhino took place to stock other protected areas and to reduce local populations. Trophy hunting at Jackalberry was effectively arranged to cull over-populated species and to generate revenue. In all four cases, limited culls of impala (a small, prolific antelope) were permitted in order to provide staff with rations.

Breeding rare wildlife species took place at Pretoriuskop for tsessebe and Lichtenstein's hartebeest, while on the Sabi Sands sable were bred, and local reintroductions of locally endangered and extinct species took place. In the case of Pretoriuskop, tourists colliding with wildlife as they drove carelessly on the park's tar roads caused some wildlife mortality. Despite KNP staff's use of speed-traps and imposing fines, wildlife deaths still occurred.

Changes in wildlife behaviour were observed across all three protected areas. In addition to the habituation of wildlife to vehicles – which facilitates game viewing – primates consistently caused problems raiding waste food from bins, damaging thatched roofs and vehicles. Even spotted hyena and honey badgers were observed accessing food in bins and fridges. Management strategies to deal with problematic primates involved both the translocation of individual animals, and in serious cases euthanasia. In the case of Pretoriuskop, behavioural change was also observed in amphibians that were observed breeding prolifically in the artificial chlorinated swimming pool rather than in natural wetlands!

ROADS AND ACCESS

All four enterprises maintained roads on their properties in order to facilitate access to different areas during the operation of game drives. The density of game viewing roads varied from ~0.5 km per km^2 around Pretoriuskop to ~6.9 km per km^2 around Sabi Sabi. The extent to which the roads were managed varied in relation to the level of financing and control that enterprises had over the management. In the case of Ngala, considerable levels of sheet and gully erosion had allegedly been caused by limited and poorly timed road maintenance. Due to contractual omissions, lease fees paid by Ngala to the landowner for use of the reserve were not used to finance land management activities undertaken by SANParks. These contractual oversights between the landowner and KNP not only affected the ecological quality of the land, but also had implications for the quality of experience for guests and cost of maintaining vehicles.

Historically poorly placed roads on Jackalberry and Sabi Sabi's land had led to the need for extensive civil engineering to stabilise and rehabilitate eroded areas. Some roads were closed, re-routed and rehabilitated in cases where they had crossed seeplines or sodic areas. In all four cases, gravel and sand were taken from quarries and rivers within the protected areas to provide substrate for road maintenance.

CONTROL OF COMMERCIAL ACTIVITIES

Predominantly, the commercial activities operated at the enterprises for tourists were non-consumptive photographic game drives, with optional bush walks and bush barbeques. In the case of Pretoriuskop, self-drive visitors mostly undertook the tours themselves, although escorted safari drives with trained guides were available at extra cost. The three private sector enterprises operated guided safari tours and visitors were not permitted to take unescorted tours of the reserves. The types of activities undertaken within these areas of high biodiversity, and the potential danger of working with African wildlife, had led to the development of various codes, rules and guidelines for staff and tourists at the enterprises.

The guides at Ngala and Sabi Sabi undertook intensive in-house training with probationary periods before they were permitted to escort tourists on game drives or walks. During these periods they learned about safety for both people and wildlife at sightings, and how to minimise their impacts on the environment. Jackalberry's guides had to at least hold the minimum nationally recognised qualification before they could undertake game drives. At all three private enterprises, guides received codes of conduct and rules that they had to adhere to. Off-road driving was permitted in these cases for the purpose of viewing specific charismatic species of wildlife (e.g. lion and leopard) h within certain environmental parameters. For example, driving off-road in wet conditions or over sensitive soils was not permitted, and serious penalties were enforced upon those who did not adhere to the rules. At Pretoriuskop, no off-road driving was permitted by self-drive tourists or staff, and both were required to abide by park rules that were publicly displayed. Guides monitored one another's behaviour in the PNRs, while volunteers and park staff reported any infringements of park rules around Pretoriuskop. At Pretoriuskop, guides were trained to the highest national standard before they were permitted to undertake bush walks, although students training for national conservation diplomas could escort guests on less dangerous game drives. Visual environmental interpretation material was available for tourists at Pretoriuskop and Sabi Sabi, with information regarding local wildlife, management and research activities.

ENVIRONMENTAL MANAGEMENT WITHIN THE ENTERPRISE

Although Ngala and Sabi Sabi were in the process of developing internal Environmental Management Systems, neither Pretoriuskop nor Jackalberry had addressed the environmental performance of their hospitality establishment in a systematic way. The following activities were assessed at the four enterprises:

- energy use;
- water consumption;
- waste disposal (wet and solid); and
- purchasing activities.

ENERGY USE

Three of the enterprises used electricity from the national grid to supply the majority of their energy needs. The electricity used was generated at coal-burning power stations, and therefore its use had associated environmental costs. The amount of electricity used and the associated pollutants created were calculated for each enterprise and related to the number of commercial bed/ nights (see Table 5). This indicated that Pretoriuskop and Sabi Sabi consumed roughly the same amounts of electricity in relation to the number of commercial bed/nights, while Jackalberry had more than five times their comparative consumption. In addition to electricity, the enterprises also used diesel and petrol for vehicles, paraffin for lighting, gas and charcoal for cooking, and wood for ambient fires. Pretoriuskop, Jackalberry and Sabi Sabi used solar power to electrify their fences. At Ngala, solar power had been discarded as an option for major power supply, due to the amount of power required to operate the camp. Ngala used a diesel generator for power, but at the time of assessment

TABLE 6: ENTERPRISE RESOURCE CONSUMPTION ESTIMATES (SPENCELEY, 2003A)

Ngala	Pretoriuskop	Jackalberry	Sabi Sabi
Energy consumption estimates			
Diesel generator used 255 - 292 kilo litres diesel p/a or ~16-19 litres per bed/night	2 118 MWh grid ~electricity p/a or 17 kWh per bed/night Associated annual pollutant creation of ~1800 tonnes CO_2, 17 tonnes SO_2, and 17.5 tonnes NO_x.	~370 MWh grid electricity p/a or 101 kWh per bed/night Associated annual pollutant creation of ~330 tonnes CO_2, 3 tonnes SO_2, and 1.4 tonnes NO_x	~561 MWh grid electricity p/a or 16.7 kWh per bed/night Associated annual pollutant creation of ~477 tonnes CO_2, 4.4 tonnes SO_2, and 2 tonnes NO_x.
Water consumption estimates			
~ 31 280 m^3 p/a or 2.0 m^3 per bed/night Of 83.3 million m^3 falling on the reserve p/a this equated to ~0.04% of available water	~ 44 640 m^3 p/a or 0.4 m^3 per bed/night Of 447.6 million m^3 falling on region p/a, this equated to 0.008% of available water	~ 4 380 m^3 used p/a or 1.2 m^3 per bed/night Of 28.4 million m^3 falling on reserve p/a, this equated to ~0.02% of available water	~ 54 000 m^3 p/a or 1.6 m^3 per bed/night Of 20.8 million m^3 falling on reserve p/a, this equated to ~0.03% of available water

proposals had been made to connect the camp to the national electricity grid instead.

There was limited use of natural light in the architecture at the enterprises. All four establishments used a mixture of incandescent light bulbs ranging from 60 W to 150 W, and one of the lodges at Sabi Sabi was supplied with low energy bulbs throughout. Office areas were generally lit by lower-wattage fluorescent strip lighting, and there were isolated occurrences of low-energy bulbs at Ngala, Pretoriuskop and Jackalberry. Two enterprises noted that although they had attempted to use low-energy bulbs, their fluctuating power supplies caused the expensive bulbs to fail relatively quickly. One of the enterprises left the lights in guest accommodation on constantly for aesthetic reasons, even when guests were not there.

The climate, and the demands of their international guests meant that all four enterprises had installed air conditioning units in the guest rooms. In some cases air conditioning was left on constantly, and some air conditioning units were poorly maintained – which needlessly increased their energetic expenditure.

Laundry took place on-site at Ngala, Pretoriuskop and Jackalberry, while Sabi Sabi outsourced this service to a local sub-contractor. The private sector enterprises changed linen daily and would wash towels between once and four times a day. Although the management of one enterprise stipulated that its policy was to change linen every two days, when dirty, or when new guests arrived - housekeeping staff actually changed all linen daily regardless. Active use of energetically expensive washing machines, tumble dryers and isolated use of washing lines for 'free' drying were observed during the assessments. Pretoriuskop made communal laundry equipment available to self-drive tourists, and enterprise staff changed accommodation linen every-other day, or when new guests arrived. Hot water geysers at the enterprises were set at between 50°C and 60°C throughout the enterprises, and in general each guest room had its own geyser. Energy was used to pump water from groundwater through boreholes at Ngala and Sabi Sabi, and was extracted from rivers in the cases of Pretoriuskop and Sabi Sabi. Pretoriuskop needed to pump its water from a river over 37 km away, which required a great deal of energy.

Pretoriuskop sold petrol, diesel, wood and charcoal to self-drive tourists. Wood for ambient fires was predominately sourced from bush clearing operations, flood damage and alien species. However, Ngala collected indigenous dead wood from the reserve on a regular basis to stock fires. All four enterprises used rechargeable batteries in radios used by staff.

None of the enterprises evaluated the number of 'air miles' used by guests to reach the tourist enterprise, nor did they try to offset the associated carbon-dioxide emissions through carbon-neutral schemes.

WATER CONSUMPTION

None of the enterprises practiced any form of water conservation, either through limiting use, setting guidelines or targets to reduce consumption, or practicing environmental awareness for staff and guests. This was especially interesting given the high water-pumping costs incurred by Pretoriuskop to obtain water from a river 37 km away.

In general, the enterprises had installed 9 litre toilet cisterns, which were sometimes set to lower flush volumes (e.g. 6 litres in the case of Jackalberry), but no dual-flush systems were observed. None of the faucets or showerheads at the enterprises had low-flow water saving attachments. Two of the enterprises noted that the high levels of calcium carbonate in the water led to serious 'furring' of pipes and water saving devices, and that they were therefore impractical to use. All rooms at Ngala and Sabi Sabi had baths in guest rooms, while they were fitted in only isolated suites at Pretoriuskop and Jackalberry.

Communal swimming pools were installed at all four enterprises, and one of the lodges at Sabi Sabi provided each guest room with an individual pool. All pools were chlorinated, save one saline pool at Jackalberry, and none used covers for pools to reduce evaporation when they were not in use.

The lawns and plants in landscaping schemes around the enterprises were watered regularly. The best water saving system for irrigation was found at Jackalberry, where sprinklers were used for two hours in the late afternoon (to avoid evaporation) on six cycles of fifteen minutes (to improve infiltration). Sabi Sabi only permitted lawns to be watered once a week, and all enterprises promoted the use of native, low water consumption species in their plantings.

Only Pretoriuskop formally monitored the volumes of water it pumped from its source. Although water meters were installed on some of the boreholes at one of the enterprises, not all were functioning. Meter readings had been taken for a period of time when a couple of enthusiastic staff members had promoted monitoring, but this activity had ceased once the individuals left the enterprise. The quality of water used for human consumption was tested at all of the enterprises on a monthly basis. The volumes of water use by the enterprises were estimated and equated to the amount of precipitation on the enterprise property and the number of commercial beds as benchmarks (see Table 8). The public sector enterprise had the lowest estimated consumption per bed night, while it appeared that Ngala had the highest relative level of use.

SOLID WASTE

All four enterprises operated recycling schemes and separated their waste glass, steel and tin. Considerable investment had been made in the cases of Ngala and Sabi Sabi to set up recycling centres that were wildlife-proof. Recyclables were either taken to a central recycling depot by enterprise staff (a community run depot in the case of Sabi Sabi) or were collected by external agents. Members of staff at Ngala and Sabi Sabi had jobs dedicated to the sorting of waste. The Timbavati PNR policy dictated that all solid waste should be removed from the reserve. However, the external recycling plant used by Ngala had demised for commercial reasons, which meant that there was no further incentive for the enterprise to sort its waste. The remoteness of Ngala meant that the transport costs to remove waste from the reserve were not covered by revenue generated by the recyclables sold. Local farmers in Welverdiend and Huntingdon collected food waste from Ngala and Sabi Sabi respectively, for use as fodder for their pigs. Waste oil was stored and collected for recycling at Ngala, Pretoriuskop and Sabi Sabi.

Each of the enterprises had an incinerator to dispose of additional card and plastic waste, but none of these had air filters attached, nor was any air-quality monitoring implemented. Only the incinerator at Pretoriuskop was clay brick lined, which heated waste up to 800°C in order to completely combust waste. The other three enterprises either simply dried and burned non-recyclable waste in an open pit, or adapted old oil drums for use as incinerators, without insulation or temperature monitoring. In all four cases, ash leftover from incineration was landfilled. Landfill pits within the protected areas were covered over with topsoil and left to re-vegetate after use.

Only Sabi Sabi had worked with its suppliers in order to reduce the amount of packaging that came into the reserve with the materials it purchased – and in some cases they returned packaging to suppliers. The other enterprises tended to buy in bulk where possible and therefore reduce the packaging and transportation required to obtain goods. Purchasing concentrated detergents and using re-fillable containers were also strategies employed at Ngala and Sabi Sabi.

Only Pretoriuskop quantified the volumes of waste produced and recycled. Here it was estimated that ~120,450 kg (or ~1314 m^3) waste was collected annually and 24% of this was glass that could be recycled, and 14% was recyclable steel or tin. This waste equated to just under 1 kg of waste per bed/night. However, no targets were set to reduce the volumes of waste created.

WET WASTE

Ngala, Pretoriuskop and Sabi Sabi had constructed wetland wastewater purification systems in different designs in order to treat grey- and black-water waste. The reed beds at Pretoriuskop were the most heavily engineered, with a series of six evaporation ponds and two reed beds constructed. The septic tanks and wetlands at Sabi Sabi had been carefully designed to treat wastewater to such an extent that it could effectively be recycled back to the environment. Monthly water quality testing at Pretoriuskop and Sabi Sabi permitted the release of treated water back into natural wetlands. The artificial wetland at Ngala was observed in a poor state of repair during the assessment, and electric fencing that had been used to keep game out had been damaged. Sabi Sabi purchased biodegradable detergents and soaps (including guest soaps and shampoos) in order that harsh chemicals would not adversely impact on the natural purification process. Artificial wetlands are preferable to chemical treatment plants because they require little maintenance, no chemical inputs and no electricity to operate. Jackalberry had the weakest sewage treatment system with a series of French drains (or soak-aways), which due to the geology of the area were not draining effectively.

PURCHASING

The enterprises used their purchasing power to buy some local and environmentally friendly products. Biodegradable soaps and detergents were preferentially purchased at Ngala, Pretoriuskop and Sabi Sabi, while Pretoriuskop ensured that KNP's nature conservation department approved all chemical products. Enterprises preferentially purchased items from local suppliers (although the quality, consistency and availability was often problematic), and also from historically disadvantaged people in the case of Pretoriuskop. Ngala also purchased paper that had either been produced from sustainable forests or was recycled. This enterprise also used chemicals that did not bio-accumulate in its pest control programmes (e.g. for pest rodents and mosquitoes).

DISCUSSION

The environmental results described for the four enterprises can be used to evaluate their environmental sustainability, and also to extrapolate lessons regarding best practice in nature-based tourism operations.

ENVIRONMENTAL CONTEXT

Comparisons made between the four enterprises made it clear that the existence and application of strategic environmental and development management plans promoted sustainable use. Overarching policies and plans reduced the fragmentation of approaches in relation to habitat management, while allowing coherent management of migratory wildlife to be applied. Cooperation on wildlife and habitat management between landowners promoted sustainable and strategic environmental management, while penalties applied by neighbours for infringements within a democratic process provided control and conflict resolution mechanisms. Cooperation was motivated by enlightened self-interest in the private sector cases, where they could benefit from larger populations of wildlife ranging over larger geographical areas if they remained unfenced from their neighbours.

Limited natural resources were provided to local people from the enterprises, and therefore it was perhaps inevitable in the light of conflict with wildlife that subsistence poaching occurred, that the majority of community members did not think that the protected areas or tourism compensated them for their costs. Although environmental education programmes were beneficial to local people, it was clear that they required more economic benefits such as jobs, money and compensation, coupled with better communication between themselves and the protected area. Given the need for protected areas to engage with local communities, and to provide benefits that encourage conservation, it was clear that the well-motivated efforts of the four enterprises had not been sufficient to induce favourable perceptions of wildlife. Improving this perception and providing tangible benefits to the rural poor *must* be achieved if this form of land use is to be sustainable, and if levels of poaching are to be reduced.

LAND MANAGEMENT

The case studies highlighted that there was little formal planning of the environmental management. A key factor in the sustainable environmental management of habitats was the ability to control and finance activities. Habitat management practices, in relation to the use of fire, bush clearing, mowing or *laissez-faire* approach, were inconsistent between the enterprises. Since the private sector enterprises did not monitor the ecological impacts of their activities in the long-term it was not possible to say whether their activities promoted or detracted from environmental sustainability. The use of aerial photographs to guide management activities would only be 'best-practice' if they were used in the context of the pressures that were prevalent at the time when they were taken, and in relation to changed circumstances. Extended research in KNP and the geographical extent of the park promoted a more hands-off management system. All of the enterprises provided artificial water for wildlife. According to research in KNP, this had been to the detriment of some herbivores and had benefited others, and so had skewed natural wildlife populations and species dynamics. Although KNP's policy towards artificial water had changed over time, all of the enterprises maintained too much water on their land - with no strategic or practical mechanisms to deal with the problem. The trade-off between conserving biodiversity and providing game viewing opportunities for tourists was clear.

Consumptive utilisation of wildlife appeared to be sustainable at the four enterprises, with hunting quotas for meat and trophies set in relation to population counts from aerial censuses, and controlled through the use of penalties when infringements were identified. Political pressure, public perceptions and consumer demand influenced individual enterprise's hunting and culling activities. Although changes in wildlife behaviour were observed, it is difficult to say from the data collected whether this negatively impacted upon the survivorship of the species concerned, save in obvious cases where problem animals were euthanased.

Although the relative densities of roads were evaluated around the enterprises, there was no information available to determine at what level road coverage became unsustainable - given the absence of baseline information, or research addressing the impacts of roads and small-scale fragmentation on sensitive flora and fauna. Appropriate planning of the construction and placement of roads (in addition to their regular maintenance) was required to minimise erosion. Maintaining good quality roads improved the game drive experience for tourists, while the density of roads constituted a trade-off between accessing areas of the reserve while fragmenting habitats and removing vegetation to construct them.

In the cases where guides escorted tourists on photographic safari tours, it was clear that training coupled with rules, guidelines and monitoring promoted sensitive and sustainable tourism activities. However, the lack of systematic long-term ecological monitoring of the impacts of tourism activities (e.g. off-road driving) left the practice open to debate regarding its sustainability. Where self-drive tourists undertook their own tours policing and control of adherence to rules was also necessary – although not infallible. In all cases, the key motivations behind training, rules and enforcement were improving the quality of experience for guests; minimising adverse impacts on the environment; and reducing risks of working in dangerous environments.

ENVIRONMENTAL MANAGEMENT WITHIN THE ENTERPRISE

Little action was taken by any of the enterprises to reduce their energetic expenditure or their water consumption, despite the financial and pollutant savings that would have been made. Energy was ultimately sourced from non-renewable fossil fuels, while use of renewable resources was un-monitored (as in the case of wood) or limited (in the case of solar power). Active promotion of low-energy light bulbs; the use of natural lighting and cooling systems; and water-saving technology would have reduced the financial and environmental costs of energy and water use at the enterprises. The use of more appropriate and sensitive laundry programmes, and reducing the temperature on water geysers to between 46°C and 49°C would have also saved energy. Programmes to evaluate and offset the production of carbon dioxide associated with guest flights and safari drives would also have promoted the sustainability of the activities on a global scale.

All enterprises operated recycling systems, within the constraints of local commercial capacity to deal with waste glass and steel. The donation of waste food to local pig farmers showed innovative re-use of waste, with knock-on socio-economic benefits for poor people. However, the incineration and landfill activities for other waste materials were inevitably polluting, and not implemented in line best practice standards. Only one enterprise measured the volumes of waste produced, while only one other was working with suppliers to reduce the levels of packaging brought into the reserve.

However, efforts made to remediate grey- and black-waste water were more encouraging in cases where enterprises had established artificial wetlands and were monitoring the quality of remediated water. Effectively these enterprises were sustainably recycling their wastewater, with minimal energy inputs, to an extent that water could be re-integrated into local habitats.

CONCLUSIONS

This paper has described a variety of different responsible strategies that have been used by four nature-based tourism enterprises in South Africa to promote long-term environmental sustainability. The paper has highlighted areas regarding the context, land and enterprise management that impact on the natural environment at local and global levels, and which have been addressed by enterprises with varying degrees of success.

Enterprises clearly require information and support in driving and maintaining environmental best practices – information that empowers them with sufficient information to make decisions, such as the range of technologies and techniques available, and also the relative financial and environmental costs and benefits of different options. Researchers should consider the application of locally appropriate grey literature such as the *Responsible Tourism Manual* in South Africa (Spenceley *et al.* 2002), and international sources of information such as the Conservation International/Tour Operators Initiative *Practical Guide to Good Practice* (Sweeting & Sweeting, 2003) to promote best environmental practice in destinations.

With little comparable baseline data from other nature-based tourism enterprises with which to compare the relative environmental costs and benefits, it has not been possible to evaluate how the performance these establishments compares with other similar businesses. Potentially, the widespread uptake and implementation of the Responsible Tourism Guidelines for South Africa (DEAT, 2002) and the SUNTAT (Spenceley, 2003a) could address this shortfall, and begin to address the cumulative impact of environmentally sensitive best practices - rather than the currently observed isolated and fragmented efforts. This might also allow enterprises to exploit the increasing market demand for environmentally sustainable holidays by transparently reporting on their efforts to reduce their environmental impacts.

Finally, it is critical to indicate the limitations of this report in light of the holistic nature of sustainable development. As mentioned earlier, sustainability is not only dependent upon the appropriate application 'environmentally friendly' activities, but it must also address economic, social and cultural sustainability. In the case of the four enterprises documented, these aspects were assessed and are reported elsewhere (Spenceley, 2003a). The sustainability of nature-based tourism must also be aligned to the strategic political and planning frameworks of particular countries or localities to promote sustainable development.

ACKNOWLEDGEMENTS

Many thanks to the managers and staff of Ngala, Pretoriuskop, Jackalberry Lodge and Sabi Sabi, members of the rural communities who agreed to participate, and especially Louis Hlabane and Johannes Moreko. Thanks also to Dr Harold Goodwin at the University of Greenwich in the UK, to Angela Scott at the Institute of Natural Resources, and Dr Trevor Hill at the University of KwaZulu-Natal in South Africa. The Leverhulme Trust generously funded this research, which was in part used to towards a doctorate from the University of Greenwich. This chapter is adapted from a longer paper that appeared in the Journal of Sustainable Tourism in 2005.

REFERENCES

Adams, W. M. (1990) *Green development: Environment and sustainability in the Third World*. 2nd Edition. Routledge: London and New York.

Anderson, S. H. (1995) Recreational disturbance and wildlife populations. In R. L. Knight and K. J. Gutzwiller. (eds) *Wildlife and recreationists: coexistence through management and research*. (pp. 157-168). Island Press: Washington D.C.

Anon (2002) British holiday-makers most likely to favour hotels with responsible environmental policies. *Caterer & Hotelkeeper* 1 August 2002, 6.

Archer, B. and Cooper, C. (1994) The positive and negative impacts of tourism. In W. Theobald, (ed) *Global Tourism: The next decade*. (pp. 73-91). Butterworth Heinneman: Oxford.

Ashley, C., Roe, D., and Goodwin, H. (2001) *Pro-poor tourism strategies: Making tourism work for the poor: A review of experience*, Pro-poor tourism report No. 1, April 2001, ODI/IIED/CRT. Online document: http://www.propoortourism.org.uk.

Ashworth, G., and Goodall, B. (1990) *Marketing tourism places*. London: Routledge.

Bagri, A., McNeely, J., and Vorhies, F. (1998) *Biodiversity and Impact assessment*, Paper presented at IUCN workshop on Biodiversity and Impact Assessment. Christchurch, New Zealand, 21-22 April 1998.

Beanlands, G. E. and Duinker, P. N. (1984) An ecological framework for environmental impact assessment. *Journal of Environmental Management* 18, 267-277.

Bowles, A. E. (1995) Responses of wildlife to noise. In R. L. Knight and K. J. Gutzwiller (eds) *Wildlife and recreationists: coexistence through management and research*. (pp. 109-156). Island Press: Washington, D. C.

Bramwell, B. and Lane, B. (1993) Interpretation and sustainable tourism: the potential and the pitfalls. *Journal of Sustainable Tourism* 1 (2), 71-80.

Briassoulis, H. (1991) Methodological issues: Tourism input-Output Analysis, *Annals of Tourism Research* 18, 485-495.

Buckley, R. (1991) How accurate are environmental impact predictions? *Ambio* 20 (3-4), 161-162.

Burger, J. (1981) The effect of human activity on birds at a coastal bay. *Biological Conservation* 21, 231-241.

Burger, J. and Gochfeld, M. and Niles, L. J. (1995) Ecotourism and birds in coastal New Jersey: contrasting responses of birds, tourists, and manager. *Environmental Conservation* 22 (1), 56-65.

Burton, F. (1998) Tourism development on the rampage – the Cayman Islands. *ECOS* 19 (1), 15-19.

Butler, R. W. (1996) The concept of carrying capacity for tourism destinations: Dead or merely buried? *Progress in Tourism and Hospitality Research* 2, 283-293.

Butler, R. (1998) Sustainable tourism – looking backwards in order to progress? In Hall, C. M. and Lew, A. A. (eds) *Sustainable tourism: A Geographical perspective*. Longman.

Ceballos-Lascuráin, H. (1996) *Tourism, ecotourism and protected areas: The state of nature-based tourism around the world and guidelines for its development*. IUCN, Gland, Switzerland, and Cambridge UK.

Clarke, J. (1997) A framework of approaches to sustainable tourism, *Journal of Sustainable Tourism* 5 (3), 224-233.

Cole, D. N. and Landres, P. B. (1995) Indirect effects of recreationists on wildlife, IN R. L. Knight and K. J. Gutzwiller (eds) *Wildlife and recreationists: coexistence through management and research*. (pp. 183-202). Island Press: Washington, D. C.

Commission on Sustainable Development (CSD) (1999) *Report on the seventh session*. 1 May and 27 July 1998, and 19-30 April 1999, Economic and Social Council Official Records, 199, Supplement No. 9, United Nations, New York, 1999, Copyright © United Nations Division for Sustainable Development 02/09/1999.

Cott, H. B. (1969) Tourists and crocodiles in Uganda. *Oryx* 10, 153-60.

Decision Surveys International (DSI) (1999a) *A Survey of South Africa's Foreign Visitor Market*. August 1999. SATOUR.

Decision Surveys International (DSI) (1999b) *A Survey of South Africa's Foreign Visitor Market*. January 1999. SATOUR.

Department of Environmental Affairs and Tourism (DEAT) (1996) *The development and promotion of tourism in South Africa*, White Paper, Government of South Africa, Department of Environmental Affairs and Tourism.

Department of Environmental Affairs and Tourism (DEAT) (1997) *White Paper on the Conservation and Sustainable use of South Africa's Biological Diversity*. Department of Environmental Affairs and Tourism, Government Gazette, Vol 385, No. 18163, July 28th 1997. Government Printer, Pretoria. Online document: http://www.environment.gov.za/white_paper/diversity.htm

Department of Environmental Affairs and Tourism (DEAT) (1999) *The National State of the Environment Report*, Department of Environmental Affairs and Tourism. Online document: http://www.ngo.grida.no/soesa/nsoer, Updated February 2000.

Department of Environmental Affairs and Tourism (DEAT) (2000) *South Africa National Report to the Fourth Conference of the Parties, Convention on Biological Diversity.* Department of Environmental Affairs and Tourism. Online document: http://www.environment.gov.za/chm-final/cbdrep2.htm.

Department of Environmental Affairs and Tourism (DEAT) (2002) *Responsible Tourism Guidelines for South Africa*. DEAT, May 2002.

Duffey, E. (1975) The effects of human trampling on the fauna of grassland litter, *Biological Conservation* 7, 255-74.

Edington, J. M. and Edington, M.A. (1986). *Ecology, recreation and tourism*. England: Cambridge University Press.

Elkington, J. (1997) *Cannibals with Forks*: The Triple Bottom Line of 21st Century Business, Oxford: Capstone Publishing Ltd.

Evans, N. G. and Stabler, M. J. (1995) A Future for the package tour operator in the 21st century? *Tourism Economics* 1 (3), 245-263.

Food and Agriculture Organisation (FAO) (1972) The state of marine pollution in the Mediterranean and legislative controls. *Studies and Reviews Report*. No. 51.

Gabrielsen, G. W. and Smith, E. N. (1995). Physiological responses of wildlife to disturbance. In Knight, R. L. and Gutzwiller, K. J. (eds) *Wildlife and recreationists: coexistence through management and research*. (pp. 95-108). USA: Island Press.

Goodwin, H. and Francis, J. (2003) Ethical and responsible tourism: Consumer trends in the UK. *Journal of Vacation Marketing* 9 (3), 271–284.

Gutzwiller, K. J. (1995) Recreational disturbance and wildlife communities. In Knight, R. L. and Gutzwiller, K. J. (eds) *Wildlife and recreationists: coexistence through management and research*. (pp. 51-69). USA: Island Press.

Harris, R. and Leiper, N. (1995) *Sustainable tourism: An Australian perspective*. Butterworth Heinneman, Australia.

Hay, I. (ed) (2000) *Qualitative research methods in Human Geography*. Oxford University Press.

Hulbert, I. A. R. (1990). The response of ruddy shelduck (Tadorna ferruginea) to tourist activity in the Royal Chitwan National Park of Nepal. *Biological Conservation* 52, 113-123.

Klein, M. L., Humphrey, S. R., and Percival, H. F. (1995) Effects of ecotourism on distribution of waterbirds in a wildlife refuge. *Conservation Biology* 9 (6), 1454-1465.

Knight, R. L., and Gutzwiller, K. J. (eds) (1995) *Wildlife and recreation: Coexistence through management and research*.Washington, DC: Island Press.

Knight, R. L. and Cole, D. N. (1995). Wildlife responses to recreationists. In Knight, R. L. and Gutzwiller, K. J. (eds) *Wildlife and recreationists: coexistence through management and research*. (pp. 51-69) USA: Island Press.

Lui, J. C., Sheldon, P. J. and Var, T. (1987) Resident perception of the environmental impacts of tourism. *Annals of Tourism Research* 14,17-37.

Martin, A., and Stubbs, R. (Undated) Future development in tourism, MORI.

Mathieson, A., and Wall, G. (1982) *Tourism: economic, physical and social impacts*. New York, USA: Longman.

May, T. (1993) *Sharing the land: Wildlife, people and development in Africa*. IUCN Regional Office for Southern Africa, Harare.

McCoy, M. (1995) Asian Rhinos Rhinoceros unicornis on the run? Impact of tourist visits on one population. *Biological Conservation* 73, 23-26.

Miller, G. (2001) Corporate responsibility in the UK tourism industry. *Tourism Management* 22, 589-598.

Mintel (2001) *Ethical Tourism*. © International Group Limited, October 2001.

Mowforth, M., and Munt, I. (1998) *Tourism and Sustainability. New Tourism in the Third World*. London: Routledge.

Müller, H. R. and Landes, A. (2000) *Tourismus und Umweltverhalten. Befragung zum Reiseverhalten*. Forschungsinstitut für Freizeit und Tourismus (FIF), Hans Imholz-Stiftung, Switzerland Travel Writers & Tourism Journalists Club Zürich (STW), Bern März 2000.

Myrdal, G. (1973). The beam in our eyes. In Warwick, D., and Osherson, S. (eds) *Comparative research methods*. (pp. 89-99). Englewood Cliffs, NJ: Prentice-Hall.

Noss, R. F., Quigley, H. B., Hornocker, M. G., Merrill, T., Paquet, P. C. (1996) Conservation biology and carnivore conservation in the Rocky-mountains. *Conservation Biology* 10 (4), 949-963.

Perdue, R. R., Long, P. T. and Allen, L. (1990) Resident support for tourism development. *Annals of Tourism Research* 17, 586-599.

Peterson, E. B., Chan, Y. H., Peterson, N. M., Constable, G. A., Caton, R. B., Davis, C. S., Wallace, R. R., and Yarranton, G. A. (1987) *Cumulative effects assessment in Canada: An agenda for action and research*. Canadian Environmental Assessment Research Council, Hull, Quebec.

Poultney, C. and Spenceley, A. (2001) *Practical strategies for pro-poor tourism, Wilderness Safaris South Africa: Rocktail Bay and Ndumu Lodge*, PPT Working paper No. 1, CRT/IIED/ ODI. Online document: http://www.propoortourism.org.uk

Robson, C. (1993) *Real world research*. Blackwells: Oxford.

Roe, D., Leader-Williams, N., and Dalal-Clayton, B. (1997) Take only photographs, Leave only footprints. *IIED Wildlife and Development Series* No. 10, October 1997.

Rogers, C. (1981) Caribbean – coral reefs under threat. *New Scientist* 5 November, 382-7.

Sindiyo, D. and Pertet, F. (1984) Tourism and its impact on wildlife conservation in Kenya. *UNEP Industry and the Environment* January-March,14-19.

Speight, M. C. D. (1973) Outdoor recreation and its ecological effects: a bibliography and review. *Discussion papers in Conservation* No. 4, University College: London.

Spenceley, A. (1997) *Strategic environmental assessment of tourism at Hwange National Park, Zimbabwe*. MSc thesis, Imperial College Centre for Environmental Technology: University of London.

Spenceley, A. (2000) Sustainable Nature-based Tourism in Transfrontier Conservation Areas: A Delphi Consultation Study. *Institute of Natural Resources Working Paper WP134*: South Africa.

Spenceley, A. (2001) *Integrating Biodiversity into the Tourism Sector: Case Study of South Africa*. United Nations Environment Programme – Biodiversity Planning Support Programme (UNEP-BPSP).

Spenceley, A. (2003a) *Managing sustainable nature-based tourism in Southern Africa: A practical assessment tool*. Doctoral thesis. University of Greenwich, UK.

Spenceley, A. (2003b) Tourism, Local Livelihoods and the Private Sector in South Africa: Case studies on the growing role of the private sector in natural resources management. *Sustainable Livelihoods in South Africa Research Paper 8*. Institute of Development Studies: Brighton UK. February 2003.

Spenceley, A., Goodwin, H., and Maynard, W. (In press) The development of responsible tourism guidelines for South Africa, In Diamantis, D. and Geldenhuys, S. (eds) *Ecotourism: Management and Assessment*, Continuum International.

Spenceley, A., Relly, P., Keyser, H., Warmeant, P., McKenzie, M., Mataboge, A., Norton, P., Mahlangu, S., and Seif, J. (2002) *Responsible Tourism Manual for South Africa*. Department for Environmental Affairs and Tourism, July 2002.

Stankey, G. H., McCool, S. F, and Stokes, G. L. (1984) Limits of acceptable change: a new framework for managing the Bob Marshall Wilderness complex. *Western Wildlands* 103 (3), 33-37.

Stueve, A. M., Cook, S. D. and Drew, D. (2002) *The Geotourism Study: Excerpts from the Phase 1 Executive Summary*. National Geographic Traveller/Travel Industry Association of America. Online document: http://www.tia.org/survey.pdf.

Sun, D. and Liddle, M. J. (1993) A survey of trampling effects on vegetation and soil in eight tropical and subtropical sites. *Environmental Management* 17 (4), 497-510.

Sun, D. and Walsh, D. (1998) Review of studies on environmental impacts of recreation and tourism in Australia. *Journal of Environmental Management* 53, 323-338.

Sweeting, J. E. N. and Sweeting, A. R. (2003) *A practical guide to good practice: Managing Environmental and Social issues in the accommodation sector*. The Centre for Environmental Leadership in Business. Tour Operators Initiative for Sustainable Tourism Development.

Tearfund (2001) *Guide to Tourism: Don't forget your ethics!* 6 Aug 2001. Online document: http://www.tearfund.org/homepage/index.asp.

Tearfund (2002) *Worlds Apart: A call to responsible global tourism.* January 2002. Online document: http://www.tearfund.org/acting/tourism.pdf.

Therivel, R., Wilson, E., Thompson, S., Heaney, D., and Pritchard, D. (1992) *Strategic Environmental Assessment*. London: Earthscan.

Tosun, C. (2001) Challenges of sustainable tourism development in the developing world: The case of Turkey. *Tourism Management* 22, 289-303.

United Nations/DESA (2002) *Key outcomes of the Summit, Johannesburg Summit 2002*, World Summit on Sustainable Development, Johannesburg South Africa, 26 August – 4 September, United Nations.

Van der Duim, R., and Caalders, J. (2002) Biodiversity and Tourism: Impacts and Interventions. *Annals of Tourism Research* 29 (3), 743–761.

Van der Zande, A. N., TerKeurs, w. J., and van der Weijden, W. J. (1980) The impact of roads on the densities of four bird species in an open field habitat – evidence of a long-distance effect. *Biological Conservation* 18, 299-321.

Wang, C. Y. and Miko, P. S. (1997) Environmental impacts of tourism on US national parks. *Journal of travel research* Spring 31-36.

Whittaker, D. and Knight, R. L. (1998) Understanding wildlife responses to humans, *Wildlife Society Bulletin* 26 (2), 312-317.

Wilkinson, D. (2000) *The researcher's toolkit: the complete guide to practitioner research*. Routledge Falmer.

World Commission on Environment and Development (WCED) (1987) *Our Common Future*. Oxford University Press, Oxford.

World Travel and Tourism Environment Research Centre (WTTERC) (1993) *World travel and tourism environment review: 1993*. World Travel and Tourism Environment Research Centre, Oxford.

7

OPPORTUNITIES AND PITFALLS IN ECOTOURISM DEVELOPMENT

IAN ROTHERHAM

ABSTRACT

Ecotourism is a rapidly growing sector of the tourism industry but reality and vision differ. Much activity is wildlife- or nature-based tourism, not ecotourism, but with economic impacts recognized in developed countries such as the UK and the USA, the World's emerging economies are cashing in on the benefits. Tourism providers often do not understand their industry's resource base, and conservation bodies disengage from tourism and economics. Joining tourism, local people, and land management is central to resolving this. Tourism economic benefits must feed back to environment and community.

Resolution is vital for tourism evolving within sustainable development. In the UK, land management links local distinctiveness of hospitality to tourism experience and visitor attractiveness. Sustainable rural tourism relates landscape and community character to distinctive visitor experience. Local food supply and traditional cuisine join wildlife tourism to land and species conservation, supporting local farmers and extensive farming methods. Marketing of local crafts and local products produced sustainably supports traditional, land use. There are issues of commitment to the local supply chain, and quality assurance of product and experience.

Solving these difficulties makes economic and social benefits flow, with scope to exchange ideas and best practice between stakeholders and actors in developed and emerging economies. Recognising ecotourism opportunities, we can avoid the pitfalls.

Keywords:* *ecotourism; wildlife tourism; tourism economics; community; sustainability

INTRODUCTION

Ecotourism is a fast growing component of tourism (Higgins, 1996; Herath, 2002) "*one of the fastest growing sectors of the tourism industry worldwide*" according to the World Tourism Organisation. Described as a niche market (Bell and Lyall, 2002), Preece *et al.* (1995) questioned time and resources dedicated to ecotourism, a small component of tourism. In 1996 Brandon claimed: "*... ecotourism and nature-based tourism have not lived up to expectations.......*". Ecotourism and nature-based tourism may 'green' mainstream tourism (Preece *et al.*, 1995), Stucker Rennicks (1997) suggesting nature-based tourism had come of age for 'green', cultural, and nature tourists and mainstream tourists enjoying nature-based experiences on holiday. This nature-based tourism, wildlife tourism, adventure tourism, are increasingly significant, but not all is ecotourism.

The World Tourism Organization (WTO) estimated over 595 million international travellers in 1997 spending US$425 billion. Tourist arrivals grew 4.3% a year, international tourism receipts at 6.7%. Tourism economic impact was recognised and adverse impacts of mass tourism obvious. The tourism, leisure, and recreation industries are at a crossroads. Recognised as one of the world's largest industries they face issues of sustainability and environmental compatibility, with local communities, and cultural heritage. Addressing tourism, the environment, and sustainability there are five key challenges (modified from McCool (1995) :

(1) Improved understanding of tourist values, motivations, and behaviours related to 'natural' environments;

(2) Enhance community wellbeing through leisure and tourism activities;

(3) Identify key social and environmental impacts of leisure and tourism;

(4) Establishment of management systems by the industries to address these impacts;

(5) Maximize benefits and minimise damage.

THE NATURE OF THE CHALLENGE

The leisure, tourism, and recreation industries face difficult development choices. Decisions affect the sector, its participants and providers, and the lives and economic opportunities of tourism destination communities. Such decisions may be irreversible should communities lose their distinctive character and competitive edge that attracts visitors and income. This affects the industry but the providers often move to pastures new. Tourism and leisure are potentially fickle and parasitic on their host community.

Tourism can support service and retail sectors with economic benefit to local communities (accommodation, transport, food, and retail sales), without concern for changes in the industry. This assumes stability of traveller values and preferences, and of tourism product and destination. It avoids questions about leisure and tourism products, scale, development acceptability, sustainability, quality of life, and host community needs. With rapid social change, and global social, economic, and environmental transformation, these questions are increasingly important.

Tourism worldwide has changed fundamentally due to the experiences and settings that travellers require, to government and international regulations, to globalisation and information technology revolution. These permeate the industry and policies of governments, agencies, and NGOs. Transformation of demand and values (both a cause and a consequence) leaves no choice but to respond. This must address critical questions of objectives, purpose, values, opportunities, barriers, policies, and strategies.

Decisions about tourism development are difficult, involving many stakeholders, but often few decision-makers. They ask questions of future visions for communities and how these are affected by tourism. The abilities or inabilities of host communities to absorb or influence changes are often overlooked, and decisions adversely affecting traditional natural resource utilisation, land management, or custom are controversial. They affect people who benefited from traditional practices, and cause declines in local culture, traditional crafts, and landscape quality. Distinctive, traditional culture can become a museum showcase for visitors with loss of community pride, and a decline in basic economy, skills, trades, crafts, and land use. Local people, especially the young, may leave rural areas for nearby towns. Distinctive character and culture are diluted and '*Disneyfied*', as a worst-case scenario. Change and decline often occur anyway, with global urbanisation and rural de-population. Tourism or leisure activities and associated investment, carefully planned and implemented may halt declines. In a world of rural change and globalisation, many deep-rooted cultural changes are inevitable, even if economic and de-population problems reduce.

THE BACKDROP OF LAND USE AND PLANNING

The World has human intervention of varying degrees and intensities. Even the most 'natural' landscapes witness conflicts of resources exploitation, economic development, and ecosystem or cultural integrity. Ecotourism and heritage tourism are key pieces in a sustainable development jigsaw. Political imperative is mostly short-term determined by economic necessities; so economics drives land use and strategic planning, with token gestures to quality of life and biodiversity. Conservationists and environmentalists often fail to engage with or understand economic and planning processes, or win political debates.

THE OPPORTUNITIES OF ECOTOURISM

Ecotourism development is a response to these challenges, and has grown rapidly in recent decades. The Ecotourism Society's Bibliography has information on over 400 papers, from books, journal articles, conference proceedings, and other publications. Research by the Ecotourism Society (1998) and by Fillion *et al.* (1992) highlighted the market size, with 20% to 40% of international tourists being nature-tourists, and for 20% to 40% their holiday wildlife-related. By 1994, worldwide there were 106 million to 211 million wildlife-related tourists (Ecotourism Society, 1998). They defined nature tourists as people visiting a destination to experience and enjoy nature. Wildlife-related visitors were tourists at a destination to observe wildlife. However, there are issues of definition and description, with studies not indicating the proportion of a tourist's activity that was wildlife or nature dependent. Reynolds & Braithwaite (2000) considered this in detail. A complication often ignored in pure tourism studies is the potential importance of local visitors and regional day visitors to attractions such as nature reserves or country parks (Rotherham *et al.*, 2004; 2005).

Ecotourism is nature-based speciality travel defined by the Ecotourism Society (ES) as "*responsible travel to natural areas, which conserves the environment and sustains the well-being of local people.*" This definition is widely accepted in principle, but is not a functional definition for gathering statistics. There is no globally accepted mechanism for gathering ecotourism data. Many workers consider ecotourism as a speciality segment of the larger nature-tourism market. However and here confusion arises, many researchers and practitioners use the terms inter-changeably.

Driml and Common (1995) noted tourism as an important economic activity in Australia, with parks and protected areas amongst its major tourism attractions. They estimated tourism economic value in five Australian World Heritage Areas with tourism expenditures in 1991-1992 of Australian $1,372,000,000, total management budgets of $48,700,000, and user-fee income to management agencies of $4,160,000. Overall management budgets were 3.5% of the tourist expenditure but government revenue through user fees represented only 8.5% of the government expenditures. This demonstrated the financial value of tourism in World Heritage Areas and some associated problems.

Lindberg and Enriquez (1994) described economic impacts of ecotourism in Belize, and links between protected area use, associated ecotourism income, and local attitudes to conservation. Tourism was and is a major component of the Belize economy, worth an estimated US$211,000,000 per year in sales in 1994 including US $41,000,000 in payments to local households. Local people, even those without direct economic benefits reported positive experiences from tourist contacts. Structural change in the tourism industry could increase the benefits, and support for protected areas increased over time. This reflects basic aspirations of ecotourism, with community benefits seemingly more important than household benefits, suggesting strong community cohesion.

This demonstrates positive conservation attitudes and protected area support increasing with genuine ecotourism.

THE OPPORTUNITIES - WILDLIFE SPECTACULARS

People enjoy wildlife spectacles if available relatively easily. This is generally wildlife and nature-based tourism and not specifically ecotourism. Neither is it necessarily sustainable often depending on private car transport. If relying on international travel then there are impacts of flights *etc*. Travel once at the destination may be relatively environmentally friendly, but there is still the need to get there.

The spectacle might be watching breeding seabird colonies at the RSPB Bempton Cliffs nature reserve in Yorkshire, a wildlife safari in Kenya, whale watching off Canada, or raptor watching on the Bosphorus. Activities and experience may be very organised and packaged such as seeing the winter swans fed by floodlight at Welney Wildfowl and Wetlands Trust reserve in Cambridgeshire, or very informal when thousands of birdwatchers gather to see hundreds of ospreys wintering site on the Potomac River in Washington DC.

By providing conditions for wildlife and watcher, the spectacle can be created. In recent years, this has been done to improve wildlife habitat, provide recreational experiences and visitor opportunities, and to kick-start local tourism, and boost the economy.

OPPORTUNITY TO SPEND

For an ecotourism or nature-based tourism activity to benefit local people through economic impact there must be '*opportunities to spend*'. At the RSPB's Dearne Valley Nature Reserve, this includes a shop, garden centre, café, and meeting rooms. These opportunities employ local people, become tourism attractants, and deliver core educational messages of the organisation. If supply chains for purchase and provision of goods and services are local, the benefits increase.

LOCAL FOOD AND DRINK

Destinations can link sustainable and traditional land use, and maintenance of environmental quality through the marketing and financial benefits of locally distinctive produce. This is particularly so in terms of producing and promoting local food, drink, and hospitality. It is possible to offer the visitor a distinctive hospitality experience with enhanced benefit to conservation land management (Rotherham, 2003). Managed carefully and developed effectively, this values local culture and expertise, and helps sustain local farming and cuisine. The same approach applies to local crafts and products. For a destination, this raises critical issues of balance between mass tourism short-term economic incentives and sales of mass-produced, imported 'tat', and less lucrative but more sustainable quality local goods and services markets.

ADDED VALUE - A CRITICAL DIFFERENCE

Locally distinct cultures, crafts, and cuisine, provide 'added value', help local communities, and grow local economies. Effectively marketed and supported they enhance destination attractiveness and celebrate regional character. For rural areas in the UK, these benefits can be the difference between local services such as shops being viable and closing. The wildlife and nature-based tourist can make this difference. With mass tourism, souvenir shops and bars often replace local services.

Local Fare At RSPB Dearne Valley Nature Reserve

COMMUNITY ISSUES

Local people may be vital to success or failure of ecotourism. Even the most carefully planned and executed project changes the host community, but often social and cultural changes are inevitable anyway. Even without tourism, change and rural decline may happen. Communities and culture evolve, and settlements wax and wane. Modern society struggles to accept the evolutionary not static nature of culture. We expect host communities, and destinations to remain the same despite global changes. A reaction is to visit remote areas before they change and decline as modern, contemporary culture, Disney and Macdonalds, do their worst. The role of the host community in driving change, taking responsibility to determine their own worth and their futures is critical to sustainable or ecotourism.

THE SIZE OF THE ECOTOURISM MARKET

Nature-based leisure and tourism are dynamic sectors of the tourism industry with recent growth up to 30% *per annum* (Wright, 1996; Lindberg, 1991). In 1993, a WTO estimate was that nature-based tourism generated 7% of international travel expenditure. The World Resources Institute in 1990 found tourism grew at 4% per annum, but nature related travel at between 10% and 30% (Lindberg, 1997).

Fillion *et al.* (1994) deduced the ecotourism market from general tourism statistics, qualifying ecotourism as "*travel to enjoy and appreciate nature*". From the Ecotourism Society definition, this is nature-based tourism not ecotourism. Through analysis of inbound tourist motivations to worldwide destinations Fillion found 40-60% of all international tourists were 'nature tourists' and 20-40% 'wildlife-related tourists'. Economic multipliers gave the impacts below. 'Nature tourists' were 'visiting a destination to experience and enjoy nature' and 'wildlife-related visitors' were 'observing wildlife (e.g. bird-watchers)'.

Numerous literature examples support the size of the market. In Nepal trekking tourism numbers increased by 255% from 1980 to 1991 (Wight in Gurung and De Corsey, 1994). Costa Rica became a top ecotourism destination during the 1990s with 781,000 tourism arrivals in 1996, 66% visiting a protected natural area (Instituto Costarricense de Turismo, 1996 in ETS, 1998).

In Honduras, nature-related visitors increased 15% (of 200,000 tourists) in 1995 (Dempsey, 1996). Visitors to Kenya from 1983 to 1993 grew by 45% (372,000 to 826,000) the Kenya Wildlife Service (1995) estimating 80% of Kenya's tourist market was attracted by wildlife and revenue from wildlife parks at US$11.8 million (in 1995). Tourism generated one-third of the country's foreign exchange.

	1988	**1994**
Total International Tourism Arrivals:	393 million	528.4 million
Nature Tourists	157-236 million	211-317 million
Wildlife-related Tourists	79-157 million	106-211 million
Total International Direct Economic Impact *	US$388 billion	US$416 billion
Nature Tourists	US$93-223 billion	US$166-250 billion
Wildlife-related Tourists	US$47-155 billion	US$83-166 billion

* Total International Direct Economic Impact = money spent on travel by tourists travelling abroad.

Many examples are global and involve long-distance tourism from rich developed countries to poorer emerging economies. This is not always so and nature-based or wildlife tourism and leisure are massive in the USA and the UK. These activities are increasingly important in all countries and societies, ranging from local day visits to long-distance holidays. They are often not ecotourism in the strictest definition.

NATURE-BASED LEISURE AND TOURISM

Countryside leisure day visits and tourism have huge economic impacts. Many depend on nature and landscape, a significant proportion related to nature reserves and other protected areas. In 1999, UK countryside day visits generated £9.2 billion expenditure (77% of the countryside tourism total in England), and in 2003-4 the total expenditure on leisure day visits was £71.1 billion, with countryside spend of £17 billion per year in England. In 1998, 24% of leisure trips were to the countryside, hikers and ramblers making up 15% of tourists in England.

Countryside recreational walkers spent £6.12 billion on trips, generating over £2 billion income, supporting 245,000 full-time jobs in England. Overnight stops increase local economic benefits.

Research for the National Trust found 40% of tourism-based employment depended on high quality environments. In rural areas, dependency is 60% to 70% (The National Trust, 2001). For Wales, £6 billion GDP depends directly on the environment. In Cumbria, the Trust spent £3.5 million on staff costs, £33.4 million on goods and services, supporting 2,700-4,600 full time equivalent jobs (FTE's) or 15% of the total jobs in Cumbria's visitor economy. Rayment and Dickie (2001) reviewed UK case studies on the economic benefits of nature conservation and tourism.

- Bempton Cliffs RSPB Nature Reserve, East Yorkshire: 44,093 visitors; £407,000 p.a. to the local economy;
- Blacktoft Sands RSPB Nature Reserve, East Yorkshire: 23,706 visitors; £93,000 p.a. to the local economy;
- Leighton Moss Nature Reserve in North Lancashire: 22 staff; 100,000 visitors per year.
- Abernethy (Osprey Visitor Centre in Scotland): 11 staff; £1.7 million p.a. to the local economy supporting 69 jobs in the local economy.

Total economic values are under-estimated and analysis ignores wider leisure and tourism, and the wider context of countryside recreation and sports. This is an increasingly sophisticated sector, with diverse impacts. Most conservation bodies are unaware of this, and the tourism industry overlooks them too. Activities involve specialist equipment, training, services, clothing, catering, guidebooks, magazines, and other media, with increasing economic and social impacts. Mintel (2004) estimated UK expenditure on sports clothing including for outdoor activities increased to £4,480 million in 2003, with £72 *per capita*. The Ramblers' Association (2004) found UK outdoor clothing and equipment sales rose from £25 million (1980) to over £1 billion (2000).

PROMISES AND PERILS OF TOURISM IMPACTS

Tourism as a growth industry is a development tool to halt economic and social declines, through increased employment, income potential, and diversification (Saeter, 1998; Sharpley, 2000, 2002a & 2002b; Fleischer and Felsenstein, 2000). It is described as a development 'growth pole' and accepted uncritically (Sharpley, 2000). However, it is not necessarily benign and negative impacts on communities and environment have driven demands for 'ecotourism'. It offers alternative income but as a resource-dependant industry (McKercher, 1993) makes demands and competes with established industries (Mazzanti, 2002).

Tourism can displace established activities, adversely affecting employment and skills. Service-based export industries displace commodity-based exports (Andrew, 1997; Fleischer and Felsenstien, 2000; Zhou *et al.*, 1997). Mainstream tourism may involve inappropriate development, excessive visitor numbers, resource depletion, and environmental degradation. These impacts can generate negative images of an area, leading to declines in visitor numbers and quality. If tourism becomes central to the economy, then a decline causes serious problems. Tourism, particularly long-distance 'ecotourism' can have negative environmental impacts through travel and traffic pollution. Ecotourism and related activities seek to address these negative impacts to environment and local community.

THE PROBLEMS OF DEFINITION - WHAT IS ECOTOURISM?

Much literature centres on tourism and development, but terminology generates confusion, with alternative and contradictory use of tourist, visitor, wildlife tourism, nature-based tourism, and ecotourism. Academic literature generally has tourism-related terms used with specific meanings and in particular contexts. Practitioner literature mixes tourist and visitor, and academic differentiation is lost. Definitions can be considered trivial, diversions from the real interest. However, definitions are important in data collection and interpretation. Many UK datasets are 'day visits' and 'visitors' not 'tourists'. Other statistics including regional Tourist Boards are 'tourists', specifically visitors from outside the administrative region. Information from differs significantly with key trends masked. The spatial areas assigned to impacts or activities are problematic, 'local' communities, 'local' economies, and 'local' impacts, without definition.

The literature presents definitions of what tourism and tourists are, including sustainable tourism and ecotourism (Blamey, 1997; Sharpley, 2002b; Sirakaya *et al.*, 1999). Conceptually hard to define (Holloway, 1998) terminology is often vague and without consensus of meaning ((Mathieson and Wall, 1982; Sharpley, 2002b). Various criteria are suggested including 1) 24-hour, overnight stop (Law, 2002); 2) Travel at least 80 km from home; 3) Outside 'usual environment' - a minimum distance of 160 km (WTO, 2000).

SUSTAINABLE TOURISM

Tourism developed regardless of negative impacts may be short-lived and so researchers developed sustainable tourism concepts as a continuum of sustainable development (Wight, 1997; McCool *et al.*, 2001; Eagles, 1995; Harrison, 1996; Bramwell and Lane, 1993). The Bruntland definition of sustainable development (WCED, 1987) was described as ill defined and multifaceted by Stabler and Goodall (1996), and over 300 sustainable development definitions suit different disciplines (Heinen, 1994, in Sharpley, 2000). Sustainable tourism, ecotourism, and nature-based tourism all face similar issues (Sirakaya *et al.*, 1999; Briguglio *et al.*, 1996). Political imperatives, personal opinions, experiences, and values, influence perception and definition producing different outcomes (Sharpley, 2000).

There are many definitions of sustainable tourism (Bramwell and Lane, 1993) some including economic, social, and environmental factors, others just tourism. McCool *et al.* (2001) asked what should tourism sustain? In a rural location needing long-term economic stability and predictability, tourism alone cannot be sustained or sustainable. New income generation based around visitors' service and commodity demands is a strong incentive for tourism development, becoming more sustainable with benefits shared by the local, host community.

NATURE-BASED TOURISM, WILDLIFE TOURISM, AND ECOTOURISM

Nature-based, wildlife tourism, and ecotourism are often used interchangeably (Preece *et al.*, 1995; Blamey, 1997). Other related activities are heritage tourism, alternative tourism, and adventure tourism (described as 'hard' (wilderness trekking, bush walking) and 'soft' (scenic driving, nature reserve visits) nature-based experiences (Potts and Rourke, 2000; MacLellan, 1999; Fennell and Weaver, 1997). Brandon (19960 suggested that "*there is no standard nomenclature......and much of the literature fails to differentiate between nature-based mass tourism and nature-tourism, which is small and limited*". Confusion is frequent with a lack of agreed definitions, on what ecotourism is (Herath, 2002; Blamey, 1997; Sirakaya *et al.*, 1999). Much in the literature is on ecotourism, but often the approach does not match definition. Nature-based tourism has been reported less often but this is changing. Both nature-based and ecotourism are described as occurring in natural or near-natural environments. Ecotourism emphasises community and cultural issues (Newsome *et al.,* 2002; Wight, 1997; Fennell and Weaver, 1997). MacLellan (1999) felt nature-based and ecotourism labels were misused to promote a 'green' tourism market. Ecological practice and ecotourism profit margins are seen as incompatible (Sirakaya *et al.*, 1999) with deliberate misrepresentation, or 'green-wash' of tourism activities (McLean, in Lindsey, 2003; Wight, 1997).

At the University of Brighton Conference (2002) on *Tourism and the Natural Environment,* speakers raised serious doubts about the validity and worth of ecotourism. Jefferies based on ecotourism projects in the South Pacific suggested it was hard to find examples of pure ecotourism that worked. Projects were not sustainable beyond the first few years. Jim Butcher took the issues further and expanded this theme in his paper of 2005. He argued the impact of ecotourism supporting economic development was erroneous and it could damage host communities (Butcher, 2005). He suggested the promotion of nature-based tourism to facilitate development reflected a degraded development agenda. Development always involves transformation of relationships between people and nature. Planners dismiss development as 'unsustainable', but encourage ecotourism. This ties development potential to a largely Western vision of the environmental values that places innate worth on traditional cultures of developing countries. Poor rural communities gain economic development but based on pre-existing environmental relationships. Perhaps not always, but Butcher's arguments raise important issues.

CONCLUSIONS: IMPACTS AND BENEFITS

Growing rapidly ecotourism is poorly defined, the reality often different from the vision. Much activity is actually wildlife- or nature-based tourism, not really ecotourism. With potential economic impacts increasingly recognised in developed countries such as the UK and the USA, the World's emerging economies look to cash in on the benefits. However, there are basic problems. Many tourism providers fail to understand the wildlife resource of their industry and nature conservation bodies understand little of tourism or economics. Many tourism and leisure activities have no direct economic link to conservation land management and so fail the most basic tests of sustainable development.

The ties between tourism, local community, and land management are central to problem resolution. Tourism often reaps economic rewards that do not feed back to environment or community. The case studies noted underpin these arguments and highlight possible solutions. Resolution of these issues is important for tourism evolve within the framework of sustainable development. In the UK, progress land management and local distinctiveness of hospitality product (food and cuisine) are linking to tourism experience, and visitor attraction. Initiatives promoting sustainable rural tourism relate landscape and community character to a distinctive visitor experience. Through local food supply and traditional cuisine, these projects join wildlife tourism to land and species conservation, supporting farmers and extensive farming methods. Marketing of local crafts and local products produced sustainably supports traditional, sustainable, land use. There must be opportunities to spend for financial benefits to occur. The necessary infrastructure developments may then be controversial in a sensitive environment. However, from a socio-economic perspective without some pain, there can be little gain.

If the difficulties are resolved then economic and social benefits flow. There is scope for the exchange of ideas and best practice between stakeholders and actors, in the developed and the emerging economies, with obvious and significant mutual benefits. In recognising the opportunities, we can avoid the pitfalls in ecotourism development.

ACKNOWLEDGMENTS

Colleagues are thanked for encouragement and guidance. Simon Doncaster and Colin Avison helped find many references and sources.

REFERENCES

Andrew, P. (1997) Tourism & the Economic Development of Cornwall. *Annals of Tourism Research*, 24 (3), 721.

Bell, C. & Lyall, J. (2002) *The Accelerated Sublime. Landscape, Tourism and Identity.* Praeger Publishers, Westport, Connecticut, USA.

Blamey, R. K. (1997) Ecotourism: The Search for an Operational Definition. *Journal of Sustainable Tourism*, 5 (2), 109-130.

Bramwell, B. & Lane, B. (1993) Sustainable Tourism: An Evolving Global Approach. *Journal of Sustainable Tourism*, 1 (1), 6-16.

Brandon, K. (1996) *Ecotourism and Conservation: A Review of Key Issues.* Environmentally and Socially Sustainable Development. Environment Department Papers: Biodiversity Series, Paper 033. Global Environment Division, The World Bank, Washington D.C.

Briguglio, L., Archer, B., Jafari, J. & Wall, G. (Eds.) (1996) *Introduction: Sustainable Tourism in Islands and Small States. Issues and Policies.* Pinter, London, England.

Butcher, J. (2004) The Moral Authority of Ecotourism: A Critique. *Current Issues in Tourism*, 8 (2&3), 114-124.

Department for Culture, Media and Sport (1999) *Tomorrow's Tourism. A growth industry for the new Millennium.* Department for Culture, Media and Sport (Tourism Division), London.

Driml, S. and Common, M. (1995) Economic and Financial Benefits of Tourism in Major Protected Areas. *Australian Journal of Environmental Management*, 2 (2), 19-39.

Eagles, P. F. J. (1995) *Understanding the Market for Sustainable Tourism.* In: McCool, S. F. & Watson, A. E. (1995). *Linking Tourism, the Environment and Sustainability: topical volume of compiled papers from a special session of the annual meeting of the National Recreation & Park Association.* October 12-24, 1994. Minneapolis, MN, USA.

Ecotourism Society (1998) Ecotourism statistical factsheet.

http:www.ecotourism.org/textfiles/stats.txt 08/02/1999

English Tourism Council (2002) *Definitions of Sustainable Tourism.* English Tourism Council, London, England. www.englishtourism.org.uk/default.asp?id=527 Visited 25/2/2003.

Fennell, D. A. & Weaver, D. B. (1997) Vacation Farms and Ecotourism in Saskatchewan, Canada. *Journal of Rural Studies*, 13 (4), 467-475.

Fillion, F.L.,Jacquemot, A., Du Wors, E., Reid, R., Boxhall, P., Bouchard, P., Gray, P., and Bath, A. (1994) *The Importance of Wildlife to Canadians: Econmic Significance of Wild-life Related Recreational Activities 1991*. Ottawa: Supply and Services Canada.

Fillion, F.L., Foley, J.P., & Jaquemot, A.J. (1992) *The economics of global tourism*. Paper presented at the Fourth World Congress on National Parks and protected Areas, Caracas, Venezuela, 10-21

Fleischer, A. & Felsenstien, D. (2000) Support for Rural Tourism: Does it make a Difference? *Annals of Tourism Research*, 27 (4), 1007.

Harrison, D. (1996) *Sustainability and Tourism: Reflections from a Muddy Pool.* In:

Herath, G. (2002) Research Methodologies for Planning Ecotourism and Nature Conservation. *Tourism Economics*, 8 (1), 77-101.

Higgins, B. R. (1996) The Global Structure of the Nature Tourism Industry: Ecotourists, Tour Operators, and Local Businesses. *Journal of Travel Research*, Vol. XXXV, (2), 11-18.

Holloway, J. C. (1998) *The Business of Tourism.* Fifth Edition. Addison Wesley Longman Ltd., Harlow, England.

Law, C. M. (2002) *Urban Tourism. The Visitor Economy and the Growth of Large Cities.* Second Edition. Continuum, London.

Lindberg, K. (1991) *Policies for Maximising Nature Tourism's Ecological and Economic Benefits.* World Resources Institute.

Lindberg, K. and Enriquez, J. (1994) *An Analysis of Ecotourism's Economic Contribution to Conservation and Development in Belize.* World Wildlife Fund, Washington, D.C.

Lindsay, H. E. (2003) *Ecotourism: the Promise & Perils of Environmentally-Orientated Travel.* Cambridge Scientific Abstracts. http://www.csa1.co.uk/hottopics/ecotour/oview.html Visited 13/3/2003.

MacLellan, L. R. (1999) An Examination of Wildlife Tourism as a Sustainable Form of Tourism Development in North West Scotland. *International Journal of Tourism Research*, 5, 375-387.

Mathieson, A. & Wall, G. (1982) *Tourism: Economic, Physical and Social Impacts.* Longman Scientific & Technical, Harlow, England.

Mazzanti, M. (2002) Tourism Growth and Sustainable Economic Development: A Note on Economic Issues. *Tourism Economics*, 8 (4), 457-462.

McCool, S. F. (1995) *Linking Tourism, the environment and concepts of sustainability: setting the stage*. In: McCool, S.F., Watson, A. (Eds.) (1995) *Linking Tourism, the Environment and Sustainability: topical volume of compiled papers from a special session of the annual meeting of the National Recreation & Park Association*. 1994 October 12-14; Minneapolis, MN. Gen Tch Rep INT-GTR-328. Ogden, UT: US Department of Agriculture, Forest Service, Intermountain Rescue Service.

McCool, S, F., Moisey, R. N., & Nickerson, N. P. (2001) What Should Tourism Sustain? The Disconnect with Industry Perceptions of Useful Indicators. *Journal of Travel Research*, 40, (November 2001) ????.

McKercher, B. (1993). Some Fundamental Truths about Tourism: Understanding Tourism's Social and Environmental Impacts. *Journal of Sustainable Tourism*, 1 (1), 6-16.

McKercher, B. & Robbins, B. (1998) Business Development Issues affecting Nature-based Tourism Operators in Australia. *Journal of Sustainable Tourism*, 6 (2) 173-188.

Newsome, D., Moore, S. A. & Dowling, R. K. (2002) Natural Area Tourism: Ecology, Impacts & Management. *Aspects of Tourism Series*, No. 4, Channel View Publications, Clevedon, England.

National Trust (2001) *Valuing our Environment: The economic benefit of the National Trust's work in Cumbria*. Report by SQW Ltd & System Three for the National Trust, June 2001. Located at URL: http://www.nationaltrust.org.uk/main/policy/documents/env_cu_full.pdf

Potts, T. D. & Rourke, T. A. (2000) *Nature Based Tourism Enterprises: Guidelines for Success.* Strom Thurmond Institute of Government & Public Affairs, Clemson University, South Carolina, USA.

Preece, N., van Oosterzee, P. & James, D. (1995) *Two Way Track. Biodiversity Conservation & Ecotourism: an investigation of linkages, mutual benefits and future opportunities.* Biodiversity Series, Paper No. 5. Environment Australia: Department of Environment and Heritage, Canberra, Australia.

Ramblers' Association (2004) *Walking makes money*. Ramblers' Association. Located @ URL: http://www.ramblers.org.uk/info/factsandfigures/economic.html

Rayment, M. & Dickie, I. (2001). *Conservation Works.....for local economies in the UK.* RSPB. Sandy, England.

Reynolds, P.C. & Braithwaite, D. (2000) Towards a conceptual framework for wildlife tourism. *Tourism Management*, 22, 31-42

Rotherham, I.D. (2003) *Lunching on landscapes of leisure, history and location: eating the view as an opportunity for sustainable hospitality.* In: Ball, S. (Ed.) *Trends and Developments in Hospitality Research.* Proceedings of the 12th Annual CHME Hospitality Research Conference. April 23-24 2003, Sheffield. 332-341.

Rotherham, I. D., Doncaster, S. & Egan, D. (2004) Issues and Approaches in Valuing Wildlife Recreation and Leisure - in the context of countryside recreation. In: *Demonstrating the Economic Value of Countryside Recreation*, 2004 Countryside Recreation Network Seminar Proceedings, Bristol, 11th March 2004, Bull, M. (Ed.) 59-66.

Rotherham, I. D., Doncaster, S. & Egan, D. (2004) Valuing Wildlife Recreation and Leisure. *Countryside Recreation*, 12, 12-19.

Rotherham, I.D., Doncaster, S. & Egan, D. (2005) *Nature-based Leisure and Tourism in England's Humberhead Levels. Annals of Tourism Research*, 8 (2-3), 214-230.

Saeter, J, A. (1998) *The Significance of Tourism and Economic Development in Rural Areas: a Norwegian case study.* In: Butler, R. W., Hall, C. M., & Jenkins, J. M. (Eds.) (1998) *Tourism & Recreation in Rural Areas.* John Wiley & Son, New York, 236-245.

Sharpley, R. (2000) Tourism and Sustainable Development: Exploring the Theoretical Divide. *Journal of Sustainable Tourism*, 8 (1), 1-19.

Sharpley, R. (2002a) Rural Tourism and the Challenge of Tourism Diversification: the Case of Cyprus. *Tourism Management*, 23, 233-244.

Sharpley, R. (2002b) Tourism: A Vehicle for Development? In: Sharpley, R. & Telfer, D. J. (Ed.) (2002) Tourism and Development; Concepts and Issues. *Aspects of Tourism Series*, No. 5. Channel View Publications, Clevedon, England. 11-34.

Sirakaya, E., Sasidharan, V. & Sönmez, S. (1999) Redefining Ecotourism: The Need for a Supply-side View. *Journal of Travel Research*, 38 (2), 168-172.

Smith, S. L. J. (1995) *Tourism Analysis. A Handbook.* Second Edition. Longman Publishing Ltd., Harlow, England.

Stabler, M. J. & Goodall, B. (1996) *Environmental Auditing in Planning for Sustainable Island Tourism.* In: Briguglio, L,. Archer, B., Jafari, J. & Wall, G. (Eds.) (1996) *Sustainable Tourism in Islands and Small States. Issues and Policies.* Pinter, London, England.

Stucker Rennicks, J. (1997) Nature-based Tourism. *Business & Economic*

Review, 43, (2) http://research.moore.sc.edu/Publications/B&EReview/be43_2/toursm.htm Visited 17/4/2003.

Wight, P. (1997) *Sustainability, Profitability and Ecotourism Markets: What are They & How Do They Relate?* Conference proceedings; *Ecotourism - Balancing Sustainability & Profitability*. 22-23 September, 1997. Pärnu, Estonia.

Wright, P. (1996) North American ecotourism markets: motivations, preferences and destinations. *Journal of Travel Research*, 34 (4), 2-10.

WCED (1987) *Our Common Future. (The Bruntland Report) - Report of the 1987 World Commission on Environment and Development.* World Commission on Environment and Development. Oxford University Press, Oxford, England.

WTO (2002) *WTO Think Tank enthusiastically reaches consensus on frameworks for tourism destination success.* News release. World Tourism Organisation, Madrid, Spain. December, 2002. http://www.world-tourism.org/education/news/news_releases/newsrelease_thinktank_pressrelease2.htm Visited 16/1/2003

WTO (2000) *System of Tourism Statistics.* World Tourism Organisation, Madrid, Spain. http://www.world-tourism.org/statistics/tsa_project/basic_references/index-en.htm Visited 14/2/2003.

Zhou, D., Yanahida, J. F., Chakravory, U. & Leung, P. (1997) Estimating Economic Impacts from Tourism. *Annals of Tourism Research*, 24 (1), 76.

8

THE IMPACT OF ECOTOURISM DEVELOPMENT IN KENYA: ENVIRONMENTAL ISSUES OF PLANNING AND MANAGEMENT

ROSELYNE NYAWIRI OKECH

ABSTRACT

The ecotourism phenomena is currently entering a crucial phase of its development. In the past years, ecotourism has attracted significant attention from consumers, conservationists, economic development specialists, and others. However, we are entering a period during which ecotourism will undergo a more careful scrutiny to determine whether it provides as many benefits as its proponents suggest. Ecotourism has played, and will continue to play, an important role in terms of providing private business opportunities, creating jobs, and generating financial and political support for the protection and management of natural areas. some general themes in the field of ecotourism such as the need for co-operation between the public and private sectors, the need for more rigorous data on ecotourism's impacts, and the need to maintain quality products as the supply of ecotourism destinations increases.

Conservation and management of our natural resources is therefore a matter of concern for all of us, since we are aware that humanity, which exists as a part of nature, has no future unless nature and natural resources are conserved for the benefit of present and future generations. Sound management of our natural resources is as important as visitor management in our national parks and reserves, to ensure that we maximise benefits with minimum environmental impact.

Keywords: Ecotourism, Kenya, Planning, Management, Development

INTRODUCTION

Tourism has long played an important role in the economy of Kenya, representing the second highest single source of foreign exchange after tea. Tourism is not only a powerful social and economic force but also a factor in the physical environment as well. It has the power to protect natural attractions, enhance the environment, provide funds for conservation, preserve culture and history and set sustainable use limits. It also has the power to contribute towards negative, social, economic and environmental impacts, especially in the host countries. Eagles (1995a) and Khan (2003) state that within the tourism industry worldwide, ecotourism is one of the fastest growing sectors and has received considerable attention both in literature and international marketplace. A frequently cited definition of ecotourism originated with The International Ecotourism Society (TIES), which states that ecotourism is responsible travel to natural areas, which conserve the environment, and sustains the well being of local people (Ecotourism Society, 2000).

According to Sindiga (1999 citing several authors such as Boo, 1990; Hvenegaard, 1994 and Lindberg and Hawkins, 1993), ecotourism has generated great interest from governments, tourism enterprises, tourists, conservation groups and other stakeholders in the industry. Cater (1994) observed that one of the reasons for this interest is the availability of pristine natural environments, especially in Africa. Also, ecotourism is sensitive to the fragile nature of ecosystems and cultural systems. These qualities of ecotourism call for greater attention to destination planning, management of resources in line with consumer tastes as well as the quality and price of tourism products (Hvenegaard, 1994; Sindiga, 1999).

The broad goals of ecotourism dovetail with ideas of sustainable development in the sense that natural resources are utilised for tourism according to local aspirations and local knowledge. However, there are few examples to demonstrate that the development of ecotourism destinations has gone according to plan as noted by Hvenegaard (1994) and Sindiga (1999). The need for more rigorous data on economic, environmental and social impacts of ecotourism development has been observed. We need a better understanding of ecotourism's impacts, and how those impacts are affected by various development and management strategies. The Kenyan government gives priority to environmental conservation and management in tourism development. It is committed to finding solutions to beach pollution and the deterioration of certain national parks and reserves through the efforts of the Kenya Wildlife Service (KWS) in wildlife conservation and management.

The Kenyan government sees ecotourism as having the potential of becoming a moderately useful tool for locally directed and participatory rural development based on a rational utilisation of environmental and cultural resources on which tourism is based. Efforts will be made towards ensuring community participation with a view to achieving commitment and motivation to the conservation and sustainable use of the ecologically delicate natural resources.

ECOTOURISM IN THE BROADER TOURISM CONTEXT

Notwithstanding its potentially negative consequences, ecotourism has come to be closely associated, and even sometimes synonymous, with equally controversial and much-debated terms such as sustainable tourism and alternative tourism. Weaver (1999) proposes that all tourism forms, in theory, can be differentiated as either sustainable or unsustainable, acknowledging that an understanding of the indicators for measuring and monitoring sustainability is still in its infancy, and that tourism which appears to be sustainable in the short-term may prove otherwise over a long period of time. Most tourism forms can be classified as high volume or mass tourism and this mode has been widely perceived as being unsustainable in the long-term, given its emphasis upon large corporations, unfettered free markets, high density development, short-term profits, and the like. Alternative tourism is commonly defined, at least in its ideal configuration, as a set of characteristics diametrically opposed to mass tourism. Thus, where the latter tends toward external control, generic architecture and psycho centric tourism markets, alternative tourism is constructed as a locally controlled sector adhering to vernacular architectural norms and attracting a more allcentric type of client (Weaver, 1999).

The aims of ecotourism include ecological and socio-cultural integrity, responsibility and sustainability and its major characteristics outlined in Table 1 reveal that it is soundly grounded in alternative tourism.

Table 1. Characteristics of Ecotourism Actors

ACTORS	CHARACTERISTICS
Tourists	A tolerance for the inconveniences of remote travel
Tour operators	Focus holidays they provide on flora, fauna, landscape, native culture and archaeology and sport
Host communities	Require local involvement in planning and operating tourism
Host governments	Concerned with national planning to exploit natural environments and culture for development
International conservation groups	See ecotourism as a means to ensure conservation
Academics	Debate precise meaning of ecotourism

Source: France (1997: 18).

EFFECTS OF TOURISM DEVELOPMENT WITHOUT PLANNING

Except perhaps for Tunisia there has been no serious sectoral planning of tourism in any African country (Lea, 1993; Sindiga, 1999). Even Kenya with a relatively strong tourist industry, the assessment made about two and a half decades ago is still largely true. Very frequently, national plans show lists of "hoped for outcomes" in the tourism sector rather than agenda for implementation (Lea, 1993: 74). Planning for tourism serves a number of other purposes: minimising potential conflicts with competing land uses; developing desired tourism; and projecting its impact on environment and society now and in the future. In order for tourism to be sustainable, its planning must be based on local capacities and community perspectives without which it cannot succeed (Murphy, 1985; Sindiga, 1999). Planning requires baseline information about the tourism sector, its history, its functioning, how it has been changing over time, its performance potential for further development and how optimal use can be obtained (Sindiga, 1999). Only this way can the positive and negative contributions of tourism be pinpointed with a view to formulating policies and projects, which could enhance the positive role and ameliorate the negative consequences.

Such planning which is practical and action-oriented combines planning with implementation as a single process (Gunn, 1988). The nature of tourism demands that plans be oriented towards rapidly changing situations, which may not be anticipated in periodic conventional planning. This is what is called strategic planning and is focused, selective and concerned with handling unexpected events (Gunn, 1988; Inskeep, 1994; Sindiga, 1999).

TOURISM AND THE ENVIRONMENT

The relationship between tourism and the environment is often taken for granted. It is clear, however, that attitudes towards the environment, in the context of tourism and in the context of many aspects of human development, have changed very greatly over time. The ways that humans regard environment, the ways in which they use and abuse it, and the ways in which they try to protect it are continuously changing over space as well as time (Butler, 2000; Sisman, 1994). Similarly, several authors such as Davis (2001), Dieke (2001a), Lea (1993) and Wight (1994) take note of a relatively large literature on the interrelationship between various tourist activities and the environment. This ranges from the effects of walking on coral reefs, to the destruction of beaches and parks caused by trail bikes and off-road vehicles.

The environmental impacts of tourism include energy costs of transport, loss of aesthetic value, air pollution, water pollution and the generation of waste, disruption of animal breeding patterns and habits, deforestation, impacts on vegetation through the collection of flowers and bulbs, destruction of beaches, dunes, coral reefs and many national parks and wilderness areas through trampling and/ or the use of vehicles, change of landscape-permanent environmental restructuring and seasonal effects on population densities and structures (France, 1997). The long-standing popularity of national game parks in Africa has given rise to many studies documenting the impact of tourism on wildlife. This ranges from adverse effects such as the disruption of animal feeding and breeding patterns to a general recognition that tourism has greatly assisted the process of nature conservation (Dieke, 2001a).

At issue is the dilemma of how to cater for the tourists without causing lasting damage to the fragile ecology of the parks. Another important effect of tourism on the environment, as noted by Bramwell *et al*. (1998) is related to travel and the use of energy. Many tourist facilities are highly energy-consuming. Indirectly, the huge demand for energy increases pollution (from electric power plants and transportation) and may aggravate serious environmental problems such as greenhouse effects and acid rain.

Very frequently, environmental deterioration is also caused by the behaviour of tourists themselves and this situation is not restricted to mass tourism only. Litter left behind by tourists detracts from the aesthetic quality of an area. Consequently, Bramwell *et al*. (1998) assert that the effects of tourism on the environment do not necessarily have to be negative particularly if there is pro-active planning and management. For example, tourists can be a source of funding for the conservation of national parks and also for more widespread environmental conservation. Environmental gains from tourism may also include an enhanced concern for the environment among the residents of a host area as a consequence of both the improved local interpretive provision and also the recognition among residents of the economic value of the environment for tourism. It can be argued, however, that there is a wider range of potential negative than potential positive environmental impacts associated with tourism.

Prosser (1994) argues that the concerns over the environmental impacts of tourism has grown alongside the emergence of the global environmental movement and as all components in the tourism system-tourists, destinations and operators, acknowledge their reliance upon finite and vulnerable environmental resources. Similarly, Holden (2003) notes that the negative environmental impacts that tourism development can sometimes have, for example, leading to the draining of wetlands, destruction of coral reefs, increased rates of deforestation, pollution, and aesthetic blight, has led to increased pressure for stakeholders to evaluate their positions relative to nature. This pressure originates both from tourism pressure groups and from a changed context of international policy on development, which supports sustainable development and environmental conservation.

It is necessary here to re-emphasize the differing priorities between rich western nations which generally see the destruction of the environment as a pressing problem affecting everyone in the world, and poor developing countries, whose priorities are first to raise their own living standards to acceptable levels. Many examples from all over the Third World suggest that much of the attraction for foreign visitors is an unspoilt natural environment and traditional way of life of a kind, long passed in Europe and North America. Such attractions, however, are also a sign of under development and rarely tolerated just because they meet with the approval of visitors (Lea, 1993).

CONSTRAINTS TO LONG-TERM PLANNING OF ECOTOURISM IN KENYA

Tourism and the preservation of natural ecosystems/ habitats are mutually dependent because tourism uses environmental resources, and a healthy environment promotes tourism in Kenya and the world at large. Ecotourism simply defined is the synchronization of the tourism sector development needs with programmes for long-term sustainable environmental management. Namwalo (1992) and Shelley (1992) identified the constraints on the long-term planning of ecotourism in Kenya and are still currently observed by several authors such as Dieke (2001a), Sindiga (1999) and Weaver (1999). The constraints are discussed below:

Demographic Factor

Led by rapid population growth, the demand for land for agriculture, settlement and expansion of urban areas increases pressure on areas reserved for wildlife and poses a serious threat to the future of ecotourism in Kenya. To survive, most of Kenya's wildlife seasonally moves out of protected areas into dispersal areas that are inhabited by people. Present examples are the expansion of wheat farming or intensification of sedentary farming in the Masai region, Kitengela (South-East of Nairobi National Park) and in the group ranches around Masai Mara National Reserve.

Pollution

The disposal of untreated solid and liquid wastes and the leaching of agro-chemicals from farms cause water pollution. It is especially serious when the pollutants are released near to or within protected areas. Pollution is already a problem of some magnitude in the Malindi / Watamu Marine Park/ Reserve and in Lakes Naivasha and Nakuru.

Water Resource

Erosion, the siltation of water bodies, over-tapping of water resources and degradation of the environment is happening in water catchment areas essential to the survival of life in some parks and reserves. This problem in the Malewa, Nderit, Makalia and Njoro river catchments is affecting the volume of water discharged into Lakes Naivasha and Nakuru respectively.

Global warming and depletion/ drying of some underground water resources/ aquifers

This explains the changes in water table levels and the diminishing size and depth of Lakes Nakuru, Naivasha and Turkana over the years.

Over-Utilization

Some tourist resources have become degraded, leading to reduced visitor satisfaction in a few national parks and game reserves such as Amboseli, Masai Mara and Nairobi. The growth of the tourist industry in Kenya is reflected in the number of tourist vehicles in protected areas. While destinations such as Mt Elgon and Meru, which have sustainable ecosystems, are under-utilised, others such as Amboseli, Nairobi, Masai Mara and Samburu, with fragile ecosystems, are over-utilised. An uncontrolled inflow of tourists and vehicles into these areas imposes a serious challenge to environmental conservation.

Legislation

Both inadequate legal instruments and lack of political will to enforce existing legal provisions/ by-laws create obstacles to planning. This is noticeable especially in cases concerning land tenure and use in wildlife dispersal areas and those concerning private plots adjoining other protected areas such as beaches. There have been instances of private development and fencing of seafront plots aimed at reducing public access to protected areas. Fencing of national parks and game reserves sometimes may be justified but it ultimately deprives wildlife access to dispersal areas.

Destruction of Human Life and Property by Wildlife

This occurs, without adequate compensation, in areas of high agricultural potential adjoining protected areas like Amboseli, Masai Mara, Aberdares and Mount Kenya.

Absence of Detailed Research

There is a lack of research findings and data on capacity of land to sustain wildlife, livestock and human populations. Excessive (above optimum) wildlife, livestock and human populations in some protected areas and their adjoining wildlife dispersal zones will have deleterious effects on the habitats in question.

Adverse Media Coverage

Adverse/over-blown reports in local and foreign media of a few isolated instances of insecurity and of the ecological impacts of tourism, have an effect out of proportion to their true value.

Plan

There is lack of a detailed national tourism master plan with appropriate development strategies and policies. Such a plan should minimise incompatibilities between short-term increases in tourism earnings and long-term sustainable development of the tourist sector on the basis of zoning of areas for different types of tourist use. Investments in tourist facilities presently seem to be dictated more by private profit than by a need for broad national economic and social gains.

ENVIRONMENTAL CONCERNS IN ECOTOURISM

Ecotourists have high levels of environmental conscience. Their internal environmental philosophy dictates that nature must be protected and celebrated within a natural context, resulting in a superabundance of environmental protection rules, policies and laws (Eagles, 1995b). According to Casagrandi and Rinaldi (2002), the quality of the environment *E(t),* in the absence of tourists and capital, is described by a classical logistic equation:

$$\dot{E}(t) = E(t)\left[\frac{1 - E(t)}{K}\right]$$

Where the net growth rate *r* and the carrying capacity *K* are influenced by all activities except those related to tourism industry. In other words, K is not the quality of the environment in unrealistic (pristine) conditions, but, instead, the quality of the environment at the equilibrium in the presence of all civil and industrial activities (except for tourism) characterising the site under study. If tourists and facilities impact negatively on the environment, the complete dynamics of *E(t)* is:

$$\dot{E}(t) = E(t)\left[\frac{1 - E(t)}{K}\right] - D[T(t), C(t), E(t)]$$

Where *D [T(t), C(t), E(t)]* represent the flow of damages induced by tourism. Generally, this flow is positively correlated with tourists and capital. Moreover, the damage is higher when the environment is still unexploited. The simplest functional form consistent with these properties is the following:

$$D = E(\beta\ C + \gamma\ T)$$

Where two parameters â and ã are positive. For example heating of hotels, which impacts on air pollution, has a first component which is basically independent upon the number of tourists (heating the hall, cafeteria and restrooms) and a second component which is proportional to the number of visitors (heating the bedrooms). The same is true for many other touristic facilities, like ski lifts and discothèques (noise pollution), bus services (air pollution), artificial snow facilities (downstream water pollution) and many others. Exceptionally â and ã can be negative, for example, when high reclamation efforts are associated with tourism development. This means that if T and C would be kept constant, the environment would still be described by a logistic equation:

$$\dot{E}(t) = r^* E(t)\left[\frac{1-E(t)}{K^*}\right]$$

with

$$r^* = r\left[1 - \frac{\beta C + \gamma D}{r}\right]$$

$$k^* = k\left[1 - \frac{\beta C + \gamma D}{r}\right]$$

In other words, if â and ã are positive, tourism activities (C and T) reduce the carrying capacity and the net growth rate of the environment in the same proportion. The impacts of ecotourism depend on what ecotourism is. Definitions and characteristics have been reviewed extensively by several authors including Buckley (1994), Fennell (1999) and Honey (1999). The critical issue, however, is that ecotourism should involve deliberate steps to minimise impacts, through choice of activity, equipment, location and timing, group size, education and training, as well as operational environmental management.

Under these circumstances, which are regrettably more of an ideal than a practical reality in most cases, the impacts of ecotourism should therefore be those of nature tourism and recreation which incorporates best practice environmental management. Biodiversity and environmentally intact lands form the basis of ecological stability. But this has already been severely affected by industrialisation, urbanisation, unsustainable agricultural practices and mass tourism. While ecotourism sounds comparatively benign, one of its most serious impacts is usurpation of "virgin" territories national parks, wildlife sanctuaries and other wilderness areas which are then packaged as green products for ecotourists. Hence, with the tremendous expansion of commercialised ecotourism, environmental degradation, including deforestation, disruption of ecological life systems and various forms of pollution, has in fact increased. Even its proponents concede that ecotourism is far from a panacea for environmental destruction (Buckley, 2001).

The Masai Mara National Reserve and Amboseli National Park are both excellent examples of ecological disasters arising from tourism. In both the areas, lodges and camps have heavily deforested the small riverine forests that existed with their hunger for firewood for cooking and heating. The number of motor vehicles crisscrossing the park areas keeps growing as tour drivers search for rare animals such as lions and rhinos. An unsightly network of roads and tracks for "game drives" disrupts the grass cover, with serious consequences for plant and animal species. Often overlooked is the fact that ecotourism is a highly consumer-centred activity catering to the lifestyles of the new urbanised middle-class societies (Sindiga, 1999).

Several authors such as Anderek (1995), Hall and Lew (1999), Honey (1999), McLaren (1998), Mowforth and Munt (1998) and Stabler (1997) realised that recent efforts to rearrange existing mass tourism into ecotourism have failed due to a general reluctance to limit the growth of tourism; lack of controls and sustainability; and lack of thorough examination on the environmental impacts of tourism, including the impact of environmental resource utilisation, the consumptive nature of tourism, and its continuous discharge of pollutants through increased road and air traffic. There are broader environmental issues relating to the impacts of long-distance air and ground travel to and from an ecotourism destination, and to accommodation in urban hotels before and after an ecotour.

MANAGEMENT OF ENVIRONMENTAL QUALITY

Ecotourists seek high levels of environmental quality (Eagles, 1992). Most ecotourism is concentrated in national parks, wildlife reserves and similar types of protected areas. Each of these protected area systems has environmental integrity goals. Therefore, the inherent thrust of the ecotourist travel motives and the management philosophy of the park agencies' are similar. However, visitor use has the potential to degrade environmental quality through overuse, damaging behaviours, unplanned access to sensitive sites, and inappropriate use levels.

Gakahu (1992a) and Sindiga (1999) found that recreation in Amboseli and Masai Mara leads to soil erosion and compaction, vegetation damage, water pollution, increased fire, vandalism and noise. Considerable experience gained in methods of tourism development help produce socially acceptable levels of impact (Eagles, 1997). As tourism numbers continue to increase, Kenyan needs for site-specific management plans and policy increase as they require zoning plans, more regulation of access, site hardening and visitor education. Throughout Africa, protection of the globally significant wildlife and ecological resources is a major goal of the protected areas. In the case of most national parks, resource extraction is not allowed or is restricted and controlled, while in a game reserve, hunting is allowed. Langholz (1996) reporting on the growing number of private nature reserves, finds that the average African reserve is 11,436 ha in size, which is very small compared to national parks and game reserves, but significant nevertheless.

Private owners argue that the two most important goals of the reserves are to protect nature in general, and to preserve a specific species or habitat. Management of natural resources and visitor use ideally aims to maintain ecological integrity.

COMMUNITY PARTICIPATION AND CONSULTATION IN ENVIRONMENTAL INITIATIVES

The sustainability of nature-based tourism in Africa over the longer term depends on the support of local communities, especially in wildlife areas. Bramwell *et al.* (1998), Gakahu (1992b) and Villiers (2002) observe that sustainable development is based on the ethic of care for the whole community of life now and in the future, and emphasises that development must be people-centred and conservation-based. This approach rests on improving the quality of individual human lives through providing health care, education, and economic advancement, and on empowering local communities to manage their environment and resources effectively. Nature-tourism is a relatively new form of land-use. To a large extent, Gakahu (1992b) and Sindiga (1999) argue that its rapid growth has excluded local communities including the Masai in Kenya.

Fortunately those concerned with the management of the environment and natural resources have come to realise that local people, who are owners and users, must be involved for any resource management system to be sustainable. Local people have the greatest knowledge of their ecosystems which, when blended with modern techniques, gives the best results. Jones *et al*. (1999) make an observation that all across Africa there are examples of community development gone wrong and this is because the community was never sufficiently involved so as to acquire the necessary development benefits. Therefore, the degree of truly local participation is often limited not only in terms of ownership and control, but also in terms of enjoyment of the natural attraction.

Viewed as a form of alternative tourism, the emphasis in ecotourism development should be on small-scale, locally owned activities. Cater (1994) reports on three important repercussions. Firstly, the facilities in terms of infrastructure and superstructure are simpler and less expensive than those demanded by conventional mass tourism, and are consequently less of a drain on the limited financial investment available. Secondly, locally owned and operated businesses are not enmeshed in the need to conform to the corporate Western identity of the multinational tourism concerns, and, therefore can have a much higher input of local products, material and labour. Thirdly, the profits made should accrue locally instead of flowing back to the parent country. Communities located near major attraction sites, such as nature parks and reserves and archaeological and historic sites, should have the opportunity to participate in tourism related to the attraction. These communities can provide hotels, restaurants, shops, transportation and guide services and other tourist facilities and services. Also, they can be employed in management and operation of the attraction feature. Community participation in tourism can take various forms depending on the local types of tourism resources and social circumstances, and often these forms will overlap.

CONCLUSIONS AND RECOMMENDATIONS

Tourism must be planned at all scales with such restraint that travelers can be free to obtain the enriching rewards of discovery, adventure and achievement. Planning policies, concepts and processes are merely tools, not ends. Therefore, several important conclusions regarding destination ecotourism planning can be drawn:

Basic Principles

- Tourism planning must encompass all travel-business and pleasure
- Planning objectives, processes and outcomes vary from macro-to microscales.
- Integration of planning at all scales is essential
- Planning of the supply side should meet the needs of market demand
- Supply side planning must be directed toward the three developer sectors (business, nonprofit and governmental)
- Planning must integrate all components of the supply side
- Urban-rural planning must be integrated
- Traffic and pedestrian functions need integration
- Clustering is basic principle of planning and design

Environment and Resources

- Global environmental deterioration demands tourism's attention
- Park protection and tourism can be compatible
- Sustainable development is a planning principle for tourism
- Planning and design can resolve visitor impact management issues
- Appropriateness is a planning and design fundamental
- Ecotourism requires special site, area and regional planning and design
- Ecotourism can foster conservation
- Economic success of tourism depends on resource protection
- Placeness is a tourism planning fundamental

Policies and Goals

- Economic development cannot be an exclusive goal
- Tourism planning policies should be directed toward quality as well as growth
- Tourism policy must be more than promotion

- Tourism planning policy requires greater public-private cooperation
- Regional tourism policies can strengthen all planning
- Regional policies for development incentives can stimulate business
- Policy should link business with government and nonprofit attractions

Processes

- Processes for plans and continuous planning need integration
- Geographic heterogeneity requires destination identification
- Process techniques can assist identification of potential destinations
- Destination planning processes encompass cities and surrounding areas
- Destination cooperation of leadership and organization is essential
- Place making is essential to destination planning processes
- Site scale design is interrelated to all tourism planning
- Design professionals do not have exclusive control of design
- New design paradigms require new kinds of designers
- Site design must meet several design criteria
- Site design requires special design processes

Future Challenges

- Entrepreneurship is essential to future tourism plans
- Plans should foster low-impact development
- Much greater intersector cooperation is needed
- Greater support for research, education and training will become evident

- A new proactive environmental protection planning policy is needed
- A new catalytic professional planning role is needed
- Creativity and innovation characterize future tourism planning and design
- A new planning and design principle of land use stewardship is needed
  - Federal to local government roles need to be clarified
  - Societal objectives pose a major challenge to planners
  - Tourism must not be overplanned

REFERENCES

Anderek, K.L. (1995) "Environmental Consequences of Tourism: A Review of Recent Research". In: S.F. McCool and A.E.Watson (eds.) *Linking Tourism, the Environment and Sustainability*. US Forest Service Intermountain Research Station. General Technical Report INT-GTR-323. Ogden, Utah.

Boo, E. (1990) "Ecotourism: The Potential and Pitfalls". Washington, DC: World Wide Fund for Nature (2 Volumes).

Bramwell, B., Henry, I., Jackson, G. and Straaten J. van der. (1998) "A Framework for Understanding Sustainable Tourism Management". In: B. Bramwell., I. Henry., G. Jackson., A.G. Prat., G. Richards and J. Straaten. van der (eds.) *Sustainable Tourism Management: Principles and Practice*. Tilburg University Press. pp. 23-71.

Buckley, R. (1994) "A Framework for Ecotourism". *Annals of Tourism Research* 21, 661-665.

Buckley, R. (2001) "Environmental Impacts". In: D.B. Weaver (ed.) *The Encyclopedia of Ecotourism*. Wallingford: CAB International. pp. 379-394.'

Butler, R.W. (2000) "Tourism and the Environment: A Geographical Perspective". *Tourism Geographies* 2 (3), 337-358.

Casagrandi, R. and Rinaldi, S. (2002) "A Theoretical Approach to Tourism Sustainability". International Institute for Applied Systems Analysis, Austria. Interim Report IR-02-051.

Cater, E. (1994) "Ecotourism in the Third World – Problems and Prospects for Sustainability". In: E. Cater and G. Lowman (eds.) *Ecotourism: A Sustainable Option?* John Wiley and Sons. pp. 69-86.

Davis, J.B. (2001) "Commentary: Tourism Research and Social Theory

– Expanding the Focus". *Tourism Geographies* 3 (2), 125-134.

Dieke, P.U.C. (2001a) "Kenya and South Africa". In: D.B.Weaver (ed.) *The Encyclopedia of Ecotourism*. Wallingford: CAB International. pp. 89-105.

Eagles, P.F.J. (1992) "The Travel Motivations of Canadian Ecotourists". *Journal of Travel Research* 11 (2), 3-7.

Eagles, P.F.J. (1995a) "Key Issues in Ecotourism Management". Paper presented at the State of Western Australia Annual Tourism Conference, Perth, Western Australia.

Eagles, P.F.J. (1995b) "Understanding the Market for Sustainable Tourism". In: S.F. McCool and A.E. Watson (eds.) *Linking Tourism, the Environment and Sustainability*. Topical Volume of Compiled Papers from a Special Session of the Annual Meeting of the National Recreation and Park Association, 1994 October 12-14 Minneapolis, Report INT-GTR-323. Ogden, UT:US.

Eagles, P.F.J. (1997) "International Ecotourism Management: Using Australia and Africa as Case Studies". Paper Prepared for the IUCN World Commission on Protected Areas, Protected Areas in the 21st Century: From Islands to Networks, Albany, Australia, November 23-29.

Ecotourism Society (2000) Ecotourism Statistical Fact Sheet. Alexandria, V.A: Ecotourism Society.

Fennell, D.A. (1999) "Ecotourism: An Introduction". Routledge, London

France, L. (ed.) (1997) "The Earthscan Reader in Sustainable Tourism". Earthscan Publications.

Gakahu, C.G. (1992a) "Framework for Establishing Potential Visitor Capacity".' In: C.G. Gakahu (ed.) *Tourist Attitudes and Use in Maasai Mara National Reserve*. Wildlife Conservation International. pp. 62-65.

Gakahu, C.G. (1992b) "Participation of Local Communities in Ecotourism: Rights, Roles and Socio-economic Benefits". In: C.G. Gakahu and B.E. Goode (eds.) *Ecotourism and Sustainable Development in Kenya*. Wildlife Conservation International. pp. 117-123.

Gunn, C.A. (1988) "Tourism Planning". New York: Taylor and Francis.

Gunn, C.A. (1994) Tourism Planning Basic Concepts, Cases 3rd Ed.

Hall, C.M and Lew, A.A. (eds.) (1999) "Sustainable Tourism: A Geographical Perspective". Longman: London

Holden, A. (2003) "In Need of New Environmental Ethics For Tourism?" *Annals of Tourism Research* 30 (1), 94-108.

Honey, M. (1999) "Ecotourism and Sustainable Development: Who owns

Paradise?" Island Press.

Hvenegaard, G.T. (1994) "Ecotourism: A Status Report and Conceptual Framework". *Journal of Tourism Studies* 5 (2), 24-35.

Inskeep, E (1994) "National and Regional Tourism Planning: Methodologies and Case Studies". WTO Publication. London and New York: Routledge.

Jones, D., Openshaw, R. and Robinson, J. (1999) "Travel and Tourism". Collegium Educational Publishers, Volume 3, 51-61.

Khan, M. (2003) "ECOSERV Ecotourists' Quality Expectations". *Annals of Tourism Research* 30 (1), 109-124.

Langholz, J. (1996) "Economics, Objectives and Success of Private Nature Reserves in Sub-Saharan Africa and Latin America". *Conservation Biology* 10 (1), 271-280.

Lea, J. (1993) "Tourism and Development in the Third World". Routledge, First Published in 1988.

Lindberg, K. and Hawkins, D.E. (eds.) (1993) "Ecotourism for Planners and Managers". North Bennington, Vermont: The Ecotourism Society.

McLaren, D. (1998) "Rethinking Tourism and EcoTravel: The Paving of Paradise and What You Can Do To Stop It". Kumarian Press, Connecticut.

Mowforth, M. and Munt, I. (1998) "Tourism and Sustainability: New Tourism in the Third World". Routledge, London.

Murphy, P.E. (1985) "Tourism: A Community Approach". New York and London: Routledge.

Namwalo, E.L. (1992) "Constraints on Long-term Planning of Ecotourism in Kenya". In: C.G. Gakahu and B.E. Goode (eds.) *Ecotourism and Sustainable Development in Kenya*. Wildlife Conservation International. pp. 23-32.

Prosser, R. (1994) "Societal Change and the Growth in Alternative Tourism'. In: E. Cater and G. Lowman (eds.) *Ecotourism, A Sustainable Option?* John Wiley and Sons. pp. 19-37.

Sindiga, I. (1999) "Tourism and African Development: Change and Challenge of Tourism in Kenya". African Studies Centre Research Series.

Sisman, R. (1994) "Tourism: Environmental Relevance". In: E. Cater and G. Lowman (eds.) *Ecotourism, A Sustainable Option?* John Wiley and Sons. pp. 57-67.

Stabler, M.J. (ed.) (1997) "Tourism and Sustainability: Principles to Practice". Wallingford: CAB International.

Villiers, D. De. (2002) “Tourism A Tool for Poverty Alleviation”. In: *Tourism a Catalyst for Sustainable Development*. Published by WTO. pp. 50-53.

Weaver, D.B. (1999) “Magnitude of Ecotourism in Costa Rica and Kenya”. *Annals of Tourism Research* 26 (4), 792-816.

Wight, P. (1994) “Environmentally Responsible Marketing of Tourism’. In: E. Cater and G. Lowman (eds.) *Ecotourism: A Sustainable Option?* John Wiley and Sons. pp. 39-55.

9

TOURISM DEVELOPMENT AS AN ALTERNATIVE FOR AGRICULTURAL PRODUCTION – The Case of E. Slovakian Wine Tourism

GEJŽA M. TIMCAK

ABSTRACT

The paper deals with the prospects of wine tourism development in E. Slovakia that has excellent tradition of wine production. The analysis of Tokay wine growing area – Slovakian part. The pros and cons of turning to wine production instead of usual agricultural activity that dwindled due to EU quota system. Problems of unemployment and HRD in rural areas of Zemplin. Risks of orientation to wine-production. Wine tourism development in E. Slovakia. Cooperation and EU projects in wine tourism. An outline of further wine tourism development strategy. Prospects of wine tourism development in E. Slovakia.

Keywords: ***Tourism, rural tourism, wine-tourism, wine produc-tion, HRD in rural areas, EU projects, strategic planning***

INTRODUCTION

The general trend in Europe - where there is an agricultural overproduction - is either to change agricultural production to ecological production, or to secure employment in alternative areas. One of the viable alternatives is tourism (cf Timcak 2004, Zolovcikova et al, 2005). Tourism is a special industry inasmuch as the client comes to collect the product and usually takes with him/her only the immaterial part of the product.

The Kosice County and within it the Zemplin region is rich in beautiful natural environment, history and culture (Fig.1). Thus recreational tourism, wine tourism and rural tourism are easy to develop there.

A successful transformation of the human resources that were used to deal with agricultural works to tourism is not an easy task as new skills and new professional culture need to be acquired (Torma 2003). Further, new investments are needed into the infrastructure both general and tourism related one. Presently, the County office chairmen of the Presov and Kosice County are trying to intervene in Brussels in order to allow the creation of regional programmes that would aim at the development of cross-sectoral funds. From these the Eastern part of Slovakia could develop e.g. the general infrastructure (http://www.sme.sk/clanok.asp?cl=2424520).

By the time all this is accomplished, the image of the region (and country) should be well established in all the regions targeted as source of clients. Presently our survey has shown that e.g. in the USA and Canada, Slovenia and Slovakia are usually mixed up. In Taiwan we found that Slovakia was mixed up also with countries like Somalia. Until the image of Slovakia is firmly rooted in the world-perception of at least the Europeans, one cannot expect a marked increase of tourist influx.

Our studies also indicated that for Slovakia, the ideal tourist target group would be young to middle age, medium income group that likes natural, geomorphologically well articulated landscape (up to 2600 m. over the sea level) with generous woodlands, relatively simple boarding conditions, admirable history and interesting ethnics.

Fig.1. Aerial View Of The Romanesque Church In Svinica. In The Back Part Of The Image Is Herlany, With Its World Famous Cold Geyser (Photo R. Klik).

In E. Slovakia we have traditionally Hungarians, Germans (Zippsers, Mantas), Rusins, Gorals and Gipsies (Romas). In the southern part of Zemplin, the Hungarian ethnics is dominant and this can help in extending cross-border tourism products – like an integrated Hungarian-Slovakian Tokay wine trail (see www.landmarkagency.sk/; http://www.tokaji-borut.hu/) (Hajdu 2004).

As the natural and historical environment has to be preserved for future generations, sustainable forms of tourism would be preferred. The concepts of sustainability is, however still not firmly established within the Slovakian tourism industry. However, the conclusions of Saethorsdottir (2004) as regards what clients like or do not like to see in a natural environment, hold largely true also in Zemplin.

THE EAST SLOVAKIAN REGION

East Slovakia in terms of NUTS classification belongs to NUTS 2. On the NUTS 3 level, it is composed of the Presov and Kosice County. The Kosice County Office commissioned the Geotourism Department to design the Zemplin wine route as a part of their efforts to make the region known and to intensify the tourism activities in this region (Timcak et al. 2003). This is important also because the high unemployment rate (33 to 50% in this area). Wine production in the area includes also the world famous Tokay wine.

The area is well modulated, the mountains are usually covered with woods and there is a significant proportion of arable and viticultural land. The river network is relatively dense, but only river Bodrog is navigable. The area can be reached by plane (Kosice Airport), and a new airport is about to be built in the Kralovsky Chlmec area. Zemplin is well accessible by rail and road. There is one large water reservoir in the region (Sirava). There are two protected areas (Jablonska, Timcak 2005). Other points of tourist interest are: the only cold-water geyser in Herlany, localities where opal is found, summer and winter sports resorts plus places and objects of historical interest (battlefields, Romanesque to Baroque style churches, buildings, manors). The archaeology is also very interesting there. Together with folk-lore and other events, this gives a very good programme possibilities for attracting tourists.

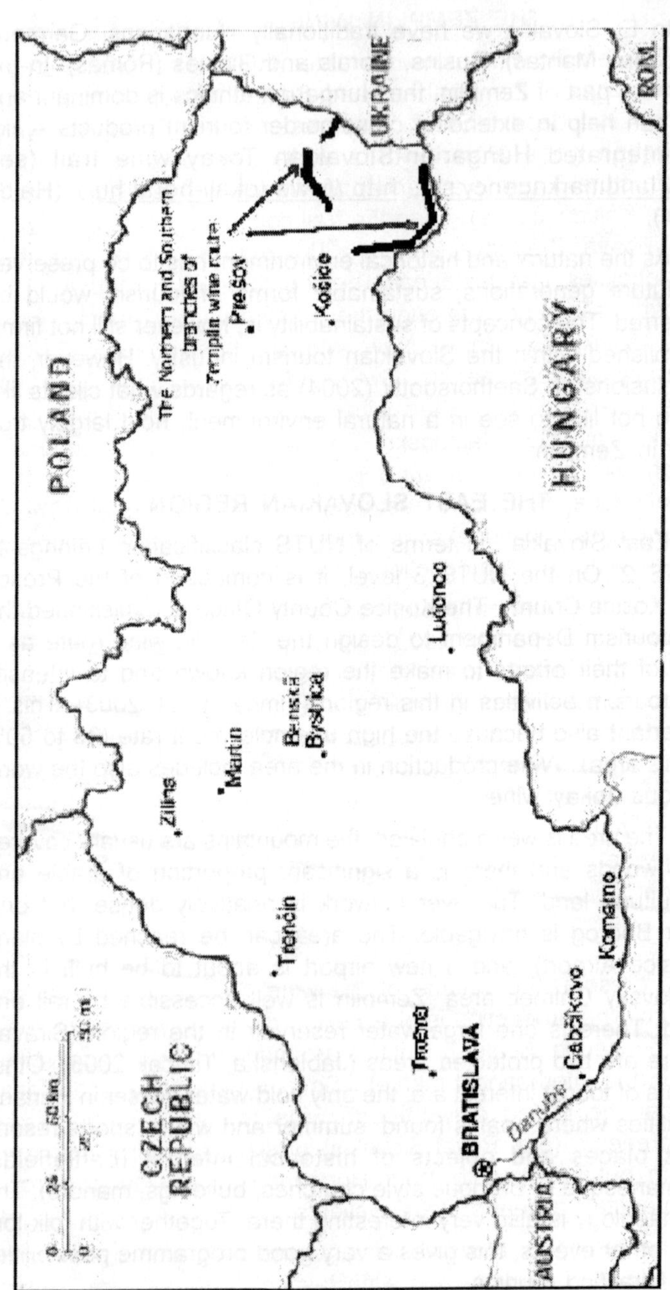

Fig.2: Map Of Slovakia With An Indication Of The Zemplin Wine Route

THE ZEMPLIN WINE ROUTE

The Zemplin wine route is situated in Kosice county and has two branches – the Northern and Southern ones (Fig.2). The Northern includes the Sirava water reservoir area, and here wine production goes along with a well-developed recreational infrastructure. There is a number of villages, where wine is grown (Vinne, Kaluza, Jovsa). Then the trail continues to the Sobrance area (Tibava, Orechova, Krcava). This branch thus incorporates also localities that historically belong to the Uh County. The southern branch goes through the Tokay area (V. Trna, M. Trna, Bara, Vinicky, Slovenske Nove Mesto) and continues to the Kralovsky Chlmec area (incl. Svatuse, M. Hores). Some of these areas were famed for their wine since prehistorical times (cf. Timcak et al. 2003, Jablonska, Timcak 2005). In the southern branch, the volume of wine production is greater, but the recreational and service infrastructure is not yet adequate. There is, however a vocational school in Vinicky, which offers tuition in wine growing, wine production and catering.

Along the Northern route, both white and red wine types are produced (see Hronsky 2001). No large scale production exists and the wine cellars are of the family type. In the Tibava area, medium scale wine production (dry white and red wines) exists. The southern branch is famous for its *Tokay aszu* wine (special sweet, dessert wine first produced in the 16th Century) and for dry and semi-dry white wines. Six medium size companies produce high quality wine. In the Kralovsky Chlmec area, small entrepreneurs produce both red and white wines with special regional flavour.

WINE TOURISM

At present, the volume of the wine production is small to medium. The production is of excellent quality. Those wines that are produced in greater quantities are marketed both in Slovakia and on the international market. Small wineries produce wines that can be tasted only through wine tourism. Some of the entrepreneurs (e.g. Royal Slovakia) prepare for extensive wine tourism, but they have to import Hungarian Tokay wines to satisfy the quantitative needs of their clients.

The region is now adjusting to the new skill needs and gradually the boarding- and wine tasting capacities are getting extended. Efforts are made to use river Bodrog for international passenger transport (via Tisza river). Investments into the renovation of the historical sites (e.g. the Rakoczy castle in Borsa), extension of wine cellars, establishing new hotel and catering facilities are well on their way.

Still, there is a considerable risk for the local population, if they will rely solely on wine production. The first question is calibrating the volume of wine production. In Slovakia, Act. No. 153/1998 regulates the geographical extent of regions usable for specified regional wine brand production. Thus the production volumes cannot be extended deliberately. The wine market is fluctuating and competes with the beer with varying result. The *Tokay aszu* wines have also medicinal properties, so they have an additional marketing edge. Cheap imported wines tend to satisfy the mass needs, so education of customers is also a very important task if high quality, more expensive wines are to be sold. In Slovakia, the habit of consuming distilled alcohol is giving way to wine and beer consumption, what supports the development of wine production.

Nevertheless, the strong point of the Zemplin wine route is in having charming, usually very old wine cellars that can cater for small to medium size tourist groups (cf. Jablonska, 2005). Te people are very hospitable. They offer unique wine brands of excellent quality, the majority of which will never appear on mass-markets.

Some villages in the Tokay area started a programme for educating farmers for organic agriculture. This – apart from satisfying local needs – may have a balancing effect on the economy, as there are no export quotas on such products. A number of EU project proposals have been submitted to finance these activities.

The nature, archaeology, history and culture related places and events are an attraction that adds spice to the wine tourism. The two protected nature areas in Zemplin host a number or rare zoological and botanical species. If the results of the Saethorsdottir survey are taken into consideration, Zemplin would not come under the "unspoiled nature" category (Table 1), but wood covered- and protected areas would satisfy most of the requirements for such category.

Table1. Choice Of Sighted Items Acceptable In An "Unspoiled Nature/Wilderness" Area (Saethorsdottir 2004)

Sight/item	Affirmative responses
Traces of off-road driving	30
Damaged natural phenomena	30
Damaged vegetation	30
Dams/power plants	50
Reservoirs	70
Electric power lines	72
Hotels/guest houses	100
Roads	130
Fences	135
Service centres	170
Tracks	290
Designed footpaths	292
Trails made by walkers or domestic animals	355
Mountain huts	370

WINE TOURSIM DEVELOPMENT STRATEGY

The Kosice Conty Office in cooperation with the local government and other organisations designed a development strategy (Zolovcikova et al. 2005) that can lead to a tourism development master plan (Timcak 2005). A thorough in situ investigation is needed in order to determine what can be sustainably developed at the individual tourist destination localities. Therefore at the Geotourism Dept. we started a research programme where we map the tourism and human resource potentials of the more than 400 villages and towns of the Kosice County and thus also those places in Zemplin, where wine tourism can be developed. Naturally, their natural environment is also assessed. The results are integrated into a GIS.

To indicate the present state of tourism in the region, Table 2 shows the average utilisation of lodging facilities in Kosice county. The underlined cities are at the starting point of the 2 branches

Table 2. Degree Of Utilisation Of Lodging Facilities In Kosice County

Average utilization (%)

District	**Year**							
	1997	**1998**	**1999**	**2000**	**2001**	**2002**	**2003**	**2004**
Kosice County	28,3	17,1	14,2	11,9	14,5	19,3	13,9	13,9
Gelnica	5,5	39,8	33,6	26,7	26,6	18,8	19,5	22,5
Kosice I	32,6	26,3	26,5	28,7	32,2	31,8	28,5	26,7
Kosice II	52,0	37,5	39,5	29,3	16,8	34,1	29	21,8
Kosice IV	16,8	16,2	12,5	17,2	18,1	20,1	24,9	24,6
Greater Kosice	34,8	37,1	35,3	23,2	22,3	21	20,5	20,5
Michalovce	24,9	8,6	7,2	4,9	6,7	11	6,5	6,3
Roznava	28,3	26,0	27,0	25	25,1	27,5	24,2	16,1
Sobrance	15,0	11,2	no data	11,4	15,3	5,4	5,9	7,4
Sp. N. Ves	29,3	38,8	20,3	18,5	19,5	30,6	22,6	17,4
Trebisov	29,4	9,9	5,3	3,3	8,7	8,1	8,4	8,1

Source: Statisticky urad SR.

of the Zemplin wine route. We can see, that recently, the rate of utilisation became very low. The rate of utilisation in villages is usually similarly low. Thus a new influx of tourists is a must, if the tourist industry and local wine production is to survive there.

According to www.czechtourism.cz survey carried out in 2005 (8000 respondents; 4x2000 interviews in Germany, Austria, Slovakia, Poland), 90% of the travels abroad are for holidays, 11% of incoming travellers travel up to 5x per year for holidays., 27% of the respondents however, do not travel at all. The average length of vacations is 11-13 days. The greatest frequency of travel is to South European countries (e.g. Spain, Italy, Croatia). The most frequent holiday destination for Slovaks it is Croatia (see Table 2).

The underlined cities are the starting points of the Northern and Southern branch of the Zemplin wine route. If the data of this table are compared with the data for Germany (http://www.destatis.de/basis/e/tour/tourtab2.htm), we can see that there, 36% is the usual average utilisation).

On the average, 48% of travellers travel mostly by car; 43% by plane. 16% of respondents gave the first place to buses. Thus road conditions have a significant impact on tourist turnover. The availability of airports in Kosice, Poprad and in the near future also in the Kralovsky Chlmec area is thus a valuable asset.

Table 3. Main Outgoing Travel Destinations Of Slovakians (www.czechtourism.cz)

Destination	%
Czech Republic (Bohemia)	7
Greece	8
Egypt	8
Italy	10
Croatia	16

The finding, that „New" EU countries are not much known to 11% to 24% of respondents strengthens our results indicated above. The survey has shown that one of the reasons of not visiting Bohemia was the lack of up to date, comprehensive and easily available information (32%). This holds true also for Slovakia (cf Table 3). Thus image making and marketing is one of the most important tasks for Slovakia. The Slovak Agency for Tourism Development (SACR) has recently stepped up its activities in this area. When we compare the survey results with the statistical data for Kosice County for the period of 1997-2004 (Table 5), we can see that most tourists are Slovakians and then come the Czechs, Poles and Hungarians.

Table 4. Reasons For Not Visiting Bohemia (www.czechtourism.cz). Similar Reasons Are Expectable Also In Case Of Slovakia.

Reason stated	Proportion in %
Inadequate facilities for sports, inadequate number cultural events	2
Difficult transport	5
Low quality of services	13
Too great distance to travel	19
Little known destination, too few information	32

From this we can conclude that the greatest tourism potential is still in the inland tourism and that the Zemplin region is most likely to be visited by foreigners from Bohemia, Poland and Hungary. As they share a lot of common history, these groups are also perhaps the easiest to satisfy. Wine tourism packages would, however be an excellent product also for Austrians and Germans. In W. Slovakia, Austrians already form the most significant clientele of the Carpathian wine growing region (cf. http://www.mvc.sk/topic.php?topic=mvc&id=intr).

CONCLUSIONS

Intensified wine production and wine tourism in the Zemplin region is a viable alternative to classical agricultural production that was the main occupation of the inhabitants. This is supported by the long-standing tradition of wine production, the support of the Government, of the County Office and of the local entrepreneurs. The process however is labour intensive and the result depends also on weather conditions and trade situation. Still, it is a risk that can hardly be avoided. As the unemployment

Table 5. Tourist Turnover In Kosice County By Countries.

No. of visitors

Country of origin	Year							
	1997	1998	1999	2000	2001	2002	2003	2004
Slovakia	183 086	202 784	182 699	177 707	186 302	209 962	196 769	182 925
Belgium	640	508	576	no data	1 843	1 362	890	1 237
Cech Rep.	22 671	23 099	19 647	19 642	20 921	38 011	29 240	30 171
France	927	997	818	1 039	1 398	1 435	1 780	2 678
The Netherlands	1 440	1 355	1 488	1 487	1 164	1 566	1 945	2 395
Hungary	5 760	6 703	6 153	6 415	6 936	11 581	13 126	15 763
Germany	7 088	7 675	5 440	5 255	5 486	6 592	6 989	8 694
Poland	9 197	11 929	15 297	16 317	19 511	28 199	21 421	17 466
Austria	2 031	2 338	1 803	1 797	2 060	2 434	2 310	2 648
Russia	2 074	1 611	589	923	834	650	602	522
Italy	1 877	2 237	1 867	1 522	1 679	1 844	2 145	2 111
Ukraine	8 875	5 597	4 673	3 363	2 385	2 705	2 061	1 875
G. Britain	1 869	1 723	1 511	1 244	1 512	1 713	1 659	1 969
USA	2 163	3 467	2 202	2 567	2 964	2 772	2 453	2 642

Source: Statisticky urad SR

rate is high in Zemplin, and the possibility of industrial employment is low, if the character of the rural areas is to be preserved and migration after labour is to be prevented, wine production, wine tourism and ecological farming seem to be the natural solutions.

Investment into both the infrastructure and to HRD are, however necessary. Steps are being taken on the level of Government, the County Office and by private entrepreneurs to create an attractive environment for international wine tourism. Functioning cross-border cooperation would be very much needed, but presently the wine route associations in Slovakia and Hungary could not mobilise enough momentum to attract sufficient public interest in their products.

REFERENCES

Hajdu M. (2004), *Impact of cross-border cooperation within EU member states on the development of off-center regions in E. Slovakia*, Proc. GEOTOUR 04, Herlany, pp. 57-62

Hronsky V. (2001), *Slovenské vina (Slovakian wines)*, Belimex. Bratislava

http://www.czechtourism.cz/files/statistiky/analyza/motivace_turistu.pdf

Jablonska J., Timcak G.M. (2005), Zemplinska vinna cesta, EKO, Vol. 16, No.4, pp. 12-14

Jablonska J.,(2005), *In vino veritas – Rozvoj cestovného ruchu v Malom Horesi*, Ekologie a spolecnost. Vol. XVI/5

Saethorsdottir A.D. (2004), *Adapting to change: maintaining a wilderness experience in a popular tourist destination*, Tourism today, No.4, Autumn 2004, pp.52-65

Timcak G.M. (2004), *EU and the future of tourism development – the Slovakian perspective*, Proc. GEOTOUR 04, Herlany, pp. 2-12

Timcak G.M. (2005), *Tourism development strategies in E. Slovakia*, Abstracts, GEOTOUR 05, AGH Kraków, p. 118

Timcak G.M. et al. (2003), *Pre-feasibility study "The Zemplin wine route"*, Kosice County Office and Geotourism Dept., Kosice, 250pp

Timcak G.M., Jablonska J. (2004), *Tourism development potentials in the Zemplin region*, Proc. GEOTOUR 2004, Herlany, pp. 38-45

Torma P. (2003), *HRD in rural tourism*, Proc. GEOTOUR 03, Herlany, pp. 114-118

Zolovcikova M. et al. (2005), *Tourism development strategies in Kosice County for the years 2005-2009*

SECTION C

ECONOMIC IMPLICATIONS OF HOSPITALITY AND TOURISM DEVELOPMENT

10

IMPLICATIONS OF DEVELOPMENT OF HOSPITALITY AND TOURISM IN THE ECONOMY: Micro and Macro Level

WACLAW KOTLINSKI

ABSTRACT

In recent years one may notice a sudden growth of tourism in the world. Its development is not only caused by fulfilling the needs of tourism but also it is stimulated by the supply. Tourism yields profits to international, national, and regional budgets, but also to enterprises and households. Therefore, the economic meaning of tourism should be discussed on two levels: micro and macroeconomic one.

On the microeconomic level of the tourism development very significant processes influence on the different stage of touristic consumption. In the literature there are mentioned four stages: preparation, travel, supply, travel. The development of tourism is particularly important for the reception areas. It makes them more active, causes the capital flow, new places of work are set up, local people become richer and there are higher taxes which come into the budget. It is active so-called multiple effect which stimulates to take actions to further development of tourism.

On the macroeconomic level of tourism development the most important and decisive are profits, which are brought to the budgets of reception countries. It also causes the balance of payments, stimulates international flow of capital and workforce. In this context a separate issue is touristic policy accomplished by the governments of counties, the groups of countries (e.g. within the European Union), activities of institutions and international organizations.

***Keywords:* development of tourism and hoteliering, touristic policy of the country, multiple effect of tourism**

INTRODUCTION

A very rapid development of tourism all over the world has been observed recently. Its development does not merely result from the tourists' need to practise tourism but is equally stimulated by the tourism supply party.

Available literature often uses "tourist explosion" term. According to W. Alejziak, however, the observation of present trends and tendencies that exist on the international tourism market leads to the conclusion that the term is inadequate (Alejziak, 1999).

Explosion usually means something that proceeds rapidly, suggesting at the same time that the break out will be followed by tranquillity. Yet, as shown by statistics and prognosis, the phenomenon does not lose its impetus – on the contrary- it expands very dynamically.

Tourism is a particularly complex phenomenon. One of the factors of its complexity is the fact that it exerts its impact on many aspects of social and economic life, and vice versa, its development is dependent on many social, economic and political factors.

The globalisation of tourist activities has been observed over the past years, which is influenced by the disappearance of borders to carry out business activities and the concentration of capital. Supranational enterprises started more and more to dominate new markets, setting new standards and the course of transformations that international tourism will undergo in the future.

Tourism is extremely profitable both on the international scale and the national, regional, particular firm and household budget scale as well. Therefore, the economic significance of tourism for the economy should be considered on different levels.

The author of this paper, due to its limited volume, decided to highlight only the most important economic aspects of tourism influence on economic development on an international scale and that of specific countries. In particular, the paper concentrates on the problem of tourism as an element of international economic relationships, its influence on the formation of the world's labour market and its significance for the development of economic growth in a country. Further on, it discusses the case of economic conditions of tourism development in Poland, the influence of political and economic transformation on tourism development and the factors that hinder tourism development in Poland.

1. Tourism as an Element of International Economic Relations

Due to significantly advanced globalisation processes, the international economic relations are becoming one of the quickly developing branches of modern economics. The following issues are considered in particular: international labour division, profits generated by international trade, the amount and the structure of trade turnover, balance of payments, free exchange rates, flux of capital, international co-operation, etc. Considering the fact that international tourism, due to its character, is accompanied by all aforementioned problems, it would seem that it is in the centre of interest of international economic relations. In practice, however, in spite of international scale of tourist movement and connected with it profits earned by reception countries, it is rarely of any interest or the subject of investigations on a larger scale.

The only reason for this state of affairs was, for many years, the economists' interest in trade turnover. The scope of services was treated marginally. In fact, the proceeds of non-material service scope were disregarded in national income calculations in the former communist countries (also in Poland). Being mostly interested in industry production, the economists started relatively late to appreciate the economic significance of services. Some of them (Alejziak, 1999) did not at all believe in the research data which showed that the turnover value, particularly taxes, from the activities of Abba group at the time when they were the most successful was higher than that achieved by powerful automobile syndicate Volvo.

The next reason worth to be taken into consideration results from the character alone of the services, the consumption of which takes place in the area where they are rendered, accompanied by the terminology problems, as well as those connected with keeping the record of some services.

With time, however, quickly growing participation of services in the global trade lead to the understanding of the shortcomings in the organizational system of international service trade.

It is only recently that the economic significance of travelling abroad has been appreciated, and the role of tourism in the forming of international relations has been seriously regarded. The growing number of economists started to consider the manifold economic issues resulting from international tourist activities, although many articles and manuals still disregard the problems of international tourist turnover. The reason for such a state of matters arises from the fact that tourism is a very specific branch of economy. Its nature leads to many questions that the researcher has to answer when trying to define the quantity of tourist turnover. Assessing the scale and the range of economic activities connected with tourism becomes very difficult. Equally difficult seems to be the scope of the influence of tourism on economy and international relations. This is because there are no clear border lines separating tourism from the remaining economic activity. Most definitions tackle the problem of tourism considering the demand, describing it as a whole of products bought by tourists. Therefore, it means that the same goods depending on the kind of consumer in some cases will be treated as tourist consumption and will increase the value of tourist turnover and in others will not be considered at all. Since the tourists can buy various products many branches of economy will participate in tourist turnover. The problem has been clearly stressed in one of the documents of the World Tourism Organization (WTO) in which it has been stated that ".... according to the present classification, the type of economic activity depends on the kind of goods produced by companies, whereas tourist economic activity is still classified according to the consumption of goods and services by visitors, tourists and one-day visitors" (Alejziak, 1999).

The role of foreign tourism in international relations was already described in 1934 by E. Gebert (Ha³aciñski, 1972), who stated that "....a wise, organic linking on one side- of the export of goods and active tourist movement, and the import of goods and reception tourism- on the other side, can significantly reduce the difficulties arising in economic turnover in the particular fields of international turnover, which allows the balance to be reached in that turnover". Nowadays, the role of foreign tourism in the global economy is assessed by facts showing that 23% of the world's service exports falls to the proceeds from foreign tours. Tourism holds the second position in the ranking of all services, which is second after transport. Considering the fact that part of turnover realized by international transport is connected with tourism, it can be assumed that the whole of international turnover connected with foreign tours constitutes about 1/3 of global value of the export of services.

Different sources point out to the fact that each year over 1.5 billion people, i.e. more than 30% of the world's population, set out on some tour. Financial consequences of such global tourist movements are expressed by the expenditures that equal 2 billion USD on buying different goods and tourist services. Those expenditures make about 12% of global product.

At the end of the twentieth century the prognoses of the World Tourism Organization (WTO) foresaw:

- 400-500 million people in the international tourist movement,
- 300-400 billion USD of expenditures connected with international tourist movement,
- 9-10% participation of tourist activity in the world's trade,
- about 40 million of new workplaces in tourism.

Judging from the results achieved in the year 2000, it appears that the prognoses were considerable lowered. According to the data given by WHO there were 625 million tourists who travelled abroad in 1998, which was connected with expenditures reaching 445 billion USD, with the costs of transport services excluded. The number of international tourists in 1999 was calculated as 656 million people, but in 2004 there were already 763 million. i. e. 10.7% more than in 2003. The revenue from international tourism (given in the local currency) rose in 2004 at the same rate as the number of international tours (by 10.3%) and reached its record level of 622 billion USD.

TABLE 1. THE TRENDS IN INTERNATIONAL TOURISM BETWEEN 1998-2004

Specification	1998	1999	2003	2004
International tourist movement (in milion of people)	625	656	689	763
Revenue from international tourism (in billion USD)	445	455	525	622

Source: Tourism Highlights 2000, Second edition, August 2000; World Tourism Barometer, Vol. 3, No June 2005

It is predicted that the number of international trips in 2020, according to WTO will reach 1.6 billion people and the expenditure on tourism will amount to 2000 billion USD.

The revenue from international tourism is characterized by a high degree of concentration. For example, the first twenty countries collected almost 70% of global income from arrival foreign tourism.

TABLE 2. TRENDS IN INTERNATIONAL TOURISM ACCORDING TO THE REGIONS OF WTO IN 2003-2004

The world regions	***Arrivals (in milion people)***		***Revenue (in billion USD)***	
	2003	***2004***	***2003***	***2004***
Europe	395.9	415.2	283.1	326.3
Americas	113.1	125.7	114.0	131.5
Only North America	77.4	85.8	84.3	98.1
Asia and Pacific	119.6	152.9	95.5	125.0
Nar. East	29.6	35.6	16.7	20.7
Africa	30.6	33.2	15.8	18.9

Source: WTO World Tourism Barometer Volume 2, No 3, October 2004.

Apart from the analysis of the amount of income per time, attention should be paid to the location of the expenditure on tourism taking, into account their regional distribution.

The European region still holds a very high position in the participation in all proceeds from international tourism. Several circumstances lead to the supposition that this leading position will still continue in the future. The basic circumstance seems to be the still progressing political-economic integration of European countries. The European Union countries have the decisive voice as refers the concentration scale of the world's tourist movement and the proceeds from it. The disappearance of all barriers for the people, goods and capital resulted in the formation of a large consumer market, which yielded an advantageous situation for the growth of both home and international tourism. WTO forecasts that, by 2020, the greatest growth in arrivals will refer to mid-eastern European countries (particularly those recently accepted) – 223 million, and southeastern Mediterranean countries (212 million). The region of eastern Asia and Pacific will be the second next after Europe the most frequently visited place in the world and its participation will rise up to 25%.

2. Tourism and the World Labour Market

There has been a marked increase in unemployment over the past years. It is predicted that the unemployment will still rise not only in industrial countries but also in many developing countries. International Work Organization (IWO) states that ...the fall of communist regime block caused a very sharp reduction of production, sudden appearance of massive unemployment, the progressing stratification of the society and poverty. IWO calculates that 30% of the world work supply, i.e. about 2.5 billion people, remains to be unemployed or work part-time.

In such circumstances the question arises: what role can be played by modern tourism in the process of balancing the labour market? To answer the question it is necessary to recognize the problems existing in assessing the tourist labour market. These are mainly (Gaworecki, 2000):

- part-time jobs,
- seasonal work contracts,
- labour black market,
- a common practice of treating "trade and services" as a whole in statistics which makes the calculations of the exact average for tourist sector very difficult.

In spite of those problems the effort to assess tourist labour market is still undertaken. In 1995 modern tourism generated directly and indirectly employment for 212 million people in the world, i.e. 10.7% of all employed. One in ten employed people works in the tourist sector, which means that the sector belongs to the greatest employers of the world. WT&TC experts predict that the first decade of the 21rst century will be marked by a very fast growth of employment in the widely understood tourist industry (Travel, 1995). It will rise by about 60%, which means that extra 130 million people will find work in tourism. The leading party is Asia and particularly China. In 1995 over half (about 108 million) of the people employed in tourism worked there. The authors of the report predict that Southern Asia and China will be the fastest to increase employment in this sector, by up to 83.4%. In some regions tourism is the sector of economy, which employs the greatest number of people. The Caribbean Islands best illustrate the situation where every fourth worker (24.7%) works in the tourist movement service. Excellent prospects of finding good jobs in tourism will be offered for those who look for them in the countries of mid-eastern Europe, where the chances will double in the period covered by prognosis.

As has been mentioned earlier, the employment in the tourist sector is of limited, seasonal character. The results of the research carried in 1998 by International Work Bureau (IWB) in Geneva (Gaworecki, 2000) show that the seasonal work constitutes 44.6% of all tourist employment in France, 35% in Ireland and 25% in Spain. Part time employment is particularly common in highly industrialised countries. The data of IWB show that it is 12% of all employed in this sector in Switzerland and more than 30% in Denmark, Norway and Great Britain, to 51% in Australia.

The question arises whether this seasonal employment in tourism is a harmful phenomenon. It seems that for many reasons it is not. Considering the employer's economic calculation, part time employment is often a preventive measure in the situations of increased tourist movement. The employers take on workers at the peak of the season and for jobs that do not require particular qualifications. Also for workers who have been made redundant, students, or those looking for their first job this may be a good chance for training, enhancing their qualifications or changing qualifications.

Recently, due to a high rate of unemployment in Germany (particularly in the eastern lands) lots of German people undertook seasonal work in Swiss mountain resorts as chefs or waiters.

When discussing the problem of significance of tourism in the development of labour market it is essential to discriminate between the employment created by tourism directly and indirectly. The tourist expenditures create work places directly and indirectly in many branches of economy. Direct employment refers to services consumed directly by tourists. Indirect employment, however, is connected with previous services and investments (OECD: Politique, 1995).

The investigations carried by University of Tenesee and First National Bank of Hawaii (Organisation, 1966) showed that in the USA every thousand people staying in the hotels of a given region generates 279 jobs in tourism and 107 jobs indirectly connected with tourism, whereas every thousand people staying on a camping site creates only 57 jobs in tourism and 32 jobs indirectly connected with tourism.

When analysing the importance of tourism for the development of labour market, attention should be paid to its influence on local markets, particularly those of regions and towns or tourist communes. Advantageous conditions that balance local labour market are created by tourism development since it supports the creation of new work places. This results, among others, from the fact that the characteristic feature of employment in tourism is a relatively high participation of live work and a low degree of its technical background. Tourist activation of local economy becomes a factor of the growth in the work demand in the widely understood sphere of tourist movement service. It is often recognized, from the point of view of local economy development, that tourism can be more beneficial for the development of employment than investments in industry with a low expenditure in labour and what is more, highly qualified. In the area of tourist movement service the need to employ highly qualified personnel is insignificant. The scale of job positions for the needs of tourist services ranges from jobs for unskilled workers to managerial positions. It is therefore more favourable.

The role of tourism in stabilizing the population in the tourist resorts is also of great importance. Those areas, often lacking industry and having poor conditions for the development of agriculture are often places of the migration of its population. In such circumstances tourism, absorbing local surplus of work force, makes people stay in their homeland, being the source of income for those people and their stability.

A positive feature of the employment in tourism is the significant participation of women, stimulation to activity of the retired people and the possibility of getting a job in tourist services by young people, particularly students. The growth of employment in the direct tourist economy results in the increase in the demand for jobs in the indirect tourist economy. Therefore, the employment in the area of tourist movement service becomes complementary. Tourism stimulates better use of local work power; it can greatly reduce the rate of unemployment, enabling local people to earn high income.

3. Tourism and the Economic Development of the Country

In order to define the role of foreign tourism and its influence on the development of the economies of particular countries, several indices are generally considered. The basic ones are the comparison of receipts from arrival foreign tourism with gross national product, the defining of arrival tourism participation in the export of goods and services and the determination of foreign tourism significance in the balance of payments and also in balancing of debt and liabilities of the country.

The General Meeting of the International Union of Official Tourist Organizations UIOOT (the predecessor of WTO) in Tokyo in 1966 accepted the concept of perceptibility threshold of receipts from arrival foreign tourism in the economy (£azarek, 1999). The reason for the acceptance of that index was the belief that comparing the absolute volumes of receipts did not explain much, therefore it was necessary to assure the connection with the gross national product being the basic index, which characterises the state and the development of the economy. It was accepted that the receipts from arrival foreign tourism of 1% worth of gross national product and even more exceeding that value, signals that arrival foreign tourism exerts globally perceptible influence on the development of national economy.

Dynamic development of foreign tours resulted in the growth of participation of the receipts from international tourism in the global values GNP from 0.94% in 1985 to 1.42% in 1995 (Table 3).

TABLE 3. THE PARTICIPATION OF THE RECEIPTS FROM TOURISM IN THE WORLD GNP IN THE YEARS 1985-1995

Year	No of examined countries	The receipts from inter-national tourism (in bilion USD)	Total GNP (in bilion USD)	The participation of receipts from tourism In GNP (in%)
1985	158	117	12461	0.94
1987	160	174	16583	1.05
1989	165	219	19129	1.14
1991	172	272	22101	1.23
1993	183	317	23912	1.33
1995	184	398	28060	1.42

Source: Tourism Economic Report, WTO, Madrid, 1997.

On the global scale the index of 1.42% points at the significant participation of proceeds from foreign tourism in the world GNP.

As has already been mentioned foreign tourism plays quite a differentiated role in the economies of particular regions and sub regions isolated by WTO. In 1995 the participation of foreign tourism in GNP ranged from 0.58% in the region of South Asia to 2.34% in the Southeastern one. In Europe it was also high, at 2.1%. Decidedly greater disproportion appears in sub regions. Tourism plays the greatest role on the Caribbean where its participation in GNP equalled 14.2% and in Micro and Polynesia (12.8%). It should be added that in those countries, and particularly in small island countries where the index reaches 50% the highest is also so called "leakage index", which shows, among others, what part of currency is spent on import of different goods and services connected with foreign tourist service.

The next measure of the importance of tourism in the economy of a given country is the participation of proceeds from arrival tourism in the general proceeds from export. Arrival tourism is one of the forms of so-called invisible export. The highest values of that factor are connected with the countries having the best-developed tourist industry and worse functioning economy, with a particularly poorly developed export. Therefore, countries holding the highest positions in the rankings of arrivals and income (e.g. the USA or France) occupy the last positions in the tables presenting countries with the highest participation of proceeds from foreign tourism in the export in general. The first ones on the lists are such countries as: Spain, Austria, Greece, Portugal, where tourism is one of the main sources of acquiring foreign currency and the basis of their national economy.

Present liberalization of the formalities on the borders, particularly connected with passports, visas and foreign currency due to regional partnership schemes enhances the development of trade tours particularly between the neighbouring countries. The scale of such trips is bigger when the purchasers take advantage of the differences in price, the range and the quality of goods. Such a situation is particularly favourable for short, one-day departures and arrivals to buy goods and services (as it is now between Poland and Ukraine). In some countries those one-day arrivals are more important for the economy than the arrivals of tourists. Foreign tourists consume on the spot or pay retail price for the goods which they buy as souvenirs and which, in part, are also exported within the foreign goods traffic scheme, but at wholesale prices, much lower than retail prices. In the retail trade business and particularly catering business there are often different margins and after payments. They are frequent in tourist resorts. It should be also added that in tourism most shopping is done at once, in cash, whereas in foreign trade the most typical are credit settlements (Libera, 1969).

According to official calculations the foreign tourists' expenditures in Poland are 20% more profitable export than official trade export (Zbieæ, 1996). In the mass tourist movement small unit shopping becomes sometimes a mass turnover on the national scale. That phenomenon should be taken into consideration in economic policy to make use of the positive effects, which may result for the economy.

Three fundamental issues should be taken into consideration in the range of tourist turnover being goods and services export (£azarek, 1999):

- the possibility of substituting the traditional goods export by the consumption of the same products on the spot by arriving foreigners and thereby extending the export in these groups of goods, at the same time keeping or developing the traditional forms of export. It should be remembered here that export through tourist consumption permits to avoid different quota and other limitations imposed by different countries thus safeguarding their market against foreign competition;
- the export by directly buying by foreign tourists the same or other goods which appear in traditional export, also goods that would not have any chance in that exchange, which eliminates the imposed protection restrictions;
- investment alternative, i.e. investments in the area of tourist service instead of other economy lines.

The above comments point at the necessity to notice in particular national economies the possibility of substitution between goods export and the arrivals of foreign tourists and the benefits for the particular economies obtained by taking this fact into consideration in international economic relations policy.

CASE STUDY

Economic Conditions of Development Tourism in Poland

System changes, which took place in Poland in the 1980s, have led to the development of market economy with all its characteristic features such as the introduction of private ownership, the development of the market mechanism, the change of the orientation of enterprises towards gaining profits, and so on.

The necessity to take the market mechanism into consideration became the condition of getting out of the crisis, which took place in the economy on the turn of the 1980s and 1990s. The crisis also affected the tourist trade. Socialist governments treated tourism as an element of social politics in the range of the national tourism and as a field "to be under special supervision - for the privileged people" for foreign tourism. In the socialist epoch Polish tourism was characterized by the following features (Gralec, 1996):

- Centralism of management and financing,

- division into social tourism (including the developed factory tourism) and market tourism,
- the management of tourism was subordinated by social criteria instead of market criteria, which manifested itself in a great contribution of allocations while economic processes of the tourist trade subjects were being financed. In consequence of that there was lack of correlation between the price of tourist services and the expenditures which were paid in order to create a service as well as the quality of the services,
- state form of ownership of the tourist subjects was dominant,
- restriction in the development of foreign tourism, both arriving and departing tourism, which manifested itself by the passport and visa difficulties, restrictions in the possession and spending foreign currencies.

On the turn of the 1980s and 1990s, system and structural changes in Poland gave "a green light" to the rapid development of tourism, and consequently to the profits, which were flowing from tourism. The profits began to constitute a substantial contribution in the Gross National Product (GNP) of Poland.

Characterisation of the State of Tourism in Poland

Poland was recognized as "a tourist tiger" (Migdal M., 1999) by the World Travel Organization (WTO). In the years 1990 - 1998 the number of tourists grew by 600% from 3.4 million to 18.8 million, which caused the movement of Poland in the WTO ranking from the 27th position onto the 8th position. The profits grew even more spectacularly by about 2000% from 358 million USD to 8.0 billion USD, which resulted in a jump from the 64th position onto the 12th position in the ranking.

The dynamic development of the tourist trade, which has been observed in Poland since the beginning of the processes of transformation of the economy, has got its conditions in its transformations, which completely changed the Polish tourist landscape within the last ten or twenty years. We can speak here about the all-trade "effect of the domino", which was brought about by the change of the political system and the consequence of which was the opening of the borders, annulment of foreign-currency and visa restrictions, liberalization of the principles of business activity (Kotlinski , 2004). The system of central authorities, the philosophy of the macroeconomic management of the trade and the way of the management of the tourist politics were changed in tourism. Economic effects of the tourist economy exert influence on the formation of some macroeconomic factors.

The subject system of tourism has also changed. Tourism has been dominated by private firms whereas state and co-operative enterprises, which have acted so far, have been undergoing privatization processes, restricting social functions and becoming market economic subjects, which are directed at gaining profits.

However, in the second half of the 1990s in Poland after a period of rapid development of tourism and profits, which were flowing from it, there has been noted a startling decline of those factors.

TABLE 4. ARRIVALS OF TOURISTS AND ONE-DAY VISITORS TO POLAND IN THE YEARS 1994 – 2002

(In thousands of arrivals)

Years	Arrivals of foreigners	Including tourists
1994	74253	18825
1995	82244	19215
1996	87439	19410
1997	87817	19520
1998	88592	18780
1999	89118	17950
2000	84515	17400
2001	61431	15000
2002	50735	13980

Source: Institute of Tourism in Warsaw (www.intur.com.pl).

In the first half of the 1990s, the growth of the arrival tourism (Table 4) was influenced by the so-called cascade effect in a large degree. The cascade effect is described by the theory of the economy of tourism and it is connected with different levels of prices between neighboring countries and the country, which receives tourists. In relation to Poland it caused a dynamic development of the border-areas and gave visible effects in the payment balance. As the time passes, as a result of adaptation processes of both price and quantity nature in the neighboring countries, the significance of the factor of the "cascade effect" became smaller (Szubert, 1999). As a result there appeared a new challenge for subjects of tourists economy and particularly for the national tourist office, in relation to the change in the way of carrying out marketing strategies in the Polish tourism. For this purpose it is necessary to recognize accurately the conditions and economic and non-economic factors, which decide about future directions of the development of tourism in Poland.

TABLE 5. FOREIGN CURRENCY TAKINGS OF POLAND OBTAINED FROM THE ARRIVAL TOURISM IN THE YEARS 1994 – 2002

(In billion USD)

Years	Takings in general	Including tourists	One-day tourists
1994	6.1	3.6	2.5
1995	6.6	3.3	3.3
1996	8.4	4.4	4.0
1997	8.7	4.3	4.4
1998	8.0	4.4	3.6
1999	6.1	3.4	2.7
2000	6.1	3.1	3.0
2001	4.8	2.9	1.9
2002	4.5	2.8	1.7

***Source:* Institute of Tourism in Warsaw (www.intur.com.pl).**

In the years 1994 - 1997 there occurred a permanent growth of global takings of Poland, which were obtained from the arrival tourism in the understanding of the WTO, in other words including the expenditures of one-day visitors (Table 5). The reasons for that state of affairs should be seen in the abolition of restrictions (impediments) while crossing the borders and in the advantageous price relations on various goods among others. Since 1998 you may observe a permanent gradual decline in foreign currency takings, particularly on the part of one-day visitors. The government continued to maintain a higher and higher rate of zloty, which caused that the price relations between Poland and Western Europe countries are becoming smaller and smaller. It makes unfavorable inroads upon the arrivals of one-day visitors, whose overwhelming majority used to come from the former Soviet Union countries and the purpose of their arrivals was mainly trade activity.

The profits, which are obtained from tourism, constitute a serious source of financing the social development and the economic growth in the countries in which the tourist functions are developed. The quotient of takings from foreign tourism to the national revenue is the measurement, which is applied here.

In Poland, on account of very high takings obtained from tourism, and on the other hand, a small value of the Gross National Product, the contribution of the takings in the GNP is high (Table 6). The GNP amounted to 5.22% in 1995 for the sake of comparison. Unfortunately, since 1996, when it was the highest (6.24%), it has been undergoing a permanent decline, shaping itself on the level of 3.01% in the year 2001. In spite of such a great decline, the takings from tourism constitute a substantial contribution in the GNP of Poland.

TABLE 6. CONTRIBUTION OF TAKINGS FROM ARRIVAL TOURISM AT POLAND IN THE GNPIN THE YEARS 1995 - 2001

(In Million Usd - Current Prices)

Years	Takings from arrival tourism at Poland	The size of GNP	The percentage contribution of takings in relation to the size of the GNP
1995	6600	126348	5.22
1996	8400	134550	6.24
1997	8700	143066	6.08
1998	8000	157274	5.09
1999	6100	155151	3.93
2000	6100	157585	3.87
2001	4800	159427	3.01

Source: ***The author's own publications written on the basis of the data derived from the Chief Central Statistical Office.***

The budget still remains the basic instrument of public financing in tourism. The role of the budget is systematically getting smaller and smaller (Table 7). The year 1998 was a turning point because then the government assigned most money i.e., about 19 million USD onto the development of tourism, which constituted only 0.237% of the general takings obtained from tourism this year (the contribution of takings from tourism amounted to 5.09% in the analyzed year in the GNP). These numbers show how big the disproportions are between the takings from tourism in Poland and the expenditures of the government in order to support its development. In the next years a permanent decline in the expenditures of the country spent on tourism is observed, which is at the same time accompanied by the reduction of takings from tourism. In the meantime the experts from the Central Office for Planning (The Report, 2000) claim that the budget support in the amount of about 60 - 70 million USD (prices from the year 1998), in other words about four times more, is necessary in order to realise the purposes, which are directed by the state tourist policy (for example the development of agrotourism, investments on the accommodation base) and in order to support social functions of tourism (for example school didactic tourism, recreation of children and youth).

TABLE 7. THE DEPENDENCY BETWEEN THE TAKINGS FROM TOURISM AND EXPENDITURES OF THE GOVERNMENT ONTO TOURISM IN POLAND IN THE YEARS 1994 - 2001

(In Million USD)

Years	Takings from tourism	Expenditures of the government onto tourism	Contribution of expenditures in the takings (in %)
1994	6100	6.52	0.107
1995	6600	9.8	0.148
1996	8400	15.2	0.181
1997	8700	17.35	0.199
1998	8000	19	0.237
1999	6100	14.62	0.240
2000	6100	12.25	0.201
2001	4800	10.65	0.222

Source: ***The author's own publications written on the basis of the data derived from the Chief Central Statistical Office.***

Factors, Which Block the Development of Tourism in Poland

The registered significant decline of the tourist movement to Poland creates the necessity to analyse the factors, which block the growth and cause that the scale of the development is smaller than it might result from the existing opportunities.

We can divide those factors into two groups. The first group of factors lies in the surroundings of the enterprises. The second one refers to the actions, which are directly taken in the sphere of the tourist supply. On account of the conference problems and the frames of this article, we will concentrate on the first group of factors. We can include the following ones in them (Golembski, 1996):

- the conditions to conduct the politics of development in tourism - first of all the construction and modernisation of the base,
- the possibilities of the inflow of the foreign capital to the sphere of tourism, and also the creation of equal chances of investment for both home and foreign capital,
- the possibility to create the conditions in order to manage the tourist economy in the local and regional scale,
- the development of tourist information and marketing in tourism, but on the national and regional level, exceeding the possibilities and the scale of the activity of the individual enterprises, even those, which have got a large capital.

The construction and modernization of the base is a key issue, which conditions the development of tourism. The whole difficulty consists in the fact that the factors, which enlarge the risk of making decisions, get accumulated while tourism is being developed. The following factors belong to them: the necessity to engage a large capital, as a rule, a long period of time of returning the costs, which were spent, a negative influence of the temporary turnovers in tourism onto the shaping of the profit and lack of possibility to organise the stocks of service capacity.

This issue is even more essential because the base, which was inherited after the previous political-economic system is not at all adjusted to the growing demand both in the quantity and first of all quality respect, which results from the high degree of the decapitalisation of the base. It brings about the necessity to invest vast sums of money to execute necessary alterations, which may improve the quality of the services to the level, which will enable people to run service activity. The needs to reconstruct and to develop the tourist base exceed the possibilities of many investors if we consider the today's system. They cause the delays in the privatization processes, the collapse of many owners of the old base, the reduction and even the freezing of the investment activity from Polish capitals and to the growth of prices of the hotel services.

In the meantime there are almost no stimuli, which enable petty manufacturers of services to undertake an investment and repair activity. Independently from the lack of financing stimuli, you can also notice lack of professional consulting institutes, which would enable to adjust the standard of services to the tourist need.

The development of the tourist base is connected with the influx of foreign capital. The engagement of this capital can be reflected both in the direct investments (the construction of new tourist facilities) and in the indirect investments (for example while including hotels to one's own hotel chains). Unfortunately, it results from the observations that foreign investment capital is not sufficiently interested in investing in Poland. The reasons for that lie both in the administrative-legal sphere (the system of granting the licenses for the localization, the ways of pricing the buildings and land) and, first of all, they lie in the financing sphere (the tax system the credit system, the possibilities of the capital flow).

There exists an urgent need to change the faulty system of the tourist management. The modeling of the supply for tourist services must be supplemented by the funds coming from the budget to a large degree. The supply is also integrally connected with the tourist region and the co-coordinated management of numerous different subjects of this supply can be held only on the regional and local level. With the present system of the centralization of accumulation budget means and the centralization of redistribution of those means, the integrated supply for tourist service in the regions is not possible. Lack of money in the local budgets, complete lack of correlation between the quantity of the paid taxes in the tourist trade in the given region and the returned quantity of the budget means assigned for the development of tourism, is a basic factor, which blocks the development of tourism in Poland. Apart from the budget ways of financing there were to be different types of assistance programmes from the European Union. However, in practice, the access to those means is limited on the part of the local communities, small firms, and so on, because on the one hand there are strict formal requirements and on the other hand, there is lack of one's own means for co-financing the investments. The consequence of this is that large sums of money, which were granted to the Polish investors, are not taken advantage of.

CONCLUSIONS

The analysis of the accumulated empirical material shows that in spite of the deterioration of such parameters as the size of arrivals and profits, tourism occupies a significant place in the country's economy. The acceptance of the assumption that tourism is a significant factor of social-economical development implies further statements about insufficient use of this factor in the stimulation of the growth of Polish economy, which enters the next stages of system transformations. In order to make it possible, there is a necessity for far reaching and consequent government's actions, which will indicate the frames and will create conditions for the development of tourism in Poland.

REFERENCES

Alejziak W. (1999), *Turystyka w obliczu wyzwañ XXI wieku*, Albis, Kraków

Gaworecki W.W. (2000), *Turystyka*, PWE, Warszawa

Go³embski G. (1996), *Czynniki hamuj¹ce rozwój turystyki w Polsce*, Aktualne problemy gospodarki turystycznej, Zeszyty Naukowe nr 247, AE Poznañ

Gralec R. (1996), *Turystyka w warunkach gospodarki rynkowej*, Zeszyty Naukowe nr 247, AE Poznañ

Halaciñski P. (1972), *Ekonomiczne problemy wspó³czesnej turystyki miêdzynarodowej*, Ruch Turystyczny, Monografie nr 11, SGPiS, Warszawa

Kotliñski W. (2004), *The Government's role in stimulating national tourism development: the case of Poland*, in: Tourism and transition: governance, transformation and development, CABI, Wallingford, UK

Libera K. (1969), *Miêdzynarodowy ruch osobowy*, PWE, Warszawa

Lazarek R. (1999), *Ekonomika turystyki, wybrane zagadnienia*, WSE, Wroc³aw

Migdal M. (1999), *Perspektywy rozwoju turystyki na Pomorzu Zachodnim*, Firma i Rynek, 13

OCDE (1995): *Politique du tourisme international dans les pays de l'OCDE 1992-1993*, Paris

Organisation (1966) de Nations Unies pour l'Education, la Science et la Culture: *La preservation des monuments et d'autres biens culturels en liaison avec le developpement du tourisme*, 72 KK/3 Paris, 14 avril

Raport (2000) Centralnego Urzêdu Planowania, Warszawa

Szubert-Zarzeczny U. (1999), Ekonomiczne uwarunkowania turystyki w Polsce w latach dziewiêædziesi¹tych, Wybrane zagadnienia turystyki, WSZ, Wroclaw

Tourism Economic Report (1997), WTO, Madrid

Tourism Highlights 2000, Second edition, August 2000

Travel and Tourism Economic Perspective (1995)– A special Report from The World Travel & Tourism Council, WT&TC

WTO (2004) World Tourism Barometer Volume 2, No 3, October www.intur.com.pl

Zbiec E. (1996), *Wptywy z zagranicznej turystyki przyjazdowej w bilansowaniu naleznosci i zobowi¹zañ RP*, Rynek Turystyczny, nr 1.

11

THE DECISION ABOUT THE INCREASE OF INCOME AND THE REDUCTION OF COSTS IN HOSPITALITY CORPORATIONS

DRAGAN NIKOLIC

ABSTRACT

From a short-term point of view hospitality corporations is not capable of changing the fixed inputs, while in a long-term range all the costs are actually variable and a hospitality corporation can change its capacity, human resources and all the activities, i.e. its chain of values. When the advantages of the economics of scale are exhausted, further reduction of costs can be done by an internal growth or by a horizontal, vertical and conglomerate integration with other companies. Cost efficiency resp. economy and profitability are expressed through the economic value added (EVA) and through the added value return which calculates the contribution of individual segments of a corporation in the chain of values. Through a differentiation of production-service industry programme, the improvement of quality and other attributes the increase of income is achieved on the basic of the increased value (utility value) for the consumers. During the process of costs reduction it is necessary to identify their structural and executive generators (causes) in order to provide in a strategic way for a competitive advantage of a corporation through their elimination or diminishing. Instead of increasing prices, the increase of income is more and more achieved by the improvement of quality, by the innovation of production-service industry programme and by a differentiation of products and services.

Keywords: incomes, costs, decisions, hospitality corporations, management

INTRODUCTION

A hospitality corporation, as any other, will, certainly, tend to achieve the optimum combination of input that will enable it to "make" the necessary volume of turnover with the lowest expenses or the one that will make it possible for it to maximize the volume of turnover with the same total expenses. The efficiency of expenses (economy) is achieved by maximizing the input mix.

From a short-term point of view, a corporation is not capable of changing its equipment, technology, top management staff, business premises, resp. the fixed outputs, which means that the volume of turnover changes only as the result of the operation of a greater or a smaller use of the variable (changeable) inputs, as labour or raw materials. In the analysis of the relationship between short-term costs and the volume of turnover (production) the important thing is concepts of total, average and marginal costs. The analysis of structure and behaviour of the costs of a hospitality corporations (as well as of the other ones) in the short-term, when the capacity size and other fixed inputs are given, is done on the basic of the short-term cost curve. (Hughes, 1986: 104-123).

In the long run, all inputs are variable (changeable). In the long run a corporation can change its equipment, its business executives, build new hotels, close restaurants and hotels, modify its production-service process etc.

1. Relevant Starting Point in Decision Process

The aim of a corporation is to achieve the planned volume of turnover (production) the lowest expenses which will require to choose the capacity of "the right size" (optimum or the most efficient capacity regarding, the expenses which will make it possible to acquire the planned volume of turnover with the lowest expenses). The analysis of the structure and behaviour of the expenses in the long – term, when all the inputs are varialbe (and when the corporation can modify its technology, equipment and change the use of all inputs), is carried out on the basic long term average costs curve. When the corporation has used all the advantages of the economy of scale the chosen and installed capacity (or at the level of the corporation as a whole), the additional reduction of expenses can be obtained by increasing the corporation size, namely, by the corporation growth: internal (when a corporation increases its size by itself) and external (based on taking over or merging with other corporations through the forms of horizontal, vertical and conglomerat i.e. lateral merging).

The efficiency of expenses (economy) is a prerequisite of the profitability of business operations of hospitality corporations, because when the optimum mix of input is achieved, the maximal profit is achieved at the same time. Therefore the analysis of profitability is the basic for making decisions on the volume of turnover and sale where the profit is maximized, the decision on continuing or ending of business operations and on temporary or permanent closing of the corporation as well as the decision on the crucial volume of turnover when the business operations of the corporation becomes profitable. While the accounting approach to measuring expresses the profitabilit which has been acquired, the economic approach expresses profitability through indicators such as: (Besanko et al., 1996: 12)

- Economic value added – EVA, and
- Return on value-added

Economic value added is an indicator of the achieved value in the corporation which is based on the economic concept of results. It is obtained as the difference between the operating profit after the taxation and total annual expenses of the capital, which are equal to the expected returns by the owner and creditor at the moment of rendering of accounts, and not to the effective dividends and interests presented in the official financial statements. If EVA iz positive the corporation is making some value, while on the contrary it is destroying it.

The expenses of a capital depend on the sources from which it is provided. For example, the difference between the debt costs and the costs of owner's equity is because a debt isn't taxed, while the dividends are, which means that a debt is cheaper than owner's equity. The calculation of the capital costs is most often carried out according to the sources from which the capital is provided and they depend on a relative participation of each of these three sources in the overall expenses of financing. EVA means greater returns than capital costs. As long as the rate of returns on the invested capital is higher than the capital expenses, the corporation can increase the profit and profitability of its business operations, EVA is mostly used by the investors and top managers. The investors are more likely to invest into the corporations which measure its profitability by means of EVA and the indicators that can show if the rate of returns on the invested capital is higher than the capital costs. Namely, when returns are higher than capital costs, i.e. economic value added, it means that more profit is obtained, without the use of more (new, additional) capital. Thus EVA begins to be applied for determining the bonus and salary of managers (Besanko, et. al.,1996: 12).

Return on value added measures the profitability of each segment of the production-expenditure chain of a corporation and it shows how much a corporation has contributed to make the value. Return on value-added is the relation between profit (before taxation) and added value. Therefore, added value presents the difference between the sale income and overall costs of bought material inputs of every segment of the chain of value, from the purchase of raw materials and all other inputs, through production, up to the distribution of products-services to end users.

2. The Decision About the Increase of Income

The decision about the increase of income is made by a hospitality corporation on the basis of the indicators of net profitability (it is calculated by dividing the profit after taxation by the value of sale and it shows the sale return). The increase of income in hospitality corporations can be achieved by: the increase of the sale volume; the rise of the products and services price and by combining the increase of sale and the change of price. The volume of sale can be increased by: the improvement of the quality of the services; finding new ways of the use of the products (the use of the services); better distribution and "larger" scope of services; more efficient promotion by which the sale increase without the increase of costs; more strict control of overall business transactions; more successful collection of claims; better placement of cash and other liquid assets etc. The increase of income can be achieved by increasing the price of products-services. However, more and more corporations today agree that for the increase of income the most important factors are the quality of services and other attributes, reliability in "delivering" services. Instead of the rise of prices, the increase of income is more and more achieved by the improvement of quality, by the innovation of production-service programme and by the differentiation of products (services).

The aim of the differentiation is to make the customers become attached to a product (service), namely to the attributes which are incorporated into a product or the terms of offering products (services). The customers find satisfaction or utility not in the products, but in the attributes that it includes. A product differentiated in such a way, is, then, considerably different from the same or similar products-services of the competition.

While choosing among the possible ways of *value added services* a hospitality corporation must estimate how a customer will react to that benefit. The preparation is a process that includes three steps (Kotler Ph., 1997: 281):

1. ***Defining a model of values for customers***. Corporations first determine all production-service factors which can influence the concept of value by target customers.
2. ***Building a hierarchy of values for a customer.*** A corporation develops every factor in one of the four groups: basic, expected, desired and unforeseen. When applied to a restaurant it looks like this:
    a) **Basic:** The food is eatable and served on time. (However, if it is all that a restaurant does well, a customer, still, will not be satisfied).
    b) **Expected:** A restaurant has good dishes, tablecloths and towels, flowers discrete staff and well-prepared food. (These factors make the offer acceptable, but not a special one).
    c) **Desired:** A restaurant is pleasant and quiet, and the food is especially good and interesting).

d) **Unforeseen:** A restaurant unexpectedly serves coffee' between two courses and puts candies on the table after the last course has been served.

3. ***Deciding about the set of values for customers***. Now a corporation chooses a combination of tangible and intangible valves, experiences and results formed in such a way to be more efficient than the competition and to gain the loyalty and respect of customers.

To succeed, or simply to survive, corporations need a new philosophy. To win in today's marketplace, corporations must be *customer centered*; they must deliver superior value to their target customers. They must become adept in building customers, not just building products. They must be skillful in market engineering, not just product engineering. (Kotler Ph., 2003: 383)

The aim of hospitality corporations, therefore, should be the creation of superior benefits that can make it possible to keep the present and to attract the new customers. Parallel to that, the spending of resources in those corporations must be subject to this aim. To say it more precisely, every expense that is made in a corporation must be in the function of creating distinguished benefits which meet the requirements and needs of customers. The efficient strategic managing in modern corporations assumes the connecting of the income from the created utility value for the buyers with the generated costs, which is different from the period, not a long time ago, when the greatest number of strategic decisions were made in the area of marketing, production planning and engineering. (Drury, 1996: 215). Namely, in the conditions of dynamic business operations and competitive surroundings the level of income that a corporation can make on the market does not depend only on characteristics but, also on the level of utility value that its products respectively services provide for the buyers (customers). Since the characteristics of products-services, benefits for buyers, the income and costs of a corporation represent the variables of the degree of performance which are very much interconnected; there is a great need, in the practice of the developed business world, to evaluate them simultaneously. For such purpose it is necessary to have an analysis which deals more with buyers than with products, resp. with the services of a corporation. This, it could be said the crucial requirement of a management is greatly helped by the strategic analysis of costs, because it is primarily concentrated on the process of making values for buyers, resp. customers.

3. The Decision About the Reduction of Costs

When the price-elasticity of demand is high, when a corporation does not have any control over the prices of the services or when the change of prices can cause unwanted and unexpected reactions of the competition, it is unavoidable to start with the reduction, resp. with the cutting down of costs. The aim is to increase the sale returns by the reduction of costs. The reduction of costs will enable the corporation to increase its profitability without the change of prices. But the reduction costs can make it possible to reduce the price of products resp. services as well, which can result in the increase of sale, income and higher returns on the invested funds. The reduction of prices, on the basis of reduced costs, attracts also the buyers of competing corporations and leads to the increase of sale, and to a greater presence on the market. However, it is necessary to take care that the reduction of prices isn't a drastic one, because it can have as a consequence a cheap service and low quality of services. It is necessary to have in mind that a radical reduction of costs may generate costs. Therefore a prevention, control and managing of costs are a more effective approach to reduction of costs. To have a preventive influence on costs means to determine i.e. point out the generators resp. the causes of costs. The generators of costs can be:

- ***Non-economies of volume.*** They appear in every segment of the chain of costs activities (production-service cost chain). They can be eliminated by measures of simplifying the service programme with a smaller number of services that will satisfy the needs of a chosen market segment. The limitation of the range of services leads to the reduction of costs, shortening of the time of using funds and increasing the profitability of business operations. Also, by the reorganization of sale it is possible to spare the sale costs (smaller number of employees).
- ***Productivity and the effects of education and experience.*** The control and analysis of the productivity of labour and by using the effect of education and

experience the costs of business operations can be considerably reduced. Thus, during a research applied on a hotel 16 factors of productivity which a hotel manager must have in mind while analyzing (staff recruitment and selection; staff morale and satisfaction; staff training and qualifications; staff pay, bonuses and incentives; management training; customer perceptions and satisfaction; quality of service and product; advertising and promotion; forecasting; hotel facilities; new technology; weather; economic climate; competition; local events; property overheads). (Sasse et al., 1996: 154). The effects of education and experience lead to the decrease of costs (because of fewer stoppages, greater productivity of labour, faster completion of work assignments, acceleration of work process, redesigning of business process etc.).

- ***Occupancy rate*** can be a significant cause of costs, especially with hotel corporations (capital- intensive activity). If the production capacities are not used enough, fixed costs per one unit are higher and therefore the increase of the degree of utilization of production capacity is a very important source of the reduction of costs.
- ***The degree of connection in the chain of values.*** The chain of values identifies strategically relevant activities which make value and costs in business operations. If the costs of the activity in the degree chain of values significantly depend on the way some other activities are done, the connection can lead to a more significant reduction of costs.
- ***Complementary and interdependence of organizational units of a corporation***. If those parts are closely interconnected and complementary, then significant savings can be achieved if you take advantage of the economy of volume (better use of capacity by applying the knowledge which has been acquired earlier in one organizational unit and which is conveyed to the other one in respect of the reduction of costs etc,),
- ***Location as a significant cause of costs.*** It is well known how a location, for instance of a hotel influences

the degree of performance of its business operations.

- ***The effects of daily i.e. operational decisions from different levels of managing and different domains of business operations.*** They can be significant causes of costs as, for example, the decision about the costs or reduction of the programme of services; the increase or the decrease in the number of services; incorporation of a greater or smaller number of accomplishments in a service; the level of salaries and other compensations; the increase in productivity and economy; changes of the conditions things (groceries, drinks).
- ***The attributes of products i.e. services*** (products, i.e. the services of a corporation are not regarded as an entity or one unit, but as a collection of separable benefits of a greater number of attributes which attract both the existing and the potential buyers. Each product-service can be alternatively defined as a set of carefully chosen attributes which are offered to customers and which must be adjusted to their needs. These are visible and invisible benefits of a product or a service which are at customer's disposal. Attributes, therefore, represent a wide range of the elements of quality, such as reliability, functionality, safety etc.).

For the purpose of strategic analysis all the activities of a corporation that create value can be divided into: organizational with two sub-groups: structural and procedural (executive) and operational. (Hansen at al., 1997: 357). Organizational activities define the organizational structure and business process of a corporation. Within them, structural activities point out the economic structure (for example, the construction of a hotel building, the choice and structure of management, the choice and arrangement of workers, vertical integration and sl.), while procedural activities give a closer definition of the business process itself (providing capacities, engaging workers, securing quality, designing the process of providing services e.t.c.). Operational activities include daily activities which take place in a corporation (reception and checking of the material, providing services to customers, and sl.). Since the subject of the strategic analysis of costs is dealing with a long-term analysis, the focus of its interest must be organizational (structural and executive) activities.

Therefore, while determining the generators and causes of costs it is necessary to make a clear distinction between structural and executive generators of costs. Structural generators of costs appear as a consequence of the choice of activities which a corporation makes in regard to its economic structure. With regard to that, in front of each, as well as in front of a hospitality corporation there are five strategic choices which, at the same time "influence" the costs of any product resp. service, and they are: scale, scope, experience, technology and complexity. (Shank at al., 1993: 21-23).

The executive generators of costs are, also, in the function of determining long-term expenditure position of a corporation. The executive causes of costs comprise those factors which are related with the capability of a hospitality corporation to direct its services successfully towards the buyers' resp. customers. Among those factors of executive generators of costs that can improve the cost position of the corporation the following ones could be mentioned: motivation and devotion of employees by permanent improvement of the business process; total quality managing; the use of capacities; plant layout efficiency; the position of product; exploitation of the connections with buyers and suppliers.(Nikoliæ, 2005: 50-59).

The long-term expenditure position of a hospitality corporation will improve more significantly if its workers are motivated and concentrated on the permanent improvements of a business process. It is similar with governing the overall quality and the use of capacities. Costs can be reduced also by increasing the plant layout efficiency (external and internal marketing logistics). The designing of services with a smaller number of components can reduce many costs. Finally, establishing and using the relationship with suppliers and buyers resp. customers make it possible to reduce costs and, in that way, improve the competitive position of a corporation on the hospitality (tourist) market.

While making short-term decisions about the costs the usual practice in scientific literature is mainly that the costs of a corporation should be regarded through the focus of only one provoker: the scale of business activity. As a consequence of such view, a rather great number of categories (and concepts) of costs and analytical techniques have been developed (for example, fixed and variable costs, average and marginal costs, cost –scale-profit analysis, contribution analysis etc.) which, more or less were relying on the scale of business activities as the only factor which ''pushes'' or ''pulls'' the costs of a corporation.

Hospitality corporation must identify three primary functions of cost management systems: (Cooper at al., 1999: 1)

1. Measure cost of goods sold and value inventory for the financial reporting function,
2. Estimate cost of activities, products, services, and customers,
3. Provide economic feedback to employees and operator about process efficiency.

CONCLUSION

More and more corporations in hospitality today agree that for the increase of income the most important factors are the quality of services and other attributes, reliability in ''delivering'' services. Instead of the rise of prices, the increase of income is more and more achieved by the improvement of quality, by the innovation of production-service industry programme and by the differentiation of products (services).

Competitive advantage in relation to direct competitors can be gained by reducing costs and (or) increasing the value, in the course of which the mentioned ways can also be combined. In that sense it is necessary in the corporation, by means of a so-called internal chain of values, to identify mutual relationship between the activities to make it possible to adjust them in such way so that they result in the reduction of costs and the increase of the value. Reconfiguration of the chain and relocation or elimination of some activities in the chain can then lead to the improvement of competitive position of the corporation.

The reorganization of the business activities of a corporation which significantly affects the increase of income is related to the changes of a hospitality corporation services programme. The decision about the change of the programme of services is made by reexamining the services and the market and it comprises redefining as well as the change of the range of services. It means the elimination of the existing services which are little profitable and the introduction of new ones.

Under the conditions of the emerging of a new economic global structure which makes the competition even more severe, global hospitality companies are forced to change radically their attitude towards suppliers. Business organization is concentrated on key activities in the chain of values (core competence), while the other activities are carried over to those external collaborators who can do them in the best and cheapest way, contributing, in that way, to a more efficient and competitive business.

REFERENCES

Besanko, D. and Dranove D. and Shanley M. (1996) *Economics of Strategy.*New York: John Wiley & Sons, Inc.

Cooper, R. and Kaplan S.R. (1999) *The Design of Cost Management Systems - Text and Cases.*New Jersey: Prentice Hall.

Drury, C. (1996) *Management Accounting Handbook*. Oxford: Butterworth Heinemann.

Hansen, D. and Mowen M. (1997) *Cost Management*. Ohio: South-Western College Publishing.

Kotler, Ph. (1997) *Marketing Management – Analysis, Planning, Implementation, and Control:* New Jersey: Prentice-Hall, Inc.

Kotler, Ph. and Bowen, J. and Makens, J. (2003) *Marketing for Hospitality and Tourism.* New Jersey: Prentice Hall.

Nikoliæ, D. (2005) *Costs and Marketing Politics in Tourism.*: Valjevo: Valjevo Print.

Sasse, M. and Harwood-Richardson, S. (1996) Productivity Management in Hospitality and Tourism. In N. Johns (eds.) *Influencing Hotel Productivity*. London: Cassell.

Shank, J. and Govindarajan, V. (1993) *Sstrategic Cost Management:The New Tool for Competetive Advantage*. New York: The Free Press.

12

THE IMPACT OF MANAGEMENT ACCOUNTING SYSTEMS ON PERFORMANCE: AN EXPLORATORY STUDY OF HOTELS IN SLOVENIA

SLAVKA KAVCIC and GORDANA IVANKOVIC

ABSTRACT

Nowadays organizations find themselves in turbulent conditions which are mostly a reflection of growing globalization and internationalization, development of information technology, spreading of the idea of importance of knowledge as the basic element of a business process, as well as the owners' pressure to increase income and the pressure from the general public and other interested parties to hold someone accountable for socially (ir) responsible activities. All this has also an effect on the importance of accounting and accounting information. An increasingly greater emphasis has been laid upon the accounting providing information needed for making decisions. Decision-making information must be adjusted to business decisions, which in hotel organizations are of very special nature and are different from those in other business organizations, due to the special character of their activities on one hand and their international involvement on the other hand. Therefore the general accounting information determined by accounting standards (in Slovenia "Slovenian Accounting Standards") is of very little significance for decision-making. Organizations engaged in activities governed by special conditions need to develop a special accounting information system for decision-making. This is based on economic categories determined by standards, yet their combination and size must be adjusted to the specific conditions of the activities or even to the organization itself. Although nowadays various techniques are available enabling the gathering of information necessary for making decisions, the development of an appropriate information system is very expensive and the Slovene hotel industry being permanently on the brink of survival finds it difficult to cover those costs. Unfortunately, they are not aware that information leads to the establishment of conditions necessary for a more efficient business in the future. The aim of this paper is to present how developed is management accounting in Slovene hotel organizations and to prove or reject the hypothesis that organizations with a developed system of management accounting for different levels of decision-making are more efficient than those lacking this system. The article is based on the research carried out in Slovenia in hotels with over 100 rooms. First the necessary information for various decision-making levels will be introduced together with the criteria for efficiency measurement and then the basic hypothesis will be tested by relevant statistical methods.

Keywords:* *hotel industry, decision-making information, performance, Management Accounting System (MAS), financial and non-financial measures

Introduction

Accounting today is more than just an activity offering support to the management in their decision making, but rather an activity reflecting - in its solutions - wider processes in the society, thus epitomising the philosophy of each individual company. An important novelty in the developing theory of accounting is that it is not only about monetary evaluation of economic categories or about the calculation of business performance, but it tends to extend to the area of corporate social responsibility. The idea is substantiated by the fact that companies and other organisations also have social responsibility, which reaches beyond generating money for shareholders. If the interests of all the stakeholders (management, employees, customers, suppliers, the government and wider communities) are not taken into consideration, such groups could turn away from co-operating with a company, which could threaten its future performance. The operating circumstances on the one hand, which have changed in the past decade because of advances in technology - particularly IT - and the political changes on the other, brought about the globalisation of business (Kavèiè and Ivankoviè, 2004b: 134).

The first consequences of globalisation in the hotel industry can be identified in the enforcement of hotel standards as a benchmark for quality in the hotel business. Hotel chains have definitely most of the merit for such enforcement.[1] Standardisation in the hotel industry does not affect only the quality of hotel services, but influences entire business processes, as well. The current system of categorisation of hotels by quality (number of stars) and size (number of rooms), and particularly the Uniform System of Accounts for the Lodging Industry, 1996 - USALI, offers the possibility to compare hotels in terms of quality and other factors regardless of any individual hotel's location on the world map.

The business environment in the hotel industry is characterised by fierce competition and constantly changing circumstances. Each hotel is in direct or indirect competition with every other hotel. Strong competition forces the management to try to get closer to their guests' wishes, since it is the only way to achieve success. Numerous authors claim that the lodging industry lacks a sufficiently developed management accounting system (MAS) (Phillips, 1999; Mia and Patiar, 2001; Banker et al., 1999; Brander Brown and McDonnell, 1995 and others), which could offer valid information for adopting relevant decisions.

An adequate MAS helps the management to meet their customers' demand and achieve business objectives (Damonte et al., 1997). Chenhall and Morris (1986) and Mia and Chenhall (1994) state that MAS information is strongly needed, since it helps the management to pass valuable decisions, thus contributing to better achievements (cf. also Downie, 1997). MAS must therefore supply information that the management is asking for (Dent, 1996; Govidarajan, 1984; Mia and Chenhall, 1994; Simons, 1990). In the paper, we give a brief illustration of Slovenia, its hotel industry, the level of development of MAS in Slovenian hotels and its influence on performance.

SOME INFORMATION ON SLOVENIA AND SLOVENIAN HOTELS

Slovenia is a Central-European country, which up to recently has been part of Yugoslavia. The country - located between Croatia, Hungary, Austria and Italy - became independent in 1991. There over 2 million people living on an area of 20,273 km^2. The country's capital is Ljubljana with around 300,000 inhabitants. On 1 May 2004, Slovenia became a member country of the European Union. Slovenians speak Slovenian, which is a Slavic language. The currency is the Slovenian tolar (SIT) (1€ = 240 SIT) and the euro is expected to be adopted as the national currency in 2007. In 2004, per capita gross national product amounted to € 12,977 and was 5.3 percent higher than in 2003.

Economic growth in Slovenia is strongly affected by tourism, which is one of the major economic opportunities creating an additional market for selling Slovenian products and services abroad. The tourism capabilities of a country are limited by the features of the tourism offer, one of the most important components of which are the lodging capabilities available. Such capabilities are defined in the international hotel industry as the number of rooms (USALI). Hotels play a predominantly important role in the overall lodging capabilities, which increased since 1990. Detailed figures regarding Slovenia's lodging capabilities in the past five years are shown in Table 1. We can see that in 2004 hotel rooms accounted for over 60% of all lodging capabilities, while in 1990 their share amounted to less than 40%.

The research done by Kavèiè et al. (2001: 40) shows that almost one half of all the hotel rooms' fall within the three-star category, mostly in coastal, thermal-bath and other hotels. Thermal-bath hotels hold a 25.2% share of all the rooms; coastal hotels have 24.1%, while others have the remaining 50.7% of rooms (Kavèiè et al. 2001: 38)

The characteristics of the hotel industry (60% share of fixed costs) make the occupancy rate and important factor for success. In 2000 - 2004, the average occupancy rate was 47.2% (the highest in 2004 at 49.6% and the lowest in 2000 at 43.2%). The figure is well below the European average of 66% (Kavèiè and Ivankoviè, 2003: 21). The number of overnight stays increased together with the occupancy rate: from 4,223 in 2000 to 4,619

TABLE 1: ROOMS IN HOTELS AND OTHER LODGING FACILITIES[2]

Lodging facilities	**1990**	**1995**	**1999**	**2000**	**2001**	**2002**	**2003**	**2004**
Hotels	13,311	13,840	13,350	13,642	12,639	12,684	13,290	13,566
Other lodging facilities	20,626	14,115	16,250	16,600	17,447	17,590	16,941	8,893
TOTAL	33,937	27,955	29,600	30,242	30,086	30,274	30,261	22,495

Source: http://www.stat.si/doc/statinf/2005/si-90.pdf/ (11.9.2005)

in 2004 (Reports of the Statistics Office of the Republic of Slovenia, 2005)

The increased number of overnight stays and the improved occupancy rate should have brought about better performance of Slovenian hotels. The actual figures are shown in Table 2, which contains data on the economic growth of hotel companies, broken down by various economic categories.

Data in Table 2 show that in most of the years in the period concerned, hotel companies in Slovenia operated at a loss. Only 2002 and 2003 were an exception, when the overall performance was positive. The change is the result of thermal baths being included in the hotel industry. If we compare the performance of Slovenian hotels with that of the average economy, we see that an average Slovenian company achieved positive results, since the average share of profits in operating revenues amounted to 2.18% and the average growth rate was 21%. Added value per employee amounted to € 25, while the growth rate in the period 2000 - 2004 was 6%. What are the reasons for such a situation? We can find them both on the side of revenues and of the expenses. Data show a positive trend on the revenues side, since net sales revenues in the period concerned increased on average by 7% On the other hand, the analysis of operations in the period concerns tells us that costs were growing more rapidly than the revenues. The average increase in costs in the period 2000-2004 was almost 9%. This means that the reasons for poor performance of the hotel industry are to be found on the costs side.

Hotels are able to manage their costs if they have a good information system. Such a system must be adapted to be used by people having the possibility to manage costs at various levels, i.e. General Managers (GMs) and Department Managers (DMs) - Food & Beverage Departments and of Rooms Department; at lower levels of responsibility. Both need a MAS that could help them make decisions. Our fundamental assumption is that one of the reasons for the poor performance of hotels are inadequate MAS, which - in the Slovenian hotels - are used by people, who make decisions at various levels. (Ivankoviè, 2004: 3-4)

TABLE 2: SOME ECONOMIC PERFORMANCE INDICATORS FOR HOTEL COMPANIES IN SLOVENIA IN 2000 - 2004

Economic Categories	2000	2001	2002	2003	2004	Average growth(with 2000 as baseline)
Net sales revenues (in €)	230,100	243,612	266,782	281,716	306,957	7.27%
Net profit or loss for the financial year (in €)	-11,636	-575	4,863	11,710	-9,549	
Average number of employees on the basis of hours worked in the accounting period	6,461	6,293	6,302	6,340	6,578	2.16%
Added value per employee (in €)	20	21	24	24	25	1.7%

***Source:* *http:/www1.gvin.com/FinancniPodatki/* (9.9.2005).**

WHAT IS AN ADEQUATE MANAGEMENT ACCOUNTING SYSTEM?

Proper MAS are an ever-greater need in the hotel industry. The reason for that is fierce and increasingly global competition. Adequate MASs offer hotel managements the possibility to make decisions that could ensure the best possible results, taking into account the special characteristics of the hotel business. Such special features show in the high share of fixed costs in overall expenses and in the need to be focused on marketing (Brander Brown and Harris, 1998; Kotas, 1975; Harris, 1995). Services in the hotel industry are complex, personal, intangible, heterogeneous and simultaneous (Jones and Lockwood, 1989; Fitzgerald et al., 1991). The same can be said about the products, which feature elements of services, as well as those of retail and manufacturing (Harris, 1995). An idea gaining ground (Brander Brown and Atkinson, 2001: 130) is that the key factor of success in the hotel industry is focus on people: employees and guests.[3] The starting point for creating an adequate MAS is to know the objectives of an individual hotel and the strategies to achieve them (Geller, 1985a, b, c[4]; Brotherton and Shaw, 1996, Croston, 1995; Jones, 1995; Brander Brown, 1995) and the recognition of the factors that are of critical importance for the achievement of the objectives. If we equal success with achieving goals, we can say that the critical factors for achieving objectives are the same as the CSFs.

Since the demand for computerised information needed for budgeting, making decisions, supervising and comparing, MAS proves to be an important reason for introducing a high-quality IT system. Such a system will not ensure the results wanted if the responsibilities for making decisions are not clearly divided among the various levels of management before the introduction of an IT system. Hotels usually have different decision-making levels. Managers at each level make decisions within their areas of competence and responsibility. MASs must supply information to each decision-making level that is customised for the purpose and the subject of decisions. We believe that MAS information is useful as much as the management are satisfied with them. If the information is not supplied on time, the management will not use it, even if it would like to do so. The opposite is also true: If the management are not satisfied with the information supplied, they will not use them (Kavèiè and Ivankoviè, 2004a: 550). Satisfaction with the MAS is therefore very important.

Kaplan and Norton (1992) have proven that organisations operating in today's dynamic circumstances need to resort to different criteria (financial and non-financial indicators and indices) and also take into account multiplication performance measures. Only by taking into account both financial and non-financial measures, such as profitability, customer satisfaction, response time, team work and productivity, we are able to create a consistent MAS that will also offer a more effective system of supervision. The lodging industry is a people-oriented industry. The economic and financial success of a hotel therefore depends on the attitude and behaviour of employees, the development of new products and services, as well as on customer satisfaction. Hotel companies must think of their performance in a wider sense (from the point of view of employees, customers, suppliers, management etc) and not only from a merely financial perspective, which is only the epitome of all the aspects of success. Hotel General and Department Managers must recognise equal importance to the goals of all the stakeholders and not only of their shareholders. The achievement of the objectives of all the stakeholders (i. e. guests, employees, strategic partners, community) can be measured by both financial and non-financial measures.

Hotel companies usually work in a very competitive environment. Competition brings about threats, as well as opportunities. Proactive companies study their environment very carefully and take into consideration all the economic, social and technological changes, accepting them as opportunities and challenges (Rolfe, 1992: 33). As hotels prepare a new product on the basis of the opportunities perceived, the new idea is often copied by competitor hotels, which shortens the useful life of such product or service. Hotels that are market leaders must therefore constantly progress if they want to keep their cutting edge. New competitors can easily enter the hotel industry, since almost every hotel is able to manipulate prices through special discounts and packages. Managements are aware that hotels need to catch the interest of customers, turning customer satisfaction into a priority. If they want to be successful at it, they have to know their competition well and know which differentiated products or services (at low costs) can be their competitive advantage. Hotels will be able to ensure long-term success, if they have satisfied customers that keep returning and thus contributing to hotels' good performance. Another key factor for every hotel are the business strategy adopted, alongside with Strategic Management Accounting (SMA), which supplies information for monitoring the implementation of the business strategy.

After having taken into consideration the theoretical assumptions, we have formulated ***our basic hypothesis that hotels with an adequate MAS perform better than those without one.***

In order to test our hypothesis, we first had to define what adequate MAS should look like. We have maid the claim that a company has an adequate MAS, if the MAS meets the following requirements:

1. General Managers - GMs and Department Managers - DMs (Food & Beverage Departments and Rooms Department) of the hotel:
   - 1a) use the information of the MAS frequently;
   - 1b) both management levels are satisfied with the timeliness and usefulness (contents) of the information.
2. When evaluating their performance, top management and heads of units of a hotel pay equal attention to monetary and non-monetary measures.
3. The hotel:
   - 3a) has a well-defined business strategy - measured by its mid-term budget (3 years or more); and
   - 3b) uses SMA for making decisions - measured by its own market share and the market shares of its main competitors and their prices.

We were also aware that Slovenian hotels might fulfil one, two or all the conditions above. For this reason, we had to counter balance some of the conditions. Having made a thorough analysis of the importance of individual factors, the experts of the Faculty of Economy at the University of Ljubljana, those of the Slovenian

Institute of Auditors, along with experts in the areas of tourism, agreed that it would be better to compare factors with comparable importance.

The next step in our analysis was to check whether Slovenian hotel companies have MASs. This would enable us to conclude whether inadequate MASs are to be blamed for the poor performance of some Slovenian hotels. The analysis of such verification is given below.

METHODOLOGY

We analysed the development level of MASs in Slovenian hotels. In 2002, we decided to survey the managements and the guests of Slovenian hotels. For this purpose, we have prepared two questionnaires: one for the guests and one for the hotel's management. In the first questionnaire, we asked the guests about their opinion on the quality of a hotel, their satisfaction, while classifying the guest (thermal-spa, domestic, foreign etc). The questionnaire for hotel managements was divided into eight chapters: general information on the hotel, use of MAS at various level of decision-making, marketing information, information about the employees, company owners and IT systems, performance measures, implementation of SMA and methods used for budgeting. Both questionnaires were sent to 51 hotels, which accounts for all the hotels in Slovenia with more than 100 rooms. The questionnaires were filled out by 39 hotels or 76% of the entire section of the industry.[5] Of all the hotels included, 61% have three stars, the others have four.

Below, we are giving a list of the criteria that we used for evaluating the development of MASs in Slovenian hotels, along with the connections between the use of MASs and performance.

CRITERIA FOR EVALUATING VARIABLES

Consistently with the definition of the development level of MASs and their importance for the performance of a company, we also had to define our relative and absolute variables.

Definition of Independent Variables:

1) **We measured the importance of MASs** in making business decisions separately in the case of hotel General

and Department managers (Food & Beverage and separately rooms), through:

- Frequency of use of MAS information[6] in taking short- and long-term business decisions (condition 1a)
- Satisfaction with the timeliness and usefulness of MAS information[7] (condition 1b); and

2) **Evaluation of the importance of goals**[8], which we adapted from Kaplan's and Norton's BSC (1992) (condition 2).
3) **The hotel has a well-defined business strategy and SMA,** if it has a long-term strategy, a consequent strategic plan for three or more years, and if it follows its own market share and the market shares of its main competitors, as well as their prices (condition 3).

Definition of Dependent Variables:

We have defined the business performance of a hotel to be a dependent variable, measure by financial and non-financial measures.

1) In order to guarantee comparability, we have chosen two financial indicators in the period of the preceding five years and we have de-flationed the figures: average net sales revenues per room (USALI, 1996; Kwansa and Schmidgall, 1999: 90) and average profit or loss per room.
2) Among the non-financial criteria we have taken into consideration: the number of new products in the preceding two years, the average share of return guests in the preceding five years (Foster et al., 1996) and the average number of employees per room in the period of the preceding five years (USALI, 1996).

RESULTS OF THE ANALYSIS OF THE DEVELOPMENT LEVEL OF MASS AND ITS INFLUENCE ON THE PERFORMANCE OF SLOVENIAN HOTELS

We started by verifying the first condition to be met by a hotel, if we are to say that it has a developed MAS. So, we first checked how frequently MAS information is used in Slovenian hotels by directors and heads of units for taking short- and long-term decisions. By applying the reliability rate of a measuring scale (Cronbach's alpha), we first verified the internal consistency of the measuring scale, composed by the variables used to check the frequency of use of MAS information. We obtained a high value for the rate (0.92), which proves that the variables have been chosen correctly.

Table 3 shows that **(condition 1a)**, on average, General and Department Managers of hotel use the information for taking decisions with the same frequency, which is above average, since the arithmetic mean was 3.9 on a five-degree scale. General and Department Managers do not show considerable statistic differences in using information on customer satisfaction ($t = 0.96$; $p>0.5$) for making short- and long-term decisions.

Table 4 shows the levels of satisfaction with the MAS information, in terms of timeliness and usefulness (contents) of the information supplied to General and Department Managers (condition **1b**)

Table 4 shows that General Managers tend to be more satisfied with the timeliness and usefulness of information than the Department Managers. Both groups show a combined rate of 74%.

The second condition for having an adequate MAS, is to pay the same level of attention to financial and non-financial goals when General and Department Managers evaluate the performance of their hotel. When checking the difference between General and Department Managers in terms of goal importance, we see a considerable statistical difference between General and Department Managers in giving more importance to financial goals than to non-financial ones ($t=3.97$; $p<0.5$), while there are no statistically relevant differences between the treatment of non-financial goals by General and Department Managers ($t=-0.176$; $p>0.5$) The arithmetic mean of the answers on a five-degree scale is shown in Table 5.

The data show (Table 5) that top management, i.e. General Managers, pay the same amount of attention to financial and non-financial goals, while heads of units tend to be more focused on non-financial than on financial objectives. The results make sense, since Department Managers are faced with non-financial issues (customers' complaints, fluctuations of staff and quality of

Table 3: Use of Mas Information for Taking Short- and Long-term Decisions

VARIABLES	Decision-making level	AM-S	AM-L	AM Total
Effectiveness of promotion and sales	GMs	3.9	4.1	4.0
	DMs	3.1	3.2	3.1
Costs of goods and services	GMs	4.5	4.5	4.4
	DMs	3.7	3.7	3.7
Booking system and marketing strategy	GMs	3.7	4.0	3.9
	DMs	3.2	3.2	3.3
Guest satisfaction	GMs	4.5	4.6	4.5
	DMs	4.2	4.1	4.1
Profitability of department	GMs	4.3	4.6	4.5
	DMs	3.5	3.6	3.6
TOTAL	GMs	4.2	4.4	4.3
	DMs	3.6	3.6	3.6
TOTAL (GM + DM)		3.9	4.0	3.9

Legend:
GMs = General Managers
DMs = Department Managers of Food & Beverage and of Rooms
AM-S = arithmetic mean of a short-term decision
AM-L = arithmetic mean of a long-term decision

services) on a daily basis, while financial questions are more remote to them.

Table 4: Satisfaction Of Hotel Management's With the Timeliness and Usefulness of Mas Information

VARIABLES	Decision-making level	AM
Timeliness of MAS information	GMs DMs	3.9 3.4
Usefulness (contents) of MAS information	GMs DMs	4.0 3.5
TOTAL	GMs DMs	3.9 3.5
TOTAL	(GM + DM)	3.7

Table 5: Importance Of Financial And Non-Financial Goals For Hotel General And Department Managers

VARIABLES	Decision-making level	AM
Financial goals	GMsDMs	4.23.4
Non-financial goals	GMsDMs	4.24.2
TOTAL	GMsDMs	4.23.8
TOTAL	(GM + DM)	4.0

The third condition that we have set for good MAS is composed of a well-defined business strategy and the use of SMA. Business strategy was defined as the adoption of a long-term strategy, while SMA meant that the management knew their market share and the market shares of their main competitors along with their prices.

The analysis of the answers received is shown in Table 6.

The figures show that most Slovenian hotels meet the third condition for a good MAS.

The level of compliance with the three conditions is shown in Table 7.

Table 6: Use of SMA and Definition of Business Strategy

VARIABLES	AM
Long-term strategy	3.8
Knowing one's own market share	3.5
Knowing the market shares of the major competitors	3.0
Knowing the prices of the main competitors	4.6
TOTAL	3.7

Table 7: Level of Development of Mass in Slovenian Hotels

Condition	AM
Frequency of use of information (1a)	3.9
Utility of information (1b)	3.7
Use of monetary and non-monetary measures (2)	4.0
Long-term strategy and SMA (3)	3.7
TOTAL	3.8

If we consider the presence of all the conditions set out for good MAS in Slovenian hotels, we can conclude that 74% of hotels have well-developed MAS. The level of development of MASs in Slovenian hotels indicates that they should be successful.

The following step was to verify whether the hotels with a good MAS perform better than those that do not. In order to answer this question, we gathered information on the average performance of the hotels surveyed in the preceding five years. In line with the definition of performance measures, the financial and non-financial measures are shown in Table 8. We have divided the hotels in coastal, thermal-spa and others.

The data indicate that thermal-bath hotels are the most successful in terms of net sales revenues per room, while the others do not perform that well. Thermal-bath hotels also tend to have a larger number of new products. In terms of profit or loss and a lower number of employees per room, the coastal

TABLE 8: HOTEL PERFORMANCE MEASURES

Type of hotel	Net revenue per room (in €)	Net profit per room (in €)	No. of employees per room	Portion of return guests	No. of new products
Thermal baths	17,283	1,933	0.68	0.15	10
Coastal	16,233	2,004	0.54	0.04	8
Other	12,142	-1,104	0.37	0.15	1

hotels are more successful than the thermal baths. Other hotels tend to achieve the worst financial results, in spite of having, on average, fewer employees per room.

According to our hypothesis that hotels with a good MAS tend to perform better, the figures would indicate that thermal-bath and coastal hotels have good MASs, while the others have not. Therefore, the next step was to verify the level of development of MASs in the different types of hotels. We have discovered that thermal-bath hotels have comparably developed MASs (3.82 on a five-degree scale), followed by coastal hotels (3.80 on a five-degree scale), while the other hotels are in the last position (3.23 on a five-degree scale). The result proves that the hotels with better-developed MASs do perform better than those without one.

Since several equally important factors have been taken into consideration in defining adequate MAS, we had to verify the connections between individual factors of MAS development with performance. For this purpose, we have calculated the Pearson's correlation rate. The results have shown that none of the MAS factors can considerably affect the level of success. Neither rate that we have calculated has exceeded the value of 0.0368. The only factor to achieve this value was the correlation rate between net sales revenues per room and the frequency of use of a MAS for making long-term decisions by hotel General Managers. The rates calculated therefore have no explanatory value. The results have confirmed our expectations, since figures on the business performance of Slovenian hotels show that most of them perform poorly, in spite of having relatively well-developed MAS.

DISCUSSION

Figures show that in most cases Slovenian hotels show poor economic performance. This could lead us to say that they have inadequately developed MASs. The analysis of the answers showed that the average level of MAS development is comparably good, since it reaches 3.8 on a five-degree scale.

The fundamental assumption of our paper was that the hotels with better developed MASs perform better than those without one. The hypothesis has been only partially proven. Thermal-bath hotels have the highest net sales revenues per room and the largest number of new products. Coastal hotels have the highest profit per room and the lowest number of employees per room. Both types of hotels have MASs at similar levels of development, while the other hotels, with less developed MASs, also tend to perform worse. When we verified the correlations between individual factors of MAS development against performance, we did not find any . We have to conclude therefore that the development of MASs does not affect the performance of Slovenian factors as other factors do. This conclusion has also been proven in the case of thermal-bath hotels. The reason for their success is mostly their monopolistic position in the market, since most of their guests are supplied by the government's Health Insurance Institute. The hotels have agreements stipulated with the Institute, on the basis of which they have better occupancy rates, revenues and cash flows. The agreements also guarantee prices and timely payments. For this reason, the thermal baths pay less attention to costs and achieve lower profits in spite of higher revenues. The opposite can be said about the coastal hotels, which operate in market conditions and therefore have to be more focused on managing costs. For this reason, they have better profits per room in spite of lower revenues per room. Thermal-bath hotels use their MASs mostly to define the prices for their services that can be charged to the Health Insurance Institute.

The results of our research of Slovenian hotels failed to confirm our hypothesis, which is something unusual. There have been many researches published in the world about the issue that we have investigated in Slovenia and their conclusions were that MAS development levels affect the performance of hotels. (Brander Brown and McDonnell, 1995; Mia and Clarke, 1999; Mia and Patiar, 2001; Brander Brown and Atkinson, 2001; Phillips, 1999; Denton and White, 2000; Huckestein and Duboff, 1999; Collier and Gregory, 1995; Dunn and Brooks, 1990; Noone and Griffin, 1997; Brotherton and Shaw, 1996; Croston, 1995; Jones, 1995). One reason for different results in Slovenia is probably due to the fact that in the system of self-management socialism - in force in Slovenia up until 1990 - there was no global competition, which would force companies to weight the positive and negative sides of individual business decisions. The need for considerate decision-making based on adequate information only made its appearance in Slovenia once the economic system has been changed in all the companies, including hotels. Hotels, as other companies as well, gather information for making decisions. The question remains, whether such pieces of information are relevant and whether they are being used. An answer to this question will have to be given by future studies.

FOOTNOTES

1. Eight great hoteliers have to be credited with the development of hotel chains and hotel standards: Cesar Ritz, Elsworth Statler, Conrad N. Hilton, Ralf Hitz, Ernest Henderson, Howard Dearin Johnson, Willard Marriot and Kemon Wilson (for more about that cf. Avelini, 1998, p. 64-70).
2. The Statistics Office of the Republic of Slovenia classifies the following facilities as other types of lodging: boarding houses, motels, inns, overnight accommodations, apartments, camping sites, mountain huts, company vacation facilities, vacation facilities for youth, other vacation facilities, tourist farms with accommodation, private accommodation, other accommodation facilities, temporary accommodation facilities and marinas.
3. Also rising is the belief that hotels need a higher level of information among employees, since the employee's morale and customer satisfaction are two key areas.
4. By taking into consideration the characteristics of individual companies, Geller identified the goals that are typical of the entire industry, such as critical success factors (CSF) and criteria.
5. Hotels who did not answer are located in different parts of Slovenia and differ in size. This means that the unanswered questionnaires do not imply that hotels of a certain size or in a certain region in Slovenia have been left out .
6. The frequency of use of MAS information was measured by using a five-degree scale of importance (ranging from 1-never to 5-very often), previously used by Mia and Patiar (2001); ibid. Also Chenhall and Morris (1986); Mia and Clarke (1999); Simons (1990). We measured the use of MAS information in five different units separately: effectiveness of advertising and marketing, prices of products and services, booking systems and marketing strategies, customer satisfaction and profitability of units.
7. The level of satisfaction with MAS information was measured with a five-degree scale, ranging from 1-not satisfied to 5-very satisfied.
8. We have grouped the goals in financial (monetary achievements and results compared to the budget) and non-financial goals

(customer complaints, fluctuations in staff numbers and quality of services).

REFERENCES

Avelini, H.I. (1998) *Kontroling: Upravljanje poslovnim rezultatom.*Opatija: Faculty of tourism and hospitality management.

Banker, R., Potter, G. and Srinivasan, D. (1999) An empirical investigation of an incentive plan based non-financial performance measures. *The Accounting Review* (forthcoming).

Brander Brown, J. (1995) Management Control in the Hospitality Industry: Behavioral Implications. In P.J. Harris (ed.) *Accounting and Finance for the International Hospitality Industry* (pp. 183-201). Oxford: Butterworth-Heinemann.

Brander Brown, J. and Atkinson, H. (2001) Rethinking Performance Measures: Assessing Progress in UK Hotels. *International Journal of Contemporary Hospitality Management* 13 (3), 128-135.

Brander Brown, J. and Harris, P.J. (1998) Organizational Culture and Control in a Strategic Planning Context: Implications for the International Hospitality Industry. In R. Teare, B. Farber and G. Brown (eds) *Global Directions for Hospitality and Tourism Development*. (pp. 105-131). London: Cassell.

Brander Brown, J. and McDonnell, B. (1995) The Balanced Score-card: Short-term Guest or Long-term Resident? *International Journal of Contemporary Hospitality Management* 7 (2-3), 7-11.

Brotherton, B. and Shaw, J. (1996) Towards an Identification and Classification of Critical Success Factors in UK Hotels plc. *International Journal of Contemporary Hospitality Management* 15 (2), 113-135.

Chenhall, R. and Morris, D. (1986) The Impact of Structure, Environment and Interdependence on the Perceived Usefulness of Management Accounting Systems. *The Accounting Review* LXI (1), 16-35.

Collier, P. and Gregory, A. (1995) The Practise of Management Accounting in Hotel Groups. In P.J. Harris (ed.) *Accounting and Finance for the International Hospitality Industry* (pp. 137-159). Oxford: Butterworthe-Heinemann.

Croston, F.J. (1995) Hotel Profitability: Critical Success Factors. In P.J. Harris (ed.) *Accounting and Finance for the International Hospitality Industry* (pp. 295-315). Oxford: Brookes University.

Damonte, L., Rompf, P., Bahl, R. and Domke, D. (1997) Brand Affiliation and Property Size Effects on Measures of Performance in Lodgings Industry. *Hospitality Research Journal* 20 (3), 1-16.

Dent, J. (1996) Global Competition: Challenges for Management Accounting and Control. *Management Accounting Research* 7, 247-269.

Denton, G.A. and White, B. (2000) Implementing a Balanced-scorecard Approach to Managing Hotel Operations. *The Cornell Hotel and Restaurant Administration Quarterly* 2, 94-107.

Downie, N.J. (1997) The Use of Accounting Information in Hotel Marketing Decisions. *International Journal of Hospitality Management* 16 (3), 305-312.

Dunn, K.D. and Brooks, D.E. (1990) Profit Analysis Beyond Yield Management. *The Cornell Hotel and Restaurant Administration Quarterly* 31 (3), 80-90.

Educational Institute of the American Hotel & Motel Association (1996) *Uniform System of Accounts for the Lodging Industry*. New York.

Fitzgerald, L., Johnston, R.S., Brignall, T.J., Silvestro, R. and Voss, C. (1991) *Performance Measurement in Service Businesses*. London: Chartered Institute of Management Accountants.

Foster, G., Gupta, M. and Sjoblom, L. (1996) Customer Profitability Analysis: Challenges and New Directions. *Cost Management* (Spring), 5-17.

Geller, A.N. (1985a) Tracking the Critical Success Factors for Hotel Companies. *The Cornell Hotel and Restaurant Administration Quarterly* February, 76-81.

Geller, A.N. (1985b) The Current State of Hotel Information Systems. *The Cornell Hotel and Restaurant Administration Quarterly* May, 14-17.

Geller, A.N. (1985c) How to Improve Your Information System. *The Cornell Hotel and Restaurant Administration Quarterly* August, 19-27.

Govindarajan, V. (1984) Appropriateness of Accounting Data in Performance Evaluation: An Empirical Examination of Environment Uncertainty as an Intervening Variable. *Accounting Organization and Society* 9 (2), 125-136.

GV IN Finanèni podatki. Online documents at URL http://www1.gvin.com/fipo2005 [11.9.2005].

Harris, P.J. (1995) A Development Strategy for the Hospitality Operations Management Curriculum. *International Journal of Contemporary Hospitality Management* 7 (5), 29-32.

Huckestein, D. and Duboff, R. (1999) Hilton Hotels: A Comprehensive Approach to Delivering Value for All Stakeholders. *The Cornell Hotel and Restaurant Administration Quarterly* August, 28-38.

Ivankovic, G. (2004) Performance measurement in the hotel industry. PhD thesis, University of Ljubljana.

Jones, T.A. (1995) Identify Managers Information Needs in Hotel Companies. In P.J. Harris (ed.) *Accounting and Finance for the International Hospitality Industry* (pp. 163-182). Oxford: Butterworth-Heinemann.

Jones, T.A. and Lockwood, A. (1998) Operations Management Research in the Hospitality Industry. *International Journal of Hospitality Management* 17, 183-202.

Kaplan, R.S. and Norton, D.P. (1992) The Balanced Scorecard: Measures that Drive Performance. *Harvard Business Review,* January-February, 71-79.

Kavcic, S. and Ivankovic, G. (2003) *Vzpostavljanje razmer za pridobivanje raèunovodskih in drugih podatkov potrebnih za metodologijo USALI v Sloveniji*. Research Report. Ljubljana: Faculty of Economics - University of Ljubljana.

Kavcic, S. and Ivankovic, G. (2004a) Influence of management accounting of efficiency of tourism and hospitality management in Slovenia. In Z. Ivanoviæ (ed.) *17th Biennial International Congress Tourism & hospitality industry 2004: New trends in tourism and hospitality management: congress proceedings* (pp. 659-678). Opatija: Faculty of tourism and hospitality management.

Kavcic, S. and Ivankovic, G. (2004b) Performance measurement in the hotel industry. In E. Monèekova (ed.) *International conference: Tourism in the process of the european integration and globalization* (pp. 134-140). Bratislava: Dom techniky ZSVTS.

Kavcic, S., Ivankovic, G., Klobuèar, N. and Vidic, D. (2001) *Raziskava Analiza mo□nosti spremljanja uspešnosti poslovanja po metodologiji Horwath v slovenskih hotelskih podjetjih*. Research Report. Ljubljana: Faculty of Economics - University of Ljubljana.

Kotas, R. (1975) *Market Orientation in the Hotel and Catering Industry*. London: Surrey University Press.

Kwansa, F. and Schmidgall, R.S. (1999) The Uniform System of Accounts for the Lodging Industry. *The Cornell Hotel and Restaurant Administration Quarterly*, December, 88-94.

Mia, L. and Chenhall, R. (1994) The Usefulness of MAS Functional Differentiation and Management Effectiveness. *Accounting, Organization and Society* 19(1), 1-13.

Mia, L. and Clarke, B. (1999) Market Competition, Management Accounting Systems and Business Unit Performance. *Management Accounting Research* 10 (2), 137-158.

Mia, L. and Patiar, A. (2001) The use of management accounting systems in hotels: an exploratory study, *International Journal of Hospitality Management* 20, 111-128.

Mia, L. and Patiar, A. (2001) The Use of Management Accounting Systems in Hotels: An Exploratory Study. *International Journal of Hospitality Management* 20, 111-128.

Noone, B. and Griffin, P. (1997) Enhancing Yield Management with Customer Profitability Analysis. *International Journal of Contemporary Hospitality Management* 9 (2), 75-79.

Phillips, P.A. (1999) Performance Measurement System and Hotels: A New Conceptual Framework. *International Journal of Hospitality Management* 18 (2), 171-182.

Rolfe, A.J. (1992) Profitability Reporting Techniques Bridge Information Gap. *The Journal of Business Strategy* 13 (1), 32-37.

Simons, R. (1990) The Role of Management Control Systems in Creating Competitive Advantage: New Perspective. *Accounting, Organizations and Society* 15, 127-143.

Statistièni urad Republike Slovenije. Online documents at URL http://www.stat.si/doc/statinf/2005/si-90.pdf [11.9.2005].

WTO Tourism Higlights, Edition 2003. Online documents at URL: http://www.hotelbenchmark.com/Features/articles/031013 WorldT ourism Org_Highlight... [31. 5. 2004].

13

THE CRETAN RESORT CYCLE FROM WEALTHY EXPLORERS AND CRUISERS TO MASS TOURISM

KONSTANTINOS ANDRIOTIS

ABSTRACT

The increasing demand of international tourists for holidays has resulted in a rapidly increase of the number of tourist destinations. To explain destinations development the life cycle approach has been widely adopted. According to Butler (1980) destinations pass through a predictable sequence of six stages. These stages are: exploration, involvement, development, consolidation, stagnation and decline or rejuvenation. In each life cycle stage there are changes in the morphology, the types of tourists' visitation, and residents' attitudes towards tourism. Through the presentation of historical data from the start of the 20th century up to now, it is the aim of this paper to document these changes by providing evidence from the island of Crete. Five stages of tourism evolution are evident, namely: the era of 'wealthy' explorers, the era of cruisers, the Second World War and the Civil War, the reconstruction of the tourism industry, and the era of mass organised tourism. The findings confirm that today the island is on the maturity stage, tourism has resulted on substantial changes on the island's coastal resorts and various attempts are required by the private and the public sectors to avoid decline.

Keywords: ***resort cycle, tourism, Crete***

INTRODUCTION

Various studies (e.g. Gilbert, 1939; Defert, 1954; Stansfield, 1978; Young, 1983) have attempted to illustrate the various stages of resort evolution through the concept of the life cycle. However, up to date Butler's (1980) hypothetical model of resort evolution is the most widely accepted model suggesting that "resorts become unattractive with the passage of time, as visitor numbers increase and their carrying capacities are exceeded, and are unable to compete with other newer resorts" (Smith, 1991: 192). According to this model the stages of resort evolution are: exploration,

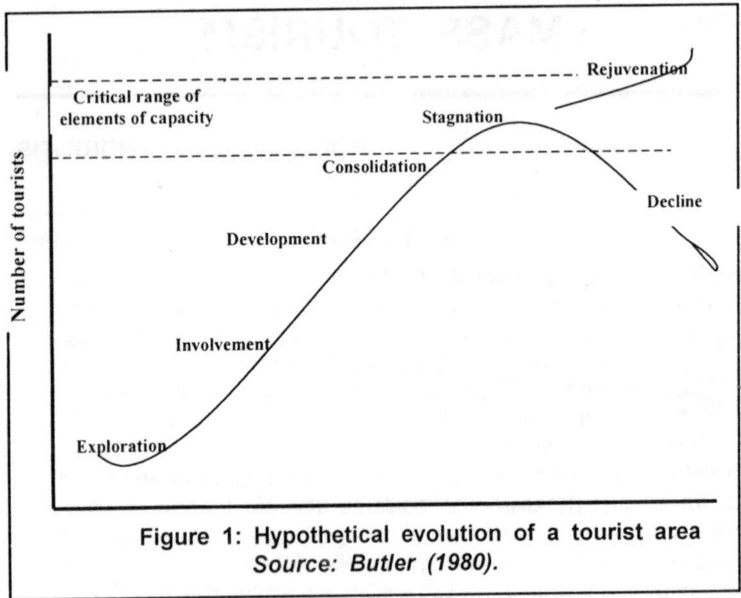

Figure 1: Hypothetical evolution of a tourist area
Source: Butler (1980).

involvement, development, consolidation, stagnation and decline or rejuvenation (Figure 1).

Crete is a Greek island that has experienced significant levels of growth in tourism over the last 30 years. As a result, tourism is now the largest economic activity of the island and many coastal resorts have been developed. Although the island has undergone significant changes between the early arrivals of tourists and today, there is a remarkable negligence of research towards these changes. Despite the significance of tourism for the island, not many studies have been conducted to investigate whether Crete, as a tourist destination, has passed through the stages identified by Butler's life cycle model. As a result, it is not known the stage of the life cycle that Crete is today, and what attempts are required to develop further its tourism industry and avoid negative effects in the future. To address this research negligence this study was undertaken with the aim to review Butler's resort cycle of evolution and test this model in the case of Crete. This paper is divided into three sections. Section one reviews the stages of Butler's model of resort evolution. Section two presents the life cycle stages of the island of Crete. The final section provides the conclusions of the study.

RESORTS CYCLE OF EVOLUTION

According to Butler (1980), resort areas undergo an evolutionary cycle of six stages. These stages are analysed below.

In the *exploration stage* the resort is isolated with a 'sleepy' appearance and with little or no development. Prior to the commencement of tourism development a settlement, perhaps a village, which is fishing and or agricultural orientated is present. A limited number of businesses exist. The provided facilities are used and owned by locals. The beachfront is not developed, and may consist of only one or two houses erected for the sea view and the proximity of the beach. Tourists are restricted by lack of access and facilities. There is only a road that connects the settlement with an urban centre and some smaller roads for access to farming land and the fishing port. Only small numbers of adventure tourists (explorers, allocentrics, poets and painters) discover the destination, making individual, non-institutionalized travel arrangements and having limited impacts on the area. These tourists are welcomed by the locals.

In the *involvement stage* visitors from the overcrowded urban centres are attracted by the relaxing and unspoiled landscape of the resort. Local entrepreneurs realise the economic significance of tourism and begin to provide facilities and services to tourists. The first hotel, built to higher-than-local standards, is constructed that according to Johnston (2001: 16) can be termed a 'pioneer hotel' and its opening represents a critical event because it catalyses tourism development at the destination. This hotel draws a new sort of tourists to the destination, tourists' numbers increase, as well as tourism impacts. Some jobs are created for locals and the demand of foreigners' leads to the production of local handicraft, and art items for sale to tourists. Pressures may be placed on the public sector to provide infrastructure, and a seasonal pattern emerges. At this stage community begins to adapt to the tourist trade and advertising to attract tourists can be anticipated (Andriotis, 2001a). A coastal road is constructed for access to the hotel and the second houses on the shore.

Given the success of the first hotel in attracting tourists, there is a kind of "neighbourhood effect" with the increase in the construction of more accommodation, infrastructure, commercial, and recreational facilities and second homes facing the sea. As a result, the resort expands and reaches the stage of *development*. The number of tourists increases and at peak periods far outweigh the size of the local population. Many locals appear to tolerate tourism unwanted effects because of its substantial economic effects (Bramwell, 2003). The increase in tourist arrivals is helped by the improvement of accessibility to the resort through the extension of the road network. It is more profitable for locals to sell their land for the construction of tourist enterprises than to continue traditional activities. Consequently, residences are displaced away from the beachfront in order to provide space for tourism development. The number of incoming workers increases and more residences are constructed to accommodate the imported workforce. Local agricultural and cattle production cannot provide the quantity and perhaps the quality of food demanded by enterprises and many foods are imported. Likewise the local handicraft production is not enough and imported souvenirs are sold in the shops of the resort. Large-scale investments are undertaken and local involvement and control of development declines rapidly and the tourist trade is taken over by outsiders. With the increase of tourist arrivals, most traditional houses are converted for business purposes.

In the *consolidation stage* a drastic reduction of beach width occurs because of the construction of more accommodation establishments and businesses. The indigenous population is being pushed further away from the beachfront. "A well delineated business district has taken place, some of the older deteriorating facilities are perceived as second rate", and local efforts are made to extend the visitor season and market area (Agarwal, 1992: 196). Building construction follows international standards of garish and conflicting architectural styles rather than the traditional local one. As the amount of capital for construction increases, buildings are getting greater and taller and high-rise hotels along and at back of the beach indicate the resort has reached the 'international' form" (Johnston, 2001: 14). The road network expands further in order to provide access to the accommodation establishments, businesses and residences. Residential areas, displaced away from the beachfront, continue to increase in size in order to accommodate the incoming workforce. Some businesses directed to the passing trade are also constructed on the road leading to the beach. Many beaches become inaccessible for the locals because of the ribbon development of accommodation establishments, businesses and second homes along the shore. A major part of the local economy is tied to tourism, but native residents may find themselves excluded from major attractions. The resort expands in a contiguous manner, without satellite development (Smith, 1991: 197). The rate of increase in the number of visitors declines, although total numbers are still on the rise and exceed permanent residents. As a result of an oversupply of hotel rooms and other tourist facilities, prices fall and the market attracted is the four S's market (sun, sea, sand and sex) exclusively organised by foreign tour operators. The community perceives some negative effects and antitourist sentiment may emerge.

When the resort reaches the *stagnation stage*, the tourism landscape becomes dominant and little room is available for further expansion. As a result, accommodation establishments are constructed in inland areas. The resort has become urbanised and its capacity levels are reached or exceeded, to the extent that it loses the local quality that made it attractive in the first place Tourism related developments along the beachfront and the inland areas, as well as the increasing tourist activities have led to the degradation of the resort complex and the tourist product has been seriously weakened or diminished (Young, 1983).

Although the resort now has a well-established image, it is no longer in fashion and property turnover is high. Few new establishments open, facilities depreciate in value and local ownership of tourist facilities increases. "A direct result of the lack of direction and regulation of resort growth has been the proliferation of environmental and social problems, poor infrastructure provision and deteriorating resort ambience as these destinations sprawl in an uncontrolled manner" (Smith, 1992a: 209).

The end of the cycle is marked by the *post-stagnation* phase, which may result in *decline,* if the tourist market continues to wane and the resort is not able to compete with newer resorts, or *rejuvenation*, through the development of an artificial attraction, e.g. the introduction of casinos, as Stansfield (1978) reported for Atlantic city.

Butler contended that most tourist destinations evolve in this pattern and cited Mexico as an example. Numerous other studies have suggested that Butler's life cycle model applies to various destinations, such as Lancaster County (Hovinen, 1981), Laurentians, Quebec (Lundgren, 1982), the Grand Isle resort of Louisiana (Meyer-Arendt, 1985), Malta (Oglethorpe, 1984), Vancouver Island (Nelson and Wall, 1986) and Minorca (Williams, 1993).

Other researchers found Butler's model incapable of explaining the tourism evolution of some resorts and proposed modifications or alternative models that better fitted the development process of particular resorts. Among these studies Haywood (1986) proposed a variety of possible tourist-area cycles of evolution that mav occur as opposed to Butler's model. Similarly, Choy (1992) suggested that it is better to treat each destination individually, as a unique entity, and taking the case of Pacific island destinations, proposed that different approaches may be required from those, which have been applied to other regions of the world. Exceptions to the process may also occur in case authorities decide to control development and limit the construction of tourist facilities before the destination reaches the stagnation stage. In this case the resort remains in the involvement, development or consolidation stage and is slow to reach the remaining stages of evolution. In addition, there is a possibility to jump stages

(Prideaux, 2000). As Goncalves and Aguas (1997: 13) state about more recently developed destinations; the first stage is being gradually reduced and sometimes even disappears, giving as example the Cancun of Mexico, where the resort has been transformed rapidly to a mass tourist destination without passing the first stages of resort cycle.

THE CRETAN RESORT CYCLE

Through the presentation of historical data from the start of the 20th century up to now the following stages are evident for the island of Crete, and more specifically, for the island's tourism developed north coast.

The Era of 'Wealthy' Explorers:

The thirst of knowledge and the fascinating quest for and discovery of the ancient Greek world attracted the first travellers to Crete. As Greger (1988) notes: "small numbers of archaeologically or classically educated foreigners came on what amounted, for them, to a sacred pilgrimage" (p.112). The Minoan ruins, the environment, art, history and literature of Crete, and the Greek legends of 'gods and heroes' made the island famous abroad. As Kardasis (undated) states "for archaeologists, architects, painters, classicists and amateur historians, one of life's goals was a journey to Greece: to locate ancient sites, to discover ancient monuments and churches, to meet and talk to the contemporary Greeks". Enlightened by their trips to Crete, many wealthy artists and men of letters originating mainly from western European countries wrote books about the island (e.g. Pashley, 1837; Sieber, 1823; Spratt, 1865).

The small number of visitors was accommodated by locals, since there were no hotels to accommodate them. Private accommodation was available only in large cities and villages, mainly in the form of inns of an unacceptable quality. As Aetoudakis (1968) reports before 1900 only eight-accommodation establishments with a total capacity of 173 beds were available in Crete. These establishments were mainly attracting peasants with their animals and passing-by traders (Ethniki Foni, 1971).

The Era of Cruisers:

Improvements in the sea transport shortened the time required for journeys and reduced costs, "meaning that it could be made by larger numbers of people and indeed from social strata that had been excluded in the past" (Kardasis, undated). As a result, it became possible for Western societies to organise cruises to the Eastern Mediterranean with Crete one of their stopovers. The first organised tourists to Crete arrived in the early 20th century. They used to arrive at the capital city of Heraklion to visit a few antiquities, such as Knossos Palace and the Museum of Heraklion, and the same day departing to other Greek or Mediterranean destinations. Visitors' consumption was very low (less than 2 to 3 dollars), mainly because of the short stays and the type of all-inclusive holidays offered by the cruisers. The limited amount of money spent by tourists on the island stayed within the local economy since imports were limited. For example, in 1932 a local newspaper reported a loss of foreign exchange from the French navy's arrival, due to beer shortage, since beer was not produced or imported in Crete (Drasis, 1932).

Before the Second World War, tourists to Crete numbered only a few thousand. To increase tourist arrivals and length of stay, 17 hotels of a total capacity of 371 beds were established between 1920-1940. Although the share of local ownership within these hotels is not known, foreigners played a major role in developing the island's hospitality industry. For example, the first to realise the need for hotels in the city of Heraklio and to take the initiative to construct the first hotel of the 19th century was the flour merchant Dimitrios Zeis who came from Konstantinoupolis in 1901. Likewise, many other foreigners invested in hotels, such as the hotel Anatoli in Heraklio that was owned by an Italian and the only hotel in Ierapetra, named the hotel of France, was owned by the French lady, Madam Gitar.

The Second World War and the Civil War:

Attempts by the Greek authorities to increase the number of tourist arrivals, such as the opening of Heraklion airport in 1939, came to an end with the emergence of the Second World War. The fierce resistance of Cretans against German occupation from 1941 to 1944 resulted in the destruction of the modest infrastructural facilities of the island. For example, three of the best hotels of Heraklion (Knossos, Pallas and Minos) and the airport of Heraklion were destroyed by bombing (Stavrinidis, 1983). Even after the end of World War II a savage civil war between the Right and the Communist movements did not leave any opportunities for tourism development. As a result, between 1940 to 1950 only three new hotels of a total capacity of 82 beds were constructed in Crete.

The Reconstruction of the Tourism Industry:

After the end of the Civil War in 1949, Crete enjoyed political stability, and the island's infrastructure was partially restored. The Greek National Tourism Organisation played a significant role in increasing visitation to Crete by chartering cruisers that included Crete as one of their stopovers.

As a result of political and economic stability in the 1950s nine new hotels enriched the island's hospitality industry. Statistics indicate that altogether 2,315 hotel beds were available in Crete during 1962. Most of them were for local traffic and only 950 were of an acceptable quality. Nearly 60% of the latter were in the city of Heraklion and its surroundings, 15% in Chania, 15% in Agios Nikolaos, and only 10% in Malia, Archanes, Souda, Ierapetra, Sitia and Paleochora. In 1963, visitors to Crete were originated from the USA (27,3%), the United Kingdom (19,4%), Germany (17,1 %) and France (11,2%).

Through the spread out effect, small seaside villages, dispersed in close proximity to the urban centres of the island, started to attract the first excursionists. A large number of accommodation establishments were built during the 1960s in the northern coastal areas to take advantage of sandy bays and proximity to the main urban centres and the airports. As a result, between 1960 to 1967 41 hotels with modern facilities added 1615 beds in the existing capacity that totaled in 1968, 4,185 beds (Aetoudakis 1968). The expansion of the island's tourism industry has resulted in changes in local economic activity. As Kousis (1989) found in Drethia with the arrival of tourists, "the number of farmers decreased dramatically, while the number of small shopkeepers and wage earners increased considerably" (p.332). Likewise, once contact with tourists developed, the local population started to demand imported products, previously consumed only by tourists, and as a result, per capita consumption of local wine and raki (the local spirit) diminished and foreign/ imported drinks, such as beer, whisky, and vodka have replaced them (Andriotis, 2003a; Moore, 1995; Wickens, 1994).

The Era of Mass Organized Tourism:

When the airport of Heraklion became international in 1971, and charter flights started to land, the mass organised tourists started a new era of commercialisation for Cretan tourism. Tourism in Crete was characterised by a rapid growth of tourist arrivals, increasing from 211,000 in 1973 to 728,000 in 1980, and slightly more than 2.5 million tourists in 2003 (Figure 2). The upturn in arrivals encouraged further hotel construction (Figure 3), since the Government attempted to spread building activity towards under developed regions which had seen little development in the 1960s.

After Greece's accession to the EU in 1981, significant amounts of funds started flowing to the island and pushed its economy forward (Briassoulis, 2003: 102). Many of these funds came from foreign companies. Although, the share of foreign ownership of the island's tourism industry is not known, the local elite of oil-merchants and soap-makers in Rethymno still owns five out of the six large hotel establishments and 25% of the hotel beds, although they own only 7.9% of the hotel units (Papadaki-Tzedaki, 1997).

The problem of foreign dominance in terms of tourist arrivals is evident in Crete. In 2003, 24.2% of the tourists who visited the island were from Germany, 18.9% from Britain and 15.7% from Scandinavian countries. On the other hand, the share of Greek nationals bednights was only 7.2%. Although the island is a mixture of civilizations and cultures from the past, there is an increasing dominance of tour operators in the Cretan tourism industry, reflecting high external influence on the island's tourism industry (Andriotis, 2003b). In 1997, it is estimated that on average each tourist spent during his holidays in Crete 365,349 GRD, approximately €1,072 (TEI, 1998). Forty-two percent of this expenditure was paid to foreign tour operators for the purchase of the tourist package (transport and accommodation). Of the remaining 58%, 24% was spent on shopping, 17% on catering, 12% on local transportation and five percent on services (TEI, 1998). As a result, foreign tour operators keep a high share of tourist consumption, and, metropolitan tourism companies play a crucial role in the island's tourism industry because they determine tourists' choice through advertising and promotion and

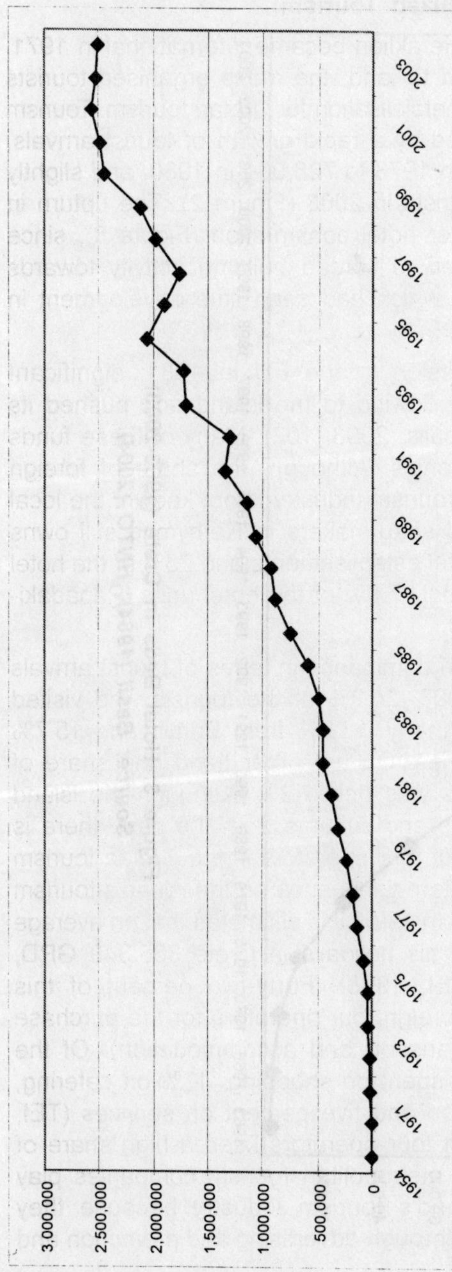

Figure 2: Tourist arrivals in Crete (1954-2003)
Source:* *Basil (1964); HNTO (2004).

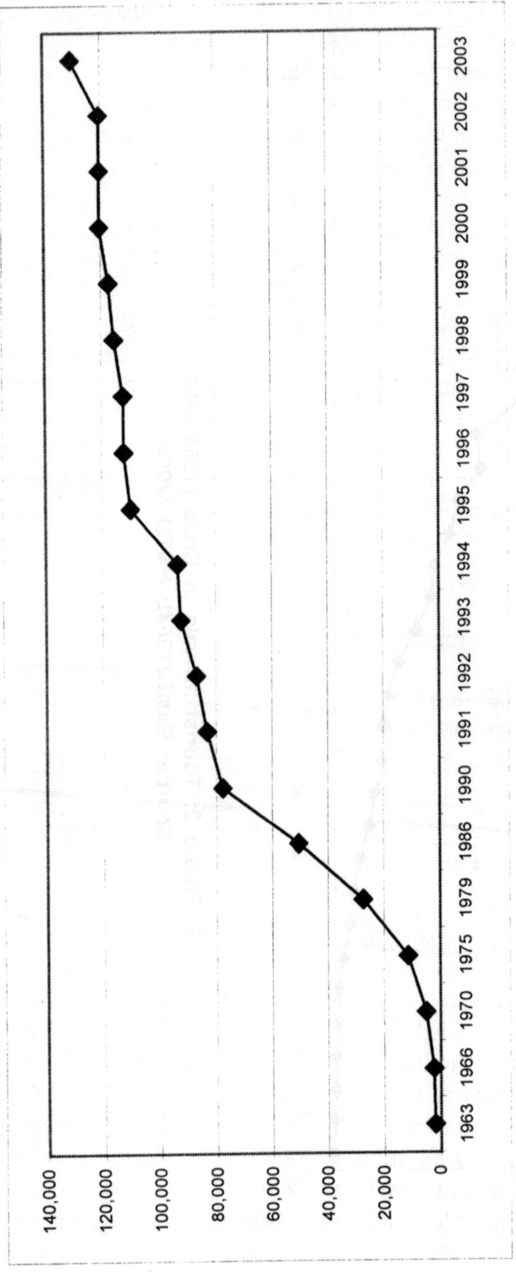

Figure 3: Hotel Beds in Crete (1963-2003)
Source: Basil (1964); HNTO (2004).

due to the trend toward inclusive tour packages organised exclusively in origin countries (Andriotis 2000; 2003b; 2003c). Briassoulis (2003) estimates that foreign tour operators control 70% of tourist beds through various arrangements. This weakens self-reliance and local control of development, and there is high leakage of money out of the local economy, seriously reducing the industry's potential for generating net financial advantages and growth of the local economy.

CONCLUSIONS

This paper has tried to outline the evolution of Cretan coastal resorts by applying Butler's model in the case of Crete through the presentation of historical data from the start of the 20th century up to now. Despite the constrain of data availability for the island of Crete, it is evident that the most important change in Crete since World War II has been the development of tourism, at first slowly, then at increasing pace under the dictatorship of Colonels from 1967 to 1973 (Hopkins, 1977: 235). Although the discussion undertaken in this paper formed a basis for the understanding of Cretan tourism, it was not clear enough the identification of life cycle stages and their turning points. In reality, Butler's model application in the case of Crete was constrained by data availability. In addition, the plethora of resorts in Crete, each of which may vary in terms of timing of foundation and rate of development, made difficult the detailed determination of the turning points that the island's coastal resorts passed through each stage of the resort cycle. For example, many locations of the Southern coast are in the early stages of the life cycle mainly due to access difficulties.

Nevertheless, the exploration stage, characterized by farming and traditional activities, was very long, not only because of the lack of infrastructure, but also because of the Second World War and the subsequent Civil War. The mid 1960s was the time that most resorts started to reach the involvement stage and there has been a fast growth of tourism places by the construction of tourist accommodation, businesses and other types of buildings frequently functioning as second home areas for the population of the island's urban centres. During early 80's most of the island's coastal resorts started to reach the development stage and tourism started to be a dominant economic activity for the island.

Today, most Cretan resorts are at the point of maximum touristic impact and have either reached consolidation, or leading towards stagnation. The Greek government has recognized many areas of the island as saturated and no further construction of accommodation establishments is allowed. Concurrently, local authorities seek to increase the product appeal and tourist spending by promoting alternative forms of tourism, the environmental and cultural resources of the island and attempting to diversify the tourist product through construction of golf courses and the improvement or construction of infrastructure (Anagnostopoulou et al., 1996; Region of Crete, 1995; 1998). By doing this, an attempt is made to forestall the decline stage of the island's tourism industry.

However, current attempts are not sufficient. Future tourism development of the island should be directed towards economic, social and environmental sustainability by increasing economic benefits and involve residents in the decision making process, preserve culture and environment and provide a diversified product to the tourist traffic. In order to avoid negative impacts, there is a need to draw a master plan with listed priorities and strategies for the future development of the island (Andriotis, 2001b). Tourism should be seen as a development strategy that uses local resources, but, if carefully managed, and residents maintain sufficient control of the development process, it can remain in place for future generations for the local population, as well as incoming tourism.

To conclude, despite the negative consequences of unplanned evolution of tourism in Crete the island has some of the limited unspoiled beaches in the Mediterranean. Many coastal areas, mainly in the underdeveloped southern part, have kept their natural beauty. The economic significance of coastal resorts for the local communities suggests that their number will increase in the future. Therefore, there is a need for careful planning, financing, and policy implementation if the problems of past unplanned resorts development are to be avoided or at least minimized (Smith, 1992b: 319).

BIBLIOGRAPHY

Aetoudakis, D.E. (1968) Tourism Infrastructure in Crete - Hotels. Athens.

Agarwal, S. (1992). The resort cycle revisited: implications for resorts.

In: Cooper, C.P. and Lockwood, A. (eds). *Progress in Tourism, Recreation and Hospitality Management*. Vol. 5. Chichester: Wiley, 194-208.

Anagnostopoulou, K., Arapis, T., Bouchy, I. and Micha, I. (1996) *Tourism and the Structural Funds - The Case for Environmental Integration*. Athens: RSPB.

Andriotis, K. (2000) *Local Community Perceptions of Tourism as a Development Tool: The Island of Crete*. PhD thesis. Bournemouth: Bournemouth University.

Andriotis, K. (2001a) Strategies on resort areas and their life cycle stages. *Tourism Review* 56(1/2), 40-43.

Andriotis, K. (2001b) 2001 ENVIRONMENT AND SUSTAINABILITY: Tourism Planning and Development in Crete. Recent Tourism Policies and their Efficacy. *International Journal of Sustainable Tourism* 9(4), 298-316.

Andriotis, K. (2003a) Tourism in Crete. A form of modernisation. *Current Issues In Tourism* 6(1), 23-53.

Andriotis, K. (2003b) Dependency on Tour Operators. Problem Faced by the Cretan Tourism Businesses and the Views of their Owners/ Managers'. *International Journal of Hospitality and Tourism Administration*, 4(3), 23-48.

Andriotis, K. (2003c) Problems Faced by the Cretan Tourism Industry as Perceived by the Business Sector. *Tourism: An International Interdisciplinary Journal* 51(1), 21-30.

Bramwell, B. (2003) Maltese Responses to Tourism. *Annals of Tourism Research* 30(3), 581-605.

Butler, R.W. (1980) The concept of tourism area cycle of evolution: implications for management of resources. *Canadian Geographer* 24 (1), 5-12.

Choy, D.J.L. (1992) Life cycle models for Pacific island destinations. *Journal of Travel Research* 30(3), 26-31.

Defert, P. (1954) Essai de localisation touristique. *Tourist Review* 9(1), 110-119.

Drasis (1932) The Arrival of the French Navy, 15th April, p. 1, [in Greek].

Ethniki Foni (1971) The Inns. 22nd March, [in Greek].

Gilbert, E.W. (1939) The growth of inland and seaside health resorts in England. *Scottish Geographical Magazine* 55, 16-35.

Goncalves, V.F.C. and Aguas, P. M.R. (1997) The concept of life cycle: an application to the tourist product. *Journal of Travel Research* 35(1), 12-22.

Greger, S. 1988 Village on the Plateau: Magoulas - a Mountain Cretan Village in Crete. Warwickshire: Brewin.

Haywood, K.M. (1986) Can the tourist-area life cycle be made operational? *Tourism Management* 7(3), 154-167.

Hopkins, A. (1977) *Crete: Its Past, Present and People*. London: Faber and Faber.

Hovinen, G.R. (1982) Visitor cycles: outlook for tourism in Lancaster county. *Annals of Tourism Research* 9(4), 565-583.

Johnston, C.S. (2001) Shoring the foundations of the destination life cycle model, part 1: Ontological and epistemological considerations. *Tourism Geographies* 3(1), 2-28.

Kardasis, V. (undated) *Greece - Travels through time*. Athens: Hellenic National Tourism Organisation.

Kousis, M. (1989) Tourism and the Family in a Rural Cretan Community. *Annals of Tourism Research* 16(3), 318-332.

Lundgren, J.O.J. (1982) The tourist frontier of Nouveau Quebec: functions and regional leakages. *Tourist Review* 37(2), 10-16.

Meyer-Arendt, K.J. (1985) The Grand Isle. Louisiana resort cycle. *Annals of Tourism Research* 12(3), 65-73.

Moore, R.S. (1995) Gender and alcohol use in a Greek tourist town. *Annals of Tourism Research* 22(2), 300-313.

Nelson, R. and Wall, G. (1986) Transport and accommodation: changing interrelationships on Vancouver Island. *Annals of Tourism Research* 13(2), 239-260.

Oglethorpe, M. (1984) Tourism in Malta: a crisis of dependence. *Leisure Studies* 3, 147-162.

Papadaki-Tzedaki, S. (1997) *Endogenous Tourist Development in Rethymno: Development or Underdevelopment*. PhD thesis. Rethymno: University of Rethymno, [in Greek].

Pashley, R. (1837) *Travels in Crete*. London: John Murray.

Prideaux, B. (2000) The resort development spectrum – a new approach to modelling resort development. *Tourism ManagemenT* 21(3), 225-240.

Region of Crete (1995) *Plan of Regional Tourism Policy for Crete*. Unpublished, Heraklio, [In Greek].

Region of Crete (1998) *Regional Strategy 2000-2006*. Unpublished, Heraklio, [In Greek].

Sieber, F.W. (1823) *Travels in the Island of Crete in the Year 1817*. London: Sir Richard Phillips.

Smith, R.A. (1991) Beach resorts: A model of development evolution. *Landscape and Urban Planning* 21, 189-210.

Smith, R.A. (1992a) Beach Resort Evolution: Implications for Planning. *Annals of Tourism Research* 19 (2), 304-322.

Smith, R.A. (1992b) Review of Integrated Beach Resort Development in Southeast Asia. *Land Use Policy* 9, 209-217.

Spratt, A.B. (1865) *Travels and Researches in Crete*. London: John Van Voorst.

Stansfield, C.A. (1978) Atlantic city and the resort cycle. Background to the legalisation of gambling. *Annals of Tourism Research* 5(2), 238-251.

Stavrinidis, N. (1983) Roidi's Casino. Heraklio: Knossos, [in Greek].

TEI (1998) *Expenditure of Incoming Tourists, Its Level and Articulation in the Region of Crete*. Heraklio: Technological Educational Institute of Heraklio and EC, [in Greek].

Wickens, E. (1994) Consumption of the authentic: the hedonistic tourism in Greece. In A.V., Seaton, ed., *Tourism: The State of Art*. Chichester: Wiley, pp. 818-825.

Williams, M.T. (1993) An expansion of the tourist site cycle model: The case of Minorca (Spain). *Journal of Tourism Studies* 4(2), pp.24-32.

Young, B. (1983) Touristisation of traditional Maltese fishing-farming villages. *Tourism Management* 4(1), 35-41.

SECTION D

DESTINATION MANAGEMENT

14

POLITICS OF PLACE AND THE ROLE OF POLICY MAKERS IN THE CREATION OF OPPORTUNITIES FOR COMMUNITY ORIENTATED EVENTS AND FESTIVALS

RAZAQ RAJ

ABSTRACT

This article explores how local policy makers use community events and festivals to secure political power and influences among local residents and businesses. Qualitative data was collected on the social and political impacts of festival on their local community. Festivals are seen principal platform for collective participation in expressions of traditional and contemporary culture in the United Kingdom and around the world.

The findings of this research show us that Notting Hill carnival creates the different cultural diversity for the local community and enhances party-goers to enjoy the sights and sounds of the spectacular costumed troupes and parading traditional Caribbean music. The case study demonstrates how the Notting Hill carnival has developed to become a centrepiece event for the local economy each year. It is now strongly viewed by the local community and small businesses that carnival is the significant part of the attracting tourism to the area and value the tourist market as a vital tool for the development of local economy.

Keywords: policy makers, local identity, local economy, community festivals

INTRODUCTION

This paper initially reviews literature related to the politics of place and the role of policy-makers in the creation of opportunities for community orientated events and festivals, which contrast with tourist orientated events, which have tenuous links with local communities. Within the review of literature related to politics and events we consider the issue of 'festivalisation' and the creation of festivals for politically expedient applications such as for regeneration and economically driven purposes. Moreover, paper will argue that community based events and festivals provide an opportunity for the celebration of local identity and community empowerment and create tourism for the local area.

The case study within this paper explores the political and policy dynamics of the multi-cultural festivals and events with the UK, and the positive contribution that these events play in solidifying community relations with public policy makers. The discussion in the case study is included on how the social and political impacts of festival on their local community can be measured as an aid to funding sustainable local festival.

The desire for festivals and events is not specifically designed to address the needs for any one particular group. The hosting of events is often developed because of the tourism and economic opportunities addition to social and cultural benefits. Many researchers have contested that local community's plays vital role in development of tourism through festivals. (E.g. Getz, 1997, Key Leisure Markets, 2001, Stiernstrand, 1996). It was thought in the past that the political and policy makers have relatively modest implications on the event and tourism. However, this is been changed in the last two decades. The local festivals do have political impact on them to show local dignitaries and politicians fulfilling their purpose, but also on the revitalisation of the social identity, through festivals, celebration of local culture and art, crafts and music. According to the WTO Business Council, the current trend in almost all regions of the world is towards semi-public but autonomous tourism organisations involving a partnership with both private sector and regional and/ or local authorities.

The community festivals are seen by the local politician a great educational settings for all cultures. Festivals in the community setting help to teach different culture to all groups in a community. The festival is a good concept to use in order to share ethnic minority cultures and values through dance, music, art, and foods with the larger community.

DEVELOPMENT OF FESTIVALS AND CELEBRATIONS IN THE LOCAL COMMUNITY

Today the Festivals are seen principal platform for collective participation in expressions of traditional and contemporary culture in the United Kingdom and around the world. The festivals attract increasing numbers of visitors to each festival from within the region; country and they also develop links with the global community worldwide. Getz (1997) provides this definition of festivals "A festival is a public themed celebration". Smith (1990, p.128) provides a more detailed definition of Festival.

> **"A celebration of theme or special event for a limited period of time, held annually or less frequently (including one-time only events), to which the public is invited"**

These definitions make it is possible to consider festivals as a celebrations of a theme or event, held annually, infrequently, or as a one off an individual or historic event and that they are open to the general public. The festivals and celebrations in local community has generally been accepted and recognised. The local festivals create entertainment for residents and visitors, but also contribute to a sense of community, building bridges between diver's community groups and giving them an opportunity to come together and celebrate their history, diversity and the place they live in. The major festivals in the United Kingdom have become a major tourist attraction over the last decade. As stated by Prescott (2003):

"We live in one of the most urbanised countries in the world and our cities play a critical part in our national and regional life. They are home to many millions of people, they are the backbone of our economy, and they are centres of learning, of culture, sport and invention. All this brings richness to our cities that give them a unique status".

(Leeds: *A Business City*, p3.)

Goldblatt (2002, p.1) introduces festivals events as a:

"Kaleidoscope of planned culture, sport, political, and business occasions: from mega-events like Olympics and World fairs to community festivals; from programs of events at parks and attractions to visits by dignitaries and intergovernmental assembles; from small meetings and parties to huge conventions and competitions."

Yeoman, Robertson, Ali-Knight, Drummond & McMahon-Beattie (2004) states that culture is central to promoting the continued renaissance of the city and has a role to play in creating a more inclusive and sustainable community. They go on to describe that the use of cultural events has become an even more important economic and culture drive for towns and cities. Research has shown that that it is possible that public sector marketing strategies can utilise events for pre determined objectives that bring benefits to the location and the community (Gold & Ward, 1995).

"Culture has both a material and a value dimension and includes a wide range of activities including arts, media, sports, parks, museums, libraries, the built heritage, the countryside, pay grounds and tourism".

(*Guidance to Local Authorities*, December 2000.)

Enhancing Leeds' cultural offer is a key factor in creating the vibrant and liveable environment that helps attract and retain knowledge economy workers and residents (The Leeds Initiative: The Business City, p22). Yeoman, Robertson, Ali-Knight, Drummond & McMahon-Beattie (2003) stated that culture and festivals brings distinction to the image and profile of the city; it enriches the experience of the city centre and makes each community unique in its history or sense of place.

The Centre of Urban and Regional Development Studies (CURDS), 2001, identified in their 'Building the Regions Knowledge Economy' Report (2001) that cosmopolitan cities attract knowledge intensive activity, skilled labour international tourists and business elites, all of which in turn introduce new ideas and creativity and generate a demand for quality and high value added goods and services, which in turn creates a more attractive environment capable of attracting more activity.

TOURISM DESTINATION IN LOCAL COMMUNITIES THROUGH FESTIVALS AND EVENTS

Festivals can be big business for a destination. Festivals become part of destination tourism strategies because they can bring in new money to the local economy. Also, now, it seems the importance of cultural events is higher than ever. Festivals can act as a spectacle in attracting the tourist attention and concentrating their focus on a particular city during a short intense period; this can enable the hosts to showcase their destination on a world stage and highlight key attractions and activities they offer. The local authorities are using events to position their destinations in the market, and thus fulfil their cultural, tourism, festivals and arts strategies. (Bowdin, 2001, Yeoman, (2004). Over the last decade local authorities identify in their strategies, the importance of using festivals to covert their obligations to meet the demand of tourist. The Department for culture media and sport stated:

> **"The value of domestic and inbound UK tourist trips was over £74 billion in 2002. The UK's attractions are at the very heart of the tourism industry, with the top twenty major paid attractions accounting for 45 million visits alone in 2003."**
>
> (http://www.culture.gov.uk/)

The Belfast City Development program aims to use the events as tool to promote destination tourism.

> **"Develop high quality sustainable inclusive programme of public access events, in a safe enjoyable environment in order to raise the profile of Belfast in support of regeneration."**
>
> (Belfast City Council, 2000, p.2)

Leeds experienced this on the 8th of July 2000 when The Radio 1 Love Parade was staged at Roundhay Park in the city. Leeds fought off competition from London, Manchester and Liverpool to stage the Love Parade UK that council leaders said they had "no hesitation" in backing (Yorkshire Evening Post, July 6th, 2000). The Event attracted around 200,000 – 250,000 people and was deemed a success with Phil Cook, Leeds City Council's Executive Director for development, saying,

> **"At least 200,000 young people came to Leeds, had a good time and went away with a favourable impression of the City."**
>
> (*Yorkshire Evening Post*, 13th July, 2000).

Mr Cook also went on to describe how in the days preceding the event the gateway Yorkshire Tourist Information Centre received numerous inquiries about weekend breaks in the city from people who had attended the event and had been impressed by Leeds.

The Leeds carnival organisers suggested that the event is becoming more and more a tourist attraction, in the last decade have developed as a natural outgrowth and benefited the local economy. This is due to the better press coverage by the local and national press, previously carnival relied on local visitors over the years, but in last five years with the growth and size of the carnival increasing, it is now seen as one the major tourism attractions in the area.

Kim (2002) stated that a community festival will become a tourist trap and the authenticity of the event is replaced by overcrowding and commercialism. Frisby & Getz (1989) argue that community events are more likely to survive if marketed to the visitors beyond the local area. Jeong & Faulkner (1996) and Hall (1992) name the strengthening of regional values and traditions, with the increase in participation of activities associated with the event.

POLITICS OF PLACE AND ROLE OF POLICY MAKERS

Events have been commonly used for political ends throughout history. Rulers and Monarchs have used events to popularise themselves and the area they rule. Some of the major events of recent times involved Royal weddings and Jubilee celebrations.

Governments use events particularly hallmark ones to punctuate the end of their term in office because they create nationalism, enthusiasm and most importantly votes. These events not only promote the city, area and country they provide economic benefits and jobs. Prime Minister, Tony Blair quoted:

> **'The British Government is delighted to give its full support to the London Bid for 2012. Winning the Games would be good news for London and for all of the UK. I hope everyone in the country will get behind the campaign.'**
>
> [*London 2012 Olympic Bid* (2003, p.1)]

Politically, as London has declared a bid to host the 2012 Olympic Games, there has never been more recognition by the Government of the potential benefits to the host region. The festivals and events help to develop social and economic cohesion, confidence and pride that connect local community and local authorities together. The local authorities secure political power and influence through events to gain moment among the local residents and businesses.

> **"Politics and politicians are an important part of the equation that is contemporary events management"**
>
> (McDonnell, Allen and O'Toole, 1999 p.26)

Research into political implications of events may assist in improving their planning and management (Hall, 1992 p.15). Delemere et al, (2000) suggest that it is important to determine the priorities of the residents and the community leaders to establish whether they are compatible and thus representative.

McDonnell, Allen and O'Toole (1999) believe that events have the ability to raise the profile of politicians and the cities that they govern. Hall (1994), however, argues that although this is an aspect of tourism, the relationship between politics and tourism is not primarily concerned with political parties and elections and their influence on tourism policy.

Hall (1994) explains that politics is unalterably the study of power, concerning who gets what, where, how and why. There is unarguably an element of politics surrounding the festival. The local authorities undertake the development and direct delivery of festivals to pursue specific economic and community development objectives. Given their responsibility for public spaces, local authorities have some advantages in presenting outdoor public events. The Mayor for city of Toronto stated,

> It is estimated that five to six hundred community-based festivals and events a year are assisted by Economic Development, Culture and Tourism Department staff. This support recognizes the key role festivals and events play in strengthening communities, business districts, cultural, heritage and arts resources, and in attracting tourists and visitors to the City. They help promote awareness of Toronto's rich history and dynamic and diverse cultural identity for City residents and visitors alike. They provide the opportunity for communities to come together, build alliances, celebrate and educate. They also are an important economic development tool, used by local business districts to build identity and attract shoppers.
>
> http://www.city.toronto.on.ca/legdocs/1999/agendas/council.htm

The local authorities use community-based festivals and events in strengthening communities, business districts, cultural, heritage and arts resources, and in attracting tourists and visitors to the City. In addition, the festivals and events are important economic tool for local authorities to increase development in the local area, by attracting people from around the globe to attend the festival. The festival organisers are now using the historical and cultural themes to develop the annual events to attract visitors and creating cultural image in the host cities by holding festivals in the community settings. The event organisers do not take into account the social and environmental impact in to consideration. It is argued that there is a clear need to adopt a holistic approach:

> **In any location, harmony must be sought between the needs of the visitor, the place and the host community**
>
> (*English Heritage*, 2000 p.29).

Host communities play a major role when running a major sporting event or any other large scale events. Also, major sporting events play a major role in host communities. The work of Getz (1997) was concerned with the event manager gaining support and resources from the host community, while also looking at the local benefits and costs, cultural meanings of their event and also the political factors. If all this is taken into consideration then it can lead to a good event and even a good relationship between event and local community.

A festival that is started by the community can evolve into a festival of vital importance, in terms of impacts in economic and social terms on the host community. This can happen to an extreme that it can be hijacked by the local authority or council for there own benefit and development, this can sometimes be detrimental to the values of the event. In the context of these considerations this paper now considers the following case study to analyse the social and political impacts of festival on their local community.

NOTTING HILL CARNIVAL

The Notting Hill Carnival, formed in 1964 as an opportunity for West Indians to celebrate their ancestors freedom from slavery, with an attendance of 200. Today the Carnival is organised by the Notting Hill Trust, a charity set up in 1990 to pursue the development of the Carnival. Behind the colour and music of the carnival there is a deeper meaning rooted in the experiences of Caribbean people arriving in England around a time of great change in late 1950s and early 1960s. So it was a search for identity, for community and belonging that led to carnival being developed early 1960s in the area of Notting Hill in London. As stated by the William Stewart the founder of initial Caribbean carnival in this country.

This great festival began initially from the energies of black immigrants from the Caribbean, in particular, Trinidad, where the Carnival tradition is very strong, and from people living locally, who dreamed of creating a festival to bring together the people of Notting Hill, most of whom were facing racism, lack of working opportunities and poor housing conditions resulting in a general suppression of good self-esteem.

Source: http://www.mynottinghill.co.uk/nottinghilltv/carnival-countdown.htm

The carnival has created that platform for the Caribbean people to come together and share their social and cultural differences with the local community. It is about people coming together and people having fun. Michael Conally argues the Notting Hill Carnival has been sold out to commercialism and it is no longer about people celebrating their culture.

Perhaps because the third phase has begun to reveal the enormous commercial possibilities of the event and Carnival is gradually being turned into a huge money-spinning spectacle (and not necessarily for Black people).

It does not have the political centre that it used to have. People used to feel that it was their Carnival. Now there is a perception that it belongs to Lilt.

Source: http://www.yush.com/rewind/yush0107/lilts.htm

POLITICAL CHANGES BY POLICY MAKERS FOR CARNIVAL

The Mayor of London ordered a Carnival Review in 1999 to address the process of staging an event, which has lacked political and financial support over the years. The purpose of Carnival Review Group was to look at how performers and festival spectators able to enjoy cultural experience from this unique festival. Moreover, Carnival Review Group was asked to look at the following issues.

Public safety and density of people

Carnival location and procession/route

Travel to and from Carnival

Police presence

Cultural, social and economic impact

Content of Carnival

Provision of facilities

Carnival is managed and financed

Adequate communication and signage

The Mayor had set up Carnival Review Group to promote culture and customs of carnival goers and change the image of Notting Hill carnival's journey. The Notting Hill carnival has very mix political history. Daily Mail columnist Lynda Lee-Potter (1991), cited in The Guardian (2002) described the carnival as:

"A sordid, sleazy nightmare that has become synonymous with death"

The Guardian (2002)

Notting Hill carnival's journey from a response to race attacks in 1958 to pride of place on the Mall in 2002, passing revelry, riot and resistance en route, is both powerful and painful. It is the tale of how a marginalised community built, protected and promoted what is now the largest street party in Western Europe, using the radical cultural politics of the Caribbean to confront Britain's racist political culture.

Over the last few decades calls was made to ban the carnival from all nature of the British society. The Notting Hill carnival in late seventies and early eighties had very bad image among the local, national media and political parties. The Tory Shadow home secretary Willie Whitelaw (1977) cited in The Guardian (2002) said,

"The risk in holding it now seems to outweigh the enjoyment it gives."

"Then it is up to their leaders to take steps necessary to ensure its survival."

In addition, the Notting Hill carnival received good support from Prince Charles, who backed the carnival.

"It's so nice to see so many happy, dancing people with smiles on their faces."

The Guardian (2002)

Moreover, Notting Hill carnival creates the different cultural diversity for the local community and enhances party-goers to enjoy the sights and sounds of the spectacular costumed troupes and parading traditional Caribbean music. It also, brings together the people of races and nationalities to enjoy the great day of fun with people of all ages. Notting Hill carnival gives the opportunity for residents to interact with the performers and volunteers from the event as well as giving residents the greater opportunity to interact socially.

THE SOCIAL AND ECONOMIC IMPACTS OF THE NOTTING HILL CARNIVAL

The carnival is all about people coming together and people having fun. This year over 750,000 people enjoyed the mixture of local and international talent. This magic music was mixed with the wonderful smells of Caribbean cooking. The carnival creates the different cultural diversity for the local community and enhances party-goers to enjoy the sights and sounds of the spectacular costumed troupes and parading traditional Caribbean music. It also, brings together the people of all different races and nationalities to enjoy the great day of fun with people of all ages. The report produced by The Royal Borough of Kensington and Chelsea 2004 stated the following figures to highlight the environmental impacts of the Notting Hill Carnival.

ACTUAL FACTS AND FIGURES

Attendance Figures:

	2004	2003	2002	2001	2000
Sunday	**250,000**	150,000	450,000	100,000	400,000
Monday	**500,000**	500,000	850,000	400,000	1,000,000

The Carnival Procession:

	2004	2003	2002	2001	2000
Bands registered	73	68	67	69	80
Bands actually appearing	62	60	Not recorded	Not recorded	Not recorded
Bands past the judging point by 9.00pm	56	60	53	59 by 11.00pm (NB judging point at Westbourne Grove)	Not recorded

Refuse Collection:

	2004	2003	2002	2001	2000	1999
Tonnes of refuse collected in RBKC	**203**	192	168	210	250	211
Tonnes of refuse collected in WCC	**155**	N/a	N/a	N/a	N/a	N/a

Complaints About Noise:

	2004	2003	2002	2001	2000
Complaints about noise in RBKC	**60**	63	66	74	201

Source: The Royal Borough of Kensington and Chelsea.

The carnival organisers suggested that the event is becoming more and more as tourist attraction, compared to before. This is due to the better press coverage by the local and national press, previously carnival relied on local visitors over the years, but in last five years with the growth and size of the carnival, it is know seen as one the major tourism attraction. It is now strongly viewed by the local community and small businesses that carnival is the significant part of the attracting tourism to the area and value the tourist market as a vital tool for the development of local economy. Therefore, carnival has seen as a key development event for true tourist attraction to bring the local, national and international tourists to this unique event.

Moreover, the carnival has generated significant economic impact on the local area over the last 20 years. It is difficult to analyse the economic benefits the carnival brings to the host community, no detail financial analysis have been carried out after the carnival in previous years. In 2004 the London Development Agency has carried out detail research on looking at the economic impact of carnival. The report highlight that the Notting Hill Carnival economic impact is key resource to the development of local businesses and local community. Commenting on the report, Michael Ward, LDA Chief Executive, stated:

'Carnival brings visitors and businesses to London. It is one of Europe's most spectacular tourist attractions. It could bring even more benefits with support. We will be working with the Mayor and the organisers to try to implement these proposals."

Source: http://www.london.gov.uk/view press release

ECONOMIC ANALYSIS OF CARNIVAL

£93 million	London's economy
3,000	Full time Jobs
1.16 million	People attended Carnival over three days
£45 million	Spend by Carnival goers in three days
£50 million	General financial boost to firms and individuals involved in Carnival

The economic impact to local business community is very significant the local business community benefit from the carnival in large. The above table indicates that the carnival generated huge economic benefits to the area. Moreover, the carnival organisers believe the publicity and promotion of event generate benefits for London in the form of improved image and repeat visitation. There is no doubt the Notting Hill Carnival plays an important part in developing the economic benefits for the local community and local businesses. The London mayor and other local politician see carnival a great income generation for London and it provides cultural diversification to community settings. Lee Jasper, Mayor's Policy Director and Chair of the Carnival Review Group, stated:

'Carnival is now regarded as London's premier cultural event and a symbol of the ease with which Londoners have embraced their city's diversity. This report identifies that carnival generates millions of pounds in revenue and makes a significant contribution to London's tourist economy.'

Source: http://www.london.gov.uk/view press release

It is vital for event organisers and other agencies to develop a practical and co-operative approach to take this event to next level of cultural, social and economic growth.

CONCLUSION

The findings of this research show us political and policy dynamics of the multi-cultural festivals and events with the UK, and the positive contribution that these events play in solidifying community relations with public policy makers. The research suggests that the community festivals are seen by the local politician a great educational settings for all cultures. Festival is a good concept to use in order to share ethnic minority cultures and values through dance, music, art, and foods with the larger community.

Moreover, festivals and events help to develop social and economic cohesion, confidence and pride that connect local community and local authorities together. The local authorities secure political power and influence through events to gain moment among the local residents and businesses. The study also found that some leading authors, Kim (2002), Jeong & Faulkner (1996), Hall (1992) and Frisby & Getz (1989) argues that a community festival will become a tourist trap and more likely to survive if marketed to the visitors beyond the local area. Festivals increase the regional values and traditions, with the increase in participation of activities associated with the event.

The findings show us that Notting Hill carnival creates the different cultural diversity for the local community and enhances party-goers to enjoy the sights and sounds of the spectacular costumed troupes and parading traditional Caribbean music. It also, brings together the people of different races and nationalities to enjoy the great day of fun with people of all ages. This research has highlight that the Notting Hill carnival have become a centre piece events for the local economy each year. The local hotels, restaurants, taxis, public transports and small stall traders have planned their business activities around these events. The case study within this paper demonstrates how the Notting Hill carnival has developed to become a centre piece event for the local economy each year. It is now strongly viewed by the local community and small businesses that carnival is the significant part of the attracting tourism to the area and value the tourist market as a vital tool for the development of local economy. Therefore, carnival has seen as a key development event for true tourist attraction to bring the local, national and international tourists to this unique event.

REFERENCES

Bowdin Et al (2001) *Events Management*. Oxford, Butterworth-Henemann

Blair, T. Prime Minister, London 2012 Olympic Bid (2003). <http://www.london2012.org> Accessed on [29/1/05]

Belfast City Development, Belfast City Council, (2000), www.belfastcity.gov.uk> Accessed on [29/1/05]

Conally, M. <http://www.yush.com /rewind/yush0107/lilts.htm> Accessed on [29/1/05]

Daily Mail columnist Lynda Lee-Potter (1991), cited in *The Guardian* (2002)

Delemere, T.A, Wankel, L.M. Hinch,T.D Development of a scale to measure resident attitudes toward the social impacts of community festivals, Part II: verification of the scale. *Event Management*. Vol 7 Pp 25-38

Dwyer, L. et al (2000) A Framework for Assessing "Tangible" and "Intangible" Impacts of Events and Conventions. *Event Management* Vol. 6 pp.175-189.

English Tourism Board (1991) *Tourism and the Environment: Maintaining the Balance*. English Tourist Board.

English Tourism Council (2001) Time for action: a strategy for sustainable tourism in England London: English Tourist Board [Internet] Available from < http://www.english tourism.org.uk> Accessed on [29/1/05]

Frisby, W. & Getz, D. (1989) "Festival Management: A Case Study Perspective." *Journal of Travel Research*, Vol 28 pp 7-11.

Getz, D. (1991), *Festivals, Special Events and Tourism* New York:Van Nostrand Reinhold.

Getz, D. (1997). *Event Management and Event Tourism*. New York, Cognizant Communications Corporation.

Goldblatt, J. (1997), *Special Events Best Practices in Modern Event Management 2nd Ed.* New York: International Thompson Publishing Company.

Guidance to Local Authorities, (2000) <http://www.odpm.gov.uk> Accessed on [24/2/05]

Hall, C. (1994) *Tourism and Politics: Policy, Power and Place Chichester*. John Wiley and Sons Ltd.

Hall, C. (1992) *Hallmark Tourist Events: Impacts, Management and Planning Chichester*. John Wiley and Sons Ltd.

Identified in their 'Building the Regions Knowledge Economy' Report (2001)

The centre of Urban and Regional Development Studies (CURDS).

Jeong, G.H., Faulkner, B. (1997) Resident Perceptions of Mega-Events Impacts: The Taejon international exposition case. *Festival Management & Event Tourism*, Vol 4 Pp 3-11.

Jasper, L. Mayor's Policy Director and Chair of the Carnival Review Group, <http://www.london.gov.uk> Accessed on [15/2/05]

Kim, K. Uysal, M. & Chen, J. (2002) Festival visitor motivation from the organisers point of view. *Event Management.* Vol7 pp 127-134.

Key Leisure Markets (2001) *Tourism in the U.K. London: MarketScape Ltd*

McDonnell, I. Allen, J. and O'Toole, W. (1999) *Festival and Special Event Management*. Brisbane: John Wiley and Sons Australia Ltd.

Mayor for city of Toronto, <http://www.city.toronto.on.ca.htm> Accessed on [24/2/05]

Notting Hill Carnival (2001) [Internet] Available from <http://www.mynottinghill.co.uk.htm > Accessed on [18/2/05]

Prince Charles , cited in *The Guardian* (2002)

Prescott, J. (2003) Leeds: *A Business City*, Leeds City Council.

Smith, S.L.J. (1990). "A Test of Plog's Allocentric/Psychocentric Model: Evidence From Seven Nations". *Journal of Travel Research*, vol28(4)40-42.

Stiernstrand, J. (1996) The Nordic Model: A Theoretical Model for Economic Impact Analysis of Event Tourism, *Festival Management & Event Tourism* Vol 3 pp.165-174

The Department for culture media and sport, <http://www.culture.gov.uk/ >Accessed on [15/2/05]

The Royal Borough of Kensington and Chelsea, <www.rbkc.gov.uk> Accessed on [15/2/05]

The Leeds Initiative: *The Business City*, (2000) Leeds City Council

Willie Whitelaw (1977) cited in The Guardian (2002)

Ward, M. LDA Chief Executive, <http://www.london.gov.uk> Accessed on [15/2/05]

Yorkshire Post Newspaper (2002) [Internet] Available from <http://www.ypn.co.uK/>Accessed on [29/1/05]

Yeoman Et Al (2004) *Festival and Events Management*. Oxford, Elsevier Butterworth Heinemann.

15

THE CLUSTER EFFECT OF THE TOURISM INDUSTRY IN PEARL RIVER DELTA

ZHANG MU

ABSTRACT

The Pearl River Delta is an area with fast economy development and tourist industry cluster. Now more and more theme parks cluster in this area and promote the tourist industry development in China. The paper discussed the main characteristic of the theme parks cluster such as the spatial cluster, dynamic and network etc over there. Then the mechanism about this cluster has been analyzed and the authors consider that the open policy, knowledge innovation and local economic growth are the main drive force to promote the tourist industry cluster. Finally, some suggestions about expanding the sustainable effect of the tourist enterprises cluster have been put forward.

Keywords: Tourist industry; industry cluster; effect; drive mechanism; Pearl River Delta

INTRODUCTION

The industry cluster is a geographic phenomenon in the course of one industry evolvement that means more similar enterprises gathered in certain area in order to get the cluster scale effect and benefit. This industry congregativeness not only takes place in the manufacturing industry but also is suitable for the tourist industry. Tour industry cluster means a regional aggregation with Embedded ness by more tourist enterprises or the relative corporations based on their specialization and collaboration. Since the spatial aggregations of tourist cluster are not simple enterprises dense collection but it composes a cooperation network by the local tourist corporations even as including the surrounding area and foreign countries or district. For example, there are several successful tourist cluster zone in the world including the Kansai area In Japan, Tour collective area of San Francisco and Los Angeles in the Untie State, the Overseas China Town in Shenzhen bay of China, that all promoted the local economic development.

Guangdong Province is all along in the forward position of China reform and open, in which the economic growth capacity is higher and tourist develop faster in the Pearl River Delta than other regions of province. It still possesses rich human and nature tourist resources and has 3368.1 kilometers of coastline and more open port. The tourist industry in Guangdong Province also have clear interior difference, but best developed tourist area mainly gathered in the Pearl River Delta which have advantages of urban cluster brand and neighborhood with the Hong Kong and Macau, then it also showed the superiority of the large scope tourist enterprises cluster.

DESCRIPTION OF STUDY AREA

The Pearl River Delta is the mainstream of the foreign-oriented economic development model of Guangdong Province economy society, and also is an important economic vigor growth pole of China. It located in the southeast of Guangdong Province and faced towards the southern China Sea, and included 14 cities or counties, namely Guangzhou, Shenzhen, Zhuhai, Foshan, Jiangmen, Dongguan, Zhongshan, Huizhou, Huiyang, Huidong, Boluo, Zhaoqin, Gaoyao and Shihui. It has 41500 square kilometers of land area and total population over 23650000. The Pearl River is looked as the third river in China, which has the close dimension tributary like the spider web and spreads all over on the delta area. This landform makes the delta plain appear the dense network of rivers, rivulets, lakes and ponds. Under this nice nature environment the convenient transport facilities linked to the Hong Kong and Macau, so this area become the richest and most populous district of China. More people named it golden triangle of Guangdong Province. This golden triangle still is the pioneer tourism development region and got another name means the tourism golden triangle because it's dense spatial cities cluster, advanced traffic conditions, numerous input and output port, perfect tour service and various new resorts and destinations.

From the broad sense, Hong Kong and Macao are looked as the two wings of the Pearl River Delta all along. The Pearl River Delta developed close relation with them and composed the cooperative macroeconomic. This superiority extends to the tourism and makes the Pearl River Delta become famous tour destination for domestic and foreign tourists in China.

LITERATURE REVIEW

A scholar put forward the idea of "industry cluster" in which he analyzed the industry cluster form the view of enterprise competition force and given the reason (Michael. E. Porter, 2000). On this topic, more peoples work mainly fix attention on the research about the large scope regional collaboration as well as the influence occurred from this regional cooperation, such as the cooperation between East Asia and the Pacific region and the tour cooperation developments in the Big golden triangle area etc (Chirathivat et al.; Bramwell 1996 et al., 1997,2000).

More Chinese scholars also focus on this research field. Wang Xuzhang concludes different methods of industry cluster (Wang Xuzhang, 1998). Gai Wenqi pointed out that the regional innovation network is very useful for the high-tech middle and small enterprises development in China (Gai Wenqi et al., 1999). Qiu Baoxing described a definition about the small industry cluster when he considered more people's opinion (Qiu Baoxing, 1999). Shi Peizhe also concluded out the major reasons of the industrial cluster (Shi Peizhe, 2000). Che Weihan summarized the new characteristic of industrial cluster in the time of knowledge economy (Che Weihan, 2000). Liang Xiaomeng founded that the industrial cluster not only gets benefit from the outside scale economy but also from the inner scale economic (Liang Xiaomeng, 2000). Zhang Yuanzhi analyzed the main superiority in the enterprises that located at the industrial cluster district (Zhang Yuanzhi, 2001). Wu Yonghong and Bao Jianyun studied the regional effect of the industry cluster and expansion of the enterprise, and they found that the spatial cluster and expansion of some enterprises had great influence on the local economic development when it droved by benefit and government control in some period. (Wu Yonghong et al., 2001). Ding Yunlong and Li Yugang found out that the industrial cluster play an important role to raise the enterprise innovation ability (DingYunlong et al., 2001).

Few researches paid attention to the tourist industry cluster. Yuan Li discussed the cluster effect of the tourist industry (Yuan Li et al., 2003). Fan Xinyou analyzed the scale tourism economic phenomenon during the golden week holiday in China (Fan Xinyou, 2004). Deng Bing summarized the influence factors of tourist industry cluster (Deng Bing, 2004). Someone still put forward some innovation measure for the tourist industry cluster (Ma Xuefeng, 2004).

In summary, few documents studied the mechanism if the tourist industrial clusters at present. More problems such as the tour cluster comparison to the traditional industry, its formation mechanism, its particularity and the future development trend all are more important and need to be studied further. From the case study of the Pearl River Delta, this paper wants to find out some answers according to the above problems.

METHODOLOGY

The formation of the industrial cluster needs the support of the region economy theory which chiefly associate with the Gradient Transference theory and the Growth Pole theory.

(1) The Gradient Transference theory quoted the Lifecycle theory of the manufacturing industry into the region economy development and its core idea is that the most important factors such as the industrial structure, new technology application and productivity are followed the law that transfer from the height gradient to the lower. This theory also believed that the center cities usually locate at high gradient and they can accelerate the technology innovation and R & D progress through the cluster economic.

(2) In the theory of the Growth Pole, the economy growths do not have proportional spatial distribution. Some growth point or pole for example the center city or capital, always

> first develop their local economic, then expand and affect to the other areas. In different period, the high economic growths usually take place in the key industry and innovation enterprises and the growth pole would locate at these areas. In a word, the growth pole theory emphasizes the difference of the urban grade in regional city system because it represents the urban cluster economic capability.

From above we can make out that the regional economic development always pursue benefit occurred in the industry cluster and its scale economic effect. More and more enterprises gather in a certain district because of the close relation among manufacture and distribution among them, and then compose a regional manufacture system. In this system, each corporation can get profits from the system cooperation. The overall output of the system is always bigger than the total income received from the every enterprise.

According to these theories, the structure of the tourism industry cluster in the Pearl River Delta can be shown as the Figure 1.

FINDINGS

The features of the tourist cluster in the Pearl River Delta

The tourism cluster in center cities as a long line

The tourism cluster mainly depends on the radiation and driving capability of the local center cites such as Guangzhou, Shenzhen and Zhuhai. These center cities make use of the superiority of the geographic and location to compose a large tourist destination system, and they can get the scale tourist economic exterior effect and benefits from the tourism cluster in Pearl River Delta. The other tourist enterprises in the surrounding area also share the interest from the tour cluster. The expansions of the tour cluster here due to the more Theme Park corporations appear in these center cities. Then these growth poles promote the development of the whole tourist industry in the Pearl River Delta.

The successful Theme Park in China almost chiefly gathered in the Pearl River Delta. The first Theme Park in China is the

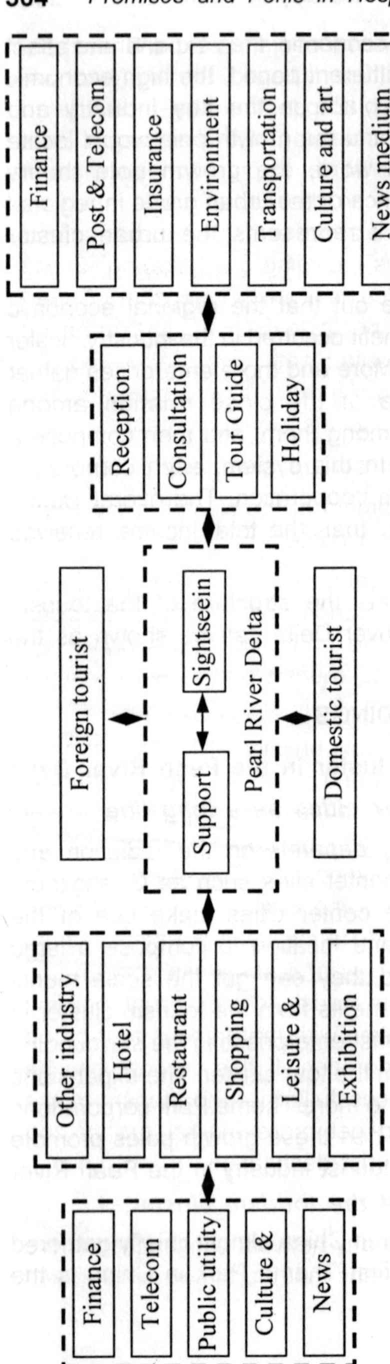

Fig 1 Network Of The Tourist Cluster Structure In Pearl River Delta

Splendid China that droved the theme parks cluster in Shenzhen. Thereafter the China Folk Culture Village, World Windows, Shenzhen Ocean world and Happy Kingdom had been completed and open to the market in succession. So the theme park construction had become the tourist development mainstream in the Pearl River Delta especially in the center cities such as Guangzhou and Zhuhai. Now there are over 20 theme park spread in this area in which the famous including the following: Flying Dragon World, Grand World Scenic Park, Guangzhou Ocean World, Aerospace Marvelous Spectacle Park, New Yuanming Palace and Panyu Xiangjiang safari park and the newcomer, Disneyland Resort in Hong Kong. All these theme park become the lead enterprises in the local tourism development.

The tourist network has been set up gradually

The tourism network development of the cluster in the Pearl River Delta contains the following content:

(1) the close tourism cooperation with the near provinces such as Fujian, Jiangxi, Hunan and Guangxi has been built up steadily. Since the traffic conditions had been improved fast and the local tourists and ecdemic visitors can travel to the different destinations easily.

(2) The new cooperation network building also gets enhance with the foreign countries and regions. The international development trend of the tourism cluster here is to set up the tourism collaboration network including Japan, Korea, Philippines and Southeast Asia countries. Certainly this network also contains the Hong Kong, Macao and Taiwan even more expands to the western Pacific region. It is useful for participate in and share the cooperation of the international tourism industry chain through building up the reliable collaboration with that famous tour group or the multinational corporation. If this network can be set up and operate successfully that the tourism in the Pearl River Delta could get more market profits and become international tourist destination.

The dynamic characteristic of the tourism cluster

Attending by the tourist company network construction is the dynamic changes of cluster. It means that the tourism cluster and its network always in a change state. For example the network system often gets to expand and upgrade so as to hold the innovation and competition capability of those enterprises in the system. In other words, the process of the tourism cluster is that the tourist enterprises compose a network and form the special tourist industry district in the local economic system. Between the corporations there exist the competition and cooperation relations so the dynamic cluster can be set up. Since the leading companies are theme parks in the Pearl River Delta, so all other tour products could be designed to service for this subject and obey to the dynamic upgrade requirement of the cooperation network. As a result, the tourism industry always appears activated and diverse upgrade in the Pearl River Delta guided by the tourism dynamic cluster.

The formation mechanism of the tourist cluster in Pearl River Delta

The path dependence caused by the local policy

Owing to the Hong Kong industry had a transfer outside period in the 80's early last century, the Pearl River Delta recommends Hong Kong dollars and develops the export-oriented industry system rapidly. Now days the star-studded small companies have become the large enterprise group and more and more FDI select to reside in the Pearl River Delta. It is obvious that the policy is the most important factor in this development course. Now the new and coming tourist capital select here to open their economic growth pole or commercial profit also because of its experience of those predecessor. It is well known when FDI want to reside in one area or industry they always first consider where the relative industry or other foreign investment had successful developed in order to escape the commercial risk and the information search cost. That is the so-called path independence and it works in the same way to the tourist industry. The successful path independence would lead to the tourism spatial cluster that not only takes place in the Pearl River Delta but also in the Beijing and Shanghai.

The tourism cluster droved by the overflow effect of the enterprise innovation

The propagation of knowledge and absorbing is the important way of knowledge innovation so more companies make effort to absorb outside knowledge. Somebody's work indicated that the enterprise knowledge overflow and receive external complement would promote the industry cluster and form the scale economic model (Jing Xiangrong et al., 2001).

In the tourism cluster district, all companies share the public infrastructure, special technology and labour resources that are useful for saving the cost and raising the operation and management capability of the enterprises. The tourism cluster possess of the complicated and self-organized structure so it flexible fix for the environment changes. Thus the overflow effect of the industry cluster can be brought into play and the main result is that the whole system output profits is more than the total profits just added by that of the all companies in the cluster district. In the Pearl River Delta, the various combined tour production, which relate to the field of land, river, lake and ocean, emerge in endlessly through the enterprise knowledge innovation. More and more new companies want to enter into the tourism market of Pearl River Delta including the foreign airline company, tourist agent and other relative enterprises.

Finally, the external scale and scope economic would appear when the industry cluster develops into a mature stage. Because of the stronger affiliation with the correlative industry, the tourism cluster can get more profits from the cluster effect and expand in the different industrial chain. So, the tourism cluster in the Pearl River Delta would arouse the notable linkage effect and drive the tourism development of province.

Another driving force: local economic development

According to the international tourism experience, the domestic resident have the travel motivation easily when the per capita year income reaches up to 300 US dollars. If the annual average income per capita increases to the 500-800 US dollar, the domestic tourism would step into the rapid development period. Suppose that criterion reaching up to 1000 US dollar, the foreign-oriented tourist product would popularize around the country. Now the people's annual income of Guangdong Province in the cities and towns have exceeded 1000 US dollar, most residents have an appetite for traveling in the province especially in the Pearl River Delta. The statistic also indicated that the total receptive tourist more than 11969600 people-times in 2003, among them there are foreign visitors about 2457600 people-times. All these date show that the local economic rapidly development would promote the tourism cluster and growth.

CONCLUSION

According to the above analysis about the tourism cluster, this paper put forward the following suggestions to promote the sustainable tourism development in the Pearl River Delta.

(1) Promoting the regional tourism cooperation guided by the government dominant strategy. The government should constitute the economic development plan on the basis of the available or rising industrial cluster and the enterprises cluster prepense does not permitted. Cluster is a complicated organic system, so any local government who attempt to create a complicated system by way of the policy almost is impossible. The local government had better participate in the cluster procedure indirectly rather than control its progress.

(2) Getting rational development of the tourist resources and optimizing their spatial distribution. The different grade highway and local road especially linked to the different cities and destinations should be finished and improved in order to form more tourism corridor in Pearl River Delta. These projects would work for the whole tourism cluster and become real tourism golden triangle in China.

(3) Expanding the tourism cluster effect by ways of design new tour products. The innovation capability is a major viewpoint of the industrial cluster theory and also expresses the competition ability of the enterprise, district and country. It is necessary that attract the foreign capital investment for the regional economic development. But only relying on the external import would serious limit the auto-development of the local enterprisers. The industrial cluster provides the sustainable way through the enterprise innovation.

(4) Building up destination brand and stepping in the way of sustainable tourism. The brand sometimes means the image of enterprise and productÿin other words it is a sign of indicator of concision but elegant design. The

brandization is one way to make one or a series of products to be differing from the other product of competitor.

REFERENCES

Bramwell B. Lane B. et al (2000) *Tourism Collaboration and Partnerships, Policiesÿ Practice and Sustainability*. New York, Channel View Publications.

Bramwell, Bill. (1997) European Collaboration in Sustainable Tourism. *Annals of Tourism Research* 24(2), 440-442.

Che Weihan. (2000) New Changes in Enterprise management Models and Assemblage of Estates under Intellectual Economy. *Academic Journal Graduate School Chinese Academy of Social Sciences* 6, 15-19.

Chirathivat Suthiphand. (1996) ASEAN-India Cooperation in Trend and Tourism, Trend and Prospects. *Journal of Asian Economics* 7(4), 743-757.

Deng Bin Yu Xi Wu Bihu. (2004) Tourism Industry Cluster and its Influential Factors. *Journal of Guilin Institute of Tourism* 15(6), 53-57

Ding Yunlong, Li Yugang. (2001) On the upgrading models of industrial structure from the standpoint of technological innovation. *Journal of HIT (Social Sciences Edition* 3(1), 78-81.

Fan Xinyou. (2004) Analysis on the Economics of the Capacity of tourism Environment —Concurrently Discuss the Phenomena of Economics of Scale in Golden weeks. *Research Resource Development & Market* 20(2), 90-92.

Gai Wenqi, Wang Jichi. (1999) The influence on the High-tech enterprise development by regional innovation network. *Journal of China Soft Science* 9, 102-106.

Jin Xiangrong, Ye Jianliang.(2001) The cluster effect of the knowledge overflow and enterprise network organization. *The Journal of Quantitative & Technical Economics* 10, 90-93.

Liang Xiaomeng. (2000) Scale economics, industry cluster and regional harmony. *Journal of Reform and Strategy,* 5, 12-16.

Ma Xuefeng. (2004) The research about the tourist industry cluster. *Market Forum* 8, 62-63.

Michael. E. Porter. (2000) Cluster and new competitive economics. *Journal of the economic and society comparison* 2, 21-31.

Qiu Baoxing. (1999) *Study on the cluster of smallness enterprises*. Shanghai: Fudan University Press.

Shi Peizhe. (2000) Study on the cause of formation of the industry cluster. *Journal of Economist* 3, 18-19.

Wang Xuzhang. (1998) Research on the selection, aggregate and expand of the regional key industry market. *Journal of Suzhou Railway Teachers College* 15(5), 24-27.

Wu Yonghong, Bao Jianyun. (2001) Study on the regional effect of the enterprise cluster and expansion. *Journal of Southwest University for Nationalities(Philosophy and Social Sciences)* 22(3), 152-153

Yuan Li, Tian Dingxiang, Liu Yan. (2003) Research on the cluster effect of the tourist industry. *Journal of Hunan Social Science* 3, 117-118.

ZhangYuanzhi. (2001)Industry Centralization, Competitive Superiority & West Development. *Journal of Xidian University (Social Science Edition)* 3, 5-10

16

AN ANALYSIS OF TOURISM INFRASTRUCTURE IN MADHYA PRADESH, INDIA

AMITABH MISHRA

ABSTRACT

Since ages, the incredible land of Madhya Pradesh has attracted tourists from far and wide. Madhya Pradesh has been well known for its hospitality and rich cultural heritage. In order to experience the unique combination of tradition with trend, Madhya Pradesh is the state to visit and there is no doubt that the trip to Madhya Pradesh will offer something more than just a trip. The objective of this study was to examine spontaneous destination images of Madhya Pradesh. This study also aimed to assess the distribution of hospitality and tourism infrastructure spread in the state. The study is based on the secondary analysis of the literature on the tourism and hospitality industry in Madhya Pradesh. In addition to this a primary study was carried out with 300 questionnaires covering the popular destinations during the D.Phil. survey. The finding of this research work will be helpful for the planner's academicians and entrepreneurs willing to work in the Madhya Pradesh.

Key Words: ***Accommodation units, motels, infrastructure, budget hotels and wildlife.***

INTRODUCTION

Tourism is a diffused and complex activity, consisting of a variety of elements. These may be developed in different contexts by a broad spectrum of developers like attractions, infrastructure, etc. These elements are then consumed by tourists who exhibit a diversity of demands. Infrastructure is the backbone of tourism anywhere in the world and Madhya Pradesh is no exception. By infrastructure, we mean facilities and services made available to tourist to make his / her visit comfortable. These include power supply, transportation, accommodation, information centers, security and city development body. However, there is no uniformity in infrastructural facilities provided by government or public.

Madhya Pradesh is a big state and offers a number of attractions for tourists. From the ancient times, Madhya Pradesh has been the centre for art and culture. There were a number of rulers who ruled this state and built various beautiful monuments, religious temples and Dharamshalas, etc. Beside this, there are also a number of natural and manmade spots, which are very important from tourism point of view. These include the Marble rocks of Bhedaghat-Jabalpur, Panna Diamond mines and National Park at Panna, Pachmarhi Hills, Mandu, Orcha, Bharhut and Sanchi stupas, Gwalior, Shivpuri, Datia, Chachi, Purva, Bahuti, Quoti and Raneh water falls, Bansagar dam, Amarkantak, Chittrakoot, Ujjain and Govindgarh Lake. There is no doubt that Madhya Pradesh is full of natural and manmade tourist attractions. unfortunatly the Government of Madhya Pradesh is not very conscious about tourism development in the State. At places like Khajuraho, Gwalior, Indore and other important places are well provided by infrastructural facilities, places like Pachmarhi and Amarkantak provision of infrastructural requirements are far from satisfactory. The following are the factor that influences the provision of tourism infrastructure in Madhya Pradesh.

The geography of the region or the place has an eminent effect on the infrastructure. For example, places, which are located in high altitude and in region where it is difficult to reach, facilities are less than these at places, which are located in plain region. The difference in geography of regions include distance from river or lake and composition of soil. The proportion of vegetation in the regions is also responsible for the infrastructural difference in the region. This can be noticed within a particular place itself. The area, which is nearer to the lake, is for most developed than the area, which is farther. Madhya Pradesh consists of about 90% of plain land and about 10% hilly region. Thus, there is vast scope of developing tourism infrastructure in the region. Development of tourism infrastructure in the region has to be considered before any step is taken to develop tourism. The government's attitude, historical importance, tourist arrivals, business, resources, public awareness is also a factor necessary to the overall development of the area. Table I gives the classification of tourism in the state:

Table 1: Type of Tourism Popular in Various Destinations of Madhya Pradesh

Tourism Type	Places
Cultural tourism (Heritage Sites)	Gwalior, Datia, Orcha, Khajuraho, Bhopal, Sanchi, Mandu, Burhanpur.
Wildlife and Adventure Tourism (Wildlife parks, rivers, lakes and Hill stations)	Pachmarhi, Amarkantak, Kanha, Bandhavgarh, Panna, Satpura and Pench Valley National Parks, Tigra Lake (Gwalior), Upper lake (Bhopal), Gandhi Sagar (Mandsaur)
Leisure and Business tourism (metros and major tourist centers)	Pachmarhi, Khajuraho, Bhopal, Gwalior, Indore, Jabalpur, etc
Pilgrim tourism (Places of religious importance)	Ujjain, Maheshwar, Omkareshwar, Chitrakoot, Bhopal, Sanchi, Orcha, Amarkantak, etc.

OBJECTIVES OF INFRASTRUCTURE IN TOURISM

Infrastructure is important for the development of a destination apart its historical and geographical significance, which leads to the promotion of tourism in Madhya Pradesh. The following are the objectives for which development of infrastructure in the region is necessary:

- To attract tourists, both domestic and international.
- To provide better accommodation to the tourist keeping

in mind their affordability. In other words better accommodation with reasonable tariff.

- To give variety and choice to the tourists in terms of accommodation, transportation, etc.
- To serve the tourist to the best.
- To provide better transportation to the tourist.
- Sustain tourist traffic.
- Efficient Rail, Road and Air services to the important places for the tourists.
- Well-maintained and well-designed shopping markets.
- Information centers and foreign exchange facilities.
- To provide consistent power supply to the consumer especially to commercial establishments.
- Properly maintained airports, bus routes and bus terminals, railway facilities.
- Government policies to aim for encouraging tourism.

ACCOMMODATION

The unique and incredible land of Madhya Pradesh offers plenty of accommodation options to suit all pockets. There are exclusive hotels and hotel chains with luxurious amenities and excellent facilities fragrance. In addition, there are several tourist bungalows and traveller's lodges that provide comfortable lodging and meals. For the tourists who prefer to travel by roads the rest houses or the Dak bungalows are best bets. They provide the basic comforts and are usually situated near or beside the national highways. Further, with its Royal past there is the option of staying in royal manner at the Heritage hotels. The Madhya Pradesh government has recently proposed the owners of various royal properties, forts and palaces to convert their establishments into heritage hotels. There are a number of forts and palaces in Madhya Pradesh, such as the fort of Chandra Nagar (Chattarpur near Khajuraho), the fort of Rewa, the fort of Mandu, Jabalpur, Orcha, etc. properly maintained by their owners or the government, which could serve the purpose. Some of them are open and allow tourists-such as the forts of Mandu, Orcha, and Jabalpur. Some of the forts and palaces have already been converted into heritage hotels. These hotels will give anyone the feel of being a Prince and Princess! The palace hotels, Fort hotels and the havelis of India are not only comfortable but they are captivating too. Travel to the destination of your choice anywhere in Madhya Pradesh and you will find the right kind of accommodation. Various websites, such as indiahotelsandresorts.com and travel/tour agents customize the tour packages and offer suitable hotel accommodation.

The reservation of rooms can be made well in advance. The various hotel packages offer the best of facilities. The rooms are well furnished and one can enjoy the luxury of staying at there hotels the way the erstwhile Maharajas did. The range of luxury and the budget hotels or any other kind of accommodation in Madhya Pradesh also includes the star categorized accommodation hotels, which are provided by the travel tour agencies.

HOTELS OF MADHYA PRADESH

Internationally reputed Indian hotel chains have chosen Madhya Pradesh for their luxury hotels. Some private entrepreneurs have also their properties in 5 to 1 star categories. The Madhya Pradesh State Tourism Development Corporation's units located all over Madhya Pradesh offers 3-star facilities. A detailed list of hotels in Madhya Pradesh is given in Annexure I.

Higher Category Hotels / Deluxe Hotels:

All four and five star hotels come under this category. Generally, these hotels are located in the major cities in the business districts or on the periphery of the cities. Services offered and ambiences provided are of international standards. Table 2 give details of rooms available in higher category / deluxe hotels at key cities of Madhya Pradesh.

Table 2: Rooms Available in Higher Category Hotels in Key Cities of Madhya Pradesh

Destination	Available Rooms
Indore	184 – Rooms
Khajuraho	416 – Rooms
Bhopal	93 – Rooms
Gwalior	56 – Rooms

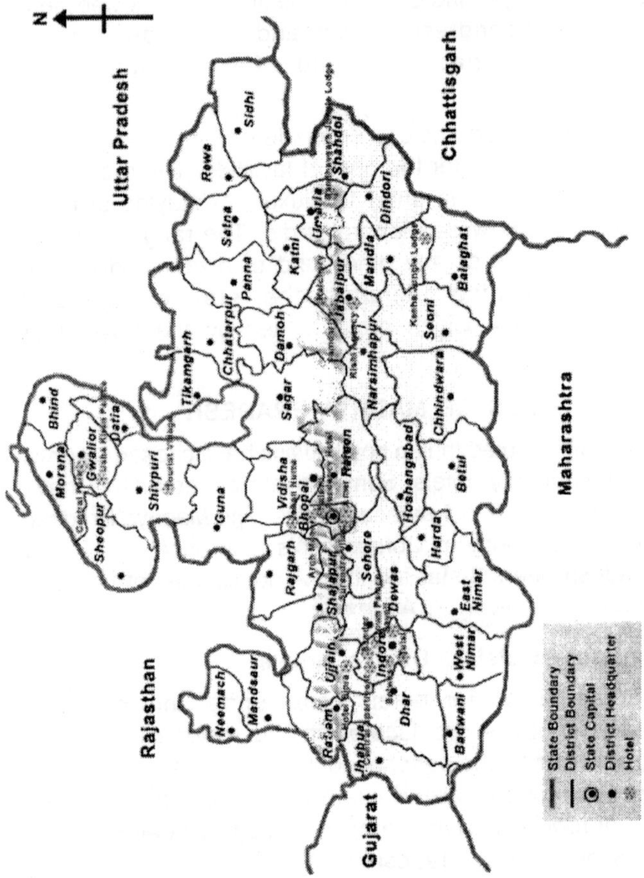

Map I Madhya Pradesh Accommodation (Hotels)

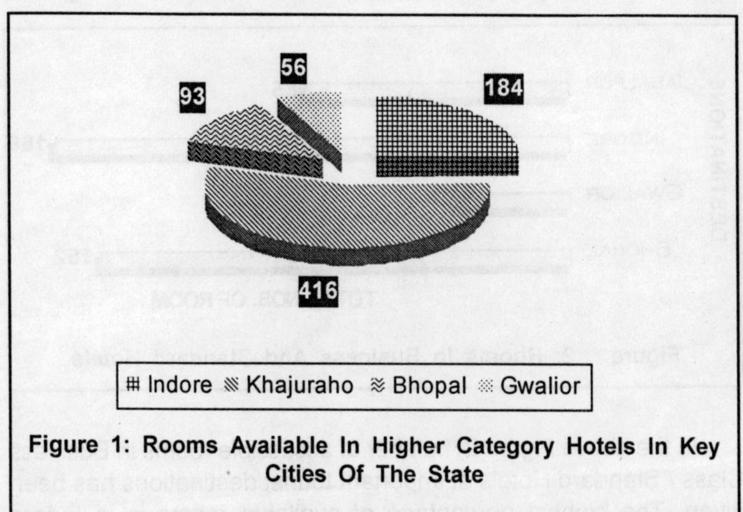

Figure 1: Rooms Available In Higher Category Hotels In Key Cities Of The State

Figure 1, gives details of number of rooms at major destinations of the State. According to the availability of rooms in higher category/ deluxe hotels at the major destinations of Madhya Pradesh, Khajuraho comes first. In Khajuraho the number of total available rooms in higher category hotels 416 followed by Indore (184 Rooms), Bhopal (93 Rooms) and Gwalior (56 rooms).

Business Class/Standard Hotels:

All the hotels in this category are of three stars classification located in the business districts of main cities. These hotels are best suitable for business travellers, who have business obligations to fulfill and whose most of the contacts are located in the business district of that particular city. The following table (Table 3) gives details of total numbers of rooms in the Business and standard Hotels located at major tourist destination in Madhya Pradesh.

Table 3: Number Of Rooms In Business And Standard Hotels Located At Major Tourist Destination In Madhya Pradesh

Destination	Available Rooms
Bhopal	152
Gwalior	36
Indore	166
Jabalpur	85

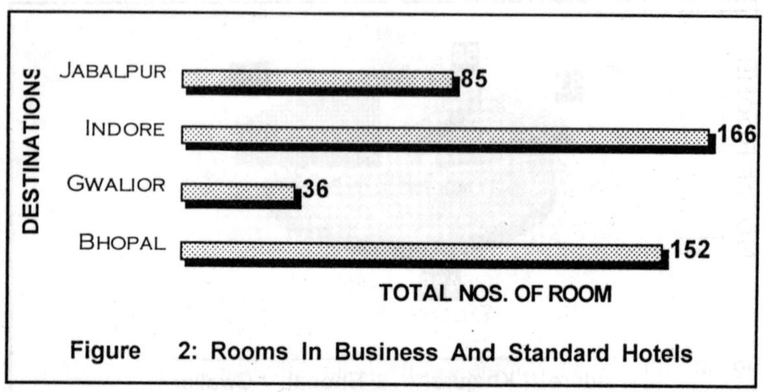

Figure 2: Rooms In Business And Standard Hotels

In the above Figure 2, number of accessible rooms in Business Class / Standard Hotels at important tourist destinations has been given. The highest percentage of available rooms is in Indore (166 Rooms) following Bhopal (152 Rooms), Jabalpur (85 Rooms) and Gwalior (36 Rooms). In this chart only government, approved rooms have been shown.

Luxury / Heritage Hotel:

If tourist wants to enjoy the best in life while traveling and experiencing new cultures, luxury hotels / Heritage hotels are best to stay in. The services and ambience offered are much better or even best in the world, making the tourist forget about the world outside. The grandeur and royal treatment in these hotels is the most remarkable thing to observe and enjoy. All these hotels are above five star rating and heritage properties come under the Heritage category. Table 4, given below, gives details of total number of available rooms in Luxury / Heritage Hotels situated at major destinations of Madhya Pradesh.

TABLE 4: NUMBER OF ROOMS AVAILABLE IN LUXURY / HERITAGE HOTELS IN MADHYA PRADESH

Destination	Available Rooms
Bhopal	130
Indore	39
Gwalior	61

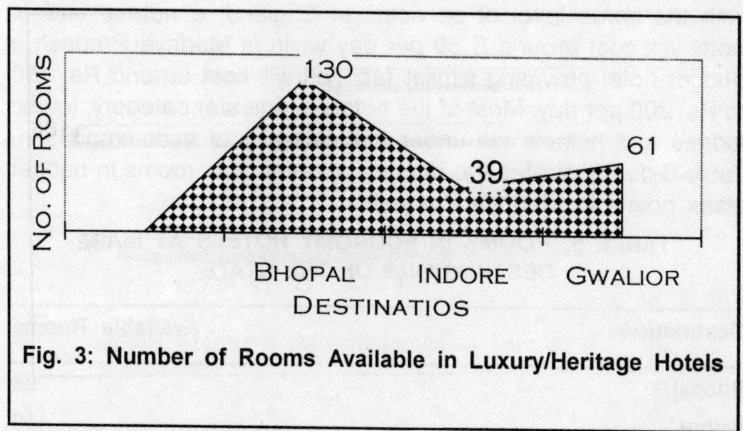

Fig. 3: Number of Rooms Available in Luxury/Heritage Hotels

According to this Figure 3, the top honor goes to Bhopal, which has 130 rooms, and the minimum numbers of rooms are in Indore (39 Rooms). Gwalior, which has 61 rooms.

Economy Class Hotel:

These hotels are for travelers light on their pocket but high in spirit. Most of the hotels are in the two or three star category. These hotels provide clean airy rooms with basic but quality services. At many places, the services offered by these hotels are comparable to services offered by higher categories hotels. Most of the hotels under this category are smaller units and are located in smaller cities and towns. Economy hotels have maximum percentage of occupancy because of their good quality services and cheap tariff. Table 5 below gives an idea about the rooms in Economy class hotels at main tourist destinations of the state.

The above Figure 4 indicates the number of rooms in Economy class hotels at some of the important tourist destinations in Madhya Pradesh.

Budget Class Hotel:

If a tourist wants to travel economically, but still needs a clean place with basic services, budget hotels are best to stay in. There are many such hotels near the major transportation hubs in big as well as smaller cities. Most of these hotels are cheap compared to their counterparts in the western countries with the same level of services. In England, a normal budget hotel will cost around £ 80 per day while in Madhya Pradesh a budget hotel providing similar facilities will cost around Rs. 150 to Rs. 200 per day. Most of the hotels in one star category, tourist lodges and hostels fall under this category of accommodation. Table 6 demonstrates the number of obtainable rooms in budget class hotels in Madhya Pradesh.

TABLE 5: ROOMS IN ECONOMY HOTELS AT MAIN DESTINATIONS OF THE STATE

Destination	Available Rooms
Bhopal	98
Indore	199
Pachmarhi	45
Ujjain	25
Amarkantak	24
Gwalior	36
Khajuraho	84
Jabalpur	52
Mandu	20

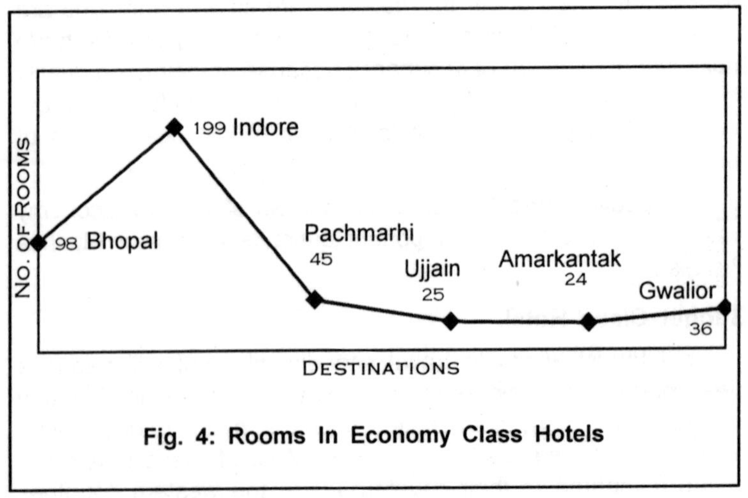

Fig. 4: Rooms In Economy Class Hotels

TABLE 6: NUMBER OF ROOMS AVAILABLE IN BUDGET CLASS HOTELS IN MADHYA PRADESH

Destination	Available Rooms
Pachmarhi	107
Ujjain	63
Khajuraho	48
Jabalpur	28

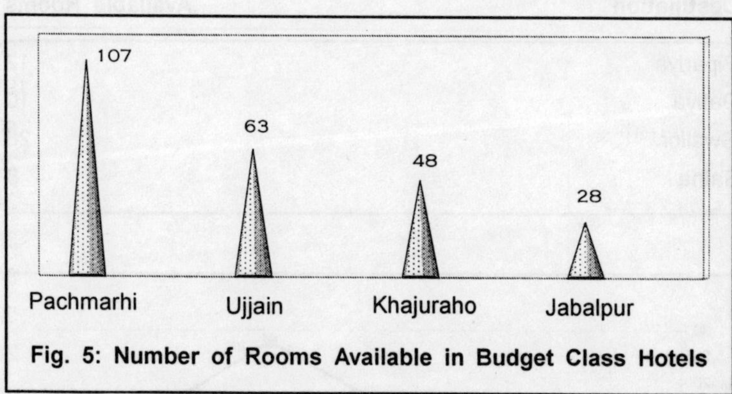

Fig. 5: Number of Rooms Available in Budget Class Hotels

Figure 5, gives the number of rooms in budget class hotels at major tourist destinations in Madhya Pradesh.

Motel:

These are roadside or placed by the national and state highway roads. They offer an opportunity to the tourists to break their journey and relax to their satisfaction. The motels provide basic facilities such as clean and hygienic environment some even offers facilities of resorts such as Swimming Pool. Table 7 below indicates availability of rooms in major motels, approved by government of Madhya Pradesh at major and minor destinations of the state.

Figure 6 below gives the availability of rooms in major motel at major tourist destination in Madhya Pradesh.

Tourist Bungalows:

Government bodies generally operate these. They normally offer services that will make tourist feel at home. These bungalows have furnished bedrooms, separate dining cum drawing room, lounge, toilets and kitchen, where a tourist can feel as if they are at home. These bungalows are especially useful for family and friends, who like to relax leaving their daily routine life aside for a time. Table 8 below indicates the number of available rooms in major tourist bungalows, approved by government of Madhya Pradesh.

Table 7: Availability of Rooms in Motels, Approved by Govt. of M.P. at Major and Minor Destinations of the State

Destination	Available Rooms
Pipariya	12
Datiya	10
Gwalior	28
Satna	8

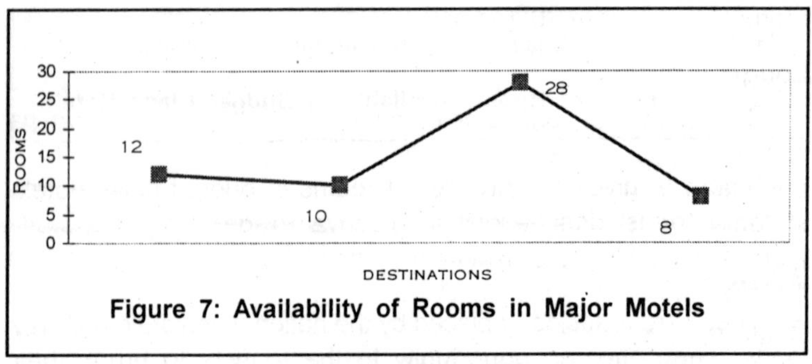

Figure 7: Availability of Rooms in Major Motels

Table 8: Rooms Available in Major Tourist Bungalows, approved by Government of Madhya Pradesh

Destination	Available Rooms
Indore	6
Pachmarhi	15
Bandhavgarh	26
Kanha	24
Orcha	10
Chitrakoot	8

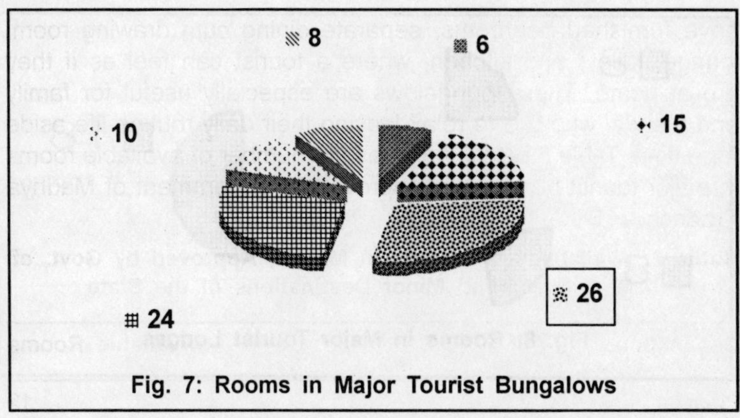

Fig. 7: Rooms in Major Tourist Bungalows

In the above Figure 7 the total no of rooms existing in tourist bungalows at major tourist places of Madhya Pradesh have been shown. It would be seen by this figure Bandhavgarh has the maximum number of rooms (26 rooms), followed by Kanha (24 rooms), Pachmarhi (15 rooms), Orcha (10 rooms), Chitrakoot (8 rooms) and Indore (6 rooms).

Lodges:

These provide one star category facilities. Lodges can be compared with the budget hotels as they provide basic facilities and clean environment at a very low price. These are especially suitable for tourists who like to travel economically. Table 9 indicates availability of rooms in major tourist lodges, approved by government of Madhya Pradesh.

Table 9: Accessible Rooms in Major Tourist Lodges, Approved by Government of Madhya Pradesh

Destination	Available Rooms
Bandhavgarh	18
Mandu	8
Sanchi	8

Dharamshalas:

Theses are operated in the name of 'Dharam' which means 'religious duties' and 'shalas' which means 'temporary residing

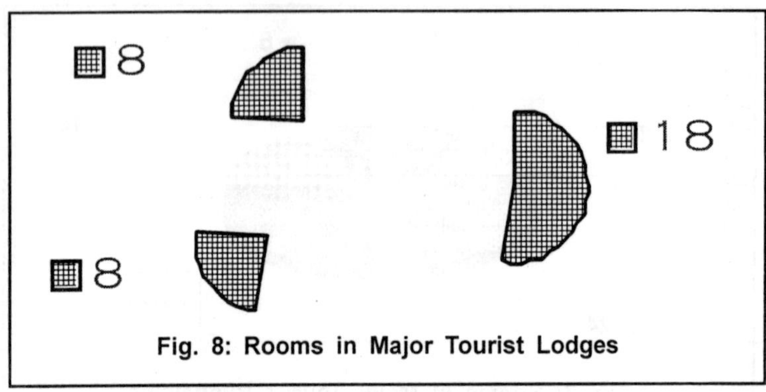

Fig. 8: Rooms in Major Tourist Lodges

place'. Thus, Dharamshalas cannot be compared with any other accommodation units, as theses are non-profit establishments and are operated as a religious duty. Dharamshalas are located in the religious places and they provide free of cost accommodation and self served food. However, if any tourist likes to add something for the cause of development of the dharamshala's infrastructure, he is most welcomed to donate money, food, household equipment etc. Table 10 gives through details of accessible rooms in major *dharamshalas* of Madhya Pradesh.

Table 10: Details of Accessible Rooms in Major Dharamshalas of Madhya Pradesh

Destination	No. Of Rooms
Amarkantak	180
Ujjain	270
Chitrakoot	210

Number of Hotel types in Madhya Pradesh – with special reference to Gwalior, Indore, Khajuraho and Amarkantak

Gwalior:

It is a city of legends and offers prime accommodation facilities for the tourists who love quality and budget and economy hotels do not want to go hard on their pockets. Gwalior provides a wide range of tourist's accommodation. The following graph 10 shows the different type accommodations available in the city.

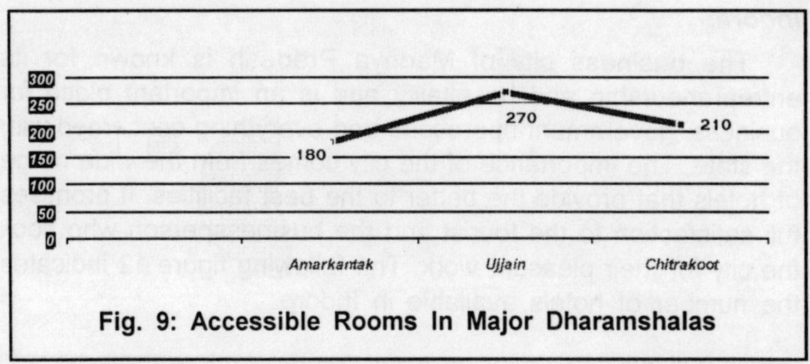

Fig. 9: Accessible Rooms In Major Dharamshalas

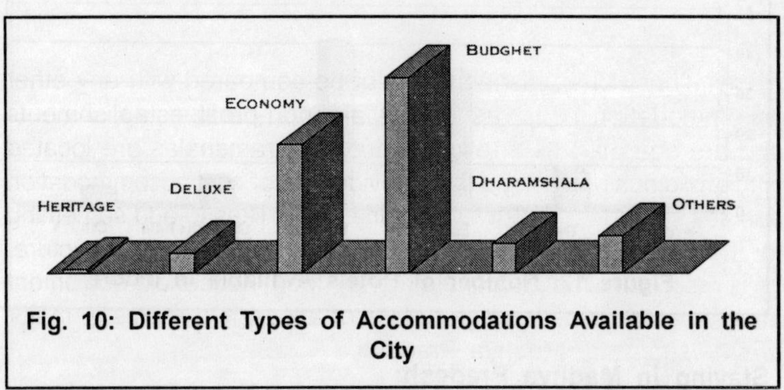

Fig. 10: Different Types of Accommodations Available in the City

Khajuraho:

Khajuraho offers the best accommodation in Madhya Pradesh. A wide range of hotels, from deluxe to the Budget category is available in plenty. Khajuraho is the most frequently visited tourist destination in Madhya Pradesh and a major proportion of tourists flock to this place to observe the cultural aspect and ancient past of the Chandellas. The following graph 11 gives the number of different type of hotels in the city.

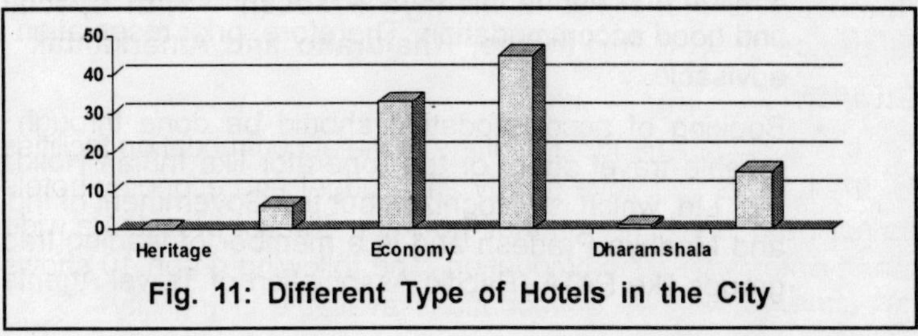

Fig. 11: Different Type of Hotels in the City

Indore:

The business city of Madhya Pradesh is known for its entrepreneurship and hospitality and is an important place for business, government operations and everything concerned with the state. The importance of the city comes from the wide range of hotels that provide the better to the best facilities. It promises full satisfaction to the tourist and the businessperson who flock the city for their pleasure work. The fallowing figure 12 indicates the number of hotels available in Indore.

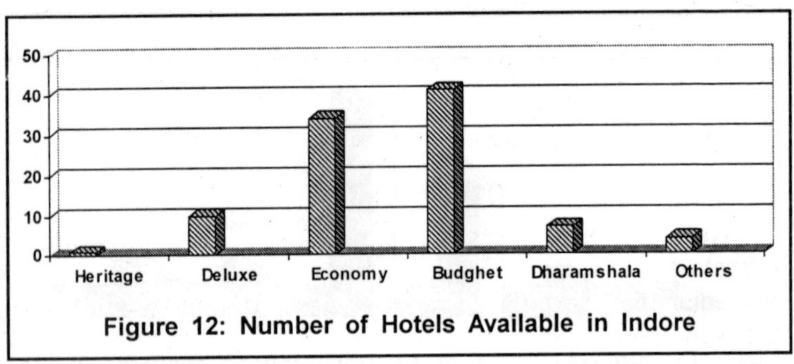

Figure 12: Number of Hotels Available in Indore

Staying in Madhya Pradesh:

Finding accommodation in Madhya Pradesh could be tough, at times, more so if one is the first timer to the region. It is essential to know exactly what to do, when one is in a difficult situation. There are some precious tips, which, if followed carefully can make tourists stay out of troubles:

- Booking of hotel should be done well in advance, especially during high season.
- In Madhya Pradesh, September to March is the high season and during this period, it is somewhat difficult to find good accommodation. Therefore, prior reservation is advisable.
- Booking of accommodation should be done through a reliable travel agent or tour operator like Indian Holiday Pvt. Ltd, which is recognized but the Government of India and Madhya Pradesh and is a member of leading trade groups like PATA (Pacific Association of Travel Agents),

IATO (Indian Association of Tour Operators), IATA (International Air Transport Association) and MPSTDC (Madhya Pradesh State Tourism Development Corporation).

- All travel documents should be preserved safely.
- Check in and check out times of the hotels should be ascertained before hand, so that problem while checking out could be avoided.
- Valuables should be kept with care and they should not be left carelessly in the hotel rooms.
- In case of problem within the hotel; hotel authority should be called for.
- Self-indulgence is not advisable.

TRANSPORTATION

Need for transportation is perhaps the most important infrastructural requirement in tourism in today's world. It acts as a medium to explore the unexplored in each and every part of the world and Madhya Pradesh is no exception. Madhya Pradesh has adequate of transportation facilities and it enables tourists to explore the incredible land of Madhya Pradesh. With new avenues, the present status of transportation is getting day by day improved in the region. Much more presentable promising and priceless facilities are available since the last decade and many more new and better facilities are aimed for the near future. Transportation by Air, Rail or Bus is as per the choice of tourists and reservation can be made easily except in high seasons. The most favourable factor in Madhya Pradesh is that, most of the places are linked with railways and national highways or state highways, which are managed by the government and public sector departments. After visiting Madhya Pradesh tourist can really stand and say that tourism infrastructure in terms of transportation is quite adequate. The services are satisfactory but require a bit more concern. The major transportation services are as follows:

Air Services:

They are few in number but adequate and most importantly uniformly distributed in Madhya Pradesh. Airports are well developed and managed by the Air Port Authority of India and state Government. The most remarkable thing in airports of the Madhya Pradesh is their management. Apart from this, these airports have tourist's information centers, so that tourists may get the right choice to opt for. Other than the above-mentioned facilities, frequent air services from far and wide distances make up for one of the best tourism infrastructure in the whole country. Major airports are situated in Gwalior, Bhopal, Indore and Jabalpur. Distribution of the airports in Madhya Pradesh can be sketched as in the map given below.

Rail Services:

Madhya Pradesh is well connected with rail services by broad gauge and it is the most frequent and commonly used service utilized by the tourists and normal persons. Major trains like Shatabdi, Rajdhani and other long distance trains like Nizamuddin-Goa Express, Ujjaini Express, Varanshi-Shikanderabad Express, Rapti-Sagar Express and Himsagar Express impart the ecstasy in transportation facilities. All major and minor places in Madhya Pradesh except Pachmarhi, Khajuraho, Mandu, Bhimbetka and Omkareshwar are well connected with the railway services.

There are specific regions for which railways services are the first choice of majority of tourists because of the following-

- Economical and suits the budget of tourists of every class.
- Safe.
- Less tiring compared to road services.
- Reservation can be made with ease through travel agents or by self.
- Established railway facilities in the region
- Primary requirement like toilet and meal available comfortably.

The above-mentioned reasons make the railway the most opted services for transportation in Madhya Pradesh for the tourists. Some of the major destinations, which have great tourist importance in Madhya Pradesh, are shown in the following table. Some major destinations are: Gwalior – it is on main central line situated in northern part of the state and is linked with Mumbai, Goa, Chennai, Delhi through mail, normal express trains, Shatabdi and Rajdhani express trains. Next destination is Khajuraho – it is very important tourist destination with world heritage site and is situated near Satna and Mahoba. Khajuraho is not directly linked by train service. The nearest railheads are Mahoba (65 kms.) and Satna (117 kms.) and these stations are well connected by good, fast and V.I.P. trains.

The following Table 11 gives the present status of railway services within Madhya Pradesh.

Table 11: Present Status of Railway Services Within Madhya Pradesh

Destinations		Major Railway Routes and Trains
Gwalior	-	It is on the central railway's main Delhi-Mumbai, Delhi-Goa, Delhi-Chennai lines.Some major trains, which can through Gwalior, include Taj, Shatabdi and Raptisagar Expresses.
Khajuraho	-	The nearest railhead is Mahoba (65 kms.).Other convenient railheads are Jhansi (176 kms.), on the Delhi-Chennai Route and Satna (117 kms.) on the Mumbai-Allahabad-Hawarah route.Shatabdi Express running on the Delhi-Bhopal route is the fastest link for the tourists coming from the Delhi, Agra and Gwalior. Detraining at Jhansi, there are convenient MPSTDC buses for transfer to Khajuraho.
Bandhavgarh	-	Nearest Railhead is Umariya (22 kms.) it is connected with regular trains on Delhi-Chennai route.
Panna	-	Nearest railhead is Satna (61kms)
Kanha	-	Nearest Railhead is Jabalpur (160 kms.).
Bhopal	-	Well connected by trains on Delhi main line. Most important trains pass through Bhopal and the fastest link it enjoys is from Delhi on the Shatabdi Express via Agra, Gwalior and Jhansi. It is also connected with Bangalore, Trivandram, Chennai, Amritsir, Secunderabad, Hawarah, Lucknow and other important places.

(*Contd.*)

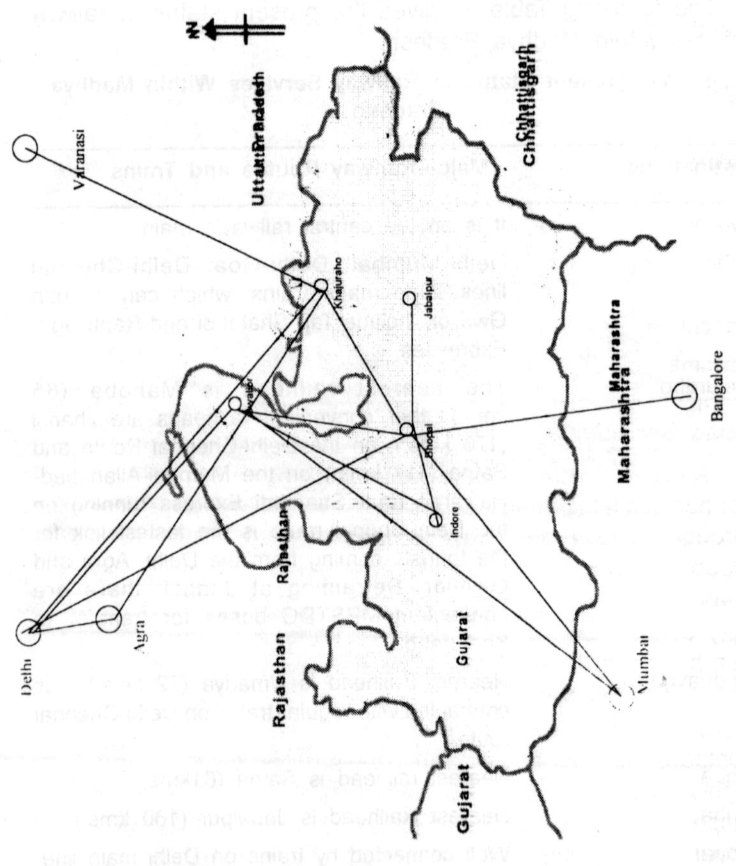

Map II: Madhya Pradesh Air Transportation

Destinations		Major Railway Routes and Trains
Jabalpur	-	Jabalpur is on the Mumbai-Hawarah via Allahabad main line and all major passengers and express trains' halt here.
Mandu	-	The nearest railhead is at Indore (99kms.) and Ratlam (124 kms.).
Ujjain		-It is on the Bhopal-Nagda sector of Western Railway.
Indore	-	Meter Gauge as well as Broad gauge lines link Indore to Bhopal, Ujjain, Mahu, Delhi, Mumbai, Hawara and Pune.
Amarkantak	-	It is connected with regular trains on Delhi-Chennai route.
Sanchi	-	Nearest railhead is Bhopal (46 kms.)
Pachmarhi	-	Nearest railhead is Pipariya (45kms.)

Road Services

Madhya Pradesh has a well-established road service which connects all the major and minor places of Madhya Pradesh through National and State highways. The highways network of Madhya Pradesh is well developed but the roads are not well maintained which is the major problem in at present. Although they connect one place to another perfectly but the roads are, turn by (except a few major highways) and tourist should be alert about irritating experience like a jump in the bus or car while traveling. Roads in Madhya Pradesh need improvement when compared to other important States. The National and State highways are maintained by the Central and State government respectively. Although great stress and strain is taken by the government to improve the present status of roads but still it lacks consistency and in the coming time, if further steps for improvement are not taken it will lead to chaotic condition and will directly affect the tourist traffic in Madhya Pradesh. These roads require much more attention from the government than what is given today.

Throughout the state, traveling by road is still preferred because of certain reasons. Firstly, many areas are still not connected by any other mode of transportation; secondly, road services are abundant and frequent. Private vehicles follow their own schedule, many prefer it, and it is much cheaper than air services and first class rail services in the state. There are certain demerits of the road service. These are: travel by roads, roads are not up to the satisfaction level, very tiring journey, frequent and better railway service, lack of mid way tourist information centers and comparatively less motels than other states or places. In spite of these demerits, road services are still preferred by a large number of tourists. Table 12 gives status of road services within Madhya Pradesh and the relevant highways.

Table 12: National And State Highways In The State

Major Places	National / State Highway
Gwalior	☐ Regular state transport and private bus services and private taxies through state highways (37 and 55) and national highways (3) to Agra, Mathura, Jaipur, Delhi, Lucknow, Bhopal, Indore, Jhansi and Khajuraho connect it.
Khajuraho	☐ It is connected by regular bus services to Agra (395kms), Bhopal (372 kms), Gwalior (287kms), Varansi (415 kms) and Allahabad (285 kms).
Bandhavgarh	☐ It is connected to Khajuraho (210 kms.) via Panna, Satna and Maihar, to Tala and Jabalpur (195 kms.) by state highway no. 11 and 14.
Panna	☐ It is connected to Satna (61kms.), Jhansi (200 kms) and Khajuraho (47 kms.) by State Highway No. 6 and National Highway no. 27.
Kanha	☐ Regular and frequent services from Mandla (65 kms.) is preferred by the tourists. It is connected to Jabalpur (160 kms.), Nagpur (255 kms.) and it is on State Highway no. 37.
Bhopal	☐ Regular services connect Bhopal with major centers within state and outside. Some important distances are Indore (188 kms.), Mandu (285 kms.), Ujjain (186 kms.), Khajuraho (387 kms.), Pachmarhi (197 kms.), Gwalior (443 kms.), Sanchi (47 kms.) and Jabalpur (310 kms.) via State Highway no. 18, 23 and National Highway no. 12.
Mandu	☐ Regular bus and taxi services connect Mandu to Dhar (35 kms.), Indore (99 kms.), Ratlam (125 kms.), Ujjain (152 kms.) and Bhopal (283 kms.)

Major Places	National / State Highway
Jabalpur	☐ It is connected with National Highways no 7, 12 and 27 and State Highway no 37 and 22.
Ujjain	☐ A regular service connects Ujjain to Indore, Bhopal, Ratlam, Gwalior, Dhar, Kota and Omkasreshwar via State Highway no. 27 and 18.
Indore	☐ It is well connected by road through National Highway no 3 and State Highway no 22 and 27 to Mumbai, Agra, Gwalior, Ahmedabad, Pune, Bhopal and Ujjain.
Amarkantak	☐ It is connected by State Highway no 22 to Jabalpur and Indore.
Sanchi	☐ It is connected to Bhopal (47kms.) by State Highway no 18 and 19.
Pachmarhi	☐ It is connected to Bhopal (197 kms.) through State Highway no 26 and 19.

Tourist Traffic

The most utilized transportation service by tourists in Madhya Pradesh is rail service followed by road and then air. Tourist traffic is affected as per the season.

Air Service

Tourists utilize lesser number of air services as compared to other transport services. The following graph 13 shows the difference in tourist traffic ratio of air service as transport in season and non-season period.

The graph shows a very small rise in the tourist traffic from 2% to 4% with the change in the season. The major reasons for air service not utilized by the tourists includes; air services are expensive and average tourist can-not afford it, these are not available in every tourist place in Madhya Pradesh and frequency of services is also too low.

Rail Transportation:

Railway is the most preferred service, which is utilized by the tourists, and the following graph 14 proves this point.

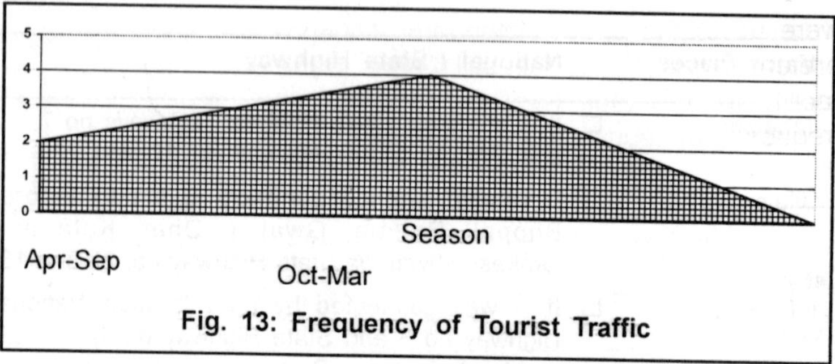

Fig. 13: Frequency of Tourist Traffic

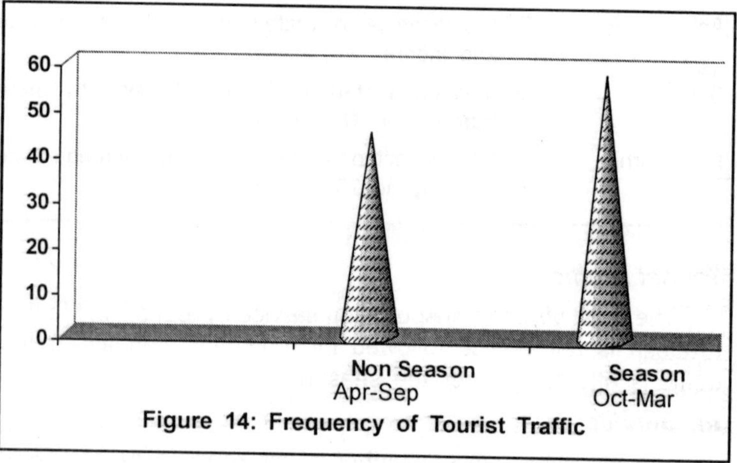

Figure 14: Frequency of Tourist Traffic

A good 10 to 15 % rise in tourist traffic is observed since the last five years, which makes the rail service the most preferred service above others. The reasons for rail service being preferred are – it provides a safe journey, not tiring, established railway facilities connecting major and minor places in Madhya Pradesh, primary requirements like toilet and meals can be met and it is economical and suits all pockets. These factors put the railways ahead of other services. The percentage of tourists utilizing rail service comes to about fifty to fifty two percent.

Road Service:

Road services in the Madhya Pradesh state is very frequent and would have been the most preferred service if the roads were up to the desired standard, Though, road service is not preferred over rail service, still it adds to the major transportation facility for the tourists. The following graph 15 explains the frequency of tourists utilizing the road services

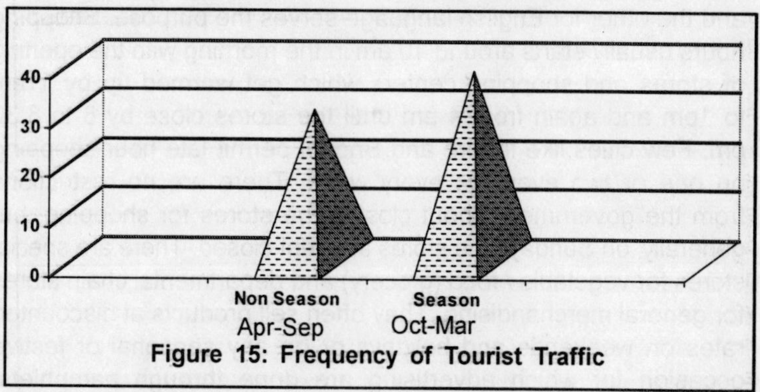

Figure 15: Frequency of Tourist Traffic

A good increase of about 8 to 10 % is observed in the percentage of tourists utilizing road service in the peak season period. The reasons why it lies below the rail service are – comparatively unsafe, it has less motels and mid way resorts as compared to other important states in the country, roads are not up to the standard and it is a lot more tiring to tour around utilizing road services than the railway services.

Shopping Facilities:

Madhya Pradesh is a shopper's paradise. The 'sale' is a way of life here, occurring in big retail stores several times in a year often on unlikely occasions. The so-called summer sales, for instance, begin immediately after the festival 'Holi' and winter cloths go on sale in late spring or early summer on the ground that, regular shoppers will have bought their wares already. Departmental stores in Madhya Pradesh are basically the same as departmental stores in the world over- only they are bigger and more varied in the selection of merchandise, Super markets sell everything from melons to set of encyclopedias. Drug stores do sell banana, cosmetics, vitamins, candies and many other items other than drugs. Shopping centers in suburban and rural areas include several stores under one roof, sharing one tremendous parking lot. Often special events, such as feat, religious festivals etc. are held in major shopping malls.

Shopping assistance to foreign visitors is furnished by hundreds of big stores across the state. Some of them have multilingual aides but in general bilingual aides of one for regional and the other for English language serves the purpose. Shopping hours usually starts around 10 am in the morning with the opening of stores and shopping centers which get warmed up by 11am to 1pm and again from 4 pm until the stores close by 8 to 8.30 pm. Few cities like Indore and Bhopal permit late hour shopping on one or two evenings every weak. There are no restrictions from the government about closing the stores for shopping, but generally, on Sundays the stores are kept closed. There are special stores for vegetable / food (grocery) and departmental chain stores for general merchandising. They often sell products at discounted rates on weekends and holidays or on any seasonal or festive occasion for which advertising are done through pamphlets, newspapers, etc. Some stars also use even done local television channel. Facilities of payment by credit card are also provided by few shopping centers in Madhya Pradesh, which the tourists find very useful.

The state is a paradise for souvenir and treasure hunters. Both expensive and inexpensive objects of utility produced all over the state, present an unending variety of skill, colour and imaginations. There are Silk Saries from Chanderi, modern and fancy wearing cloths from Khajuraho, Toys of Supari from Rewa, leather cloths from Indore, Sarees, dupattas, dress material, bed sheets, pillow covers and table cloths made by hand block printing method from Bherongarh near Ujjain, Zari work, and Juties from Bhopal.

Information Centers and Money Changing Counters

The tourist information centers and money changing counters in the state are of high utility and provide detailed information on every aspect related to tourism information on destinations adventure, wildlife, National Parks, etc. Today all the information regarding accommodation, transportation, places to be visited, natural and Man-made attractions, petrol stations and tourist information counters are available on internet websites and newspaper and magazines. It is very difficult to gather all these information at one point. Therefore, appropriate and adequate information cannot be provided to the tourists. There are several tourist information centers that are located at major tourist centers of Madhya Pradesh and most of these are well equipped and well setup. Bhopal is the headquarter of tourism department of the state and has several tourist Bureau at several places in the state that provide detailed information to the tourists. Most of the travel agents who come in contact with the tourists are not properly trained to explain the places of interest, culture, history, archaeology, geography and routes. It is just because, lack of communication skills and lack of perfect knowledge of the places.

The money exchange counters are mainly for the purpose of the foreigners who need them the most. There are number of Government and private agencies that work for the State. These agencies could act as a medium to promote tourism in Madhya Pradesh. In addition, there are several journals, articles, itineraries and guides, which are published by the government and private agencies to provide information to the tourists. The most basic travel literature for the tourist in Madhya Pradesh is the highway map, even if he or she may not be travelling by road. These are usually available from the State tourism office and also at many petrol stations run by major oil companies. At principal entry points in the State, there are some information centers, normally along the national highway, which distribute a variety of free material, including maps. MPSTDC is the most important source of information in the State and there are a few other agencies also publish guides of quality, that are sold in all standard bookshops of are available free of cost from tourist information centers. Some representative titles are Road Atlas, Vacation and Travel Guide, National Park guide, Discover India, Madhya Pradesh Travel Guide and many more, which describe the glory of the state.

State Tourism Offices

The tourist can also obtain travel information on Madhya Pradesh destinations before their departure from the travel agent but, if in case there is insufficient information about any destination or anything that concerns tourism in the State; there are State Tourism Offices, which are always there to give the best to the tourist. All agencies normally provide tourists with tourist literature and maps upon. As material often arrives in huge quantities and it is best for the tourist to specify what sort of information is required. There are number of tourist information centers in the state and the Annexure III.XIII gives description of the information centers in different parts of Madhya Pradesh.

Money Exchange Counters

The state has a number of money exchange counters for the convenience of foreign tourists. Tourist can exchange their currency into rupees at the airports anywhere in the country. Apart from this, hotels in India also provide this facility to the foreign tourists. However, there are number of banks that exchange curriries and it has been observed that foreign tourists prefer to have their currency exchanged at government banks, whose working hours are from 9 am to 3 pm. However, with the introduction of Travellers Cheques, which are safe and convenient way to carry money, more and more foreign tourists make use of it as it is accepted by luxury hotels, banks, restaurants of quality and many good category stores.

REFERENCES

Bagri, S.C., (2003), *Trends in Tourism Promotion (Emerging Issues)*, Bishen Singh Publications, Connaught Place, Dehradun, Uttaranchal

Bagri, S.C., (Ed.) (1994), *Journal of Tourism*, Vol. 2, Department of Tourism, H.N.B.G.University, Srinagar, Garhwal.

Boniface, B., and Cooper, C., (1987), *The Geography of Travel and Tourism*, Heinemann, London.

Borg, J.Vander, (1991), *Tourism and Urban Development*, Amsterdam, Netherlands.

Burkart, A.J., and Medlik, S., (1981), Tourism, Past, Present and Future, Heinemann, London.

Chakravorty, (1982), *Railways for Developing Countries*, Chetna Publications, New Delhi.

Chopra, S., (1991), *Tourism and Development in India*, Asia Publishing House, New Delhi.

Devid, steward, (1980), *The Theory and Practices of Transport*, Heinmann, London.

Government of Madhya Pradesh – *Revised District Gazetteers of Madhya Pradesh* of different districts.

Inskeep, E., and Kallenberger, M., (1992), *An Integrated Approach to Resort Development*, WTO, Madrid.

Mitchell, L.S., and Murphy, P.E., (1991), *Geography and Tourism*, ATR.

Robinson, H., (1976*), The Geography of Tourism*, Macdonald and Evance, London.

Sanghi, Vraman, (1990), *India Travel Companign*, Asia Publishing Company, College Road Market, Kolkata.

Sinha, R.K., (1999), *Growth and Development of Modern Tourism*, Dominant Publishers, South Anarkali, New Delhi.

Sinha, R.K., (1999*), Leisure Tourism*, Dominant Publishers, South Anarkali, New Delhi.

Smith, S.L.J., (1989), *Tourism Analysis*, Longman, Harlow.

ANNEXURE I
TOTAL NUMBER OF ROOMS AVAILABLE IN MAJOR TOURIST DESTINATIONS AND THEIR TARIFF

Destination	Hotel	Tariff
Indore	• Taj Residency Meghdoot Garden	Rs.2550 (Single Room) - Rs.10,750 (Deluxe Suite)
	• Hotel SayaJi Off Meghdoot Garden, Scheme 54 – C	Rs.1,450 (Single Room) - Rs.4,000 (Deluxe Suite)
Khajuraho	• Taj Chandella, Near Airport	Rs.1,800 (Single Room) - Rs.4,000 (Deluxe Suite)
	• Jass Trident, Bypass Road,	Rs.1,950 (Single Room) - Rs.4,500 (Deluxe Suite)
	• Clarks Bundela, Village Khajuraho	Rs.1,950 (Single Room) - Rs.3,700 (Deluxe Suite)
	• Clarks Khajuraho Village Khajuraho	Rs3,995 (Single Room) - Rs.5,500 (Deluxe Suite)
	• Holiday Inn, Airport Road	Rs.1,500 (Single Room) - Rs.5,000 (Deluxe Suite)
Bhopal	• Lake View Ashok Shamla Hills	Rs.1,600 (Single Room) - Rs.3,500 (Deluxe Suite)
	• The Residency 208, M.P. Nagar	Rs.1,140 (Single Room) - Rs.5,000 (Deluxe Suite)
Gwalior	• Gwalior Regency, Near New Bus Stand, Link Road	Rs.1,200 (Single Room) - Rs.2,200 (Deluxe Suite)

SECTION E

HUMAN RESOURCE MANAGEMENT IN HOSPITALITY AND TOURISM OPERATIONS

17

PAY SATISFACTION IN THE HOSPITALITY AND TOURISM INDUSTRY: THEORIES, REALITIES AND THE POSSIBILITIES

SUMEETRA M THOZHUR

ABSTRACT

The importance of researching pay cannot be stressed enough. Pay gets people to work even though other factors might make them stay. Pay is crucial from an organisational perspective as it accounts for a major fraction of organisational expenditure. According to Shaw et al (1999), compensation costs are estimated to account for between 10 to 50 percent, and in some cases 90 percent of an organisation's operating expenses. The consequences of pay dissatisfaction include both employees' physical and psychological health (depression, life satisfaction and somatic complaints), and employee behaviours and intentions (job search intent, performance, absenteeism and turnover) (McGregor, 1960; Lawler, 1971). Given the hospitality and tourism industries' concerns with service quality and employee turnover, any understanding of what causes pay satisfaction becomes central to creating good human resource policies and practices.

This research paper goes back to the drawing board to revisit pay in the hospitality and tourism industry. It attempts to understand the meaning of pay for people working in these industries. By looking at existing theories and what is happening on the ground, it identifies the ways in which pay can be used as a management tool specifically in today's hospitality and tourism industry. In trying to achieve its objective, it takes a holistic approach and brings together economic and psychological explanations as to the significance of pay for people at work. It also discovers additional factors that have not been previously identified. The investigation takes the form of a largely theoretical paper underpinned by empirical analysis, using primary data in order to explore beyond the stark figures, deviating from previous studies, which have generally been done at the macro level using secondary data.

***Keywords:* pay satisfaction, hospitality, tourism, turnover, pay research, employee satisfaction**

INTRODUCTION

Since man began bartering livestock, the face of money has come a long way but its value remains the same. Money received in return for work done or pay, continues to play an important part in people's lives. Opsahl and Dunnette (1966) state that people everywhere seem to behave as if money were a prime goal.

This chapter goes back to the drawing board to revisit pay in the hospitality and tourism industry. It attempts to understand the meaning of pay for people working in these industries. By looking at existing theories and what is happening on the ground, it identifies the ways in which pay can be used as a management tool specifically in today's hospitality and tourism industry. In trying to achieve its objective, it takes a holistic approach and brings together economic and psychological explanations as to the significance of pay for people at work.

WHY DO WE NEED TO STUDY PAY SATISFACTION?

Pay is crucial from an organisational perspective as it accounts for a major fraction of organisational expenditure. According to Shaw et al (1999), compensation costs are estimated to account for between 10 to 50 percent, and in some cases 90 percent of an organisation's operating expenses. Moreover, pay is one of the most significant techniques available to practitioners for managing employees. Kessler (2003) states that pay is a central concern and a key pillar of the employment relationship. Pay is not only a core element, but also the most conspicuous aspect of the employment relationship and thus of fundamental interest to the employers.

Furthermore, pay is immediately related to the other factors of organisational significance including job satisfaction, motivation, and performance among others. Henemann (1992) found a strong positive relationship between pay and performance, which has been supported by other researchers (Opsahl and Dunette, 1966; Lawler, 1971). Lawler (1971) believes that pay can be used to make employees feel satisfied with their job, motivate them, gain their commitment to the organisation, and keep them in the organisation. Peck, (1984) additionally states that pay is one of the main management techniques employed to improve performance and the first priority of compensation systems is to tie pay to performance. In short, it may be contended that pay is an extremely crucial factor for both employees and employers at work.

WHAT IS PAY SATISFACTION?

Pay can be defined as the sum total financial compensation that an individual receives for work done (Ehrenberg and Smith, 2000). Pay satisfaction can simply be described as satisfaction with the pay received by an individual. Locke, (1969) suggests that pay satisfaction is a function of comparison between the perceived amount of pay that one wants to receive and the actual amount received, and when congruence exists between the two, pay satisfaction results. In other words, a person's satisfaction with the fairness of the pay for his job is determined by what he wants from his job and what he perceives he is being offered. Both 'what he wants' and what 'he is being offered' are hypothesised to be influenced by personal (e.g. experience) and environmental (e.g. job characteristics) variables.

Other researchers have argued that pay satisfaction is determined by what one expects to receive rather than what one wants (Lawler, 1971, Heneman and Schwab 1985). They view pay satisfaction as a discrepancy between how much pay one feels one should receive and how much one feels is actually received. This approach combines the idea of discrepancy along with Adam's (1965) equity theory of social comparisons and has found significant support within literature (Miceli et al, 1991, Blau, 1994, Rice et al, 1991)

THEORIES EXPLAINING PAY SATISFACTION

There are numerous theories within the fields of psychology and economics that can be invoked to describe people's reaction to pay. Economic theories and psychological theories correspond in their outlook that linking pay to performance should increase performance, but disagree on the extent of importance that should be placed on pay. Economists would list pay as the one and only reason for coming to work, while psychologists would place pay among a host of personal and work variables. Heneman (1992) observes that while economic theories emphasise on the opportunity costs to the employment decisions, psychological theories give priority to the attractive outcomes to individuals as a major incentive In other words, while economists take a utility maximization approach, psychologists follow a satisfaction perspective. The following sections identify and elaborate on the major psychological theories explaining pay satisfaction.

Herzberg's Two Factor Theory:

On the basis of an extensive study involving engineers and accountants Herzberg et al (1959) classified job factors into motivators and hygiene factors. The motivators when fulfilled will lead to satisfaction, while the hygiene factors when satisfied will not. The suggestion is to focus more on the motivators and redesign jobs in order to achieve job enrichment.

Pay according to Herzberg et al (1959) is both a motivator and a hygiene factor. As Lawler (1971) observes, pay is a satisfier only as long as it is necessary to fulfil the basic requirements. Once a level of pay is achieved, it becomes a hygiene factor and no longer leads to satisfaction. This line of reasoning might not be completely justified as the amount of money required increases with increasing pay creating a higher requirement for pay. Thus current wage increases could be used to motivate people to seek the next wage increase.

Maslow's Theory Of Hierarchy Of Needs:

Maslow (as discussed in Buchanan and Huczynski 2001) posited a 'hierarchy of human needs' based on two groupings: deficiency needs (physiological needs) and growth needs (psychological needs). Within the deficiency needs, each lower need must be met before moving to the next higher level. Once each of these needs has been satisfied, if at some future time a deficiency is detected, the individual will act to remove the deficiency.

According to Maslow, an individual is ready to act upon their growth needs if and only if their deficiency needs are met. At subsistence level this means that people are more focused on attaining their basic physiological requirements and thus more focused on pay. Their satisfaction is consequently guided by the fulfilment of their deficiency needs that require money rather than their growth needs. Maslow's theory suggests that pay is extremely significant for people at the lower end of the pay scale compared to those at the upper end.

Expectancy Theory:

Expectancy theory is a cognitive theory which argues that human behaviour is directed by the conscious expectations that people have about their behaviour leading to the achievement of desired goals (Buchanan and Huczynski, 2001). In other words, behaviour depends on the outcomes that an individual values, and the expectations that a particular type of behaviour will lead to those outcomes. Consequently, according to Heneman (1992) and Vroom (1964) pay under expectancy theory is likely to lead to satisfaction when

- Performance is accurately measured in order to able the employees to perceive a direct link between effort-performance(expectancy) and performance-rewards (instrumentality)
- Increased pay is a valued outcome for employees to perceive positive valence for their output.
- The relationship between pay and performance is clearly defined to ensure that performance is seen as instrumental to pay increase by the employees.

- Opportunities to improve performance exists
- Expectancy and valence must exist within the employee

However, expectancy theory has been criticised on various grounds. Firstly, it does not effectively account for all kinds of organisational situations. Kennedy, Fossum and White (1983, as discussed in Heneman, 1992) note that expectancy theory seems to work well on individuals rather than groups. It does not account for group norms, for example, which influences productivity significantly (Buchanan and Huczynski, 2001). Secondly, it does not make allowances for the external conditions that may play a role in pay satisfaction. Economic considerations do influence pay satisfaction according to Hulin et al (1985, as discussed in Judge and Watanbe, 1993) who argue that in periods of labour over supply, employees will perceive their inputs less valuable as there are others present in the market willing to contribute their inputs for a similar or lesser rate of output. Finally, the theory does not specify how people learn what is appropriate behaviour in different stimulus situations. According to Lawler, (1971), expectancy theory does not explain how people develop their beliefs about the consequences of behaving in a certain manner nor does it explain how people develop their response stimulus subjective probabilities. Why do some people for example, believe that if they perform well, there is a high probability of a pay rise, while others believe there is a very little chance of a pay rise under similar circumstances?

Equity Theory:

Adam's (1965) equity theory unlike its predecessors suggests that satisfaction besides being influenced by pay- performance relation of the individual employee, is also affected by the pay-performance relation of significant others. If an individuals' output/ input ratio is perceived to be lower than another's' then that individual may feel under rewarded and work towards equating it with the compared individuals.

Equity theory is an important instrument to understand pay satisfaction. It makes prediction concerning four different pay inequity situations. Lawler (1971) states that an individual can be overpaid, underpaid, piece rate or hourly, and reactions will differ accordingly. For example, if an individual feels underpaid within piece rate incentives, he will react by reducing the quality (thus producing low quality goods in large numbers), whereas if he feels underpaid in hourly system, he may decrease output.

Equity theory also has its share of criticisms. Similar to most other psychological theories, equity theory does not take the external situation into consideration to account for individual motivation. For example, perception of available opportunities and the chances of getting them could influence pay satisfaction. Hulin et al (1987) found a significant relationship to exist between turnover and availability of jobs. The theory also does not account for the presence of incomplete information an individual might posses and make decisions based on them. Beach (1997) argues that individuals rarely have complete knowledge and tend to satisfy based on available facts.

PAY FOR PEOPLE IN THE HOSPITALITY AND TOURISM INDUSTRIES

People working in the hospitality and tourism industries are frequently found to be at the receiving end of low pay. They are amongst the least paid industries due to various factors. The economists mainly attribute the cause of low pay to physical and mental ability, accumulation of human capital, type of industry and nature of the job. Other factors like changes in demography and labour supply and demand, international trade and skill based technological change are said to cause the increasing wage inequality between skilled and unskilled workers. All these characteristics are prevalent in most hospitality and tourism jobs which is why they tend to be among the worst paid jobs in the market.

Just as a host of factors combine together to create low pay, a multitude of factors assist in maintaining low pay. Riley and Szivas (2003) list the major factors that keep the pay down within the tourism industry. These include occupational choice, attractiveness of the job, transferability of skills, accumulation of human capital over time, weak internal labour markets and availability of local market which in turn lead to a cultural norm of a said industry being low paid or high paid, and the industry maintaining the status quo.

The characteristics of the job and the nature of the industry aid employers by providing either a large workforce, or low skill requirements within the job as in the case of the tourism industry (Cullen, 1997). Additionally as Sharif (2000) notes that in most labour dependent economies, the reserve army of unemployed labourers maintains low pay. The kind of jobs offering low pay are ones often associated with low skills which do not allow the accumulation of skills over time. This in turn leads to a lack of bargaining power by the employees and also a lack of opportunities.

It is important to understand the difference between the input of effort for the low paid as those opposed to the high paid. An individual will accept an amount of pay and come to work if the income exceeds their reservation wage. Therefore, the labour force participation will depend on comparing market opportunities and the benefits of staying home (Ehrenberg and Smith, 2000). This explanation however, does not sufficiently explain the working behaviour of the poor who do not have a reservation wage to fall back on. Sharif (2000) argued that the susbsistency behaviour of the working poor means that they will increase their effort with a decrease in income leading to a forward falling supply curve. It means that pay for individuals in low paid hospitality and tourism jobs is extremely important not only for satisfaction but also for subsistence. As pay figures very highly on their agenda, their reactions to pay will be stronger. One reaction to low pay is turnover, which is very high in the hospitality and tourism industry and there is constant stream of staff going through the systems as people express their dissatisfaction with their pay level. It also means that these people often have low levels of motivation and job satisfaction as evident from their frequent job changes and lack of organisational commitment.

ISSUES IN PAY SATISFACTION

Level of Pay:

Level of pay is an important aspect of pay satisfaction. However, there is a lack of studies looking at pay satisfaction based on pay levels (Heneman, 1985). Porter, Greenberger and Heneman (1990) suggested that the relationship was not straightforward. They conducted an extensive study drawing upon theoretical arguments including theories of economics, political science, psychology and psychophysics. Their findings and comparisons to past studies made them conclude that there is a need to test for all theoretical relationship between pay satisfaction and actual pay for any one set of data. Relationships would be influenced by the situation and would not be a simple straightforward correlation. Any study looking at the satisfaction of the low paid would thus definitely contribute to the general pay satisfaction literature.

Conceptualising Pay Satisfaction:

One of the major issues related to conceptualising pay satisfaction is the difficulty in identifying and defining it. There are debates about the dimensionality of pay satisfaction, the components that form a part of it and the ways of identifying it. Carraher and Buckley (1996) suggest that the influences of individual differences in experiences, expectations and abilities along with cognitive complexity (Kelly, 1955) make it difficult for establishing clear definitions of the construct. Thus despite extensive research the concept of pay satisfaction itself remains vague with new boundaries forever being established. Locke (1976) criticises the attitude of researchers who draw on Hume's 'correlation without explanation', leading to observing sequences of actions but not attempting to identify the characteristics of the entities which made these actions possible. An unavoidable effect of the repeated use of this strategy of 'correlation without explanation' is scientific uncertainty, past findings repeatedly contradicted by later findings.

Another concern under the same heading is the ambiguity of the interrelation between major concepts and pay satisfaction. The relationship between job satisfaction and pay satisfaction is vague at best. Buchanan and Huczynski (2001) speak of fulfilling employee need satisfaction and improve work motivation through job enrichment with no mention of pay satisfaction in their entire book on Organisational Behaviour. Is pay a part of job satisfaction? Economists swear by pay, while psychologists are not so sure. The effect of pay satisfaction on turnover is also not clear. The only agreement among researchers is that pay is important and it causes dissatisfaction, which in turn has many behavioural consequences like turnover, job search, global satisfaction, sickness, and absenteeism among others.

PAY SATISFACTION AND ITS RELATIONSHIPS WITH OTHER VARIABLES

The inter relationships between the different variables of pay satisfaction is another source of debate. Weiner (1980) criticises the lack of empirical studies attempting to look at the relationship between determinants and consequences of pay satisfaction variables and states that those that do are atheoretical and test single or series of variables. Deckop (1992) for example, listed causes and consequences of organisational and career pay satisfaction but accepted that the model is an outcome, in that the rationale for the distinction is the presumed differences in response that depends on the source of pay satisfaction.

PROBLEMS OF MEASURING PAY SATISFACTION

Even though there is a difficulty in identifying pay satisfaction, it has been measured in numerous studies with different degrees of success. Operationally specific definitions looking at pay satisfaction in relation to level of pay, pay systems, career or organisational pay satisfaction among others are created by the researchers and used for the purpose of their research resulting in a lack of a common scale of comparison. As Deckop (1992) observes, most of the attempts to measure pay satisfaction have not been based on specific conceptual models of pay satisfaction. Despite Lawler's (1971) focus on pay fairness satisfaction, both the JDI and MSQ pay subscales include items that measure fulfilment of assorted pay desires, not just perceptions related to pay fairness like for example items 'barely live on income', 'income adequate for normal expenses' in JDI and 'the chance to make as much money as my friends' in MSQ (Deckop 1992).

The Pay Satisfaction Questionnaire (PSQ) is one model that has developed from a theoretical model, which has been validated by other researchers (Heneman, Greeberg and Strasser, 1988; Judge, 1993). However, there are criticisms of the measure as being too ambiguous as to which frame of reference respondents should use. Examples include 'My current salary', 'My most recent raise' and 'the value of my benefits'. Deckop (1992) argues that the wording of these statements leaves open the choice of referent to the individual and the results will provide no clues to the reasons behind the choices.

Using Self Reported Figures:

Another issue is the reliability of using self reported figures. Satisfaction is an individual feeling and all measures are self-reported. Given the conflicting theories surrounding pay satisfaction, and the debates surrounding 'what causes pay satisfaction', the results of any research will influence its theoretical arguments. Brown and MacIntosh (1998) suspect that in the case of job satisfaction due to the use of self-reported variables, the results although backed by theory and measurements are not completely foolproof. This argument might apply to pay satisfaction as well. Their position that it is impossible to control the level of influence of factors such as mood on the day of answering questions, whether the employee has decided to quit the job due to other reasons and what job rating scales mean to each individual among others could apply to measures of pay satisfaction as well.

THE RELATIONSHIP BETWEEN JOB SATISFACTION AND PAY SATISFACTION

Researchers agree that pay is an important aspect of job satisfaction. Heneman and Schwab (1985) found pay to be an important dimension of job satisfaction. Measures of job satisfaction (Job Descriptive Index, Minnesota Satisfaction Questionnaire, Dunham et al, 1977) always include pay as a key factor.

However, research is inconclusive on the specific role of pay in job satisfaction. The specific relationship between pay and job satisfaction is disputed. On one hand, some researchers argue that pay satisfaction is immediately related to organisational factors job satisfaction, motivation, and performance (Heneman, 1992, Opsahl and Dunette, 1966; Lawler, 1971). On the other hand, other researchers suggest that pay satisfaction may not necessarily be an active part of job satisfaction. Herzberg et al (1959) classified pay as both a motivator and hygiene factor and suggested that pay is a satisfier only as long as it is necessary to fulfil the basic requirements, and once a level of pay is achieved, it becomes a hygiene factor and so does not influence job satisfaction. Riley et al (1998) also found that people working in menial jobs in tourism separate feelings of pay from feelings about their job, thus detaching their pay satisfaction with their overall job satisfaction. In sum, researchers agree that pay is an important part of job satisfaction but disagree on the exact position of pay within job satisfaction.

SUMMARY

This chapter has described the key psychological theories explaining why people are in low paid jobs. The chapter tried to understand the meaning of pay for the low paid in the hospitality and tourism industries given their unique characteristics. It began by emphasising the importance of pay for the employer and the employee. The chapter then introduced the concept of pay satisfaction as a discrepancy between what one expects to receive and what one is receiving. The chapter summarised the key theories explaining satisfaction with pay. It identified the unique features of the hospitality and tourism industries and analysed the role of pay for people in low paid jobs and low accumulation of skills overtime. It also identified some key issues that could form the focus of much needed future research in the area of pay satisfaction.

REFERENCES

Adams, J.S. (1965) Inequity in social exchange. In Berkowitz, L (ed) *Advances in Experimental Social Psychology* (pp 267- 299). New York :Academic Press

Beach, L. R. (1997) *The psychology of decision making: people in organisations.* Sage: London

Blau, G. (1994) Testing the effect of level and importance of pay referents on pay level satisfaction. *Human Relations* 47 (10), 1251- 1268

Brown, D. and McIntosh, S. (1998) If you are happy and you know it....... Job Satisfaction in the low wage service sector. *London School of Economics, Centre for Economic Performance* Discussion Paper 405, 1- 27

Buchanan, D. and Huczynski, A. (2001) *Organisational Behaviour.* London: Prentice Hall

Carraher, S.M. and Buckley, M.R. (1991) The effect of retention rule on the number of components retained: The case of the Pay Satisfaction Questionnaire. *Southern Management Association Proceedings* 493- 495

Cullen, P (1997) *Economics for Hospitality Management*. London: Thomson Business Press

Deckop, J.R. (1992) Organisational and career pay satisfaction. *Human Resource Management Review* 2 (2), 115- 129

Dunham, R.B., Smith, F.J. and Blackburn, R.S. (1977) Validation of the Index of Organisational Reactions with the JDI, the MSQ, and faces scale. *Academy of Management Journal* 20, 320- 432

Ehrenberg, R.G. and Smith, R.S. (2000) *Modern Labour Economics.* England: Addison- Wesley

Heneman, R.L. (1992) *Merit Pay.* England: Addison- Wesley

Heneman, R.L., Greenberger, D.B. and Strasser, S (1988) The relationship between pay-for-performance perceptions and pay satisfaction. *Personnel Psychology* 41, 745- 759

Heneman, H.G. and Schwab, D.P, (1985), Pay Satisfaction Questionnaire- Its multidimensional nature and measurement. *International Journal of Psychology* 20(2), 129-141

Heneman, H. (1985). Pay satisfaction. In Rowland, K. and Ferris, G. (Eds.). *Research in personnel and human resource management.* 3 (pp. 115-139). Greenwich, CT: JAI Press,

Herzberg, F., Mausner, B. and Snyderman, B (1959) *The motivation to work.* New York : Wiley

Hicks, J.R. (1946) (ed) *Value and Capital.* Oxford

Hulin, C.L., Roznowski, M. and Hachiya, D Alternative opportunities and withdrawal decisions for the job change framework. *Journal of Career Development* 17 (1), 41- 58

Judge, T (1993) Validity of the dimensions of the pay satisfaction questionnaire: evidence of differential prediction. *Personnel Psychology* 46,(2) 331- 355

Judge, T.A. and Watanbe, S (1993) Another look at the Job Satisfaction-Life Satisfaction Relationship. *Journal of Applied Psycholog* 78(6) 939- 948

Kelly, G (1955) *The psychology of personal constructs.* New York: Norton

Kessler, I (2003) Pay and Performance. In Towers, B (2003) (ed) *The handbook of Employment Relations: Law and Practice* London: Kogan Page

Lawler, E.E. (1971) *Pay and organizational effectiveness: A psychological view.* New York: Mc-Graw Hill

Locke, E. A. (1976) The nature and consequences of job satisfaction. In M. D. Dunnette (ed) *Handbook of Industrial and Organizational Psychology.* Chicago: Rand McNally.

Locke, E.A. (1969) *What is job satisfaction.* Organizational Behaviour and Human Performance l4, 309- 336

Miceli, M.P., Greenberger, D.B., Jung, I.J. and Near, J.P. (1991) *Predictors and outcomes of reactions to pay-for-performance plans.* Journal of Applied Psychology, 76, 508- 521

Opsahl, R.L. and Dunnette, M.D. (1966) *The role of financial compensation in industrial motivation.* Psychological Bulletin 66, 94- 115

Peck, C (1984) Pay and Performance: The interaction of compensation and performance appraisal. *Research Bulletin No 155.* New York : The Conference Board

Porter, G., Greenberger, D.B. and Heneman, R.L. (1990) Pay and pay satisfaction: a comparison of economic, political, psychological and psychophysical predictions. In Jauch, L.R. and Wall, J.L. (eds) *Academy of Management Best Paper Proceedings* 289-293

Rice, R., Gentile, D. and McFarlin, D (1991) *Facet importance and job satisfaction.* Journal of Applied Psychology 76 (1), 31- 39

Riley, M and Szivas, E (2003) *Pay determination- A Socioeconomic Framework.* Annals of Tourism Research 30 (2), 446- 464

Riley, M.R., Lockwood, A., Perry, J.P. and Baker, M (1998) *Job satisfaction, organisational commitment and occupational culture: a case from the UK pub industry.* Progress in Tourism and Hospitality Research 4 (2), 159- 168

Sharif, M. (2000) *Inverted "S" – The complete neo classical labour-supply function.* International Labour Review 139 (4), 409- 435

Shaw, J.M Duffy, M.K., Jenkins, D. and Gupta, N. (1999) *Positive and Negative Affect, Signal Sensitivity and Pay Satisfaction.* Journal of Management 25 (2) 189- 206

Vroom, V.H. (1964) *Work and motivation.* New York: John Wiley,

Weiner, N (1980) *Determinants and Behavioural Consequences of Pay Satisfaction: A Comparison of Two Models.* Personnel Psychology 33, 741- 757

18

CUSTOMERS' EMOTIONAL AND BEHAVIOURAL RESPONSES TO COMPLAINT HANDLING

ATILA YUKSEL

ABSTRACT

Service failures are almost inevitable. Unless recovered appropriately, they can harm the present and future business of an organization. Proper complaint handling is vital as recovery responses can either enflame or enhance customer emotions. Broken service promises may evoke annoyance, frustration, disappointment and many other important negative emotions in customers. Certain emotions may drive specific favourable or unfavourable behavioural responses. Using two different recovery conditions (poor and full recovery), this paper examines the relationship between negative and positive emotions of customers and their behavioural responses. Results of correlation analyses demonstrate that emotions have statistically significant relationships with customers' voice, switch, recommendation, repurchase and do not complain behaviours. Regression analyses suggest that certain emotions are strong predictors of specific behavioural responses. Results further suggest that experience of certain negative emotions may lead to favourable behavioural responses. Managerial implications of the study are discussed.

Keywords: ***Service failure, complaint handling, emotional and behavioural responses***

INTRODUCTION

Failures are likely to happen even in the best-run organisations despite the service provider's attempt to provide consistent and high quality services to consumers. This is partly because service delivery is heterogeneous across service encounters and there are variety of factors that may impact on the delivery process. Customers' prepurchase expectations are negatively disconfirmed when they perceive a failure with respect to any dimensions of service quality (outcome and/or process). Broken service promise and unmet expectations will cause the customer cognitively and affectively evaluate the service failure and determine which step (e.g., exit or voice - complaining to the service provider, friends, relatives or third parties) (Day & Landon, 1977), if any, will be taken to redress the situation (Levesque & McDougall, 2000; Susskind, 2000, 2002). The manner in which recovery from service failure is managed is vital. Complaint handling is a critical moment of truth for companies in their efforts to satisfy and keep customers (Strauss & Seidel, 1998). Unfortunately, research shows that the majority of customers are dissatisfied with companies' service recovery efforts (Andreassen, 2001; Tax, Brown & Chandrashekaran, 1999).

The customer recovery experience is a blend of the physical delivery and the emotions evoked, subjectively measured across all moments of contact. Due to disruption of the consumption experience, service failure encounters can be source of such negative emotions as anger and frustration (Bigne & Andreu, 2004; Nguyen & McColl-Kennedy, 2003; Zeelenberg & Pieters, 2002). When the recovery is poor this may enflame customers' emotions (Nguyen & McColl-Kennedy, 2003). A poor service recovery is perceived as a "double deviation" in that both the initial experience and the recovery are failures (Bitner, Booms & Tetrault, 1990). Emotions - a positive or negative sensation that accompanies a reaction to a perceived or remembered object, event, or circumstance, can influence the overall degree of satisfaction or dissatisfaction with the service failure (Zeelenberg & Pieters, 2002). It is likely that emotions will also partly determine the subsequent complaining behaviour (e.g., likelihood of complaining, the degree to which customer will switch or repurchase, the extent of word-of-mouth communication they will engage in or will the customer refrain from any action?). The assumed effect on complaining behaviour could occur via overall dis/satisfaction, but emotions might also directly trigger specific behaviours (Zeelenberg & Pieters, 2002).

Research has shown that besides the cognitive component, customer (dis)satisfaction is concurrently influenced by an affective component (Barsky & Nash, 2002). Defining, designing, implementing, monitoring and managing the emotions created when customers purchase and consume the service, can provide business with a sustainable competitive advantage that rivals cannot copy or match. Barsky and Nash's (2002) study demonstrate that emotions influence customer loyalty toward hotels and that certain emotions play important role in the decision-making process in relation to willingness to pay a given rate and willingness to return. According to Barsky (2003), hospitality companies that provide certain loyalty emotions obtain higher rates and can increase prices with fewer defections. The results of their analysis even showed a significant difference between men and women. Women were more responsive to the primary emotions - comfortable, relaxed, content, secure and welcome - while the secondary emotions pampered, entertained, inspired, important, extravagant, elegant, sophisticated and hip/cool - appear to have a bigger impact on men. The effects of customer emotions on customer satisfaction and customer loyalty have been empirically verified by a number of other previous research (Liljander & Strandvick, 1997; Mattila, 2004; Smith & Bolton, 2002; Westbrook & Oliver, 1991; Yu & Dean, 2001). Some studies even reported that affective component was a better predictor of customer satisfaction and customer loyalty than the cognitive component (Yu & Dean, 2001).

The notion that people have emotional responses to their immediate environment is widely accepted in psychology researchers from different fields. The consensus is that the first response level to any environment is affective, and that this emotional impact generally guides the subsequent relations within the environment (Babin, Darden & Babin, 1998; Dolen, Lemmink, Mattsson & Rhoen, 2001; Itelson, 1973; Machleit & Eroglu, 2000, p.101). Most service failure/complaint handling studies however have not taken into account that failures and subsequent recovery attempts trigger emotional responses in addition to cognitive appraisal (Dolen et at., 2001; Yu & Dean, 2001). This is rather surprising. Customers will be more emotionally involved in and observant of recovery than in routine or first-time services (Bitner et al., 1990). For instance, customers may experience uncertainty and its associated feelings of uneasiness and anxiety in a service failure/recovery situation, particularly when they do not know how long they have to wait and what the consequence of their wait will be (Taylor, 1994). This implies that customers' behaviours during/after a complaint-handling situation may be emotionally driven (Smith & Bolton, 2002). Experience of distinct emotions may influence their expectations for and perceptions of the recovery performance, and/or their expressions and behaviours (Dube & Menon, 2000). Knowledge of emotions experienced by customers during complaint handling encounters can help managers to engineer the service recovery process to maximise satisfaction and other related positive behavioural reactions (Chebat & Slusarczyk, 2003; Machleit & Eroglu, 2000; Schoefer & Ennew in press; Zeelenberg & Pieters, 2002). In this context, the current paper explores the relationship between customers' emotions and their complaining behaviours under poor and successful service recovery conditions. The paper begins with an overview of such relevant areas as service failure, consumer complaining behaviours and affective responses. A brief description of the methodology follows and the results are presented and discussed in the third section. The paper concludes with managerial implications.

SERVICE FAILURES

Service failures are evaluated by customers as negative events and their causes can be various (Nguyen & McColl-Kennedy, 2003). Traditionally, two types of service failures -outcome and process - have been studied in the literature (Keaveney, 1995). In an outcome failure, the organisation does not fulfil the basic service need or perform the core service (Levesque & McDougall, 2000). In a process failure, the delivery of the core service is flawed or deficient in some way (e.g., receptionist treats rudely to the customer during check-in). Customers view core service failures (e.g., lost hotel reservations) as big "mistakes"- a major reason for customers switching service provider (Keaveney, 1995;

Nguyen & McColl-Kennedy 2003). Core service failures and following poor recoveries can result in loss of economic (e.g., money, time) and/or social (e.g., status, esteem) resources for customers.

Bitner et al.'s study demonstrate that service failures can be due to unprompted employee actions (e.g., rudeness), failure to respond to customer's specific needs or preferences, or core service failures (e.g., unavailable or unreasonably slow service). Manickas and Shea (1997) developed a failure classification system, which shares similarities to that of Bitner et al. (1990). Their classification consists of service failure, equipment failure, guest failure and outside interference. Service failure refers to situations in which hotel personnel do not complete the service properly. Equipment failure refers to problems associated with the physical facilities of the hotel, such as telephone problems, heat and air conditioning problem, and dissatisfaction with the decor or the size of a room. Manickas and Shea point that frequently guests make mistakes and this affects the quality of the hotel experience of others, as well as, the guest himself or herself. Problems such as guests booking the wrong room or giving unclear information to the concierge can be classified as guest failures. There are also outside interferences, which may affect the guests' stay, and they are generally beyond the management control, e.g., noise from the streets disturbing the guests' sleep (Manickas & Shea, 1997).

SERVICE RECOVERY

A service recovery refers to the actions a service employee takes in response to a service failure (Brown, Cowles & Tuten, 1996; Gronroos, 1988). The aim of service recovery efforts is basically to move a customer from a state of dissatisfaction to a state of satisfaction (Zemke, 1994). Recovery to failures can take many forms. These actions range from "do nothing" to whatever it takes to fix the problem" (Bitner et al., 1990; Hart et al., 1990; Hoffman et al., 1995; Kelley, Hoffman & Davies, 1993). The effectiveness of recovery strategies depends on the situation and is influenced by such factors as importance and type of service. Effectiveness is also dependent on the way in which the service provider handles the problem. Responsiveness, empathy and understanding improve the effectiveness of the recovery strategy (Bitner et al., 1990; Hart et al., 1990). Thus, not only what is done but also how it is done will contribute to the effectiveness of the recovery.

Customer expectations of service recovery encounters may be situation specific and they may depend on the type and amount of resources lost and gained during the exchange (Smith et al., 1999). Depending on the context, recovery expectation may be: to receive an apology for the fact that the customer is inconvenienced; to be offered a "fair fix" for the problem; to be treated in a way that suggests the company cares about the problem, about fixing the problem, and about the customer's inconvenience; and to be offered value-added atonement for the inconvenience (Zemke, 1994). Based on customer anecdotes, another study identified that attention, helpfulness, care, responsiveness, communication, and flexibility led to satisfactory recovery experiences (Johnston, 1994, quoted in Lewis & Spyrakopoulos, 2001). Immediate and speedy response, listening, courtesy, caring and honest responses, getting it right and solving the problem, and financial compensation were found to be most effective in satisfying customer complaints in other studies (Armistead et al. 1995, quoted in Lewis & Spyrakopoulos, 2001; Hoffman & Chung, 1999). It is probable that different customers may attach different levels of importance to these components. A poor recovery response may lead customers to consider what could have happened (staff could have done something else), what should have happened (staff should have behaved differently), and how would customer felt had another action been taken? (Sparks, 2003). The following section now presents a review of customers' behavioural and emotional reactions to complaint handling.

CUSTOMER COMPLAINING BEHAVIOUR (CCB)

CCB is generally considered to be a set of multiple responses arising out of purchase dissatisfaction (Day, 1984; Singh, 1988; 1990). Complaint responses are generally considered to fall into two broad categories; behavioural and non behavioural. Behavioural responses consist of any or all customer action that convey an expression of dissatisfaction (Landon, 1977). Non-behavioural responses, such as when the consumer forgets about a dissatisfying episode and does nothing, are also considered as a legitimate CCB response (Day et al., 1981). Singh (1988) notes that to the extent that some people choose behavioural responses whereas others elect non-behavioural responses in relatively similar dissatisfying episodes.

Hirschman (1970) suggested that dissatisfaction could provoke two active negative responses; voice and exit. Exit is "the voluntary termination of an exchange relationship" while voice is actual communication of the complaint to the service provider (Singh, 1988, p. 94). Loyalty - a passive response, merely accepting dissatisfaction in the hope that things will improve in the future - is one of the responses a customer has to a service failure (Hirschman, 1970). However, loyalty should not be considered as one dimensional. Customers may stay with a service provider because they have a high opinion of them and see the service failure as an aberration. 'Even when a problem is not solved, approximately half of the respondents would remain with the firm" (Levesque & McDougall, 2000, p. 22). This may be due to switching costs, lack of perceived differentiation of alternatives, locational constraints on choice, time or money constraints, habit or inertia (Hirschman, 1970). Customers may also stay after a service failure because they are spuriously loyal. That is, they feel trapped, are apathetic or there are no alternatives so they do not leave. Hence, dissatisfied customers may choose to remain with a service provider or they may exit and this is influenced by how the situation is handled by the service provider (i.e. the service recovery). Maute and Forrester (1993) found a strong support for a three-way classification of dissatisfaction responses based on Hirschman's (1970) exit, voice; and loyalty responses (loyalty being the decision to remain with the company despite dissatisfaction)

Day and Landon (1977) extended the notion of "voice" further by stating that voice can be complaining to the service provider, complaining to acquaintances (negative word-of-mouth), or complaining to third parties in order to help seek redress. Using factor analysis techniques (both exploratory and confirmatory), Singh (1988) found empirical support that consumer complaint behaviour could be viewed as falling into one of three categories: voice responses, private responses, and third-party responses. Voice responses are directed to objects that are external to the consumer's social circle and are directly involved in the dissatisfying exchange (e.g. seeking redress from the seller); private responses are the responses in which the objects are not external to the consumer's social circle and are not directly involved in the dissatisfying experience (e.g. word-of-mouth communication or exit); and third-party responses include objects that are external to the consumer but not directly involved in the dissatisfying transaction (e.g. reporting to a consumer agency or to taking legal action).

Based on categories developed by Singh (1988), Rogers, Ross and Williams (1992) conceptualised consumer complaint behaviour alternatives as follows: change future behaviour, do not buy the item or patronise the seller in the future; private complaining: warn family and friends about the product or seller; voice complaint: complain to service provider; third party: complain to customer group, take legal action, and do nothing: internalise or ignore the dissatisfaction. Customers may choose to do nothing about their dissatisfaction for a number of reasons. Among the reasons include the assumption that their complaints are unwelcome, that no one will listen to them, that they do not know who to complain and that have to wait a long time for a response (Barlow, 1996). Recently, Lam and Tang (2003) identified four complaint behaviours: personal urging, bad mouthing, complaint to management, and publicizing. This review of literature suggests mat complaint options may range from seeking redress to contacting third parties. Potential behavioural and non-behavioural responses that a customer may utilize to deal with his/her dissatisfaction were therefore included in the study. These responses were switching patronage, telling friends and relatives about the experience, telling the experience to other customers, complaining to the service employee, demanding manager's intervention, writing complaint letter to the company headquarters, complaining to an external agency, continuing to do business with the company, and do not complain.

AFFECTIVE RESPONSES

Consumption emotions are the set of positive and negative emotional responses made by consumers during product usage (Westbrook & Oliver, 1991). They are the affective responses to one's perception of the series of attributes that compose a product or service performance (Dube & Menon, 2000; Dube & Morgan, 1998). These emotions may be either negative or positive and range from anger, frustration, embarrassment, regret, disappointment to contentment, pleasure, happiness and delight. Emotions predispose individuals for actions. If one feels afraid, s/he may run away. If s/he feels resentful, s/he may be predisposed to sabotage what is being done or to take revenge. If s/he feels enthusiastic, s/he may try to move ahead, engaging in doing what s/he sees as possible. Service failures and complaint handling can therefore be a source of emotions. In a service failure situation customers first experience an expectation disconfirmation-related emotion (s) (initial failure) and then a justice-related emotion(s) (following a recovery response), and react to their emotion(s).

Emotions are complex and arise from many sources. Previous studies suggest that individuals treated fairly will experience positive emotions, whereas those under rewarded are likely to feel anger (Chebat & Slusarczyk, 2003). It is argued that too low compensation, too intricate process to get in, impolite interaction during complaint handling may lead consumers to develop negative emotions. Basically, individuals would react angrily and aggressively if what they received is below what is expected (Chebat & Slusarczyk, 2003). Previous studies reported that participants were more content (and less stressed) when they were equitably treated than when they were either underbenefited or overbenefited (Austin & Walster, 1974).

Research indicates that anger and its associated feelings of anxiety, annoyance, irritation and frustration often emerge from service failure situations where consumer goals or expectations for particular outcomes are thwarted by inappropriate responses (Berkowitz, 1989; Taylor, 1994). For example, a customer makes a booking in a restaurant for a very important special occasion. When they arrive no seats are available. Somehow the booking was not recorded. Frustration is a likely emotional response to dissatisfying elements of a service experience depicted above (Tedeschi & Felson, 1994). In a recovery situation, when customers do not receive appropriate response or sufficient information, they are likely to experience a heightened sense of uncertainty and become frustrated. In other words, as customer's expectations for service delivery are blocked, frustration may develop around the service failure (Berkowitz, 1989). Frustrated individuals may display physical and/or verbal aggression toward the object that blocked their goal attainment. Customers may also feel regretful and disappointed as a result of bad decisions and discontinued expectancies (Zeelenberg & Pieters, 2002). They may feel disappointed because actual service delivery violates prior expectations. They may also feel regret when it turns out that a foregone provider would have delivered a better service (Zeelenberg & Pieters, 2002).

Of course, customers may experience important other negative emotions during or following a disappointing complaint handling (Chaudhuri, 1997). Examples of these are anxiety, anger, embarrassment, and sadness. Sparks (2003 in Sparks 2003) identified anger, pleasure and embarrassment as three key affective responses representing typical feelings reported by customers. Unfavourable outcome, poor quality of the interpersonal treatment and the level of service provider's defensiveness would evoke anger in customers (Sparks, 2003). From everyday experiences, we know that anger is an emotion experienced often in response to failed service encounters and following perceptions of inequity. Embarrassment or feeling humiliated is another negative emotion that, broken promises and under rewarding could evoke in customers. Failure may touch an individual's ego-identity which involves self-esteem and social esteem. If one's self or social esteem is threatened such as in the restaurant case above conditions are ripe for anger, frustration and embarrassment (Peterson, 2000; Nguyen & McColl-Kennedy, 2003). The more the customer feels embarrassed about the service failure the more angry s/he will become (Nguyen & McColl-Kennedy, 2003). When the mistake is promptly rectified, customers are likely to experience such positive emotions as happiness.

Service failures and recovery responses are likely to evoke either negative (e.g., anger) or positive (e.g., pleasure) affective reactions (Nyer, 2000; Price, Arnould & Deibler, 1995), with positive and negative affect making contributions to customer recovery satisfaction and behavioural intentions (Locke, 1996; Oliver, 1997; Westbrook & Oliver, 1991). Negative emotions are expected to lead to more dissatisfaction, whereas positive emotions are expected to lead to more satisfaction (Zeelenberg & Pieters, 2002). It is possible that negative emotions will bias customers' perceptions, evaluations and their complaint behaviours. Anger may result in complaining and switching, but also in malicious attempts to hurt the service provider (e.g., intentionally spreading bad rumours about the service provider). Zeelenger and Pieters (2002) report that specific emotions - regret and disappointment - have a significant impact on satisfaction and subsequent consumer complaining behaviours. Regret was found to be directly related to switching behaviour and unrelated to complaining. They also found that the more customers experience regret, the more inert they were. In another study, Chebat and Sluarsczyk (2003) identified a strong relationship between negative/positive emotions and customers' exit and loyalty behaviours. They suggest that contact employees should be aware of the emotional climate of customer's complaints and should be trained to monitor it. They state that even if the problem, which triggered the complaint can be fixed, the customers do not necessarily remain loyal if the emotions are not properly attended to.

The reviewed literature illustrates that emotions can be influential in customers' satisfaction and behavioural reactions to complaint handling. The preceding discussion leads to the propositions that:

P1: Emotions will affect customers' recovery satisfaction evaluation and complaining behaviours.

P2: Positive emotions will lead to favourable complaining behaviours, whereas negative emotions will result in unfavourable complaining behaviours.

MEASUREMENT OF EMOTIONS

Numerous schemes for basic emotions have been proposed. The three typologies of emotions that marketers most often borrow are Izard's (1977) 10 fundamental emotions from his Differential Emotions Theory, Plutchik's (1980) eight basic emotion categories, and Mehrabian and Russell's (1974) Pleasure, Arousal, and Dominance dimensions of response. Westrbrook and Oliver (1991) in a study to identify patterns of emotional responses, found five different emotional profiles: happy/content, pleasant (positive) surprise, unemotional, negative surprise and angry/upset. Richins (1997) developed a set of emotion descriptors for measuring consumption related emotions and this contained 16 emotion clusters, including among others anger, worry, contentment, surprise and joy. With the exception of Havlena and Holbrook's (1986) and

Machleit and Eroglu's (2000) works, our knowledge of which emotional measure is most appropriate for use in marketing contexts is limited (Machleit & Eroglu, 2000).

It must be noted that emotions are context-specific. Often, emotion researchers have had to develop ad hoc measurement and classifications schemes, or revised scales, since the above measures are limited to fundamental affects and do not address more complex patterns of emotional response that often characterise contemporary experience (e.g., sentimentality, affection, confidence) (Westbrook & Oliver, 1991, p. 85). Zins (2002) adapted sixteen emotional variables from Mano and Oliver's (1993) study. Chebat and Slusarczyk (2003) borrowed four emotional variables from Plutchik (1980) study to measure negative and positive feelings. Taylor (1994) developed a set of eight emotions from a number of different scales to evaluate relations between delays, emotions and evaluations. In a recent study Bigne and Andreu (2004) used twelve emotions to segment leisure and tourism customers. Drawing from a number of previous studies (Chebat & Slusarczyk, 2003; Hui & Tse, 1996; Dube et al., 1996; Taylor, 1994; Zins, 2002), this study employed nine emotional variables. These were annoyance, anxiety, frustration, embarrassment, sadness, disappointment, uneasiness, content and happiness.

THE STUDY

The study reported here was one component of a larger project on service failure issues in the hospitality sector. Based on previous studies examining frequent failures in the hospitality industry (McDougall & Levesque, 1999; Yuksel & Kilinc, 2003), the researchers developed a scenario involving a core service failure. The use of core service failure is justified because when asked about to identify service encounters that resulted in quite dissatisfying experiences, customers frequently mentioned core service failures (Bitner et al., 1990; Kelley et al., 1993). Core service failures are situations where the customer does not receive the basic service promised by the service provider (Levesque & McDougall, 2000). Core service failures, which include lost hotel reservations, were a major reason for customers switching service provider (Keaveney, 1995). Thus core service failures are relatively serious and customers expect the service provider rectify the problem (Hart et al., 1990). The use of scenario is justifiable because this method avoids the problem of intentionally imposing service failures on customers and it minimizes memory-bias, which is common in self-reports of service failures (Smith et al., 1999). Mattila (2001) tested the impact of different relationship types on consumers' behavioural intentions following a service failure using scenario-based experimental models.

The survey was conducted with 700 conveniently selected participants in two locations. Questionnaires were distributed to 500 conveniently selected tourists staying at hotels situated in Bodrum, Kusadasi and Antalya, and to conveniently selected 200 international tourists at the departure lounge of an international airport. Participants were exposed to a written scenario describing a service failure within the context of "lost hotel reservation". The details of the scenario are presented in Table 1. The questionnaire consisted of three sections and it was written in Turkish and English. The questionnaire instructions asked respondents to assume that the situation (scenario) had just happened to them. More specifically, respondents were instructed to indicate their likely emotional and behavioural reactions in three different service recovery conditions. Respondents' attitudes to complaining were also measured by eight statements derived from Day (1984). (Analysis of attitude statements will not be discussed here). Based on different empowerment levels of the frontline employee (none, partial and full), no recovery, assistance, and compensation and assistance -the most common and frequently used service recovery responses reported in the literature (McDougall & Levesque, 1998, 1999) - were included in the study. Assistance involves action taken to resolve the problem; whereas compensation involves monetary payments for the inconvenience the customer has experienced (McDougall & Levesque, 1998, 1999). For this investigation, the primary focus was on the most dissatisfying (poor recovery) and satisfactory recovery. Hence, tourists' likely emotional and behavioural reactions when no recovery and full recovery were offered by the service provider were examined. No recovery was operationalised as the employee saying; "I am sorry for the inconvenience but there is nothing I can do to help you. If you want you may see the manager". Full recovery was operationalised as the employee saying: "I am sorry for the inconvenience; unfortunately we are fully booked today.

Let me call a nearby hotel of similar quality to see if I can make you a reservation. Please have some complimentary refreshments while I am making the call". When the receptionist returned he said: "You have a reservation at the..., a higher quality hotel, being held for you. For, your trouble, we would be happy to cover your stay expenses at the other hotel". It is expected that recovery response in which staff are empowered to deal with customer request immediately, actively and satisfactorily may lead customers to less frustrating and more satisfying service recovery experiences. In other words full recovery response is expected to bring about lower levels of negative emotions (e.g., annoyance, sadness, anxiety) and higher levels of positive emotions (satisfaction, happiness) than no recovery responses.

Table 1. Details of the Scenario

At the busiest time of the summer season, you made a reservation for a hotel that is part of a domestic hotel chain. You have decided to spend a short vacation at this hotel because it offers many features including a health club, swimming pool, quality restaurants and a reputation for giving a special attention to its guests. When you arrived at 5p.m. you found that the room would not be available for another day due to a registration mistake. However, you received a confirmation number for your reservation with a 3 p.m. check-in time. When you speak to the receptionist about this

The receptionist said:

"I am very sorry for the inconvenience, but there is nothing I can do to help. If you want you may see the manager"

How you would feel about this response...

Annoyed

Sad

Frustrated

Embarrassed

Disappointed

Uneasy

Anxious

Happy

Content

Each statement was followed by 5-point (where 1: very unlikely, 5:

very likely) scales

Please indicate how you would react to this response...

Complain to the staff

Demand immediate and active involvement of a manager

Write a complain letter to the headquarters

Talk to other customers about the problem

Complain to an external agency (travel agency, consumer group etc.,) about the problem

Do not complain

I would come to this hotel in the future

I would recommend this hotel to my friends/relatives

Switch to another hotel in the future

Each statement was followed by 5-point (where 1: strongly disagree, 5: strongly agree) Likert scales

---

Similar to previous research (Dube et al., 1996; Hui & Tse, 1996; Taylor, 1994) we adapted a set of positive and negative emotions applicable to the specific context of recovery responses under examination. Annoyance, anxiety, frustration, embarrassment, sadness, uneasiness and disappointment were the negative emotions examined in the study. Happiness and content were the positive emotions. These negative and positive emotions have already been employed in other studies (Chebat & Slusarczyk, 2003; Dolen et al., 2002; Machleit & Eroglu, 1999; Richins, 1997; Westbrook & Oliver, 1991; Zins, 2002). Respondents were required to indicate their emotional responses to the recovery response in each recovery condition tested in the study. Emotions were followed by a five point Likert type scales (where 1: very unlikely to 5: very likely).

Customer complaint behaviours were collected from published research reports (Huang et al., 1996; Levesque & McDougall, 1999; Rogers et al., 1992; Zeithaml et al., 1996) to measure the diversity of the consumer complaint behaviour construct. These are the behaviours that customers are likely to engage in when they encounter service problems (Hirschman, 1970; Singh, 1988). Following a pre-test with a convenience sample of respondents, a revised scale of nine items was developed to measure respondents' likelihood of engaging in switching to another service provider (Switch), continuing to do business with the hotel in the future (Repurchase), recommending it to friends and relatives (WoM), and Voice -complaining to the service provider, demanding manager intervention, telling other customers about the problem, telling external agencies - and do not complain. Doing nothing in response to a failed service encounter was added since often customers just do not react at all when a bad thing happens, and this might be related to their emotional experiences (Zeelenberg & Pieters, 2002).

DATA ANALYSIS

Frequency distribution of the variables was conducted in order to identify the respondents' profile, and compute means and standard deviations for each emotional and behavioural variable. A pairwise t-test was conducted to see whether customers' negative and positive emotional responses are different under no recovery and full recovery conditions. Pearson correlation analyses were then undertaken to examine the relationship between customers' negative/positive emotions and their complaining behaviours. A series of stepwise regression analyses were conducted to examine the effects of positive/negative emotions on specific complaining behaviours.

RESULTS AND DISCUSSION

There were 420 usable questionnaires. This represents a response rate of 60% (420 of 700). Twenty nine percent (N=125) of the respondents were Turkish, 24% (N= 102) were Dutch, 23% (N= 98) were Israeli, and 22% (N=95) were British. Fifty three percent of the respondents were male and the mean age was 32 years old. Thirty five percent of the respondents were married. Overall, respondents considered the scenario as being realistic (á= 4.03) and they indicated that such a failure would annoy them significantly (á= 3.96). The problem depicted in the scenario was found important (á= 4. 02). Reliability scores of the emotional scale used in no recovery and full recovery conditions were 0.79 and 0.87 respectively.

Table 2. Mean Scores for Emotions in Two Recovery Conditions

	No Recovery	Full Recovery

	Mean	SD	Mean	SD	t	Sig
Annoyed	4,06	1,55	2,24	1,25	16,612	,000
Anxious	3,16	1,48	2,18	1,49	9,111	,000
Disappointed	3,21	1,48	2,06	1,47	10,521	,000
Embarrassed	2,70	1,46	1,98	1,56	6,768	,000
Frustrated	3,57	1,58	2,33	1,56	11,066	,000
Sad	3,40	1,48	2,16	1,46	11,785	,000
Uneasy	3,73	1,65	2,40	1,36	11,075	,000
Content	2.18	1.25	3.60	1.42	10,965	,000
Happy	1,86	1,42	3,49	1,49	-13,517	,000

5 point Likert scale (where 1: Very unlikely, 5: Very likely).

Figures in Table 2 suggest that a recovery response involving "no recovery" (no assistance, explanation and/or compensation) would annoy customers most. Before proceeding with the interpretation of correlations between annoyance and CCB, it must be noted that although statistically insignificant, there is a slight difference between customers' annoyance levels measured after the initial service failure and recovery response (á: 3.96, á: 4.06, t: -.594 p>. 05). Customer annoyance measured after the recovery response is slightly higher under the no recovery condition. This provides some degree of support for the contention that customers would be more annoyed with the poor response than the initial failure (Hart et al., 1990). Pairwise t-tests were undertaken to test whether two different conditions evoke in different levels of negative and positive emotions in customers. It is clear from Table 2 that customers' negative emotional responses to no recovery condition are significantly higher than those under the full recovery situation. This indicates that doing nothing in a failure situation is likely to feed customers' anger, anxiety, disappointment and other important negative emotions.

Respondents' high scores on annoyance can be attributed to the recovery response - an unfair treatment which is unable to restore the service. The organisation has failed to deliver on an explicit promise (e.g., a room to stay). Financial costs and inconveniences would be associated with such a failure and recovery response. Customers may think that the initial failure may have been caused by a spontaneous mistake but the organisation has a chance to put things right the second time. Customer expectations in such a failure situation would be to have active and immediate rectification of the problem (Blodget et al., 1997). The response however contains only apology and it does not meet the customer's likely economic and social losses. Such a failure and subsequent recovery response, involving doing nothing, are obstacles to service experience, and when an obstacle blocks satisfaction of a need, anger and frustration result (Lawson 1965 in Taylor, 1994). In sum, offering "no recovery (doing nothing)" is likely to aggravate the situation. Scores in Table 2 indicate that customers receiving proper responses that make up for the loss would feel less annoyed than a disappointing response. Scores in Table 2 further suggest that despite the full recovery response customer may still be annoyed with the organisation. Compensation, assistance and additional services may not make the effects of initial failure just go away. Customers may be unforgiving for such core service failures that are under the control of the organisation. It may be that these recovery responses do not directly address the ways to diffuse customer anger resulting from the initial failure.

Other negative feelings on which customers appear to have high scores under "no recovery" condition are uneasiness, frustration, sadness, disappointment, embarrassment and anxiety (Table 2). This is an expected result. In a failure situation like this, customers may need to have enough information to satisfy their needs regarding the causes of the failure and subsequent recovery plans. When left without sufficient credible information regarding causes and recovery plans, consumers are likely to become anxious, uneasy and/or frustrated. In "no recovery" condition customers were not provided with information as to the cause(s) of the failure and recovery plan(s). Hence "doing nothing" would lead to a heightened sense of uncertainty (Smith, 1996). Uneasiness and anxiety can be explained largely by uncertainty as to the cause of the failure and how it is going to be remedied. Customers are likely to feel frustrated, as failed service performance has not been repaired and the response does not include any kind of assistance, explanation and /or compensation. Disappointment relates to the fact that customers' expectations have been negatively disconfirmed. Basically, despite her time and effort (sacrifices), the customer did not get what s/he had bargained for. It appears that customers accompanied by friends, relatives etc. may experience a high level of embarrassment as a result of the "no recovery action". "Doing nothing" is not an approach that shows sympathy with the situation that the initial failure puts the customer in. Customer invests a great deal of resources (both financial and emotional) and after a consideration process chooses the organisation among many alternatives. "Doing nothing" and leaving customer to fend for themselves disregards their financial and emotional (social) investments. These negative feelings are likely to be experienced when elements of the recovery remain unsatisfactory.

Two separate correlation analyses were undertaken to see whether there are statistically significant relationships between emotions and customer satisfaction and between emotions and customers' complaint behaviours under two different recovery conditions. Correlation coefficients in Table 3 and 4 suggest that there is a statistically significant relationship between customers' emotions and their complaining behaviours, and their extent and direction is different under no recovery and full recovery conditions. Although the majority of correlations under the no recovery condition are generally lower than 0.30, we can say that the relationships are statistically significant. These provide support for the first proposition of the study. Under the full recovery situation (Table 4), positive emotions are positively correlated with WoM and Repurchase behaviour, whereas negative emotions tend to correlate statistically significantly with Voice and Switch behaviours. Under the full recovery situation, there is a stronger relationship between emotions and customers complaining behaviours (Table 4). The correlation coefficients for positive and negative emotions (Table 3 and 4) suggest that negative emotions have slightly higher correlation coefficients for Voice and Switch behaviours compared to WoM and Repurchase behaviours. This provides some degree of support for the second proposition but figures in Table 3 indicate that some negative emotions do have positive relationship with WoM and Repurchase behaviours. This will be discussed later.

More specifically, positive emotion happiness is found to correlate significantly highly with Repurchase and WoM behaviours (revisiting the hotel in the future and recommending it to friends and relatives) (Table 3). It is important to note that other than

Table 3. Correlations Between Emotions and Complaining Behaviours in No Recovery Situation

	Complain to staff	Manager intervention	Written complaint	Tell other customers	Third party	Do not complain	Repur-chase	WoM Satisfaction	Switch	Recovery
Annoyed	,300**	,294**	,209**	,187**	,221**	,122	,011	-,158*	-,094	-,180**
	,000	,000	,001	,003	,000	,055	,867	,013	,139	,004
Anxious	,070	,152*	,103	,058	,098	,028	,143*	,219**	,089	,156*
	,269	,016	,107	,366	,121	,658	,024	,000	,163	,014
Disappointed	,222**	,113	,143*	,177**	,142*	,188**	,118	,045	-,105	-.011
	,000	,075	,025	,005	,024	,003	,064	,482	,099	,860
Embarrassed	,233**	,037	,162*	,246**	,219**	,234**	,126*	,123	,043	,135*
	,000	,563	,011	,000	,000	,000	,047	,053	,503	,033
Frustrated	,278**	,203**	,133*	,094	,215**	,077	-,097	,007	-,007	-.034
	,000	,001	,037	,144	,001	,229	,127	,915	,910	,594
Sad	,041	,068	,108	,163*	,103	,104	,121	,153*	,142*	,142*
	,519	,285	,090	,011	,103	,103	,057	,016	,026	,025
Uneasy	128*	,088	,061	,187**	,117	,141*	,080	,056	,080	,002
	,044	,168	,343	,003	,066	,027	,211	,378	,214	,971
Happy	,095	-,093	,055	,127*	-,077	,206**	,441**	,482**	,092	,479**
	,136	,146	,393	,047	,226	,001	,000	,000	,151	,000
Content	-,002	,120	,037	-,116	,011	,129*	,071	,215**	,091	,190**
	,973	,071	,560	,069	,857	,043	,266	,001	,153	,003

** Correlation is significant at the 0.01 level (2-tailed).
* Correlation is significant at the 0.05 level (2-tailed).

Table 4. Correlations Between Emotions and Complaining Behaviours in Full Recovery Situation

	Complain to staff	Manager intervention	Written complaint	Tell other customers	Third party	Do not complain	Repur-chase	WoM Satisfaction	Switch	Recovery
Annoyed	,565**	,485**	,560**	,554**	,410**	-300**	,375**	-.382**	-,192**	-383**
	,000	,000	,000	,000	,000	,000	,000	,000	,002	,000
Anxious	,504**	,477**	,469**	,546**	,466**	-,315**	,388**	-383**	-,221**	-,348**
	,000	,000	,000	,000	,000	,000	,000	,000	,001	,000
Disappointed	,573**	,469**	,477**	,595**	,506**	-,309**	,413**	-359**	-,192**	-,314**
	,000	,000	,000	,000	,000	,000	,000	,000	,002	,000
Embarrassed	,561**	,549**	,425**	,543**	,460**	-,274**	,370**	-341**	-,117	-.341**
	,000	,000	,000	,000	,000	,000	,000	,000	,067	,000
Uneasy	,474**	,457**	,426**	,520**	,394**	-,328**	,394**	-,417**	-,249**	-,316**
	,000	,000	,000	,000	,000	,000	,000	,000	,000	,000
Sad	,508**	,455**	,442**	,577**	,472**	-,331**	,467**	-387**	-,195**	-335**
	,000	,000	,000	,000	,000	,000	,000	,000**	,002	,000w
Frustrated	,513**	,416**	,472**	,572**	,447**	-,379**	,417**	-,413**	-,220**	-,329**
	,000	,000	,000	,000	,000	,000	,000	,000	,001	,000
Happy	-,175**	-,059	-.227**	-,133**	-,067	,208**	—,211**	,300**	,167**	,253**
	,006	,357	,000	,038	,295	,001	,001	,000	,009	,000
Content	-.168**	-,070	-.164**	-,075	-,032	142*	-,108	,154*	,097	,171**
	,008	,271	,009	,239	,620	,026	,089	,016	,130	,007

** Correlation is significant at the 0.01 level (2-tailed).
*Correlation is significant at the 0.05 level (2-tailed).

sharing with other customers no relationship between positive emotion happiness and customers Voice and Switch behaviours is found (Table 3). Compared to no recovery condition, a stronger relationship between positive emotion happiness and customers' Repurchase and WoM behaviours is found in full recovery condition (Table 4). Different from no recovery condition, an inverse relationship between positive emotion happiness and other Voice and Switch related complaining behaviours of customers is found (Table 4). These results suggest that higher positive emotions may lead to less unfavourable behaviours.

Table 3 suggests that negative emotion annoyance has statistically significant relationships with customers' Voice behaviours and an inverse relationship with WoM behaviour. Relationship found between annoyance and customers' Voice behaviours may be related to their emotional needs. Voice behaviours (complaining to staff, asking for manager's involvement, writing a complaint letter, telling the problem to other customers and third parties) may be driven by an antagonistic motive (e.g., getting even by spreading bad things about the company to friends, penalise the company through third parties). Voice behaviours may also be used as a means for approaching the service provider for information (e.g., asking the causes of the problem, plans for recovery) and for reassurances that the problem will not cause further inconvenience.

Anxiety has a positive correlation with Repurchase and WoM behaviours (Table 3). From the set of Voice behaviours, it has a statistically significant relationship only with asking for manager's intervention. Anxious customers may consider that the uncertainty surrounding the situation may be resolved only through involvement of a supervisor. Anxious customers may believe that only a supervisor can put closure to the problem, as s/he is assumed to be more empowered than a frontline staff. Embarrassment has a statistically significant relationship with Repurchase (Table 3), whereas feeling sad has a statistically significant relationship with WoM and Switch behaviours. It must be stated that feeling sad is the only negative emotion that has statistically significant relationship with Switch behaviour in no recovery condition (Table 3). There is no relationship between feeling sad and Voice behaviours other than telling the problem to other customers.

Hence, the higher is the feeling of sadness, the higher the likelihood that customer will take her business to somewhere else or talk to other customers in an attempt to find some comfort and sympathy. Customers experiencing sadness in a failed service encounter may use WoM behaviour as an emotion-coping means, namely for venting on their discontent and gaining sympathy of others (Zeelenberg & Pieters, 2002). Feeling uneasy has a relationship with complaining to staff, telling the problem to other customers and do not complain. It does not correlate with three other Voice-related behaviours. This may be because uneasiness may result in a loss of motivation for making an attempt to complaining to a manager and third parties, and writing a complaint letter.

Happiness appears to have a statistically significant relationship with do not complain. Similarly, uneasiness, disappointment and embarrassment appear to leading to do not complain. This finding has important implications. Managers should be conscious that if customers are not complaining, this may be because they are happy with the service performance, it may also because they are disappointed and do not see any benefit in making a verbal complaint. Negative emotion embarrassment does not correlate with sharing the complaint with the manager but correlates with telling it to third parties, complaining to staff and other customers. Frustration has a statistically significant relationship with complaining to staff; asking for manager's active involvement and telling the problems to third parties. These may be ways for customers venting their frustration (Nyer, 2000). Customers taking their problems to external bodies instead of just deserting at least give organisation a chance to become aware of the problem. It appears that negative emotions are likely to lead customers talking to other customers about the problem and how badly it was handled (Table 3). Negative word of mouth may be motivated by the desire to obtain emotional release (Nyer, 2000). Negative word of mouth may however affect the other customers' trust for the company.

Table 5. Emotional Predictors Oof Recovery Satisfaction and Complaining Behaviours under No Recovery Condition

No Recovery	R	R^2	Adj. R^2	Std. error	F	Sig
Complain to staff	,372	,139	,128	1,39	12,993	,000
Manager intervention	,391	;153	,142	,97	14,597	,000
Written complaint	,205	,042	,038	3,8	10,688	,001
Tell it to other customers	,335	,112	,101	1,28	10,110	,000
Third party	,322	,104	,093	1,19	9,371	,000
Do not complain	,244	,059	,055	1,47	15,326	,000
Repurchase	,483	,234	,224	1,13	24,597	,000
Recommend	,533	,284	,272	1,12	24,022	,000
Switch	,241	,058	,046	1,51	4,964	,002
Recovery satisfaction	,539	,291	,279	1.04	24,736	,000

		B	Std. Error	Beta	t	Sig.
Complain to	(Constant)	1,710	,329		5,196	,000
the staff	Annoyance	,236	,078	,200	3,013	,003
	Frustrated	,153	,065	,160	2,346	,020
	Disappointed	,136	,065	,134	2,080	,039
Manager's	(Constant)	2,931	,240		12,225	,000
(Constant)	Annoyance	,246	,049	,294	4,980	,000
intervention	Content	-.184	,045	,267	4,066	,000
Annoyance	Happiness	-,154	,046	-,218	-3,321	,001
Written	(Constant)	2,372	,283		8,372	,000
complaint	Annoyance	,219	,067	,205	3,269	,001
Third Party	(Constant)	3,025	,277		10,914	,000
	Annoyance	,164	,063	,164	2,616	,009
	Embarrassed	,200	,055	,248	3,630	,000
	Happiness	-,149	,056	-.176	-2,651	,009
Tell it to	(Constant)	2,777	,248		11,216	,000
other	Embarrassed	,225	,056	,258	4,003	,000

(contd.)

customers	Content	-,173	,056	-,194	-3,074	,002
Sad	,132	,060	,142	2,197	,029	Do not
(Constant)	2,077	,189		10,992	,000	complain
Embarrassed	,238	,061	,244	3,915	,000	
Repurchase	(Constant)	1,728	,219		7,899	,000
(Constant)	Happiness	,389	,050	,446	7,800	,000
	Frustrated	-,177	,051	-,215	-3,470	,001
	Sad	,111	,055	,126	2,030	,043
WOM	(Constant)	1,889	,274		6,905	,000
	Happiness	,425	,053	,479	8,050	,000
	Annoyance	-,170	,061	-,162	-2,807	,005
	Anxious	,140	,054	,158	2,605	,010
	Disappointed	-,124	,056	-.137	-2,216	,028
Switch	(Constant)	2,911	,294		9,901	,000
	Sad	,154	,069	,146	2,237	,026
	Disappointed	-,282	,088	-,267	-3,198	,002
	Embarrassed	,172	,084	,174	2,046	,042
Recovery	(Constant)					
Satisfaction	Happiness	,424	,048	,513	8.821	,000
	Disappointed	-.154	,051	-,183	-3,428	,003
	Annoyed	-,153	,056	-,157	-2,749	,006
	Sad	,399	,048	,112	1.978	,049

Table 6. Emotional Predictors of Recovery Satisfaction and Complaining Behaviours under Full Recovery Condition

Full Recovery	R	R^2	Adj. R^2	Std. error	F	Sig
Complain to staff	,671	,450	,443	1,06	63,789	,000
Manager intervention	,680	,462	,453	1,13	49,412	,000
Written complaint	,631	,398	,390	1,15	51,584	,000
Tell it to other customers	,581	,388	,332	1,28	59,749	,000
2Third party	,543	,295	,286	1,31	32,668	,000
Do not complain	,313	,098	,090	1,44	12,598	,000

(contd.)

Full Recovery	R	R^2	Adj. R^2	Std. error	F	Sig
Repurchase	,433	,188	,181	1,24	26,950	,000
WOM	,543	,295	,286	1,20	32,574	,000
Switch	,531	,281	,272	1,30	30,281	,000
Recovery satisfaction	,451	,204	,197	1,15	29,953	,000

		B	Std. Error	Beta	t	Sig.
Complain to staff	Constant	1,533	,221 .		6,952	,000
	Annoyance	,297	,064	,317	4,616	,000
	Disappointed	,370	,066	,383	5,626	,000
	Happiness	-,146	,049	-,146	-2,947	,004
Tell it to other customers	(Constant)	1,190	,155		7,654	,000
	Embarrassed	,501	,072	,466	6,958	,000
	Uneasy	,161	,065	,166	2,480	,014
Written (Constant) complaint	(Constant)	1,776	,238		7,478	,000
	Annoyance	,400	,069	,415	5,772	,000
	Happiness	-	,053	-,204	-3,942	,000
	Disappointed	,205	,071	,206	2,897	,004
Manager intervention	(Constant)	1,429	,238		6,008	,000
	Disappointed,	,414	,076	,397	5,442	,000
	Annoyance	,163	,078	,161	2,085	,038
	Happiness	-	,053	-,116	-2,351	,020
	Frustrated	,172	,076	,176	2,260	,025
Third party	(Constant)	1,059	,162		6,525	,000
	Disappointed	,263	,092	,250	2,874	,004
	Anxious	,189	,084	,181	2,267	,024
	Sad	,190	,088	,178	2,171	,031
Repurchase	(Constant)	3,703	,251		14,753	,000
	Frustrated	-	,052	-,381	-6,446	,000
	Happy	,176	,057	,183	3,086	,002

(contd.)

		B	Std. Error	Beta	t	Sig.
Switch	(Constant)	2,161	,259		8,346	,000
	Sad	,344	,085	,326	4,064	,000
	Happiness	-	,059	-,212	-3,813	,000
	Disappointed	,201	,083	,195	2,425	,016
WOM	(Constant)	3,446	,248		13,916	,000
	Uneasy	-,214	,077	-,243	-2,800	,006
	Happiness	,266	,055	,267	4,840	,000
	Frustrated	-,215	,079	-,235	-2,712	,007
Do not	(Constant)	3,0463,046	,299		10,193	,000
complain	Uneasy	-,245	,058	-,264	-4,232	,000
	Content	,173	,066	,164	2,626	,009
Recovery	(Constant)	3,780	,238		15,856	,000
Satisfaction	Annoyance	-	,050	-,368	-6,244	,000
	Happiness	,196	,053	,217	3,685	,000

A series of stepwise regression analyses were conducted to examine emotional predictors of recovery satisfaction and specific complaining behaviours (Table 5 and Table 6). In the first regression we separately used recovery satisfaction measures under the no recovery and full recovery condition as the dependent variable, with emotional responses as independent variables. Subsequent analyses used specific complaining behaviour as the dependent variable and emotional responses as the independent variables. Emotions were able to explain 29.1 percent of the variance in recovery satisfaction under the no recovery condition (Table 5). Under the full recovery, the adjusted R^2 = 0. 204 and F=29.953, sig = 0.000. The standardised beta coefficients are shown in Table 5 and 6, and while only 29.1 percent of the variance in recovery satisfaction (and 20.4 percent under the full recovery) is explained, the findings indicate that the emotional responses alone are important factors in explaining customers' recovery satisfaction. Regression analyses have shown that only happiness, sadness, disappointment and annoyance were strong predictors of recovery satisfaction (Table 5). The exclusion of the other emotions does not necessarily mean that they are unimportant to customers' satisfaction judgments. They may be still important in an absolute sense, but not important relative to other emotions in predicting recovery satisfaction. The results of the regression analyses showed that in general each coefficient carried expected signs (i.e., positive relationship between positive emotions and satisfaction and negative relationship between negative emotions and satisfaction). Beta scores on Table 6 indicate that negative emotion annoyance is a stronger predictor of recovery satisfaction (beta = -0.368, t = -6.244, sig = .000), with positive emotion happiness also significant (beta = 0.217, t = 3.685, sig= - 0.000). Beta scores suggest that there is a negative association between annoyance and customers' recovery satisfactions under the no recovery and full recovery conditions.

The next question of interest was the relative effect of positive and negative emotions on specific complaining behaviours. Annoyance, frustration and disappointment were better predictors of complaining to staff under the no recovery condition (Table 5). Negative emotion annoyance and positive emotions happiness were the significant predictors of asking for manager intervention (Table 5). The negative emotion embarrassment was the only significant predictor of "do not complain" under the no recovery condition (beta = 0.244, t = 3.915, sig = 0.000) (Table 5). Significant predictors of WoM behaviour under the no recovery condition were happiness, annoyance, anxiety and disappointment (Table 5). It appears that negative emotions sadness, disappointment and embarrassment would predict Switch behaviour more than other emotions analysed in the study. Figures in Table 6 also suggest that certain emotions are stronger predictors of specific complaining behaviours than others.

It appears that emotions can predict customers' recovery satisfaction and their complaining actions to a certain extent. This finding may be interpreted as different emotions may have different behavioural consequences. This may be because different emotions may cause different information processing and lead to different complaint behaviours. For example, negative emotions are usually associated with more detailed, analytical information processing (Dube and Menon 2000, p. 295). Information needs as to the cause of the failure and plans for the recovery may lead customers to Voice behaviours. Positive relations between some negative emotions (anxiety, annoyance, and sadness) and customers' WoM and Repurchase behaviours are interesting. Similarly, regression analyses identified a positive association between negative emotions (anxiety and sadness) and WoM and Repurchase behaviours (Table 5). In the literature, it is argued that emotions affect behaviour in a valence-congruent fashion (negative emotions lead to negative behaviours and positive emotions result in positive behaviours). However, correlations in Table 3 and beta scores in Table 5 suggest that this effect could be in a valence-incongruent fashion under no recovery condition. This may suggest that consumer complaining behaviours may be positively influenced by the experience of certain types of negative emotions. Research in health care and airline services indicated that the more anxious, sad or depressed the customer, the more satisfied they were with services. Taylor (1994), in a study of airline services, found that the experience of anxiety during flight delays was linked to greater consumer satisfaction with airline services. Saying to customers who are waiting for a service in the line that the service is delayed for some technical reason for two hours may evoke anxiety and disappointment in many customers. Their expectations however will be positively disconfirmed if the staff tell them half an hour after the delay announcement that the service is ready. This positive surprise (emotion) may then lead to a heightened satisfaction.

CONCLUSION

This study was concerned to explore the relationship between customer emotions in a complaint handling situation and their behavioural responses. Results suggest that evoking different kinds of emotions in customers make them less or more likely to engage in specific favourable and unfavourable behavioural responses. Apparently, the choice of customer actions (repurchase, switch, and voice) may relate to the emotions that arise as a result of recovery strategy employed in a failure situation. Significant effects of emotions on recovery satisfaction judgement and subsequent complaining behaviours suggest that emotional scales need to be included as part of customer satisfaction and complaining behaviour measurement. Managers need to emphasise how customers feel about their experiences of service delivery in a complaint handling situation. They need to explore and, as far as possible, manage emotions in order to enhance favourable customer behaviours. The results of this study (Table 4 and Table 6) show that negative emotions have a stronger effect than positive emotions on satisfaction and complaining behaviours. This suggests that situations where the customer has strong negative feelings are critical. More studies addressing the effects of emotions are needed in order to enhance our understanding of what customers will do when they are dis/satisfied.

While this research adds to the current literature on customer emotions and consumer complaining behaviour, the results should be treated cautiously due to a number of limitations. Relatively small sample size and the convenience sampling method limit the generalizability of findings. The method in which scenario is used to measure emotions and behaviours is another limitation. Despite the care in designing and pre-testing the service failure scenario, all of the details of a real world complaint handling may have not been captured by this methodology. Consumers may display different emotions and behaviours when they encounter such an incident in real life. The use of core service failure only is another limitation. Consumers' complaining behaviours and emotional responses in other failure types might be quite different. Moreover, behavioural and emotional reactions of customers from different countries to other recovery strategies might be dissimilar. Customers' coping mechanisms with negative emotions might also be different. There is a need for further emotional research on other types of services and in different user contexts.

REFERENCES

Austin, W. and Walster, E. (1974) Reactions to Confirmations and Disconfirmations of Expectancies of Equity and Inequity. *Journal of Personality and Social Psychology* 30, 208-216.

Babin, J. B., Darden, R. W. and A. L. Babin. (1998) Negative emotions in marketing research: affect or artefact? *Journal of Business Research* 42, 271-285.

Baker, J. and Cameron M. (1996) The effects of the service environment on affect and consumer perception of waiting time: an integrative review and research propositions. *Journal of the Academy Marketing Science*, 24 (4), 338-349.

Barlow, J. M. (1996) Welcome Complaints. *Executive Excellence* 13(11), 20.

Barsky, J. (2003) Market Metrix Announces First Quarter 2004 Hospitality Index Results. http://www.marketmetrix.com/newsl2..html

Barsky, J., and Nash, L. (2002) Evoking Emotion: Affective Keys to Hotel Loyalty. *Cornell Hotel and Restaurant Administration Quarterly* February, 39-45.

Berkowitz, L. (1989) Frustration-Aggression Hypothesis: Examination and Reformulation. *Psychological Bulletin* 106,156-172.

Bigne, E. J. and Andreu, L. (2004) Emotions in segmentation: an empirical study. *Annals of Tourism Research* 31(3), 682-696.

Bitner, M. J. Booms, B. H. and Tetreault, M. (1990) The Service Encounter: Diagnosing Favourable and Unfavourable Incidents. *Journal of Marketing* 54, 71 – 84.

Blodgett, J.G., Hill, D.J. and Tax, S.S. (1997) The effects of distributive, procedural, and interactional justice on post complaint behaviour. *Journal of Retailing* 73 (2), 185-210.

Brown, S. W., Cowtes, D. and Tuten, L. T. (1996) Service Recovery: Its Value and Limitations as a Retail Strategy. *International Journal of Service Industry Management* 7(5), 32-46.

Chaudhuri, A. (1997) Consumption emotion and perceived risk: a macro analytical approach. *Journal of Business Research* 39, 81-92.

Chebat, J. and Slusarczyk, W. (2003) How emotions mediate the effects of perceived justice on loyalty in service recovery situations: an empirical study. *Journal of Business Research* Article in Press.

Day R.L, and Landon, E.L. (1977) Towards a theory of consumer complaining behaviour. In Woodside, A., Sheth, J. and Bennett P. (eds.) *Consumer and Industrial Buying Behaviour*. Amsterdam: North Holland Publishing Company.

Day, R. L. (1984) Modelling Choices among Alternate Responses to Dissatisfaction. *Association of Consumer Research Proceedings* 11, 496 – 499.

Day, R. L., Grabricke, T., Schaetzle, T. and Stavbach, F. (1981) The hidden agenda of customer complaining. *Journal of Retailing* 57, 86-106.

Dolen, W., Lemmink, J., Mattsson, J. and Rhoen, I. (2001) Affective consumer responses in service encounters: The emotional content in narratives of critical incidents. *Journal of Economic Psychology* 22, 359-376.

Dolen, W., Ruyter, K. and Lemmink, J. (2002) An empirical assessment of the influence of customer emotions and contact employee performance on encounter and relationship satisfaction. *Journal of Business Research*. Article in Press.

Dube, L. and Menon, K. (2000) Multiple roles of consumption emotions in post-purchase satisfaction with extended service transactions. *International Journal of Service Industry Management* 11 (3), 287-304.

Dube, L. and Morgan, S. M. (1998) Capturing the dynamics of in-process consumption emotions and satisfaction in extended service transactions. *International Journal of Research in Marketing* 15, 309-320.

Goodwin, C. and Ross, I. (1990) Consumer evaluations of responses to complaints: what is fair and why. *Journal Consumer Marketing* 7, 39-47.

Gronross, C. 1988 Service Quality: The Six Criteria of Good Perceived Service Quality. *Review of Business* 9,10-13.

Hart, C. W. L., James, L. H. and Earl W. S. Jr. (1990) The Profitable Art of Service Recovery. *Harvard Business Review* 68, 148–156.

Havlena, W.J. and Holbrook, M.B. (1986) The varieties of consumption experience: comparing two types of typologies of emotions in consumer behaviour. *Journal of Consumer Research* 13, 394-404.

Hirschman, A. O. (1970) *Exit, Voice and Loyalty: Responses to Decline in Firms, Organizations and States*. Cambridge MA: Harvard University Press

Hoffman, K. D. and Chung, G. B. (1999) Hospitality recovery strategies: customer preference versus firm use. *Journal of Hospitality and Tourism Research* 23 (1), 71-84.

Hoffman, K.D., Kelley, S. W. and Rotalsky, H.M. (1995) Tracking Service Failures And Employee Recovery Efforts. *Journal of Services Marketing* 9(2), 49-61.

Huang, J.H., Huang, C.T. and Wu, S. (1996) National character and response to unsatisfactory hotel service. *International Journal of Hospitality Management* 15 (3), 229-243.

Hui, K. M. and Tse, D. K. (1996) What to Tell Consumers in Waits of Different Lengths: An Integrative Model of Service Evaluation. *Journal of Marketing* April, 81-90.

Ittelson, W. H. 1973 Environment Perception and Contemporary Perceptual Theory. In Ittelson W. H. (ed) *Environment and Cognition.* (pp. ...) New York: Seminar Press.

Izard, C.E. (1977) *Human emotions.* New York : Plenum

Keaveney, S. M. (1995) Customer Switching Behaviour in Service Industries: An Exploratory Study. *Journal of Marketing* 59, 71-82.

Kelley, S. W. Hoffman, K. D. and Davis M. A. (1993) A Typology of Retail Failures and Recoveries. *Journal of Retailing* 69 (4), 429-452.

Kumar, A. and Oliver, L. R. (1997) Cognitive appraisals, consumer emotions and consumer response. *Advances in Consumer Research*. 24, 17-18.

Lam, T. and Tang, V. (2003) Recognising customer complaint behaviour: The case of Hong Kong Hotel Restaurants. *Journal of Travel and Tourism Marketing* 14 (1), 69-86.

Landon, L. E. (1977) *A Model of Consumers' Complain Behaviour*. Indiana University

Levesque, T. C. and McDougall, G. H. G. (2000) Service Problems and Recovery Strategies: an Experiment. *Canadian Journal of Administrative Sciences* 17 (1), 20-37.

Liljander, V. and Strandvik, T. (1997) Emotions in service satisfaction. *International Journal of Service Industry Management* 8 (2), 148-169.

Locke, K. (1996) A funny thing happened! The management of consumer emotions in service encounters. *Organisation Science* 7(1), 40-59.

Machleit, A. K. and Eroglu, A. S. (2000) Describing and measuring emotional response to shopping experience. *Journal of Business Research* 49, 101-111.

Manickas, P. A. and Shea, L. J. (1997) Hotel Complaint Behaviour and Resolution: A Content Analysis. *Journal of Travel Research* 36(2), 68-81.

Mano, H. and Oliver, R. L. (1993) Assessing The Dimensionality And Structure Of The Consumption Experience: evaluation, feeling and satisfaction. *Journal of Consumer Research* 20, 451-466.

Mattila, S. A. (2001) The Effectiveness of Service Recovery in a Multi – industry Setting. *Journal of Services Marketing* 15 (7), 583-596.

Mattila, S. A. (2004) The impact of service failures on customer loyalty: the moderating role of affective commitment. *International Journal of Service Industry Management* 15 (2), 134-149.

Maute, M. and Forrester, W. R. (1993) The Structure and Determinants of Consumer Complaint Intentions and Behaviour. *Journal of Economic Psychology* 14(3), 219-247.

McDougall, G. and Levesque, T. (1998)The effectiveness of recovery strategies after service failure :an experiment in the hospitality industry. *Journal of Hospitality and Leisure Marketing* 5 (2/3), 27-39.

McDougall, H.G.G. and Levesque, J. T, (1999) Waiting for service: The effectiveness of recovery strategies. *International Journal of Contemporary Hospitality Management* 11(1), 6-15.

Mehrabian, A. and Russell, J. A. (1974) *An approach to environmental psychology*. Cambridge MA: MIT Press.

Nguyen, T. D. and McColl-Kennedy, R. J. (2003) Diffusing customer anger in service recovery: A conceptual framework. *Australian Marketing Journal* 11 (2), 46-55.

Nyer, U. P. (2000) An investigation into whether complaining can cause increased consumer satisfaction. *Journal of Consumer Marketing* 17 (1), 9-19.

Oliver, R. L. (1997) *Satisfaction: A Behavioural Perspective on the Consumer*. Singapore: McGraw- Hill.

Peterson, (2000, July 18) Why is everyone is so short-tempered? USA Today, 1A.

Plutchik, R. (1980) *Emotions: a psycho evolutionary synthesis*. New York: Harper and Row.

Price, L. L., Arnould, J.E. and Deibler, L.S. (1995) Consumers' emotional responses to service encounters. The influence of the service provider. *International Journal of Service Industry Management* 6(3), 34-63.

Richins, M. (1997) Measuring Emotions in the Consumption Experience. *Journal of Consumer Research* 24(2), 127-146.

Rogers, J. C., Ross, S. C. and Williams, T. G. (1992) Personal values and purchase dissatisfaction response. *Journal of Consumer Satisfaction, Dissatisfaction and Complaining Behaviour* 5, 81-92.

Russell, J.A. (1979) Affective state is bipolar. *Journal of Personality and Social Psychology*, 37, 345-356.

Schoefer, K. and Ennew, C. (In Press) Emotional responses to service complaint experiences: The role of perceived justice. *Marketing Science* 24 (4), 350-65.

Singh, J. (1988) Consumer complaint intentions and behaviour: Definitional and Taxonomical issues. *Journal of Marketing* 52, 93-107.

Singh, J. (1990) A typology of consumer dissatisfaction response styles. *Journal of Retailing* 66(1), 57-99.

Smith, A. Bolton, R. and Wagner, J. (1999) A Model of Customer Satisfaction with Service Encounters Involving Failure and Recovery. *Journal of Marketing Research* 34, 356-372.

Smith, L. W. (1996) A framework for the application of uncertainty reduction theory to service encounters. *The International Journal of Organisational Analysis* 4 (3), 299-308.

Sparks, B. (2003) Professional Lecture Series. School of Tourism and Hotel Management. Griffith University.

Susskind, A. M. (2000) Efficacy And Outcome Expectations Related To Customer Complaints About Service Experiences. *Communication Research* 27, 353-378.

Susskind, A. M. (2002) I Told You So! Restaurant Customers' Word Of Mouth Communication. *Cornell Restaurant and Hotel Administration Quarterly* 43(2), 75-85.

Tax, S. S. Brown, S. W. and Chandrashekaran (1998) Customer Evaluations of Service Complaint Experiences: Implications for Relationship Marketing. *Journal of Marketing* 62, 60-76.

Taylor, S. (1994) Waiting For Service: The Relationship between Delays and Evaluations of Service. *Journal of Marketing* 58, 56-69.

Tedeshi, J. T. and Felson, R. B. (1994) *Violence, Aggression and Coercive Actions*. Washington, DC: American Psychological Association.

Westbrook, A. R. and Oliver, L. R. (1991) The dimensionality of consumption emotion patterns and consumer satisfaction. *Journal of Consumer Research* 18, 84-91.

Westbrook, A. R.(1980) Intrapersonal affective influences on consumer satisfaction with products. *Journal of Consumer Research* 7, 49-54.

Yu, Y. and Dean, A. (2001) The contribution of emotional satisfaction to consumer loyalty. *International Journal of Service Industry Management* 12 (3), 234-250.

Yuksel, A. and Kilinc, K. U. (2003) Calisanlarin gozuyle konaklama isletmelerinde musteri sikayetleri ve kullanilan iyilestirme stratejileri (Employees perspectives on customer complaints and recovery strategies) *Seyahat ve Turizm Arastirmalari Dergisi* 3 (1), 13-25. http://stad.adu.edu.tr

Zeelenberg, M. and Pieters, R. (2002) Beyond valence in customer dissatisfaction: a review and new findings on behavioural responses to regret and disappointment in failed services. *Journal of Business Research* Article in Press.

Zeithaml, V., Berry, L. and Parasuraman, A. (1996) The Behavioural Consequences of Service Quality. *Journal of Marketing* 60, 31 – 46.

Zemke, R. (1993) The Art of Service Recovery: Fixing Broken Customers-And Keeping Them on Your Side. In Scheuing, E.E. and Christopher, W.F. (eds.) *The service quality handbook* (pp. 463-476). New York: American Management Association.

Zins, A. (2002) Consumption Emotions, Experience Quality and Satisfaction: A Structural Analysis for Complainers versus Non-Complainers. *Journal of Travel and Tourism Marketing* 12(2/3), 3-18.

19

CHANGING SCENARIO OF HUMAN CAPITAL DEVELOPMENT IN INDIAN HOSPITALITY OPERATIONS

SAURABH K. DIXIT

ABSTRACT

Hospitality business leaders have long recognized the difficulty of attracting and retaining quality employees as a continuous threat to the heath of the industry. The current bad situation is worsening. The main cause of this is the meager pay packages offered to the employees. The compensation package in the Indian hospitality industry is connected to the hierarchy of the traditional organization chart and the lower level staff or trainees are paid very less salary. The business paradigm of hospitality industry is undergoing significant changes, which have highlighted and accelerated since September 11. The hospitality education, training and research have more obvious now, when consumers are changing their habits and asking for greater product satisfaction and services. The hospitality organizations therefore need trained and educated manpower to fulfill the consumer's expectations. Current education and training suffer in many cases from a lack of depth and isolation from real practices of the industry. In view of this situation, the WTO Education Council, this comprises almost one hundred WTO members – Universities, Business Schools, and training centers throughout the world-held its 5th General Meeting in Madrid on 6 and 7 June 2004 to take action in response to these new challenges. Therefore, this paper is an effort to analyze the prevailing systems and trends of the industry mainly for the recruitment, training and compensation paid to the employees. Of course issues concerning to their problems will also be raised.

Keywords: Compensation, online recruitment, training, poaching, incentives

INTRODUCTION

Whether measured in terms of employment, total sales, value added, capital investment, or tax contributions, hospitality industry's contribution to world economic growth is clearly very significant. The battle for discretionary income is expected to become increasingly fierce during the coming decade. With growth in leisure time, combined with increasing wealth, changes in population structure and social changes – such as new values, attitudes and lifestyles – hospitality is becoming more of a priority and less of a luxury. In India hospitality is expected to generate INR 2,092.5 bn. (US$44.7 bn.) of economic activity (Total Demand) in 2005, growing (nominal terms) to INR 8, 053.4 bn. (US$121.4 bn) by 2015. Indian hospitality demand is expected to grow by 10.9% in 2005 and by 8.6% per annum, in real terms, between 2006 and 2015. 2005 total demand represents 0.7% of world market share *(WTTC forecast)*.

As demand for hospitality industry grows – an annual growth rate of 4.5 per cent worldwide in total demand over the next ten years *(WTTC)* – the industry will require an increased supply of skilled managers and staff in all sectors to deliver a consistent, quality product. Well-trained staff enhances the consumer experience, add value to the hospitality product, improve the image of individual companies and advance their own career developments. A guest experience can be greatly enhanced when the general population is receptive of visitors, when attractions and infrastructures are professionally managed, when visitors are appropriately guided and educated regarding the natural and cultural treasures of the destination, when hospitality service levels are cf the highest standard, etc.

Attracting and retaining good staff and ensuring consistent quality can only be achieved with management commitment to effective training. Investment in training and education will have long and lasting returns through increased productivity and improved staff performance. While it is not possible to single out any one aspect of education as being more important than others, it has often been said that basic service delivery with a smile is more valuable than expert service accompanied by a poor attitude. While the most appropriate mix of educational services will largely depend on the practical experience, a well-balanced mixture of skills training and attitudinal education (preferably from a young age) is important, especially for budding professionals. Labour policies have been more traditionally concerned with the administration of the workforce than with its development. As a result, there are growing shortages of skilled people in all sectors of Hospitality, and education and training systems are often ill adapted to the industry's needs.

Hospitality Industry is highly dependent upon the availability and quality of its labour inputs. An understanding of labour markets is of primary importance to tourism in both industrialized and developing countries. With the mounting competition in the hospitality industry worldwide and the market demanding higher levels of service, productivity and value- the time for investment in people, training and in education becomes increasingly important in the growth of India's hospitality industry. Alongside a hotel's location and facilities, the attitude and capability of its staff are what mark it out from the competition, and in an industry suffering from staff shortages, holding on to good employees requires a strategy that goes beyond the pay packet.

Recruiting and training staff is a costly and time-consuming business, so when you get the right staff you want to hold on to them. While the issue of staff retention is by no means a new one, it continues to top the pile of problems for hoteliers in a sector where 100% turnover of staff is not unusual in UK. In an American Express Establishment Services (AEES) survey in Europe published in February, 96% of hotel general managers polled rated the issue as one of the main obstacles facing them. There are still lots of things that can be done to improve the situation, boosting the bottom line in the progress. One way to do this is to promote flexible working and address of other things you can do to improve staff retention and motivation, and many of them are quick wins that don't cost the earth.

COMPENSATION TRENDS IN INDIAN HOSPITALITY INDUSTRY

Labor costs are increasing as hotels compete with retailing and fast food for the unskilled and semi-skilled workers. All workers are demanding greater benefits. Labor unions appear to be regaining strength, and the tightening of immigration standards in the wake of 9/11 will place an increased burden on the industry. Highly skilled and trained workers have better carrying capacity in other industries. Productivity is declining, as employees demand more favorable hours and the hotel business modernize its wage and hour policies. The spirit of hospitality is deteriorating and guest service is being compromised by turnover, lack of training, corporate earnings requirements and staff reductions.

To understand the compensation trends in India the annual compensation survey done by HVS International Journal, New Delhi proves very useful. This Survey is intended to be a one-stop reference for current and credible information on remuneration patterns, including benefits and bonuses. The Survey is based on the compensation data for the financial year 2002/03 from 106 branded hotel properties across India, ranging from the three-star category to the five star deluxe categories. More than 700 senior executives within the industry have participated in the survey. Information was compiled from responses to a detailed questionnaire framed for the purpose and sent to the corporate offices of the hotel groups. Compensation details have been presented for thirteen senior management positions in the report; this data has been further classified into a variety of categories for the purpose of comparison.

A preview of the *Federation of Hotel and Restaurant Association of India (FHRAI)* research publication on compensation trends prevailing in Indian hospitality industry reveals that a large number of hotel companies were paying very low salaries to their management trainees and new job entrants, with some amounts being outrageously abysmal. This is further aggravated with long working hours, working in shifts and arduous working conditions.

This compensation trends report, for the Indian hospitality industry is perhaps the first comprehensive study of its kind in India. It was conducted by HVS Executive Search. According to HVS International, the report was compiled with a view to provide hotel owners and operators with current and credible information regarding compensation patterns in the hotel industry in India. This survey is based on the compensation details of 160 senior executives within the Indian hospitality industry spread across different cities. Hotels ranging from five-star deluxe to three-star (budget) hotels form a part of the database. The research has compared the database on the following basis:

- Hotels with more than 150 rooms vs. hotels with less than 150 rooms.
- By designation.

The tables provided are excerpts from the main survey: ***Table 1*** reflects statistics relating to average annual compensation on a nation-wide basis for each of the thirteen designations; ***Table 2*** illustrates average annual compensation comparison by room size, for hotels with more than 200 rooms. It may be noted that the salary, bonus and retirement remuneration of expatriates has been excluded from calculations for all the positions. For each of the positions, the minimum and maximum base salary earned has been presented, as well as the base salary at the 25, 50 and 75 percentile levels. The 25 percentile can be defined as the lowest value (in this case, base salary) that is greater than 25% of the values; similarly, the 50 percentile is the lowest value that is greater than 50% of the values and the 75 percentile is the lowest value that is greater than 75% of the values. The term base salary includes basic pay, house rent allowance, conveyance allowance, education allowance and special/dearness allowance. It does not include annual bonus, which has been presented as a separate item. 'Average Retrials' indicates provident fund and/ or gratuity and/or superannuating, as applicable across individual hotel properties, while 'Average Benefits' implies medical and leave travel allowance entitlements. While most hotels provide car/ transportation facility to their senior executives as part of the total compensation due to them, it has not included this in the calculation of average benefits, as different hotel groups follow different policies with regard to this particular entitlement.

Table 1: Compensation Data - All India Figures

Position	Base Salary (Rs)					Avg Bonus (Rs)	Avg Retrials (Rs)	Avg Benefits (Rs)
	Min	25P	50P	75P	Max			
General Manager	295,000	592,000	720,000	1,180,000	2,690,000	191,000	112,000	127,000
Resident Manager	120,000	419,000	630,000	1,040,000	1,400,000	54,000	79,000	107,000
Department Head -								
Front Office	132,000	213,000	310,000	400,000	750,000	40,000	38,000	78,000
House Keeping	58,000	228,000	290,000	504,000	1,020,000	40,000	38,000	54,000
F&B Service	103,000	292,000	392,000	485,000	1,210,000	49,000	49,000	70,000
Food Production	114,000	328,000	455,000	680,000	2,000,000	71,000	58,000	94,000
Engineering	90,000	255,000	348,000	506,000	1,383,000	57,000	52,000	87,000
Sales & Marketing	100,000	311,000	442,000	687,000	1,540,000	76,000	40,000	84,000
Human Resources	105,000	215,000	361,000	474,000	1,240,000	64,000	52,000	75,000
Finance	130,000	307,000	420,000	610,000	1,440,000	73,000	59,000	88,000
Systems	90,000	144,000	206,000	312,000	750,000	22,000	27,000	36,000
Training	120,000	243,000	291,000	375,000	750,000	52,000	33,000	54,000
PR & Communications	102,000	200,000	279,000	421,000	810,000	51,000	40,600	58,000

The value of certain perks has not been included while calculating the annual compensation details. These are: accommodation on the hotel premises, loans given for car, housing, home equipment or furnishing, and other perks like duty meals, uniform and laundry facility. Retirement benefits like superannuation have also not been included. The objective of leaving out such perks and benefits in the calculations are to arrive at a database with a fair degree of uniformity. Hence the term "Annual Compensation" in this report at ***Table 1 and 2*** would represent components like the basic salary, house rent allowance, conveyance allowance, city allowance, education allowance, special allowance, medical allowance, annual bonus, leave travel allowance and reimbursements on actuals of fuel, telephone and cellular phone. Furthermore, it would also cover the value of company-leased accommodation. Adequate weightage has been provided to certain allowances keeping in view location and other parameters.

The data reflected in ***Table 1*** and ***Table 2*** confirms that compensation in the hotel industry continues to be connected to the hierarchy of a traditional organization chart. The General Manager (GM) is the highest paid executive, followed by the Resident Manager (RM). As per survey results for 2002/03, the head of Food Production is the highest paid department head, followed by the Sales and Marketing head. Taking into account all-India figures, the median (50 percentile) of the annual base salary of a GM was Rs 720,000 in 2002/03. For GMs of hotels with rooms greater than 200, the median of his/her annual base salary was Rs 1,280,000. In other words, the median basic pay of GMs of hotels with rooms greater than 200 were about 77.7% higher than the nationwide average.

Significant variations were also noticed in other designations: for example, the median basic pay of the Sales and Marketing head at hotels with rooms greater than 200 was 55.8% greater than the nation-wide average basic pay of Sales and Marketing heads. By the same comparison, the head of Human Resources at hotels with rooms greater than 200 earned 52.3% higher. The largest variation was observed in the case of Housekeeping: the median basic pay of the Housekeeping head at hotels with rooms greater than 200 was 94.8% greater than the nationwide median basic pay for this position.

Table 2: Compensation Data - Hotels With More Than 200 Rooms

Position	Base Salary (Rs)							
	Min	25P	50P Bonus (Rs)	75P Retrials (Rs)	Max Benefits (Rs)	Avg	Avg	Avg
General Manager	992,000	1,139,000	1,280,000	2,460,000	2,690,000	285,000	196,000	182,000
Resident Manager	492,000	828,000	1,051,000	1,250,000	1,400,000	84,000	111,000	177,000
Department Head -								
Front Office	230,000	372,000	442,000	584,000	750,000	61,000	60,000	154,000
House Keeping	261,000	374,000	565,000	739,000	1,020,000	50,000	55,000	90,000
F&B Service	183,000	394,000	483,000	614,000	1,210,000	70,000	71,000	71,000
Food Production	309,000	608,000	781,000	1,872,000	2,000,000	161,000	103,000	145,000
Engineering	260,000	425,000	546,000	739,000	1,383,000	73,000	79,000	93,000
Sales & Marketing	301,000	493,000	689,000	765,000	1,540,000	59,000	62,000	103,000
Human Resources	332,000	438,000	550,000	784,000	1,240,000	92,000	92,000	93,000
Finance	307,000	499,000	610,000	723,000	1,440,000	80,000	85,000	102,000
Systems	111,000	235,000	315,000	418,000	750,000	26,000	39,000	47,000
Training	240,000	276,000	363,000	456,000	750,000	59,000	40,000	67,000
PR & Communications	216,000	299,000	387,000	600,000	810,000	55,000	57,700	76,000

The research found that senior executives working in independent hotels generally have a better compensation package as compared to executives working for hotel chains. The executives in hotel chains have better benefits, perks and retirement benefits compared to executives working in independent hotels. The average bonus of a GM was about 18.4% of his/her average base salary. This is more or less in line with bonus pays for GMs in the hotel industry in the United States, where bonus as a percentage of average base salary is 20-22%. The RM's bonus was 7.3% of his/her average base salary - lower than the bonus as-percentage-of-average basic of both India-based GMs as well as RMs in the US (13%). Benefits worked out to 12.2% of the GM's average base salary and 14.6% of the RM's average base salary. Retrials as a percentage of average base salary were 10.7% and 10.8%, respectively, for the GM and the RM. For the Sales and Marketing head, average bonus as a percentage of average base salary worked out to 15.0%, while benefits worked out to 12.6%. For the Finance head, bonus and benefits as a percentage of average base salary were calculated to be 15.3% and 18.4%, respectively.

BEST HUMAN RESOURCES PRACTICES FOR INDIAN HOSPITALITY INDUSTRY

This growth in demand for hospitality industry products is stimulating competition for tourist dollars. The emergence of new, exotic destinations is putting pressure on operators to increasingly enhance the quality of their products and services to help maintain their share in the market. At the same time, travelers are becoming more sophisticated and are demanding better and more personalized service. A well-educated and well-trained workforce is essential to respond to this changing environment. The industry's poor image is being a major obstacle to attracting new staff, but a lack of understanding about what the industry has to offer new entrants is also blamed for the trend. To develop its human resource to perform their best the following points should be taken care by the industry operators:

Communication

Communication is key issue. You need to "communicate, communicate, and then communicate some more". Staff wants to know how both they and the company as a whole are doing. They want to be part of something worthwhile and be told they are making a difference. Keep them up to speed with the company direction and strategy through media such as an employee newsletter, regular meetings and staff presentations - even an intranet. Providing staff with a chance to have their say so that potential problems are picked up before they go too far is also crucial. Find ways to get staff input, even if it's only putting a suggestion box in the staff room. Conducting an employee attitude survey, preferably more than once a year, is a great way to get feedback. It also helps to benchmark your performance year on year; and follow up on staff suggestions, otherwise it's pointless. The key is to create an environment where staff feels able to highlight grievances without fear of retribution. Remember that unresolved problems can result in employees leaving the company without you ever knowing why, leaving the potential for the same thing to happen again and again. Conducting exit interviews when staff leaves the business can help here.

Financial Incentives

Offering financial "carrots" can obviously be an effective motivation tool. All the tips and the revenue from the service charge on hotel functions throughout the year and should be dished out to the staff. It goes down extremely well and it certainly helps with staff retention. The money you put in people's pockets and the way you treat them manifests itself in many different ways.

Training Advancement of the Staff

To develop appropriate and suitable manpower for the hospitality, it is essential to provide them suitable training in all aspects of HRD.The professionals need to be supported by an appropriate philosophy of man, work and work organization. Thus men or women as workers are to be viewed in dignified, egalitarian and partnership terms. Work should be seen as a process of human collaboration rather than a commodity procured with money. The work organizations are to be seen as a venue for human collaboration and growth through partnership, rather than as a place to practice authority relations, or even worse, to engage in exploitative practices through submitting others to conditions of indignity and deprivations.

To adopt and accept the normative approach to HRD in hospitality industry, it is essential to understand simple model of HRD consisting of following human development activities, namely spiritual development, intuition development, mental development, love and self attitude development. The synergy of these aspects of HRD is an essential requirement of professionals in the hospitality industry to emerge and realize their full potential. The multidisciplinary field of knowledge allows for delineation of hospitality's structure, function, operational requirements, sociopolitical strategies, and challenges and opportunities ahead, among other things. To further mobilize informed education efforts, to fully respond to human resource needs of the country, major players should be involved in order to anchor hospitality to banks of knowledge and industry. On an attempt to make SWOT analysis of the youth in India for becoming hospitality professionals, one can view the situation as shown below ***(Table -3).***

Table 3: S.W.O.T. Analysis of Present Hospitality Employees

Strength	Weakness	Opportunities	Threats
Hard Working	Lack of Communication Skills	Industrialization	Competition
Sincere	Lack Of Leadership Quality	Information Technology	Uncertainty
Loyal	Scanty Financial Support Lack Of Confidence Flimsy Technical Background	Government Schemes Credit facilities	Risk

A sustained programme of training and career development for staff at all levels, along with a communications strategy that helps the staff feel part of a company's goals, can be just as effective. There are so many other things that the staff can tell to the management and it will make them feel involved, valued and recognized. An obvious fear is that after sending employees on training programmes they will become more attractive to the competitors and leave, but this shortsighted approach must be avoided at all costs. It should be seen as an investment, not a cost. Boutique hotel chain *Malmaison* is putting online learning booths in its hotels so staff can study other subjects, such as languages, while at work; and hotel group *Mandarin Oriental* has a subsidized four-year MBA programme for "high-flying" young staff members in management positions. One method used by companies such as *Park Plaza* and the *Savoy Group* is to invite each member of staff to spend the night with a partner or friend in the hotel they work so as to experience the hotel as a guest. They then fill in a questionnaire and say what they will do differently as a result of their stay.

Staff Accommodation

Improving staff accommodation and facilities is another option. The key always is to find out what the staff wants, rather than what the management thinks they want, and to not rest on their laurels when things are going well. It's all too easy when a hotel is doing well to sit back and pat itself on its back. As guests' expectations rise, so do staff's. It's not enough to say 'more of the same'. What is really needed is to keep the foot on the pedal as the staff becomes more attractive to competitors.

Poaching

Poaching has been posing a serious problem to the hospitality industry and human resources professionals feel that it cannot be stopped unless strict measures are put in place immediately. While occupancies and ARR's are escalating, one vital characteristic in which the sector is suffering is retention of human resources. The hospitality industry is witnessing comprehensive augmentation in business with most hotels raking in the moolah owing to the vast gap in demand & supply. It may seem to be the best of times for the industry, but one vital area, which is simultaneously 'suffering', is the human resource segment. The attrition level has escalated like never before. While the industry is losing their best resources to competition, other industries like airlines and the IT sector have suddenly diverted its preference towards hospitality industry's human resource. To discourage attrition, bigger hotel chains are trying to utilize their network to send their staff to different destinations with a promotion within the chain, while small hotel groups' resort to improving the working environment. According to the industry, the problem is grave, but there is no solution until and unless the industry's manpower allocation increases, which is a distant possibility.

The Delhi-based hospitality HR Forum recently mét up to find a solution to this problem. However, the conclusions arrived at in the meeting did not find favour from the other HR personnel in the industry. During the meeting, it was suggested there should be the provision of agreement or deal that if an employee leaves one hotel/company in less than a year and joins another company, he/she will not be recruited for next the 12 months by any other hotel. However, the suggestion was ruled out. Reasons, the members didn't want to be a hindrance to someone's career or professional growth.

Poaching will be unstoppable as wherever public dealing comes into picture; hospitality professionals are the most sought after candidates. This is mainly because these candidates are capable of handling pressure, can communicate well, exhibit proper mannerism and carry a pleasant disposition. In short, they are well groomed for various jobs in the allied service industries. Earlier, employees used to quit the hotel industry to join call centers, but now people are quitting call centers to join other call centers, which are paying better packages. This can be understood by the fact that in a call center, the percentage of manpower cost out of the total may be as high as 40 per cent, while in a hotel, it is only in the range of about 12-20 per cent. In such a scenario, attrition is unavoidable. However, the hospitality industry employees are also being poached by other industries like hospitals; telecom, insurance, liquor companies and the latest to join in are the call centre and multiplex operators.

The main reason for high attrition levels is obviously the salary. Freshers from hotel management schools are paid about Rs 5000 in the first year, Rs 6000 in the second year, after which they are taken on rolls. But the difference is huge, when compared to the package given by other industries. The only way the problem can be tackled is by providing them a better working environment, giving them responsibilities and opportunities and also by making them feel important. Monetary aspects do define, but such personal issues also play an important role in deciding comfort levels.

Supply towards the industry from the hotel management colleges is coming down and it is realized that hotels have to develop from within by retention of key employees. It is mostly the young employees who tend to leave more often than the older employees, further to which the focus should be more towards them. The industry is finding it very difficult as far as retention of employees is concerned. The problem is currently more prevalent with retaining ladies, who are moving to the airline industry. Earlier it was the IT industry, which was taking most of the chunk, but now the airline industry, which is also booming, is pulling in a lot of people from the hospitality sector.

To counter the rising attrition levels, the only feasible option is to raise the bar on salaries so they refrain from even thinking of going to some other company. The industry is also applying a career progression option wherein an employee can also go to other hotels in various destinations in the country and abroad, within the group. With the group on a major expansion drive, employees are provided several options within the group. If an employee has been with a hotel for sometime, and is able to handle higher responsibility, ways to be worked out so that he gets a movement to a higher designation in a different hotel.

The management should understand that when compared to other industries, the hotel industry is a 24/7 job where an employee ends up sacrificing a lot of personal time and pleasure due to odd working hours, which is inevitable. However it is also important for the management to come out with an innovative human resource practice to compensate the staff for the same. There can be different types of compensations - be it in cash, by means of comp-offs, compensation by means of other incentives like gifts, sponsored holiday etc. Team building exercise, excellent work atmosphere, clearly defined career advancement plan for each employee, transparent management style are some essentials to maintain employee loyalty towards the company. Management should differentiate between outstanding performance and plain performance and pay better package to the outstanding performers ignoring company scheduled salary structures. There should be awareness created. There should be some commitment towards the opportunity given to them.

Proper Implementation of HR Policies

Why is it so hard to reach a goal? We usually know what do to, it's just that we lose our focus somewhere between thought and action. Little surprise, then, that many companies have exactly the same problem. And that successful companies turn out to be better at turning theory into practice. Not only do the majority of the world's most admired companies have a winning strategy—they're also able to carry it out. Once a company's plan is defined, the next step is to implement it. That means communicating the strategy to key people to make sure they know their roles and are held accountable for what they do. Clear, simple goals don't mean much if nobody takes them seriously. The failure to follow through is widespread in business and a major cause of poor execu-tion. The gap between the two was more significant when it came to accountability. Of course, it's easier to make decisions and be held account-able for them when everybody knows who is responsible for making what decision. It's when people are held accountable for their actions and know their roles that companies achieve the best results. Strategies, implementation, and execution are all important, but they're only as good as the people who realize them. That might be the first step to execution.

Proper Utilization of Online Recruitment

Recruitment is the process of identifying the prospective employees, stimulating and encouraging them to apply for a particular job or jobs in an organization. The most well known human resource system today is E- recruitment. This has been frequently practiced to ensure the effectiveness and promptness of the hospitality industry across the world. There are many opportunities throughout the online recruitment process where taking it just "one step further" can help you secure top talent for your organization. However, it is still a relatively new model and it needs a lot of attention. Many hospitality companies are taking a reactive approach and leaving it to HR administrators to just "post and pray." By doing so they are not only decreasing their chances of hiring a candidate, but they can potentially miss out on identifying the "A" player. There are many opportunities throughout the online recruitment process where taking it just "one step further" can help you secure top talent for your organization.

Searching resume databases enables employers to identify a passive candidate (someone who is happy in his current position but is willing to hear about potential opportunities). During a search, an employer may come across a perfect resume. This is a great time to "take it one step further." The nature of online recruiting as it stands now is a bit more quantity than quality. One job posting can garner hundreds of resumes, most of whom may be unqualified. It can be daunting for employers to get back to every single applicant, but it needs to be done. It may not yield immediate rewards, but eventually it will help set you apart as a best practice company. Further, you never know if someone may be a fit for your company later in their career, and you want to leave them with a favorable impression. At a minimum an auto reply should be set up for e-mail applicants. If you had spoken with a candidate and led him or her through the interview process, following up with the individual directly is a must. Depending on the search and it's complexity, you may sometimes feel are if you are more of a detective than a recruiter. Remember, diligence is the mother of good fortune. You owe it to your company to scour the market for the best possible talent, no matter what level the position.

Hospitality Education in India

National Council for Hotel Management and Catering Technology is a registered Society functioning as the apex body for education and training in Hotel Management and Catering Technology. It was set up by the Central Ministry of Tourism in the year 1982 for development of human resources for the Hotel and Catering Industry. Minister of Tourism is Chairman of the Society. The Board of Governors constituted to regulate functioning of the Council is chaired by Secretary in the Ministry of Tourism. A network of twenty four Institutes of Hotel Management located at Ahmedabad, Bangalore, Bhopal, Bhubaneswar, Calcutta, Chandigarh, Chennai, Delhi (Pusa), Delhi (Lajpatnagar), Gangtok, Goa, Gwalior, Gurdaspur, Guwahati, Hyderabad, Jaipur, Jodhpur, Lucknow, Mumbai, Patna, Srinagar, Shimla, Shillong and Thiruvananthapuram are affiliated to the Council. The six Food Craft institutes at Ajmer, Chandigarh, Darjeeling, Faridabad, Pondicherry and Udaipur are also affiliated to the Council.

The Council performs a key role in creating a modern and model training system to meet the varied and changing manpower needs for different segments of the Hotel and Catering Industry. It is the principle planning and policy formulating body responsible for co-ordinating the entire gambit of Hotel and Catering Management education in the country. Activities of the National Council include Formulation of different courses of study in the field of Food Management, Hotel Management and allied skills and crafts; affiliation of institutions conducting courses prescribed by it; prescribe norms & standards for buildings and equipment required for such institutions; prescribe educational and other standards for faculty; prescribe basic standards required for admission to various courses; prescribe manner of admission; conduct examinations for promotion from lower to higher classes; award Certificates and Diplomas and Degree in cooperation with IGNOU; promote general advancement of hospitality management education; devise and deploy means for testing skills of persons already working in the industry and grant recognition to their professional attainments; advise the Government on the coordinated growth and development of Hotel Management and Catering Technology education and training; etc.

In addition to above discussed National Council Institutes, Hotel Management education is also imparted via various Universities and private sector hospitality operators. Various Universities such as Rohilkhand University at Bareilly, Bundelkhand University at Jhansi, Nagpur University, Banglore University, Garhwal University at Srinagar Garhwal, Meerut University, and Amity Uttar Pradesh University at Noida etc. are offering Four Year Bachelor's Degree in Hotel Management and Catering Technology. Bundelkhand University and Kurukshetra University are offering two Year Masters Degree in Hotel Management. These Courses are run as per the guidelines issued by All India Council of Technical Education.

CONCLUSIONS

The paper has thrown light on various aspects of manpower employed in the hospitality sector. The country has not been able to harness the its vast potential due to lack of financial support, limited role of private sector, lack of adequate infrastructure facilities, lack of political will etc. The human resource development is now being given priority in order to make hospitality industry more efficient and employment oriented sector in India. At present

IHM's, University's Hotel Management Departments and other private hospitality education institutions should make their best effort to give much emphasis on the quality factor of training programmes for the human resources in the hospitality industry.

Actions being taken by companies to address the problems of staff attraction and retention include many different initiatives, but all seem to be designed to make existing staff and potential new recruits – especially young people – aware of the multiple career opportunities in hospitality industry. Career paths should be clearly defined at all levels, so that potential recruits know in advance how far they can progress through training and education. If qualifications mean something, it is easier to set oneself achievable goals. The different sectors of hospitality industry should be seen as separate parts of one and the same industry, rather than individual industries. This will increase opportunities for employees to switch from one sector to another, as well as from one occupation to another, thereby discouraging moves to other industries.

Development of professionalism among youth opting for hospitality industry is inevitable in the present day set up of India mainly on account of the fact that proficiency is not a genetically inherited characteristic, but socially determined endowment. It has been the general trend in India that one enters hospitality sector as a last resort when all options have failed. There is the need to inculcate the spirit of hospitality in the educational system from lower level to upper level rather than inducing it deliberately when there is no other go.

Over the next three to seven years, Indian hospitality companies have plans to either acquire or set up hotel properties across major international cities. All leading hotel companies want to invest in properties in cities such as New York, London, Dubai and Singapore. A few of them are also considering investments in prominent tourist destinations in South East Asia. With India on the global charts, hoteliers feel, it's time to make a strategic move and have a dominant presence in key global markets. To sustain themselves they need to have well trained and confidant brigade in every section.

The small hotel sector finds difficult to invest in training. The big hotels increasingly recognize the need for providing training of hotel workers to meet the new demands in terms of quality customers, multiskilling and technological innovations. Despite the availability of hospitality training institutes and programmes, more investment in training and upgrading will be necessary if the country wants to remain competitive in terms of service standards and adaptation to new technologies.

In order to make newcomers more competent there is need for the improvement of hospitality faculties. The present faculty is outdated. There is need to upgrade the teaching standards of the Hotel and Catering Management Institutes as well as orient the syllabus to include the latest techniques. Therefore, periodic courses to "teach the teacher" and "train the teacher" will have to be conducted involving the best expertise from India and abroad. The deputation of personnel from the industry to the teaching institutes may be encouraged so as to inculcate the latest developments of industry.

REFERENCES

Andrews, Sudhir (1994), India: Case study of Human Resources in Tourism, In Baum Tom (Ed.), *Human Resource*, Butterworth-Heinemann, Oxford.

Airey, D. and Johnson, S. (1999), The content of tourism degrees in the U.K., *Tourism Management*, Vol. 20,No.2, pp 229-235.

Amoah, V. and Baum T. (1997), Tourism education: policy versus practice, *International Journal of Contemporary Hospitality Management*, Vol. 9, No. 1, pp 5-12.

Andrew, R., Baum, T. and Morrison, A. (2001), the lifestyle Economics of small tourism businesses, *Journal of Travel and Tourism Research*, Vol. 1, pp 16-25.

Baum, T. (1990), Competencies for hotel management: industry expectation of education, *International Journal of Contemporary Hospitality Management*, Vol. 2, No. 4, pp 13-16.

Bradley, H., Erikson, M., Stephenson, C. & Williams, S. (2000), *Myths at Work*, Cambridge: Polity Press.

Brown, P., Green, A. & Lauder, H. (2001), *High Skills, Globalization, Competitiveness and Skill Formation*, Oxford: Oxford University Press.

Bell, R. and Weitman, S. (1995), Increasing applied skills in an introductory marketing course, *Journal of Hospitality and Tourism Educator*, Vol. 7, No. 2, pp 11-13.

Breiter, D. and Clements, C. J. (1995), Hospitality Management curricula for the 21st century, *Journal of Hospitality and Tourism Educator*, Vol. 8, No. 1, pp 57-60.

Burns, P.M. (1997), Hard Skills, Soft Skills: Undervaluing hospitality's 'Service with a smile', *Progress in Tourism and Hospitality Research*, Vol. 3, pp 239-248.

Casado, M.A. (1992), Higher education hospitality schools: meeting the need of the industry, *Journal of Hospitality and Tourism Educator*, Vol. 4, No. 2, pp 41-44.

Chirstou, E. (2000), Management Competencies for graduate Trainees of Hospitality and Tourism Programs, *Annals of Tourism Research*, Vol. 27, No. 4, pp 248-260.

Charles, R. K. and Marshall, L. H. (1992). Motivational preferences of Caribbean hotel workers: an exploratory study. *International Journal of Contemporary Hospitality Management*, 4 (3): 25-29.

Child, J. (1984). *Organisation: a guide to problems and practice*, 2nd edition, Paul Chapman Publishing: London.

Cooper, C., Fletcher, J., Gilbert, D. and Wanhill, S. (1993). *Tourism: principles and practices*, Pitman Publishing: London.

Darder, R. (1994). Six steps to creating positive motivational working environment. *International Gaming and Wagering Business*, Vol. 15, pp 17-18.

Dawson, K. M. and Dawson, S .N. (1990). How to motivate your employees? *HR Magazine*, 37 (4): 78-80.

Dale, C. and Robinson, N. (2001), The theming of tourism education: a three- domain approach, *International Journal of Contemporary Hospitality Management*, Vol. 13, No. 1, pp 30-34.

Guerrier, Y. & Deery, M. (1998), Research in Hospitality Human Resource Management and Organizational Behavior, *International Journal of Hospitality Management*, Vol. 17, pp 145- 160.

International Labor Organization (1979), *Tasks to Jobs- Developing a Modular System of Training for Hotel Occupations*, Geneva: ILO.

Ingram, A., Jamieson, R., Lynch, O. and Bent, R. (2000). Questioning the impact of the graduation of the managerial labour force upon the management of human resources in the Scottish hotel industry. *Journal of Consumer Studies and Home Economics*, Vol. 24, No. 4, pp 212-222.

Jenkins, K. A. (2001). Making a career of it? Hospitality students' future perspectives: an Anglo-Dutch study. *International Journal of Contemporary Hospitality Management*, Vol. 13, No. 1, pp 13-20.

Jafri, Zafar (1990), Research and Scholarship: the basis of tourism education, *The Journal of Tourism Studies*, Vol. 1 and No. 1.

Kelley-Patterson, D. and George, C. (2001), Securing graduate commitment: an exploration into comparative expectations of placement students, graduate recruits and human resource managers within the hospitality, leisure and tourism studies, *International Journal of Hospitality Management*, Vol. 20, pp 311-323.

Kovach, A. K. (1987), What motivates employees? Workers and supervisors give different answers. *Business Horizons*, Vol. 30, No. 5, pp 58-65.

Lu, L. (1999). Work motivation, job stress, and employees' well-being. *Journal of Applied Management Studies*, Vol. 8, No. 1, pp 61-72.

Noon, M. & Blyton, P. (1995), *The Realities of Work*, Basingstroke: Macmillan.

Rao. G. Krishna Ranga (1996), Tourism Education and Training in India, *Tourism Recreation Research*, Vol. XX, No.2.

Riley (1996), *Human Resource Management in the Hospitality and Tourism Industry*, 2nd Edition, Oxford: Butterworth-Heinemann.

Sheldon, Pauline J. (1989), Professionalism in Tourism and Hospitality, *Annals of Tourism Research*, Vol. 16, pp 492- 503.

20

EMPOWERMENT LEVELS AND COMPLAINING BEHAVIORS: A CASE OF HOTEL CUSTOMERS' BEHAVIORAL INTENTIONS

ATILA YUKSEL, MURAT HANCER AND UGUR K. KILINC

ABSTRACT

When service/product disconfirmation occurs, whether the frontline employee has been allowed to make decisions to handle the complaints becomes the key to keeping the customer satisfied. A quasi-experiment based on a scenario involving core service failure was conducted with 251 participants in order to examine the impact of different levels of empowerment on hotel customers' switch, loyalty, private communication, do nothing and third party complaint behavior. Responses were analyzed using repeated-measures MANOVA. Results brought out that empowerment affected customers' complaint behaviors significantly and customers preferred to deal with fully empowered employees who could solve their complaints relatively quickly. Managerial implications of the study are discussed.

Keywords: ***empowerment, service failure, recovery, complaint behaviour.***

INTRODUCTION

The concepts of consumer dissatisfaction (CD) and consumer complaining behavior (CCB) continue to receive growing attention from researchers and practitioners. Considering that most dissatisfied customers never bother to complain, customers seeking redress for their complaints provide destinations/ companies with opportunities to improve their management and marketing programs so as to enhance customer satisfaction and profitability (Huang, Huang & Wu, 1996). Ineffective handling of customer's complaint increases frustration and dissatisfaction, reinforces negative consumer reactions and harms a marketer's reputation (Hart, James & Earl, 1990; Hoffman & Chung, 1999; Mattila, 2001). In other words, failure to handle consumers' complaints promptly provokes consumers' unfavorable behaviors (e.g., negative word-of-mouth or exit intentions) and this can have catastrophic effects on an organization's business.

Previous studies have identified different causes and consequences of service failures (Boshoff & Staude, 2003; Jonhston & Fern, 1999). These studies note that the majority of responses to customer complaints are far from restoring customer satisfaction (Boshoff & Leong, 1998; Hart et al., 1990). Bitner, Booms and Tetrault's (1994) study indicates that the greater part of dissatisfying service encounters is the result of frontline employees' inability to respond to service failure situations. Customers often switch to an alternative service provider, not because of core service failures, but because of the unacceptable response of employees to customer attempts to redress failure (Keaveney, 1995, p. 77). This can be attributed to existence or absence of many factors - one of which is the lack of empowerment (Hocutt & Stone, 1998). Empowerment refers to "having the desire, skills, tools and authority as a frontline employee to service the customer" (Zeithaml & Bitner, 2000, p. 302). Empowering employees to solve customer complaints without first having to obtain authorization to do so has managerial implications (Boshoff & Leong, 1998). When service/product disconfirmation occurs, whether the frontline employee has been allowed to make decisions to handle the complaints becomes the key to keeping the customer satisfied (Huang & Smith, 1996; Peterson, 2000). Empowerment allows the frontline employee to make decisions concerning service dissatisfaction at the time it occurs. Thus, it is expected to address the critical issues of speed, convenience, accessibility and flexibility of complaint procedures (Boshoff, 1997; Tax, Brown & Chandrashekaran, 1999). Empowerment may not be an absolute necessity under all circumstances (Bowen & Lawler, 1992). However, empowerment is essential in effectively dealing with unanticipated incidents, which require discretionary behavior on the part of employees.

The importance of empowerment for unique and unpredictable situations in which frontline staff often find themselves cannot be questioned. Failure to ensure that complaining customers are satisfied with the service recovery response, can only lead to serious problems, as the service firm will be letting the customer down for a second time (Boshoff & Staude, 2003). Inappropriate response to the failure will lead to a magnification of the negative evaluation as the original problem was not adequately recovered (Johnston & Fern, 1999). Employees must be given the discretion in order to act immediately and sensitively to satisfy unpredicted customer requirements, recover consumer confidence by remedying service failures and delight customers by giving extra or unexpected service (Hales & Klidas, 1998).

Despite its benefits, managers are reported to be reluctant to empower their employees (Hales & Klidas, 1998). Generally speaking, employees are expected to seek approval of their supervisors or managers for the resolution of customer complaints (Boshoff & Leong, 1998; Hales & Klidas, 1998). Limited empirical information illustrating how empowerment affects customers' complaint behaviors and business performance may account for managers' unwillingness. There is a need to better understand the organizational and managerial implications of empowering frontline employees in complaint handling.

This study addresses the question of whether allowing employees to make decisions in complaint handling situations influences customers' (un) favorable behavioral intentions. Based on the classification of Bowen and Lawler (1992), three levels of empowerment (full, partial and none) were operationalized in a hypothetical scenario. A total of 251 subjects participated in this quasi-experimental study. Results suggest that empowerment levels significantly affect customers' favorable (e.g., recommending the company to others, remaining loyal to the company) and unfavorable behavioral intentions (e.g., taking legal action, complaining to other customers, switching to competitors). Customers were more likely to display unfavorable behaviors under the no empowerment condition where the frontline employee could not solve the problem at all and needed to refer the customer to management.

CONSUMER COMPLAINT BEHAVIOR

CCB is generally considered to be a set of multiple responses arising out of purchase dissatisfaction (Singh, 1988). Several different responses, ranging from doing nothing to taking legal action, can result from a dissatisfying encounter (Huang, Huang & Wu, 1996). Complaint responses are generally considered to fall into two broad categories; behavioral and non behavioral. Behavioral responses consist of any or all customer action that convey an expression of dissatisfaction (Landon, 1977). Non-behavioral responses, such as, when the consumer forgets about a dissatisfying episode and does nothing, are also considered as a legitimate CCB response (Day et al., 1981). Singh (1988) noted that some people choose behavioral responses whereas others elect non-behavioral responses in relatively similar dissatisfying episodes.

Hirschman (1970) suggested that dissatisfaction could provoke two active negative responses; voice and exit. Maute and Forrester (1993) found a strong support for a three way classification of dissatisfaction responses based on Hirschman's (1970) exit, voice, and loyalty responses (loyalty being the decision to remain with the company despite dissatisfaction). Exit is "the voluntary termination of an exchange relationship" while voice is "actual communication of the complaint to the service provider" (Singh, 1988, p. 94). Loyalty – a passive response, merely accepting dissatisfaction in the hope that things will improve in the future - is one of the responses a customer has to a service failure (Hirschman, 1970). However, loyalty should not be considered as one-dimensional. Customers may stay with a service provider because they have a high opinion of them and see the service failure as an aberration. "Even when a problem is not solved, approximately half of the respondents would remain with the firm" (Levesque & McDougall, 2000, p. 22). This may be due to switching costs, lack of perceived differentiation of alternatives, locational constraints on choice, time or money constraints, habit or inertia (Hirschman, 1970). Customers may also stay after a service failure because they are spuriously loyal. That is, they feel trapped, are apathetic or there are no alternatives so they do not leave. Hence, dissatisfied customers may choose to remain with a service provider or they may exit based on their service recovery strategy standards.

Day and Landon (1977) extended the notion of "voice" further by stating that voice can be complaining to the service provider, complaining to acquaintances (negative word-of-mouth), or complaining to third parties in order to help seek redress. Using factor analysis techniques (both exploratory and confirmatory), Singh (1988) found empirical support that consumer complaint behavior could be viewed as falling into one of three categories: voice responses, private responses, and third-party responses. Voice responses are directed to objects that are external to the consumer's social circle and are directly involved in the dissatisfying exchange (e.g. seeking redress from the seller); private responses are the responses in which the objects are not external to the consumer's social circle and are not directly involved in the dissatisfying experience (e.g. word-of-mouth communication or exit); and third-party responses include objects that are external to the consumer but not directly involved in the dissatisfying transaction (e.g. reporting to a consumer agency or to taking legal action).

Based on categories developed by Singh (1988), Rogers, Ross and Williams (1992) conceptualized consumer complaint behavior alternatives as follows: *change future behavior*: do not buy the item or patronize the seller in the future; *private complaining*: warn family and friends about the product or seller; *voice complaint*: complain to service provider; *third party*: complain to customer group, take legal action, and *do nothing*: internalize or ignore the dissatisfaction. Customers may choose to do nothing about their dissatisfaction for a number of reasons. Those reasons include the assumption that their complaints are unwelcome, that no one will listen to them, that they do not know who to complain to and that they have to wait a long time for a response (Barlow, 1996). Recently, Lam and Tang (2003) identified four complaint behaviors: personal and urging, bad-mouthing, complaint to management and publicizing.

This review of literature suggests that complaint options may range from seeking redress to contacting third parties. According to Zeithaml et al (1996) certain behaviors signal that customers are forging bonds with a company. These include expressing preference for the company over others, increase the volume of their purchase, saying positive things about the company to others and remaining loyal to the company. There are also certain behaviors signaling that customers are poised to leave the company or spend less with the company (Zeithaml et al., 1996, p.34). These behaviors include complaining to staff, friends or external agencies and contemplation of switching to another company. Solnick and Hemenway (1992) observe that voice and exit can be substitutes for each other, they often occur together. From the managerial point of view; however, any action that gives the company an opportunity to become aware of the problem and subsequently restore satisfaction can be perceived as a favorable behavior. Hence, instead of viewing it as an entirely unfavorable behavior, we have considered such voice behaviors as complaining to staff, writing a complaint letter, and demanding a higher authority as favorable behaviors. A total of nine behavioral responses that a customer may utilize to deal with his/her dissatisfaction were therefore included in the study. Unfavorable behavioral intentions were switching patronage, telling the bad experience to other customers, complaining to an external agency and do not complain. Favorable behavioral intentions were complaining to the service employee, demanding immediate intervention by a higher authority, writing a complaint letter to the company headquarters, recommending it to friends and relatives and continuing to do business with the company.

SERVICE RECOVERY AND EMPOWERMENT

Service recovery refers to the actions a service employee takes in response to a service failure (Brown, Cowles & Tuten, 1996; Gronroos, 1988). It is a "...thought-out, planned process for returning aggrieved customers to a state of satisfaction with the firm after a service or product has failed to live up to expectations". The aim of service recovery efforts is basically to maintain the business relationship with the customer by moving the customer from a state of dissatisfaction to a state of satisfaction (Zemke, 1993). Recovery to failures can take many forms. These actions range from "do nothing" to "whatever it takes to fix the problem" and they can be determined by the level of discretionary power given to the frontline employees (Bitner, Booms & Tetrault, 1990; Hart et al., 1990; Hoffman et al., 1995; Kelley, Hoffman & Davies, 1993).

Empowerment can be described as a means to enable employees to make decisions (Bowen & Lawler, 1992; Hancer, 2001; Lawler et al., 1992). While empowerment is defined as authority delegation (Burke, 1986) or a participative management technique (Likert, 1967), Conger and Kanungo (1988) suggest that empowerment is a motivational construct rather than a leader–member relational construct. The motivational approach refers to self-determination (Deci, 1975) and self-efficacy (Bandura, 1986), while relying upon goal setting and open communication (Conger & Kanungo, 1988). They define empowerment as "a process of enhancing feelings of self-efficacy among organizational members through the identification of conditions that foster powerlessness and through their removal by both formal organizational practices and informal techniques of providing efficacy information" (Conger & Kanungo, 1988, p.474).

A parallel approach to define and explore empowerment is taken by Thomas and Velthose (1990). Thomas and Velthouse (1990) conceptualize empowerment in terms of changes in cognitive variables (task assessments) which determine the motivation of individuals. They suggest that empowerment is a psychological state that exists solely within the mind of the individual person. The emphasis made in their model reveals how an empowered state of mind within an individual is reached by the perceptions of the individual. The primary differences between Conger and Kanungo's and Thomas and Velthouse's studies are: a) the concept of empowerment as motivation is identified by intrinsic task motivation; b) the task assessment causing this motivation has been deliberately identified; and, c) the interpretive processes through which workers arrive at those task assessments have been acquired (Thomas & Velthouse, 1990, p. 667).

Spreitzer (1995) emphasizes the cognitive perspective of empowerment and focused more on the psychological state of the employees who experience empowerment. Psychological Empowerment consists of four cognitions that constitute an overall construct. These dimensions are meaning, competence, self-determination and impact (Spreitzer, 1996; Thomas & Velthouse, 1990). Meaning involves the fit between a person's values and beliefs and work role requirements. Competence refers to confidence in one's job performance abilities. Self-determination reflects autonomy in the choices and decisions an individual can make regarding work allocations. Lastly, impact is a sense of being able to influence important outcomes within the organization.

The review of literature above shows that definition of empowerment may take many meanings such as, "...allowing employees to decide how they will greet a customer...[to] giving employees almost unlimited discretionary spending power to recover from any service problem" (Bowen & Lawler, 1995, p. 73). Bowen and Lawler (1992, p. 36) distinguish between four levels of empowerment. The lowest level is, in effect, no empowerment. The next level, termed suggestion involvement, implies very little change to day-to-day activities as employees can only make suggestions through formal channels and the power of decision-making remains with management. The third level does not impact on higher level strategic decision making but permits individual employees considerable freedom in terms of their daily work activities. The highest level of empowerment is called high involvement and gives the lowest level employees a sense of responsibility for the entire firm's performance.

Empowering employees to provide good service is what produces quality in both service delivery and work of life, which cascades into customer satisfaction (Coleman, 1998 cf. Boshoff, 1997). A few empirical researches investigated the relationship between staff authority and their willingness to engage in both psychological and tangible service recovery. Hartline and Ferrell (1996, p. 66) have shown that allowing frontline employees to use their own initiative and judgment, improves the quality of service they deliver to customers. Carson and Carson (1998) found that staff empowered in recovery reported the highest levels of company commitment and career satisfaction. Their study further revealed that positive job attitudes were related primarily to staff's perception of empowerment. Hocutt and Stone (1998) examined employee and customer responses to empowerment in a restaurant context. They found that empowerment via training and autonomy led to higher service employee satisfaction. Their findings further indicated that greater customer satisfaction following a service failure was created by higher employee responses and empathy during a service recovery. Boshoff and Leong's (1998) study show that once a service failure has occurred, retail customers expect the service firm to accept responsibility for the problem and they prefer to deal with staff who are fully empowered to solve their problems relatively quickly. They argue that empowerment is not an absolute necessity under all circumstances, but, to deal with unanticipated incidents, which require discretionary behavior such as initiative and imagination on part of employees, empowerment is a strategy for speedy resolutions to customer problems.

Sparks, Bradley & Callan (1996) suggested that empowerment would not do wonders on its own. Frontline staff should use a convergent style of communication (informal, personalized) during a service recovery. Frontline employees should be trained to make appropriate decisions and to develop awareness of customers' concerns (Hart et al., 1990). Training and empowering employees are interdependent (Boshoff & Staude, 2003; Hocutt and Stone, 1998). But there is no point in training employees to solve problems if it is not accompanied by the power to act on their own initiative and to fix a service failure in the way they see fit. "...it may not matter how friendly, pleasant or attentive an employee is to a customer, if she/he is not able to solve the problem or to be seen as trying to help" (Boshoff & Staude, 2003, p. 11). It is likely that under such a condition the customer will just become more dissatisfied with the service and the firm could lose a valuable customer. Boshoff and Staude's recent research provides empirical evidence for the positive impact of empowerment on customers' recovery satisfaction.

Based on the above literature and classification of Bowen and Lawler (1992), the following proposition was developed to test the link between empowerment levels and behaviors in which consumers are likely to engage in a complaint situation involving core service failures.

H_1: Likelihood of customers engaging in favorable behavioral intentions is (a) highest for customers experiencing a service problem that is resolved immediately [full empowerment], (b) next highest for customers having to wait for authorization of the staff by his/her superior to proceed with the solution [partial empowerment] and (c) lowest for customers experiencing a service problem that is not resolved at all by the employee [no empowerment].

RESEARCH APPROACH

The study reported here was one component of a larger project on service failure issues in the hospitality sector. The study was carried out in one industry in a single service setting as the complaint behaviors and outcomes of service delivery may be context specific. It will be necessary to reproduce this study in other situations before any broadly based conclusions can be reached. Given the difficulties in finding customers who would have identical failure experiences, we decided to take an experimental approach and to obtain data from a consistent context using identical failure scenarios, with differing orders of employee recovery responses. Considering its advantages, the study adopted a within-subject quasi-experimental design (Namasivayam, 2003). Within-subject design refers to involving the same individual to all conditions being tested in the study.

This approach eliminates individual differences in attitudes and personality as a source of error (Kinnear & Gray, 1994; Loos, 1995; Namasivayam, 2003). Within-subject designs can capture small changes in emotions (e.g., satisfaction) and compared to between-subject designs, it requires fewer participants for the experiment (Namasivayam, 2003). Kinnear and Gray (1994) suggest that it would be better to have just one sample of subjects and to test each subject under all conditions making up the treatment factor. Within-subject design is however not free of limitations (Sparks & Callan, 1996). In order to deal with the problem of order effects, the order of the questions and employee responses were changed (Kinnear & Gray, 1994). Such approaches have been used by Boshoff (1997) and Yuksel and Kilinc (2003).

Based on previous studies examining frequent failures in the hospitality industry (McDougall & Levesque, 1999; Yuksel & Kilinc,

2003), the researchers developed a scenario involving a core service failure. The use of core service failure is justified because when asked to identify service encounters that resulted in quite dissatisfying experiences, customers frequently mentioned core service failures (Bitner et al., 1990; Kelley et al., 1993). Core service failures are situations where the customer does not receive the basic service promised by the service provider (Levesque & McDougall, 2000). Core service failures, which include lost hotel reservations, were a major reason for customers switching service provider (Keaveney, 1995). Thus core service failures are relatively serious and customers expect the service provider to immediately rectify the problem (Hart et al., 1990). The use of scenario is justifiable because this method avoids the problem of intentionally imposing service failures on customers and it minimizes memory-bias, which is common in self-reports of service failures (Smith et al., 1999). Mattila (2001) tested the impact of different relationship types on consumers' behavioral intentions following a service failure using scenario-based experimental models.

The experiment was conducted with 500 conveniently selected customers staying in hotels of Antalya, Bodrum and Kusadasi, Turkey. Self-administered surveys were left to the room-racks of participating hotels with a cover letter and instructions. Participants were exposed to a written scenario describing a service failure within the context of "lost hotel reservation". The details of the scenario are presented in Table 1. The survey consisted of three sections and was written in Turkish and English. The survey instructions asked respondents to assume that the situation (scenario) had just happened to them. The three levels of empowerment were operationalized in the hypothetical scenario as no empowerment, partial empowerment and full empowerment, and based on the classification of Bowen and Lawler (1992) and Boshoff and Leong (1998). The level of empowerment was manipulated by changing the level of autonomy the employee had in attempting a service recovery. In *no empowerment*; the employee is not able to solve the problem at all and sends the customer to see the manager. In *partial empowerment*; the employee cannot solve the problem immediately, asks the customer to wait until she/he has been authorized by her/his superior and then offers a partial solution. In *full empowerment*; the employee does whatever it takes to fully resolve the problem.

Apology was incorporated in all responses as it is the minimum that would be offered by a service provider (Mattila, 2001). Additionally, three questions, including whether (i) the respondents find the scenario realistic, (ii) they perceive the problem critical, and (iii) they would be annoyed in such a failure situation, were asked to test the scenario (Mattila, 2001). These were assessed by five-point Likert scales. A single five-point satisfaction scale was used to measure respondents' recovery satisfaction.

Customers' behavioral intentions were collected from published research reports to measure the diversity of the consumer complaint behavior construct (Huang et al., 1996; Levesque & McDougall, 1999; Rogers et al., 1992; Zeithaml et al., 1996). These are the behaviors that customers are likely to engage in when they encounter service problems (Hirschman, 1970; Singh, 1988). Following a pre-test with a convenience sample of respondents, a revised scale of nine items was developed to measure respondents' likelihood of switching to another service provider, continuing to do business with the provider in the future, complaining to the service provider, demanding intervention of a higher authority, recommending it to friends and relatives, telling other customers about the problem, telling external agencies and doing nothing. A number of items were reverse scored in order to detect response bias. The questionnaire used a five point Likert type scale to measure responses (where 1 = strongly disagree to 5 = strongly agree).

TABLE 1. DETAILS OF THE SCENARIO

At the busiest time of the summer season, you made a reservation for a hotel that is part of a domestic hotel chain. You have decided to spend a short vacation at this hotel because it offers many features including a health club, swimming pool, quality restaurants and a reputation for giving a special attention to its guests. When you arrived at 5p.m. you found that the room would not be available for another day due to a registration mistake. However you received a confirmation number for your reservation with a 3 p.m. check-in time.
The receptionist said:

- A: "I am very sorry for the inconvenience, but there is nothing I can do to help. If you want, you may see the manager".
- B: "I am sorry for this inconvenience. Let me talk to the manager to see if we can make a reservation at another hotel of similar

(contd.)

quality". On returning the receptionist confirmed that they had an alternative reservation for you.

- C: "I am sorry for the inconvenience; unfortunately we are fully booked today. Let me call a nearby hotel of similar quality to see if I can make a reservation. Please have some complimentary refreshments in our lobby while I am making the call". When the receptionist returned, he said reservation as the Seta, a higher quality hotel, is being held for you. He also said: "for your trouble, we would be happy to cover your stay expenses at Seta"

Please state how you would react to each response*

Complain to the employee

Tell it to other customers

Demand immediate and active manager involvement

Write a complain letter to company headquarters

Tell it to external agencies

Do not complain

Switch to another hotel in the future

Recommend it to friends/relatives

Visit the hotel in the future

Recovery satisfaction

* 1 (strongly disagree) – 5 (strongly agree) Likert Scale

DATA ANALYSIS

Frequency distribution of the variables was conducted in order to identify the respondents' profile, and compute means and standard deviations for each complaint behavior variable. Repeated-measures MANOVA was used to assess the effects of empowerment levels on customers' likelihood of engaging in behaviors examined in the study. Before conducting the analysis, the distribution of the dependent variables was analyzed to check the homogeneity of variance and normality assumptions of MANOVA.

RESULTS AND DISCUSSION

A total of 251 usable surveys were collected for a response rate of 48 percent. Fifty seven percent of the respondents were male, with an average age of 31 years (SD = 10.2). Fifty percent of the respondents were Turkish, 13% from the Netherlands, 9.3% from Israel, 7.3% from England. Forty three percent of the subjects were single and 37% married. Overall, participants in this study perceived the scenario as realistic (mean = 3.9). Subjects' emotional reaction to service failure indicated that, on average, they would be upset by the situation (mean = 4.0). Rating on magnitude of problem indicated that participants had regarded the outlined situation as critical (mean = 4.08).

The appropriateness of the multivariate technique was tested by Barlett's test of spherity for all empowerment conditions tested in the study. Barlett's test (651.76 with 54 df, p=.000 for no empowerment, 698.72 with 54 df, p= .000 for partial empowerment and 1146.31 with 54 df, p= .000 for full empowerment) revealed that dependent variables were correlated and therefore MANOVA was employed to analyze the data. A summary of means under three different empowerment conditions is given in Table 2. Effects of empowerment on customers' complaint behavior were tested for significance. MANOVA results showed statistically significant differences (Wilks Lamda, p< .05) in the expected direction between means on questions about complaint behavior under three empowerment conditions.

Congruent with previous studies (Bitner et al., 1994; Boshoff & Leong, 1998; McDougall & Levesque, 1999), respondents in this study reported different levels of satisfaction with the recovery response under three empowerment conditions. Consumer satisfaction was greater under the full empowerment condition (mean = 3.79) than under the no empowerment condition (mean = 1.90, Wilks F = 146.98, p= .000). An investigation of scores in Table 2 demonstrates that the extent of customers' engaging in specific complaint behaviors tends to vary under different empowerment conditions tested in the study. Respondents' likelihood of recommending the hotel to others was greater under the full empowerment condition (mean= 3.40) than under the partial and no empowerment conditions (mean= 2.36 and 2.03 respectively). Similarly, average likelihood of customer engaging in business with the service organization in the future was found to be significantly higher under the full empowerment condition (mean = 3.55, Wilks F= 81.39, p= .000). Customer retention and positive word-of-mouth are important drivers of profit in the hospitality industry.

Table 2. Empowerment conditions and complaint behavior

	No empowerment		Partial empowerment		Full empowerment				
	Mean	*SD*	*Mean*	*SD*	*Mean*	*SD*	Wilks Lambda	F	Sig.
Complain to the employee	3.64	1.49	3.04	1.35	2.41	1.42	.702	72.36	.000
Tell it to other customers	3.37	1.36	2.92	1.33	2.60	1.58	.814	33.54	.000
Demand immediate and active manager involvement	4.15	1.05	3.24	1.25	2.61	1.54	.558	104.94	.000
Write a complain letter to company headquarters	3.27	1.34	2.99	1.37	2.36	1.48	.776	44.80	.000
Tell it to external agencies	3.95	1.26	3.02	1.31	2.42	1.56	.600	100.97	.000
Do not complain	2.74	1.52	2.62	1.34	3.10	1.51	.928	9.46	.024
Switch to another hotel in the future	3.62	1.26	2.98	1.54	2.53	1.55	.716	37.47	.000
Recommend it to friends/relatives	2.03	1.31	2.36	1.21	3.40	1.41	.649	86.50	.000
Visit the hotel in the future	2.18	1.28	2.48	1.27	3.55	1.38	.639	81.39	.000
Recovery satisfaction	1.90	1.23	2.78	1.31	3.79	1.51	.502	146.98	.000

* Based on 1 (strongly disagree) – 5 (strongly agree) Likert Scale

The results in Table 2 show that these important favorable behaviors will be at risk when customers experience a service problem that is not resolved due to a lack of empowerment. Managers are thus encouraged to employ empowerment strategies in order to reduce the risk of losing the customer after a service failure. From a strategic viewpoint, allowing employees to offer appropriate assistance and/or compensation may, at first appear costly but may be substantially beneficial when considering the long-term value of a customer. Hence, empowerment is considered a profitable strategy.

Management must be supportive in allowing frontline employees to make satisfaction–affecting decisions. It must be however noted that even under the full empowerment condition, the reported mean scores for future behavioral intentions and recovery satisfaction are not the highest. A plausible explanation for this finding may be that satisfactory service recovery, though perhaps pleasing to customers, does not cause them to entirely forget the service failure and their loss (Zeithaml et al., 1996).

Results showed that following the initial failure customers were more likely to express their dissatisfaction to staff under the no empowerment condition (mean= 3.64) than they were under the partial or full empowerment conditions (mean = 3.04 and 2.41 respectively). Verbal complaints to staff and managers should be taken very seriously. This behavior may be used by customers as a means of approaching the staff for information (e.g., asking the causes of the problem, plans for recovery) and for reassurances that the problem will not cause further inconvenience. The consumer should not be denied voicing their dissatisfaction. By voicing their complaint to the staff or managers, the consumer indicates a wish to remain with the company rather than choose the exit option. As they are likely to be more satisfied if they have the opportunity to express feelings and emotions, the voicing consumers should not experience a "frustration effect". That is, voicing should result in positive outcomes. One should remember that once a customer lodges a complaint, the original transaction may become less relevant to the consumer's ultimate satisfaction than events that follow the complaint (Goodwin & Ross, 1992). This implies that when the recovery is poor this may enflame customers' emotions (Nguyen & McColl-Kennedy, 2003). A poor service recovery response due to a lack of empowerment will be perceived as a "double deviation" in that both the initial experience and the recovery are failures (Bitner et al., 1990). Failure to act relatively quickly and actively will lead to a deterioration of consumer perceptions of the service encounter (Boshoff & Leong, 1998).

Results have shown that customers are likely to engage in indirect means through complaint letters. Compared to the partial and full empowerment conditions, scores suggest that the likelihood of customers' writing a complaint letter to the service organization is significantly higher under the no empowerment condition (mean= 3.27, Wilks F= 21, p= .000). Writing a letter to company headquarters about the experience or taking a legal action against the firm may be taken as being less confrontational. It may be seen as a way to ensure financial compensation.

MANOVA results suggested that customers were more likely to expect a higher authority to get involved immediately and actively in handling their complaints under the no empowerment condition (mean = 4.15) than under the partial or full empowerment conditions (mean= 3.24 and 2.61 respectively). An obvious benefit of empowerment is related to the time in which a problem can be resolved without requiring a manager's direct involvement. Asking the guest to wait while the staff calls for the manager is likely to prolong the response time and unexplained waiting may aggravate the situation. Hence, employees must have the power to take the necessary action in order to resolve thè problems at hand on-the-spot. Additionally, empowerment will give managers more time to deal with other organizational matters (Yuksel & Kilinc, 2003). The involvement of a higher authority may enhance the perceived value of the customers' suggestions or complaints. However, if the manager is occupied (e.g. with another customer), it is likely that the customer may view this as a service failure (i.e., s/he is made to wait longer than necessary). Some customers however may not feel that the service personnel can handle the complaint better than a manager could (Huang & Smith, 1996).

Results also demonstrate that staff empowerment has a significant influence on customers' intentions of sharing their recovery experience with other customers (Table 2). Intention of telling the experience to other customers was the highest under the no empowerment condition (mean= 3.37, Wilks F= 35.54, p= .033). Customers are likely to feel frustrated, as failed service performance has not been repaired and the response does not include any kind of assistance, explanation and /or compensation. Telling the problem to other customers may be driven by an antagonistic motive (e.g., getting even by spreading bad things about the company to friends, penalize the company through third parties). Results have shown that dissatisfied customers due to poor recovery response are more likely to get even by telling others about their dissatisfaction. This is an unfavorable behavior from the management point of view with serious consequences. Consumers who are exposed to negative word-of-mouth may form unfavorable images, and may, in turn, decide to avoid the offending seller (Blodgett et al., 1997). Thus, service organizations may unknowingly be losing potential business because of negative comments made by dissatisfied customers. The presence of a dissatisfied customer in a service setting is critical because customer-to-customer interactions can influence evaluation and satisfaction with the service experience. The presence of an upset customer due to an unresolved service failure can be intrusive and this may generate negative affects. Other customers in a service setting may feel intruded on when complainants engage in negative behaviors due to frustration fuelled by the lack of empowerment (Baker & Cameron, 1996).

Respondents were more likely to tell their dissatisfaction to an external agency under the no empowerment condition (mean= 3.95) than under the partial or full empowerment conditions (mean= 3.02 and 2.42 respectively). These findings indicate that under the no empowerment condition consumers are more likely to seek redress through an external agency. Considering that resolution of complaints involving an external agency would be more costly, it is important for service organizations to create an atmosphere that encourages dissatisfied customers to seek redress with the service organization. It is noted that not all dissatisfied customers come forward to the service provider with their complaint. It may be argued that the policy of empowerment may motivate customers to complain to the service organization. This is largely because perceived likelihood of success under full empowerment policy would be higher. Perceived likelihood of success is an important element in the encouragement of the customers to come forward with their complaint. Seeking redress through an external agency may seem as an unfavorable complaint behavior. However, compared to switching behavior, third party behaviors appear to be preferable from the management point of view. Customers taking their problems to external bodies instead of just deserting at least give organization a chance to become aware of the problem and opportunity to retain these clients.

Likelihood of doing nothing was highest under the full empowerment condition (mean= 3.10, Wilks F= 9.46, p= .000). Doing nothing in response to a failed service encounter was examined since often customers just do not react at all when a bad thing happens and this might be related to their emotional experiences (Zeelenberg & Pieters, 2002). Do not complain is an unfavorable behavior from the management point of view because the customer deprives the company of knowing what went wrong. Thus, managers should be conscious that if customers are not complaining, it may be because they are happy with the service performance or it may be because they are disappointed and do not see any benefit in making any complaint. Finally, the likelihood of customers switching to another hotel was highest under the no empowerment condition. (mean= 2.98, Wilks F= 37.47, p=.000). This is another unfavorable behavior, which is likely to affect the organization's current and future business.

CONCLUSION

The policy of empowering frontline service personnel in order to make decisions about resolving complaints has been much discussed (Bowen & Lawler, 1995). Empowerment is expected to address such critical issues as speed, cost, convenience, accessibility and flexibility in a complaint-handling (Tax et al., 1999). Although it is widely recognized that frontline employees need to be empowered to make decisions, especially in service failure situations (Bowen, 1990; Hart et al., 1990), a literature review turned up little evidence of research linking employee empowerment to customer complaint behavior in a hospitality service recovery context. This research therefore explored the link between different levels of empowerment and customers' favorable and unfavorable complaint behaviors.

The results have shown that the level of empowerment in a service failure situation is likely to determine subsequent customer complaint behavior. It must be noted that limited empowerment of frontline staff to deal with customer complaints could not only result in a lost customer but place frontline staff under considerable pressure. The conflicting demands placed on frontline staff in such situations are referred to as "role stress". They have been shown to lead to higher levels of absenteeism, labor turnover and poor job performance (Boshoff, 1997). One should note that simply acting quickly and autonomously to fix the problem may not generate positive affect unless it is accompanied by empathy and courtesy (Hocutt & Stone, 1998). In other words, dissatisfied customers expect not only to receive fair settlement, but, more importantly, to be treated with courtesy and respect (Blodgett èt al., 1997). While it is not tested in this study, it is expected that complainants who receive a fair settlement, but who are treated rudely, most likely will not visit the organization again, and are likely to tell their friends and relatives about their negative experience. As Sparks et al. (1996) noted, full empowerment would be beneficial only when the frontline staff use an appropriate style of communication during a service recovery.

While this study adds to our understanding of the relationship between staff empowerment and customer complaint behavior, its limitations should be noted. The use of a scenario may constitute a limitation, as there might be a discrepancy between stated behaviors in a paper and pencil study and actual behaviors in a real failure context. Another important issue is that effective restitution requires that service providers be both authorized and willing to respond to service breakdowns (Carson & Carson, 1998). However, it can be argued that these two dimensions are relatively independent (e.g., a provider may be empowered but s/he still not engage in service recovery). This may occur for several reasons including lack of motivation, lack of accountability and/ or lack of awareness about appropriate responses (Barner 1994 cf. Carson & Carson, 1998). Hence, future research should study the link between employee commitment, empowerment and consumer complaint behavior. The use of three different conditions may constitute another limitation, as dissimilarity in these options may create a demand bias. Emotions may be part of the service recovery encounter, as failures and subsequent delays or inappropriate responses are likely to evoke negative affective reactions. Potential impact of emotions on customers' recovery evaluations and their complaint behavior may be another interesting area of research.

REFERENCES

Baker, J. and Cameron, M. (1996) The effects of the service environment on affect and consumer perception of waiting time: an integrative review and research propositions. *Journal of the Academy Marketing Science* 24 (4), 338-349.

Bandura, A. (1986) *Social Foundations of Thought and Action: A Social Cognitive View*. New Jersey: Prentice Hall.

Barlow, J. M. (1996) Welcome complaints. *Executive Excellence* 13 (11), 20.

Bell, C. R. and Zemke, R. E. (1988) Terms of empowerment. *Personnel Journal* 6, 12-24.

Bitner, M. J. Booms, B. H. and Tetreault, M. (1990) The service encounter: diagnosing favourable and unfavourable incidents. *Journal of Marketing* 54, 71-84.

Bitner, M. J., Booms, B. H. and Mohr, L. A. (1994) Critical service encounters: the employee's view. *Journal of Marketing* 58, 95-106.

Blodgett, J.G, Hill, D. J. and Tax, S.S. (1997). The effects of distributive, procedural and interactional justice on post complaint behaviour. *Journal of Retailing* 73, 185-210.

Boshoff, C. (1997) An experimental study of service recovery options. *International Journal of Service Industry Management* 8 (2), 110 – 130.

Boshoff, C. and Leong, V. (1998) Empowerment, attribution and apologising as dimensions of service recovery an experimental study. *International Journal of Service Industry Management* 9 (1), 24-47.

Boshoff, C. and Staude, G. (2003) Satisfaction with service recovery: its measurement and its outcomes. *South African Journal of Business Management* 34 (3), 9-16.

Bowen, D. E. and Lawler, E. E. (1992) The empowerment of service workers: what, why, how, and when. *Sloan Management Review* 2, 31-39.

Bowen, D.E. and Lawler, E.E. (1995) Empowering service employees. *Sloan Management Review* 36, 73-84.

Bowen, J. (1990) Development of taxonomy of services to gain strategic marketing insights. *Journal of Academy of Marketing Sciences* 18 (10), 43-49.

Brown, S. W., Cowles, D. and Tuten, L. T. (1996) Service recovery: its value and limitations as a retail strategy. *International Journal of Service Industry Management* 7 (5), 32-46.

Burke, W. (1986) Leadership as empowering others. In. S. Srivastva (ed.) *Executive Power* (pp 51-77) San Francisco: Jossey-Baas.

Carson, P. P. and Carson, K. D. (1998) Does empowerment translate into action? An examination of service recovery initiatives. *Journal of Quality Management* 9 (1), 15-21.

Conger, J.A. and Kanungo, R.N. (1988) The empowerment process: integrating theory and practice. *Academy of Management Review* 13 (3), 471-482.

Day R.L. and Landon, E.L. (1977) Towards a theory of consumer complaining behavior. In Woodside, A., Sheth, J. and Bennett, P. (eds.) *Consumer and Industrial Buying Behavior*. Amsterdam: North Holland Publishing Company.

Day, R. L. (1984) Modelling choices among alternate responses to dissatisfaction. *Association of Consumer Research Proceedings*, 11, 496-499.

Day, R.L., Grabricke, T., Schaetzle, T. and Stavbach, F. (1981) The hidden agenda of customer complaining. *Journal of Retailing*, 57, 86-106.

Deci, E. L. (1975) *Intrinsic Motivation*. New York: Plenum.

Erstad, M. (1997) Empowerment of organizational change. *International Journal of Contemporary Hospitality Management* 9 (7), 325-333.

Goodwin, C. and Ross, I. (1992) Consumer responses to service failures: influence of procedural and interactional fairness perceptions. *Journal of Business Research*, 25, 103-123.

Gronross, C. (1988) Service quality: the six criteria of good perceived service quality. *Review of Business* 9, 10-13.

Hales, C. and Klidas, A. (1998) Empowerment in five-star hotels: choice, voice or rhetoric? *International Journal of Contemporary Hospitality Management* 10 (3), 88-95.

Hancer, M. (2001) An Analysis of Psychological Empowerment and Job Satisfaction for Restaurant Employees. PhD Thesis, The Ohio State University.

Hart, C. W. L., James, L. H. and Earl W. S. Jr. (1990) The profitable art of service recovery. *Harvard Business Review* 68, 148-156.

Hartline, M.D and Ferrel, O.C. (1996) The management of customer-contact service employees: an empirical investigation. *Journal of Marketing* 60, 52-70.

Hayes, B. E. (1994) How to measure empowerment. *Quality Progress* February, 41-46.

Hirschman, A. O. (1970) *Exit, Voice and Loyalty: Responses to Decline in Firms, Organizations and States*. Cambridge, MA: Harvard University Press.

Hocutt, M. A. and Stones, T. H. (1998) The impact of employee empowerment on the quality of service recovery effort. *Journal of Quality Management*, 3 (1), 15-25.

Hoffman, K. D. and Kelley, S. W. (2000) Perceived justice needs and recovery evaluation: a contingency approach. *European Journal of Marketing*, 34 (3/4), 418-432.

Hoffman, K.D. and Chung, G. B. (1999) Hospitality recovery strategies: customer preference versus firm use. *Journal of Hospitality and Tourism Research* 23 (1), 71-84.

Hoffman, K.D., Kelley, S. W., and Rotasky, H.M. (1995) Tracking service failures and employee recovery efforts. *Journal of Services Marketing* 9 (2), 49-61.

Huang, C. and Smith, K. (1996) Complaint management: customers' attributions regarding service disconfirmation in restaurants. *Journal of Restaurant and Foodservice Marketing* 1 (3/4), 121-134.

Huang, J.H., Huang, C.T. and Wu, S. (1994) National character and response to unsatisfactory hotel service. *International Journal of Hospitality Management* 15 (3), 229-243.

Johnston, R. (1995) Service failure and recovery: impact, attributes and process. *Advances in Service Marketing and Management* 4, 211-228.

Johnston, R. and Fern, A. (1999) Service recovery strategies for single and double deviation scenarios. *The Service Industries Journal* 19 (2), 69-82.

Keaveney, S. M. (1995) Customer switching behavior in service industries: an exploratory study. *Journal of Marketing* 59, 71 – 82.

Kelley, S. W. Hoffman, K. D. and Davis M. A. (1993) A typology of retail failures and recoveries. *Journal of Retailing* 69 (4), 429-452.

Kinnear, R. P. and Gray, D. C. (1994) *SPSS for Windows: Made Simple*. Sussex: Psychology Press.

Lam, T. and Tang, V. (2003) Recognizing customer complaint behavior: the case of Hong Kong hotel restaurants. *Journal of Travel and Tourism Marketing* 14 (1), 69-86.

Landon, L. E. (1977) *A Model of Consumers' Complain Behavior*. Indiana University.

Landon, L.E. (1980) The direction of consumer complaint research, In Olson, J. (ed) *Advances in Consumer Research* 7, 335-338 MI: Association for Consumer Research.

Lashley, C. (1995) Towards an understanding of employee empowerment in hospitality service. *International Journal of Contemporary Hospitality Management* 7 (1), 27-32

Lawler, E.E., Mohrman, S. A. and Leford, G.E. (1992) *Employee involvement and total quality management*. San Francisco: CA, Jossey-Bass Publishers

Levesque, T. C. and McDougall, G. H. G. (2000) Service problems and recovery strategies: an experiment. *Canadian Journal of Administrative Sciences* 17 (1), 20-37.

Loos, F. (1995) *Research Foundations for Psychology and the Behavioral Sciences*. Harper Collins

Mattila, A. S. (2001) The effectiveness of service recovery in a multi-industry setting. *Journal of Services Marketing*, 15 (7), 583-596.

Maute, M. and Forrester, W. R. (1993) The structure and determinants of consumer complaint intentions and behavior. *Journal of Economic Psychology* 14 (3), 219-247.

McDougall, H.G.G. and Levesque, J. T. (1999) Waiting for service: the effectiveness of recovery strategies. *International Journal of Contemporary Hospitality Management* 11 (1), 6-15.

Namasivayam, K. (2004) Repeated measures experimentation in hospitality research: a brief overview. *Journal of Tourism and Hospitality Research* 28 (1), 121-129.

Nguyen, D. T. and McColl- Kennedy, R. J. (2003) Diffusing customer anger in service recovery : a conceptual framework. *Australian Marketing Journal* 11 (2), 46-54.

Rogers, J. C., Ross, S. C. and Williams, T. G. (1992) Personal values and purchase dissatisfaction response. *Journal of Consumer Satisfaction, Dissatisfaction and Complaining Behavior* 5, 81-92.

Singh, J. (1988). Consumer complaint intentions and behavior: definitional and taxonomical issues. *Journal of Marketing* 52, 93-107.

Smith, A. Bolton, R. and Wagner, J. (1999) A model of customer satisfaction with service encounters involving failure and recovery. *Journal of Marketing Research* 34, 356-372.

Solnick, S. J. and Hemenway, D. (1992) Complaints and disenrollment at a health maintenance organization. *Journal of Consumer Affairs* 26 (1), 90-103.

Sparks, A. B. and Callan, J. V. (1996) Service breakdowns and service evaluations: the role of consumer attributions. *Journal of Hospitality and Leisure Marketing* 4 (2), 3-23.

Sparks, B., Bradley, GL. and Callan, V. J. (1996) The impact of staff empowerment and communication style on customer evaluations: the special case of service failure. *Journal of Service Management* 11, 12-26.

Spreitzer, G.M (1995) Psychological empowerment in the work place. dimensions, measurement and validation. *Academy of Management Journal* 38, 1442-1465.

Spreitzer, G. M. (1996) Social structural characteristics of psychological empowerment. *Academy of Management Journal* 39 (2), 483-504.

Tax, S. S. Brown, S. W. and Chandrashekaran (1998) Customer evaluations of service complaint experiences: implications for relationship marketing. *Journal of Marketing* 62, 60-76.

Thomas, K. W., and Velthouse, B. A. (1990) Cognitive elements of empowerment: An interpretive model of intrinsic task motivation. *Academy of Management Review* 15 (4), 666-681.

Zeelenberg, M. and Pieters, R. (2002) Beyond valence in customer dissatisfaction: a review and new findings on behavioural responses to regret and disappointment in failed services. *Journal of Business Research*. Article in Press.

Zeithaml, V. and Bitner, M. J. (2000). *Services marketing*. Boston MA: McGraw-Hill.

Zeithaml, V., Berry, L. and Parasuraman, A. (1996) The behavioural consequences of service quality. *Journal of Marketing* 60, 31-46.

Zemke, R. (1993) The art of service recovery: fixing broken customers- and keeping them on your side. In Scheuing, E.E. and Christopher, W.F. (eds.). *The service quality handbook*, (pp. 463-476). New York: American Management Association.